Visualized CHURCH HISTORY

REVISED EDITION—1962

By

SISTER MARY LOYOLA VATH, O. P., PH.D.

Social Science Department
Barry College, Miami, Florida

ST. AUGUSTINE ACADEMY PRESS
HOMER GLEN, ILLINOIS

Nihil Obstat
    John M. A. Fearns, S.T.D.
         Censor Librorum

Imprimatur
    ✠Francis Cardinal Spellman
         Archbishop of New York

New York, January 7, 1952

The nihil obstat and imprimatur are official declarations that a book or pamphlet is free of doctrinal or moral error. No implication is contained therein that those who have granted the nihil obstat and imprimatur agree with the contents, opinions or statements expressed.

This book was originally published in 1942 by The Oxford Book Company. This edition reprinted in 2019 by St. Augustine Academy Press based on the 1962 Revised Edition.

ISBN: 978-1-64051-096-8

PREFACE

VISUALIZED CHURCH HISTORY is the fruit of actual classroom experience in our Catholic high schools. It represents an attempt to apply to Church History the Unit method of organization which has proved effective in almost all other secondary-school courses. Within seven basic Units, built on both chronological and topical lines, the Author has tried to present a compact but well-rounded narrative of the principal events in the history of the Church from its founding until the present day. The book is designed primarily for secondary schools, but it is hoped that it will also be found usable in introductory college classes.

The thought content of VISUALIZED CHURCH HISTORY is not original. It has been carefully chosen not merely to provide a framework of essential knowledge, but also to increase love and admiration for the divine Founder, and for the many heroic men and women whose saintly deeds shine through the pages of history. These examples may well encourage the American Catholic youth of today to go forth and preach the Gospel by worthy lives, as well as by intelligent answers to those who seek the truth. Still another objective of this course of study is to give young people a deeper appreciation of the daily practices of their religion.

One of the distinctive features of VISUALIZED CHURCH HISTORY is the illustrations. These are the project of the art students of the Studio Angelico at Siena Heights College, Adrian, Michigan. Sister M. Helene, O.P., secretary of the Catholic Art Association, is director of the Studio. The visualizations are designed to arouse and hold the interest of the students, to clarify their thought, and to inspire them to further original efforts.

Each Unit is followed by a group of review questions and objective tests, which may be used for testing and as a basis for discussion. The Author has also supplemented each Unit with a chronological table and with a list of references for outside reading. These references are on the secondary-school level and are available in most school libraries. Many of them are of recent publication.

The Author is very grateful to many persons who have provided constructive criticism of the manuscript and have assisted with the proofreading. Among them are the Very Rev. Msgr. Carl J. Ryan, Superintendent of Schools, Archdiocese of Cincinnati; Rev. William Gauche, professor at Mount St. Mary Seminary of the West, Norwood, Ohio, and Our Lady of Cincinnati College, Cincinnati, Ohio; Rev. Alfred Stritch, professor at St. Gregory Seminary and Our Lady of Cincinnati College, Cincinnati, Ohio; and Rev. Bernard Walker, O.P., Rev. Cyril Burke, O.P., and Sister M. Paul, O.P., professors at Barry College, Miami, Florida. The permission and encouragement of Reverend Mother Gerald, O.P., afforded the only stimulus needed to begin and finish the writing. The coöperation of the Publisher has helped to make the work a pleasure.

SISTER M. LOYOLA, O.P.

BARRY COLLEGE, MIAMI, FLA.
    March, 1942.

PREFACE TO NEW EDITION

The original edition of VISUALIZED CHURCH HISTORY has been widely used throughout the United States and its possessions, and also in a number of foreign countries. It has served the needs of high school and college students, seminarians, instructors of converts, catechists, and general readers.

The stormy years since 1942, when the text was originally published, have witnessed many momentous developments in the history of the Church. To incorporate these into the presentation, the Author has undertaken a complete rewriting of the latter portion of the book, comprising Chapter 14 ("Faith Versus Unbelief in Twentieth-Century Europe") and all of Unit VII ("Catholicity in America"). Among the many topics which have been added are the persecutions of the Church in Eastern Europe, where the Communists are multiplying martyrs; the resistance to Communism in Italy and other countries of Western Europe; the marvelous missionary activity, expansion, and organization of native clergy in various parts of the world, including Japan; the Holy Year in Rome, with its promulgation of a new dogma and several canonizations; and recent developments affecting the status of the Church in the United States, including relevant Supreme Court decisions. The latest available statistical data have been used in all cases. The chronological tables, reading references, testing materials, and illustrations have been revised and supplemented to cover these recent developments. In addition, the index has been completely refurbished.

Since the appearance of VISUALIZED CHURCH HISTORY, constructive criticisms have been received from book reviewers, teachers, students, and other readers. Research has cast new light upon the Photian Schism. The Author has attempted to make revisions of the text in accordance with the guidance received from these sources.

PREFACE TO NEW EDITION

The Author wishes to thank the librarians of the Mullen Library of the Catholic University of America and the librarians of the Congressional Library, Washington, D. C. They extended every assistance and courtesy possible in carrying on the necessary research. The clergy and sisters of Puerto Rico coöperated with a questionnaire conducted in the Spring of 1951. The Author is particularly grateful to Mother Mary Gerald of Adrian, Michigan, who granted the necessary facilities for study and writing and also provided personal encouragement. The Publisher has been helpful and coöperative, as with the original edition.

SISTER M. LOYOLA, O.P.

CONTENTS

UNIT I

THE FOUNDATION OF CHRISTIANITY

CHAP.	PAGE
1. THE DIVINE FOUNDER AND HIS APOSTLES	3
Introduction	3
The Apostles and Their Labors	6
2. THE ROMAN PERSECUTION AND THE TRIUMPH OF THE CHURCH	17
The Background of the Persecution	17
The Ten Principal Stages of the Persecution	20
Practices of the Early Church	26
The Triumph of Christianity	28

UNIT II

THE GROWTH OF CHRISTIANITY

3. THE TRIUMPH OVER HERESIES	40
The Nature and Causes of Heresy	40
The Successful Struggle against Heresy	43
The Organization of the Primitive Church	59
4. THE MIGRATIONS OF THE NATIONS; THE RISE OF MONASTICISM	63
The Barbarian Invasions	63
Monasticism and Monasteries	68

UNIT III

THE AGES OF FAITH (590-1274)

CHAP.   PAGE

5. FROM GREGORY THE GREAT TO THE ELEVENTH CENTURY   79
    Introduction 79
    Gregory the Great 80
    Relations of the Church with the Frankish Monarchs   81
    Sorrows of the Church 84
    Propagation of the Faith in the Early Middle Ages . 90
    Monasticism in the Early Middle Ages 96
    Feudalism 100

6. THE GOLDEN AGE OF THE CHURCH 103
    Two Great Popes—Gregory VII and Innocent III . 103
    Heresies during the Twelfth and Thirteenth Centuries 107
    The Crusades 111
    "The Greatest of Centuries" 117

UNIT IV

THE LATER MIDDLE AGES AND THE RENAISSANCE

7. THE LATER MIDDLE AGES 137
    Introduction 137
    The Reign of Boniface VIII 138
    The "Babylonian Captivity" 142
    The Great Schism (1378-1418) 146
    Heresies of the Fourteenth Century 148

8. THE BEGINNINGS OF MODERN TIMES 151
    Introduction 151
    The Renaissance Popes 153
    The Art of the Renaissance 157
    Political Events of the Renaissance 164

CONTENTS

UNIT V

PROTESTANTISM AND THE COUNTER-REFORMATION

CHAP.	PAGE

9. THE PROTESTANT REVOLT IN EUROPE 177
   Introduction 177
   The Revolt in Germany 179
   The Spread of Protestantism to Scandinavia and Switzerland 183
   Protestantism in France 185
   Protestantism in the Netherlands 187
   Protestantism in Scotland 189
   Protestantism in England 190
   The Thirty Years' War 197

10. THE CATHOLIC COUNTER-REFORMATION 200
    The Council of Trent 200
    Popes of the Counter-Reformation 202
    Saintly Leaders of the Counter-Reformation . . 204

11. ROYAL ABSOLUTISM 211
    Nature and Causes of Absolutism 211
    The Absolute Monarchies 212

UNIT VI

FROM THE FRENCH REVOLUTION TO THE PRESENT DAY

12. THE FRENCH REVOLUTION 226
    The Background of the Revolution 226
    The Rising Tide of Revolution 231

13. THE NINETEENTH CENTURY—THE CENTURY OF CONCORDATS 236
    France 236
    Germany 243
    Italy 247

CHAP.		PAGE
	England and Ireland	249
	Other Nations of Europe during the Nineteenth Century	251
	Popes of the Nineteenth Century	252
14.	FAITH VERSUS UNBELIEF IN TWENTIETH-CENTURY EUROPE	255
	Character of the Twentieth Century	255
	France	258
	Germany	260
	Japan	263
	Italy	264
	Great Britain	265
	Poland	266
	Russia	267
	Popes of the Twentieth Century	277
	Other European Countries	275

UNIT VII

CATHOLICITY IN AMERICA

15.	MISSIONARIES AND MARTYRS IN COLONIAL AMERICA	293
	Spain in America	293
	France in America	298
	The English in America	301
16.	THE CATHOLIC CLERGY OF THE UNITED STATES	305
	The Hierarchy	305
	American Cardinals	312
17.	THE CATHOLIC LAITY IN AMERICA; CATHOLIC EDUCATION	318
	The Catholic Laity	318
	Catholic Education in the United States	329
	INDEX	xi

UNIT I

THE FOUNDATION OF CHRISTIANITY

PREVIEW

YOU are now about to begin the study of the most fascinating and inspiring story within the entire realm of human knowledge—the history of the Church. You will learn of the humble beginnings of the Church, of its miraculous growth, of its unending joys and sorrows, of the many problems it encountered, and of how these problems were faced and solved, often with glorious victories. You will learn of the divine Founder of the Church, Jesus Christ, and of what He thought and said and did. You will become familiar with the lives and works of the hosts of noble men and women who carried on the work of the Founder, in order that the Church might accomplish its divine mission. You will consider, finally, the status and problems of the Church in the troubled world of today, both in our own country and in other lands.

The infant Church first appeared in a Roman province amidst the Jewish people of Palestine. It came into existence at a time when the Roman Empire, long the master of the Western world, was entering upon the decline which led to its extinction. But although the Roman Empire failed, the Church picked up the torch of civilization, cherished all that was good in Greek and Roman culture, and changed the entire moral character of the ancient world for the betterment of mankind. Rome resisted this new power during a long era of persecution, which was systematically organized and ruthlessly enforced. But the Romans, with all their wealth and might, were merely human, while the Church is truly divine. Thus, during its first three centuries (the age of martyrs and catacombs), the Church developed like the tiny mustard seed that grows into a great tree with widespreading branches. At the end of this period, the command of the divine Father had been fulfilled: "All power in heaven and on earth has been given to Me. Go, therefore, and make disciples of all nations, baptizing them in the name of the Father, and of the Son, and of the Holy Spirit, teaching them to observe all that I have commanded you; and behold, I am with you all days, even unto the consummation of the world" (Matt. 28, 18-20).

The word *Church* is derived from a Greek term meaning "God's house." Christ and the Apostles used the word *Church* to replace the Old Testament expression "Kingdom of God" (Acts 8, 1; Matt. 16, 18). Theologians give us the following definition of the Church, adopted from the writings of Cardinal St. Robert Bellarmine (De Eccl. III, ii, 9): "A body of men united together by the profession of the same Christian Faith, and by a participation in the same sacraments under the governance of lawful pastors, more especially of the Roman Pontiff, the sole vicar of Christ on earth." As a visible organization, the Church has its code of laws, its executive officers, and its ceremonial observances. Unlike all other organizations, however, the Church is a supernatural society, divine in its origin, in its purpose, and in the means at its disposal.

VISUALIZED CHURCH HISTORY

CHAPTER 1

THE DIVINE FOUNDER AND HIS APOSTLES

"I am the way, and the truth, and the life. No one comes to the Father but through me."—ST. JOHN 14, 6

INTRODUCTION

The Charter, Constitution, and Corner Stone of the Church.—The charter of the Church is contained in the following passage from Matt. 28, 19-20: "Go, therefore, and make disciples of all nations, baptizing them in the name of the Father, and of the Son, and of the Holy Spirit, teaching them to observe all that I have commanded you; and behold, I am with you all days, even unto the consummation of the world." After nineteen centuries, this charter is preserved intact and is cherished by 400 million followers, representing one out of every five persons on the face of the earth.

The constitution of the Church is the law of Christ contained in the New Testament. This written constitution, like the Federal Constitution of the United States, has an official interpreter.

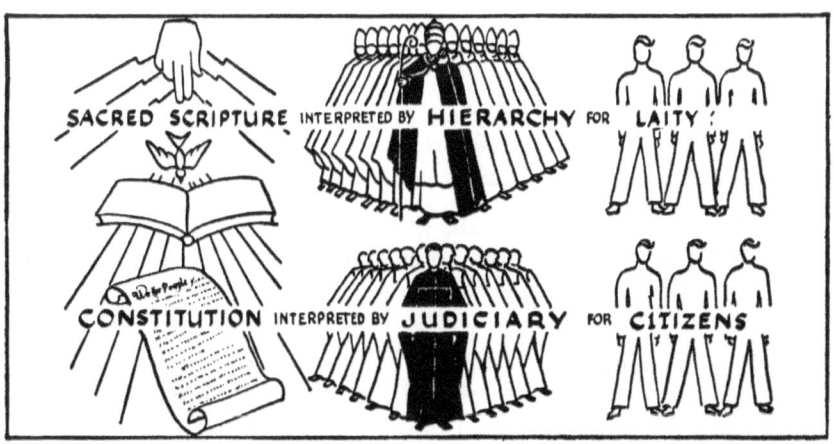

4 *VISUALIZED CHURCH HISTORY*

The Supreme Court interprets the United States Constitution; the Catholic Church, in the persons of the Popes and the Bishops, interprets the Bible. These individuals are commissioned by Christ and are authorized to teach. Catholics refer to the teaching body of the Church (including the Popes, Bishops, Priests and Deacons) as the *hierarchy*. Others are called the *faithful* or the *laity*.

The corner stone of the Church is Jesus Christ Himself. In the Psalms of the Old Testament (Psalms 117, 22), King David thus speaks of Him: "The stone which the builders rejected: the

same is become the head of the corner." St. Peter wrote at Rome, about fifteen years after Our Lord's resurrection (1 Peter 2, 6):

> Hence Scripture says,
>> "Behold, I lay in Sion a chief corner stone,
>> chosen, precious;
>> And he who believes in it shall not be put
>> to shame."

St. Peter here quotes Isaiah, the prophet, of whom we read in the Old Testament. St. Luke, in the Acts 4, 11, quotes the Psalms, as given above. The corner stone of the Catholic Church is dated 33 A.D.

A Perfect Society.—The Church is a *perfect society*. There is only one other perfect society in the world, namely, the State. By a perfect society, we mean one which is not dependent on, or subordinate to, any other. A business organization, such as the Ford Motor Company, is dependent on secular control, on laws of the State; the Army, Navy, and Air Force are subordinate to the Department of Defense, which, in turn, is subordinate to the State. Thus, none of these is a perfect society. But the Church and State are perfect societies, the one spiritual, the other temporal. The Church is not one of a series of churches, but the only true church, divinely founded.

The Founder.—During the reign of Caesar Augustus, in the Roman province of Palestine,[1] there was born a divine Child, Jesus Christ. Christ chose to be born in lowly poverty, of a Jewish mother. He lived among the poor, but during His public life of three years, He also made occasional contacts with the rich. He said, "I am the way, and the truth, and the life. Learn of Me for I am meek and humble of heart." All men, rich and poor, were to be able to fulfill His wish.

The divine Founder had been promised to men by God. The time and place of His birth had been predicted by the prophets. The purpose of His life had also been foretold: to redeem men from sin, and to found the Kingdom of God upon earth, namely, the Church. All these prophecies of the Old Testament, including the circumstances of Our Lord's passion and death, were fulfilled in every detail. He proved His divinity by words and by works, but chiefly by His resurrection from the dead.

During the three years of His public life, He preached to the Jews in the temple and the synagogues, and went about among the people doing good. The example of noble character which He left can be imitated by every human being born since His time. The keynote of His character is love.

---

[1] Palestine fell under the domination of Rome in 63 B.C. Previous to this, the Jews had been ruled by Syria, but a revolt led by the Maccabees in the second century B.C. reëstablished their independence. The Jews were then governed by their own kings until 69 B.C., when open warfare broke out between two claimants to the throne. The Roman general Pompey was in the Near East at this time with a powerful army, and both factions appealed for his aid. Pompey saw in this dispute an opportunity to extend the dominions of Rome. Utilizing surprise and treachery, he soon conquered the little country. Jerusalem was captured and the temple taken by assault; over 12,000 defenders, including many priests, were slain. Some years later, Palestine became a province of the Roman Empire.

THE APOSTLES AND THEIR LABORS

The Choosing of the Apostles.—Our Lord's public ministry was to be of short duration. Therefore, He selected some faithful assistants whom He trained lovingly and carefully. After a night spent in prayer on a lonely mountain, Jesus summoned His disciples, and chose from among them twelve poor, unlettered men to serve as His Apostles. They were to listen to our Lord's divine doctrine, to assist Him, to be witnesses of His miracles, and to propagate His religion. The lowliness of these instruments is a strong argument for the divine origin of Christianity. Holy Scripture recounts the names of the twelve Apostles in four different passages, and always names Peter at the head of the list, although he was not the first one chosen. This proves that his contemporaries acknowledged his primacy among the twelve.

Soon after choosing the Apostles, Our Lord delivered the Sermon on the Mount, the moral code of a Christian (Matt. 5-7). It contains the Ten Commandments and the eight Beatitudes, as well as explanations of them. There the perfect prayer, the Lord's Prayer, is found (Matt. 6, 9-13). The Catholic Church uses a part of the Sermon on the Mount in the Mass for November 1, All Saints' Day; the Lord's Prayer is said in every Mass at a most solemn moment, immediately after the Consecration. Christ often took the Apostles aside and instructed them minutely. He taught the multitudes in parables in the Gospel narratives.

The New Testament.—The New Testament, the inspired word of God, is an historical account, written by contemporaries who were the chosen associates of Jesus Christ. The first four books are the *Gospels;* these are narratives of the life of Christ and His doctrines written by the four *Evangelists*—St. Matthew, St. Mark, St. Luke and St. John. In addition, the New Testament contains the Epistles of St. Paul, St. James, St. Peter, St. John, and St. Jude, and the Apocalypse of St. John.

The Gospels.—The authors of the Gospels include two of the Apostles (John and Matthew), and two of their disciples (Mark and Luke). Although all the Gospels deal with the same events, they differ in their emphasis and in the character of their treatment.

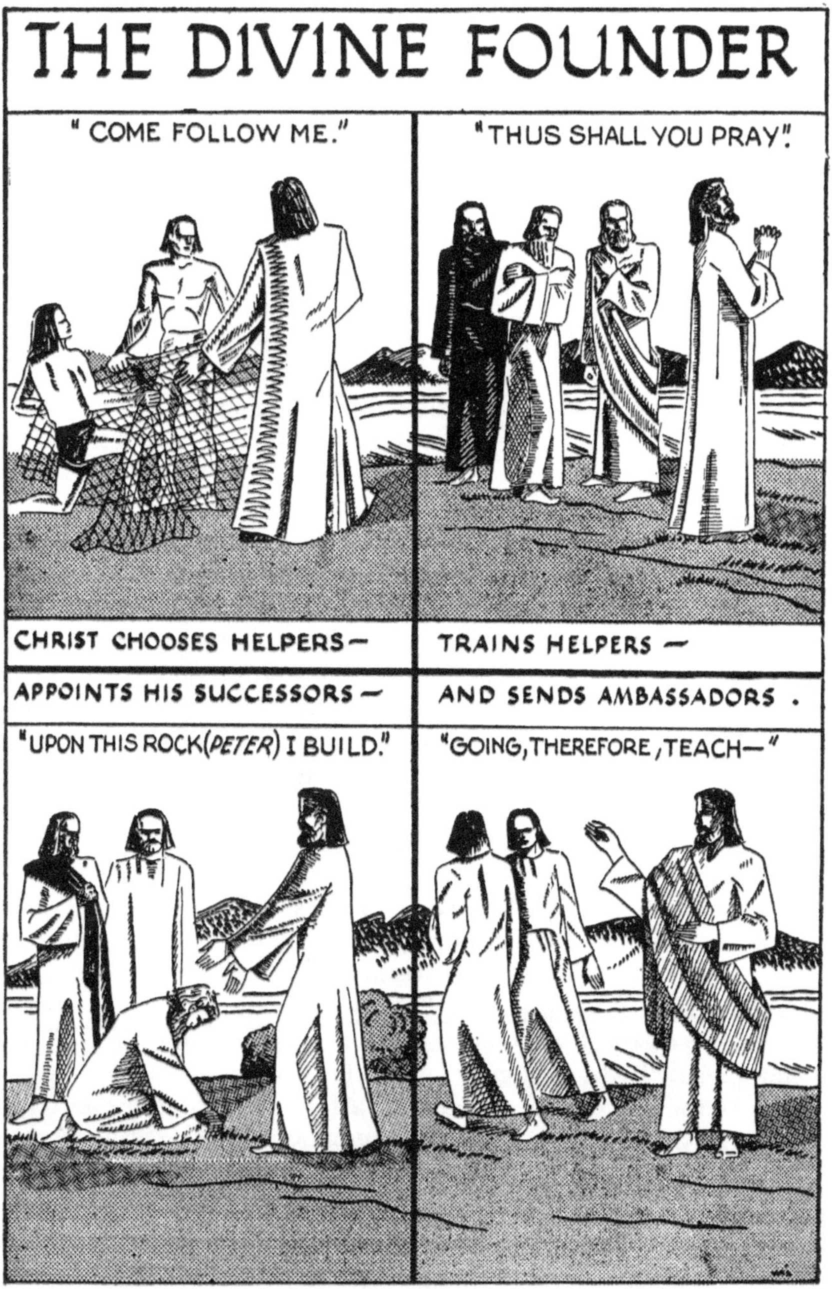

1. *St. Matthew's Gospel* opens with the *human generation* of Christ. It gives the most complete version of the passion and death of the Savior. It is symbolized in art by a young man.

2. *St. Mark's Gospel* treats of the *kingship* of Christ. It begins with the episode of St. John in the desert, and is the briefest of the Gospels. It is symbolized by a lion.

3. *St. Luke's Gospel,* which starts with a description of the sacrifice of Zachary, dwells on the *priesthood* of Christ. It offers considerable detail regarding the birth of the Savior, and emphasizes miracles of healing. It is probable that St. Luke was particularly interested in these subjects because he was a physician. Its symbol is an ox.

4. *St. John's Gospel* is a truly sublime account of the *divinity* of Christ. Since St. John soars higher than all the other Evangelists in thought and love, his Gospel is fittingly symbolized by an eagle.

Note that the symbols, inspired by a passage in Scripture, indicate the opening passage of each Gospel and suggest the principal theme of the whole.

The First Pope.—Peter was commissioned the first Pope and later became the Bishop of Rome, where he spent his last years and was martyred. With the other Apostles, he remained some years in Jerusalem. Our Lord founded the Church a year before He died when He said to Peter: "Thou art Peter *(rock)*,[2] and upon this rock I will build My Church, and the gates of hell shall not prevail against it" (Matt. 16, 18). After the Resurrection, the appointment of Peter was confirmed: "Feed My lambs. Feed My sheep" (John 21, 17). The Apostles always respected this leadership. Several instances may be mentioned. When Peter and John ran to the tomb on the Resurrection day, John, who had arrived first, stepped aside for Peter to enter. When the Apostles were gathered together to choose one to replace Judas the traitor, Peter presided. On Pentecost, Peter first preached to the multitude. At the Council of Jerusalem, a few years later, Peter took the leadership. When Peter was imprisoned in Jerusalem, an angel freed him; but James the Greater, also imprisoned, was put to death, the first Apostle to give up his life for fulfilling our

---

[2] *Peter* is actually the Greek word for "rock."

THE DIVINE FOUNDER AND HIS APOSTLES

Lord's command: "Go, therefore, and make disciples of all nations."

On Pentecost, fifty days after Easter, the Holy Ghost descended upon the Apostles. Peter then preached his first sermon about the life and death of Christ to a vast assembly in Jerusalem. Three thousand were baptized; these constituted the first con-

gregation and completed the foundation of the Church. Pentecost is, therefore, the birthday of the Church, and the second highest feast in the Church. (Liturgy gives first place to the Feast of the Resurrection.) Many of the Jews who heard the first sermon were visitors to Jerusalem and when they returned to their homes, some at considerable distances from Jerusalem, they scattered the new seeds of Faith. Although these visitors spoke several different languages, they all understood Peter's sermon delivered in his native tongue. This was the *gift of tongues*.

Propagation of Christianity among the Jews.—The first Christians were all Jews, but the Jewish authorities generally persecuted those of their brethren who had embraced the new religion. Therefore, the Apostles decided to separate, leaving James the Less to be Bishop of Jerusalem. St. Peter traveled to Antioch, and later to Rome. Ever since, the successor of St. Peter —the Pope—has been Bishop of Rome. In nineteen centuries, there have been 262 Popes in unbroken succession from Peter.

The Apostle St. John cared for the Mother of Jesus, and later went to Ephesus, where he lived until banished by the Emperor Domitian to the island of Patmos. Afterwards, he returned to Ephesus, where he died. St. John was the only one of the Apostles to die a natural death; he was miraculously saved from martyrdom when Domitian attempted to have him boiled in oil near Rome. As we have seen, he wrote one of the Gospels, as well as three Epistles, and the *Apocalypse,* which revealed the future history of the Church and described the Last Judgment. The other Apostles were true missionaries who spread the Faith throughout the Roman Empire and beyond it. The labors of St. Peter and St. Paul are related in the Acts of the Apostles by St. Luke.

The Apostles performed the duties which today are entrusted to our Bishops; they preached, offered the sacrifice of the Mass, and administered the Sacraments. Their preaching took place in the temple and the synagogues, in the open, in private homes, and in the catacombs, the underground burial places in Rome. Very often these ceremonies were held in secret because the public authorities were hostile.

Comparatively few Jews were converted to Christianity. They refused to accept the teaching of the Apostles that Jesus was the *Messias* or Savior whom they expected, and that He had fulfilled the prophecies of the Old Testament. Gradually, the Christians separated from their former co-religionists. After a time, they were not allowed in the temple and the synagogues. The Roman officials, however, regarded the early Christians as a sect of Jews, and they are so designated in the writings of contemporaries.

NOTE: In 70 A.D., Palestine was invaded by Titus, son of the Roman Emperor, Vespasian. Titus destroyed the entire city of Jerusalem. Vast numbers of inhabitants were slaughtered by the Romans, or succumbed to famine and disease. The survivors were scattered all over the known world. However, the Christian converts in Jerusalem were warned and fled in time to be saved (Luke 19, 41-44; 21, 20-24). Some of these returned to the city later to cherish the scenes of Christ's life and of the Apostolic labors.

Deacons.—When the number of Christians became so great that the twelve Apostles could no longer care for them, they chose men called Deacons to assist in many duties. (These officials, however, did not celebrate Mass.) One of the most illustrious of the Deacons was St. Stephen, who was charged by the Jewish Council with blasphemy, taken outside the city walls and stoned to death. Thus he earned the title of *protomartyr* [3] less than a year after Christ's Resurrection. One of the Jews who witnessed this martyrdom was a young man named Saul, who came from the city of Tarsus in Cilicia. Although at this time he had no sympathy for the Christians, he was soon to become St. Paul, the Apostle of the Gentiles.

Propagation among the Gentiles.—The converted Jews who fled from Jerusalem carried the Faith to far countries in all parts of the world. These missionaries came into contact with, and utilized, Greek and Roman culture. The New Testament was written in Greek [4] and traveled over the Roman roads to the most distant provinces and even beyond.

The first pagan (*i.e.*, non-Jewish) convert to Christianity was the chamberlain of Queen Candace of Ethiopia. An angel appeared to Philip, one of the seven Deacons at Jerusalem, and bade him go forth between Jerusalem and Gaza (Acts 8, 26-40). Philip obeyed and met the Ethiopian riding in a chariot, pondering over the Holy Scripture. Philip explained the prophecies concerning Christ. As they were passing a stream, the Ethiopian requested to be baptized.

---

[3] *Proto* comes from the Greek word meaning "first" or "original."
[4] The Gospel of St. Matthew was written in Aramaic, but was soon translated into Greek.

The first Roman Gentile to enter the Church was received by St. Peter at Caesarea (Acts 10-11). This convert was a Roman centurion named Cornelius. He was a man acceptable to God and was advised by an angel to go to Peter. At the same time Peter had a vision of meats, clean and unclean, and he heard a voice commanding him to kill and eat. Upon his protest, he heard a voice: "What God has cleansed, do not thou call common." While he pondered over these words, messengers came from Cornelius. Divine inspiration enlightened him to go to Cornelius. Peter said: "Now I really understand that God is not a respecter of persons." Soon the centurion was baptized with his kinsmen and special friends.

St. Paul.—The great figure whom we call St. Paul originally went under the name of "Saul of Tarsus." He was born in the city of Tarsus in the province of Cilicia, a center of Greek culture. His parents were pious Jews who enjoyed Roman citizenship. In early manhood, Paul was trained in the Jewish law by Gamaliel, a Pharisee at Jerusalem. Thus we see that "Paul was Jew, Roman and Hellenist. Birth, training and experience made him a representative of the three great cultures confronting Christianity." [5]

Before his conversion, Paul earned his living as a tent-maker, an occupation which had been chosen for him by his parents. As stated above, he witnessed the death of Stephen, the protomartyr. At this time, Paul was a bitter enemy of the Christians. Indeed, he had sought letters from authorities in Jerusalem which would authorize persecution of the Jewish Christians at Damascus, a city about 135 miles from Jerusalem. On the road to Damascus, Paul was converted by Christ Himself, and was soon baptized.

After his conversion, Paul made three great missionary journeys around the lands bordering the Mediterranean. It is for this reason that we call him the "Apostle of the Gentiles." He was to the Gentiles what Peter was to the Jews—a chosen instrument of God who inculcated men with a true faith which neither the most savage persecutions nor the craftiest wiles could ever destroy. Paul also wrote much of the New Testament, including

---

[5] Lortz, J. and Kaiser, E. G., *History of the Church.*

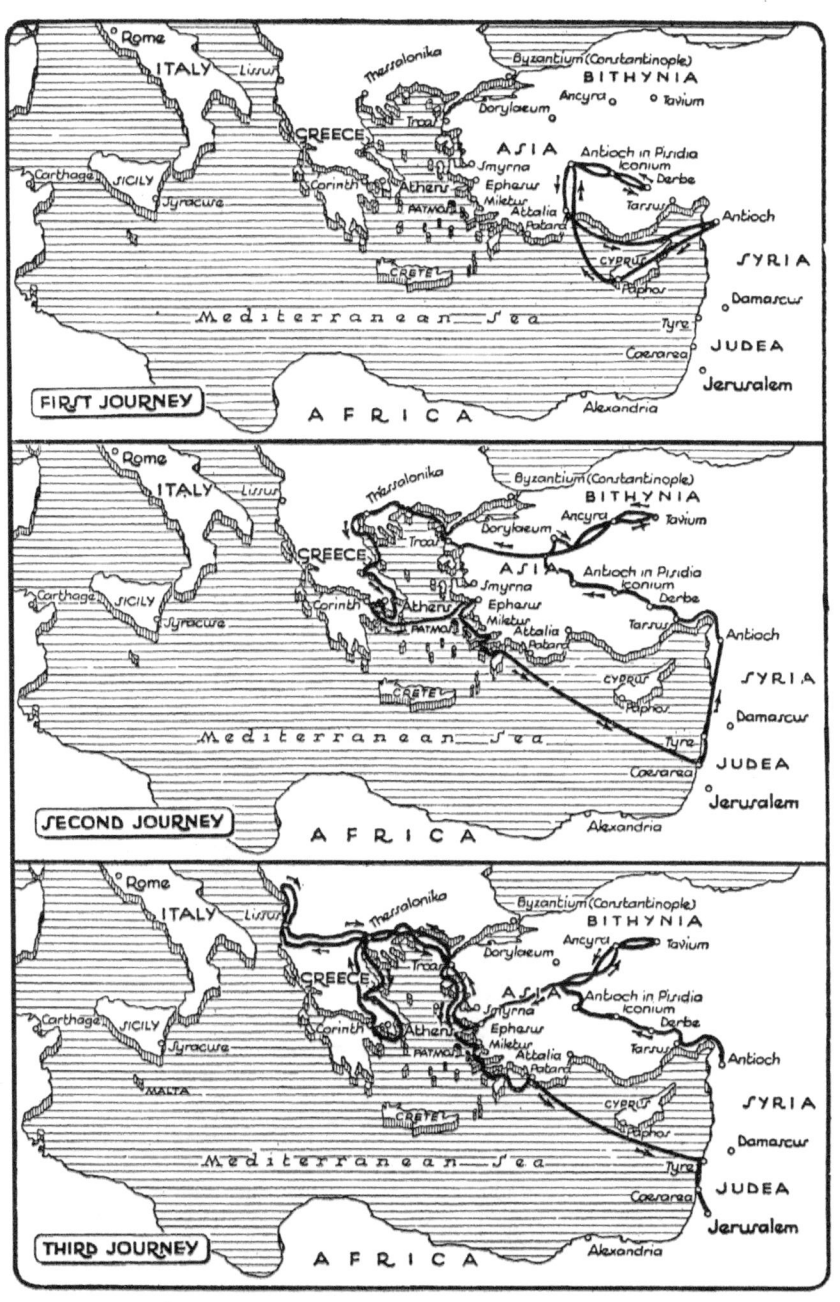

The Three Missionary Journeys of St. Paul

THE APOSTLES

Name	Feast in Latin Rite	Symbol	Scene of Apostolic Labors	Death
Peter	June 29	One or two keys	Preached in Jerusalem; Bishop of Antioch; Pope and Bishop of Rome.	Crucified by order of Nero, 67 A.D.
Andrew	Nov. 30	X-shaped cross	Scythia, Greece, Constantinople.	Crucified on X-shaped cross at Patras in Achaia.
James, Greater	July 25	Staff, wallet	Jerusalem.	Beheaded by order of Herod Agrippa in Jerusalem; first Apostle martyred.
John	Dec. 27	Eagle, chalice	Asia Minor, Ephesus, Patmos; Guardian of Mary after death of Jesus.	Escaped martyrdom of boiling oil under Domitian; died at Ephesus.
Philip	May 1	Double cross	Phrygia, Asia Minor.	Crucified at Hieropolis.
Bartholomew	Aug. 24	Knife; or shown holding his own skin in his hand	Arabia, Parthia, India, Armenia.	Skinned alive in Armenia; crucified.
Thomas	Dec. 21	Spear, arrow	India, Far East.	Martyred at Meliabor, in India.

James, Less	May 1	Fuller's club	Bishop of Jerusalem.	Stoned to death in Jerusalem.
Matthew	Sept. 21	Short sword, winged man bearing lance	Arabia, Egypt.	Martyred at Nodabar in Parthia.
Thaddeus Jude	Oct. 28	Club	Syria, Mesopotamia, Persia.	Tied to a cross and shot to death with arrows in Armenia.
Simon Zelotes	Oct. 28	Saw	North Africa, Persia.	Crucified in Persia by idolatrous priests.
Judas Iscariot	....	....	....	Hung himself, after betraying Jesus for 30 pieces of silver.
Matthias	Feb. 24	Lance	Chosen by Apostles to replace Judas; details of life not known.	Stoned and beheaded in Colchis.
Paul	June 29	Sword	As "Apostle of Gentiles," made three missionary journeys to Mediterranean countries.	Beheaded at Rome, 67 A.D.

NOTE: See Matt. 10, 1; Mark 3, 13; Luke 6, 13; Acts 1, 13.

sections replete with Christian doctrine. Today, in her liturgy, the Church never honors Peter without Paul, nor Paul without Peter.

The Council of Jerusalem.—Under the leadership of Paul, the city of Antioch in Syria was made the center of Christianity. It was here that the followers of Christ came to be called Christians. Most of the converts in this city were Gentiles, but there were also many Jews, and a violent quarrel broke out between the two groups. The Jewish law required circumcision. The Gentile converts protested, holding that baptism alone is required of a Christian. About 52 A.D., a Council was called at Jerusalem, at which Peter and Paul, together with James and other "Apostles and ancients," settled the dispute between the Jewish and Gentile elements in the Church (Acts, 15). It was decided that circumcision was not to be demanded of the Gentiles.

The Early Martyrs.—As stated above, only one of the Apostles, John, died a natural death. All the others, with the exception of the traitor, Judas Iscariot, died as martyrs. This is shown in the chart on pages 14-15. Other illustrious figures of the early Church gave their lives for the Faith—for example, St. Stephen (page 11). In addition, there were many obscure, humble Christians, among both the Jews and the Gentiles, who suffered martyrdom. Many escaped death only by fleeing to the mountains or deserts.

CHAPTER 2

THE ROMAN PERSECUTION AND THE TRIUMPH OF THE CHURCH

"Afflict us, torment us, crucify us—in proportion as we are mowed down, we increase; the blood of Christians is a seed."
— Tertullian ("Apologia," 50)

THE BACKGROUND OF THE PERSECUTION

Introduction of Christianity to Rome.—In the Acts we read that "strangers of Rome" were among those present at St. Peter's first sermon on Pentecost (page 9). We do not know who first introduced Christianity into Rome, the "eternal city." It is possible that the "strangers" mentioned brought the Faith to Rome; or perhaps the seed was carried by Roman legions who were on duty in the province of Palestine. Cornelius the centurion was a Roman who received the gift of Faith soon after Christ's resurrection (page 12). We do know that Jews and Christians were banished from Rome by the Emperor Claudius about 50 A.D. and that later they were allowed to return. We know, also, that St. Paul wrote a famous epistle to the Romans between 50 and 60 A.D., while he was preaching in Corinth on his third missionary journey. St. Peter spent some years in Rome before his martyrdom at that city in 67 A.D.

Classical writers, such as Suetonius, looked upon the Christians as a Jewish sect. The Roman government allowed the Jews to worship in their own synagogues, and this at first was a protection to the Christians. The Jews in Rome were not very numerous and they did not mingle socially with the pagan Romans. This was also more or less true of the Christians, but such obscurity was not enough to safeguard them. Christ had sent the Christians into the world as lambs among wolves and He had predicted persecutions for them. "Because you are not of the world, therefore the world hateth you."

The Nature of the Persecution.—The Roman persecution of the Christians lasted for about 2½ centuries. Historians estimate that during 129 years of this era, active persecution was taking place; during 120 years, there were intervals of comparative peace, when the Christians increased in numbers. At all times throughout this era, however, it was dangerous to profess Christianity and to practice it openly.

From the historian's point of view, the 2½ centuries during which the persecution occurred constitute a single era. We can, however, distinguish ten principal phases or stages [1] of this era, and it is convenient for us to treat each of these as an individual persecution. Bear in mind that when we speak of "Nero's persecution" or the "seventh persecution," we are merely referring to different stages of the same historical process, not to a series of disconnected events.

The aim of this savage persecution was nothing less than the complete destruction of the Christian religion. However, the Roman government, with all its great power, was merely a human agency, while the Church is divine. Thus, after 2½ centuries of organized persecution and torture, there were at least 4 million Christians. Christianity was finally granted tolerance in the Roman Empire by the *Edict of Milan* in 313.

The Church taught that it was proper to flee persecution and martyrdom, and that it was rash to seek it. None the less, the greatest glory of the ancient Church is the history of the martyrs. Their bodies were buried with the tenderest devotion whenever possible, and the days of their martyrdom were observed annually with religious ceremonies. The slabs of marble over their graves in the Catacombs became altars on which the Sacrifice of the Mass was offered. Thus, today every altar contains an altar stone with five relics of the saints; some of the relics must be those of martyrs. The Mass contains a prayer of veneration for these relics.

Causes of the Persecution.—The immediate conditions which led to the persecution of the Christians varied considerably at different times and places. However, we can distinguish a number of basic causes which are common to *all* the phases of this cruel but futile campaign to crush the Church.

---

[1] These are listed by Lactantius, an early Christian writer, in his book *On the Death of the Persecutors.*

1. The Roman pagan religion was a state religion. Every good citizen was expected to worship the pagan gods by burning incense, by offering sacrifices, and by other rites. The Christians refused to perform these rites, because they worshipped only one God, whom the Romans considered a mere man, a despised Jew. Moreover, the Romans regarded their Emperor as not only a temporal authority but also a spiritual ruler and, indeed, a god. The Christians refused to recognize this. For these reasons, the Christians were accused of treason, and of trying to undermine the state religion and the state itself.

2. The Roman law forbade secret assemblies. The innocent meetings of the Christians for their religious services were condemned as a violation of this law. This helped to fan the flames of suspicion and hatred.

3. Slanders were spread regarding the practices of the Christian religion. For example, it was reported that the Christians killed and ate little children at their religious ceremonies. No calumny was too fantastic for the ignorant, debased rabble to believe.

4. There was a conspicuous difference between the noble moral conduct of the Christians and the bestial immorality of the Romans, both poor and rich. The Romans resented the virtue of the Christians because, by contrast, it accentuated their own depravity. The pagans hated a religion which condemned their pride and their immoral lives.

5. In some cases, there was an economic reason for the persecutions. The Christian refusal to make sacrifices to the pagan gods threatened to harm the profitable business of selling sacrificial animals. The silver-smiths who drove St. Paul out of Ephesus were also impelled by economic motives.

Some persecutions were instigated by the Emperors themselves, or by lower government officials. Others were demanded by the frenzied, unthinking mob. It became customary to attribute every public calamity to the Christians. "If the Nile overflows its banks," writes Tertullian, "or if the Nile fails to overflow, if the skies are not clear, if the earth quakes, if famine or pestilence comes, up goes the cry: 'The Christians to the lions.' "

> NOTE: Tertullian was a brilliant apologist (and later a heretic) who lived through several of the persecutions. He laid the foundations of Latin Christian literature.

THE TEN PRINCIPAL STAGES OF THE PERSECUTION

Nero's Persecution.—On July 18, 64 A.D., during the reign of the degenerate Emperor Nero, a fire broke out in some storehouses in Rome near the Circus Maximus. The conflagration raged for ten days, and destroyed ten of the fourteen sections of the city. It was widely believed that Nero had started the fire himself to provide space for new construction work in the city. To clear himself of this charge, Nero blamed the fire on the Christians. This was the occasion of the first major persecution.

This persecution was pleasing to the Roman rabble, many of whom were enraged because they had lost their homes. Besides, they relished the spectacular public "entertainment" provided by the persecution. During the daytime, Christians were exposed to wild beasts in the arenas, crucified, thrown into the Tiber, and subjected to various other tortures. By night, they were smeared with pitch, after which they were fastened to stakes and set ablaze. We read of these horrible happenings in the *Satires* of Juvenal and in the *Annals* of Tacitus. Many books have been inspired by this unforgettable tragedy, among them *Quo Vadis?* by Sienkiewicz, *Dion and the Sibyls* by Keon, and *Lucius Flavius* by Spillman. In our day, the cinema has also portrayed this historical episode.

Domitian's Persecution.—After a brief interlude of comparative peace, Emperor Domitian (81-96), a vicious character, ordered a persecution aimed at Christians among the higher classes. Flavius Clemens, a Senator and a cousin of Domitian, was a victim of this persecution, and his wife was banished. Domitian attempted to kill St. John, the beloved disciple of Jesus, by having him placed in boiling oil. St. John, as we have noted above, was miraculously saved from this martyrdom, but he was banished to Patmos.

Trajan's Persecution.—Ten years later, Emperor Trajan (98-117) initiated the third persecution, which was one of the most severe. Pope Clement and two Bishops—Ignatius of Antioch, who was the first to use the term "Catholic Church," and Simon of Jerusalem—were victims of Trajan's wrath. We have a most interesting historical document relating to this persecution in the form of a letter from Pliny to Trajan, and the latter's reply. Pliny at that time was governor of the province of Bithynia, in which many of the inhabitants were Christians. He was taking drastic measures against the Christians, in accordance with an edict of the Emperor which forbade secret societies. Pliny, however, became troubled in conscience at the vast number of Christians who were suffering death, and he wrote a long letter to Trajan, in which he explained the situation and asked for advice. Trajan's reply is a classical example of following the line of least resistance, for he told Pliny not to hunt the Christians out but, if any of them were accused, to make them pay the penalty, regardless of age, sex, or position in society.

Persecution at Lyons.—There followed a period of forty or more years during which the Christians were not molested. Then came the fourth persecution, which centered chiefly in the city of Lyons, in what is now France. This persecution took place under the Emperor Marcus Aurelius (161-180), who was a Stoic philosopher and, in many respects, a high-minded man. However, he was unable to appreciate the truth and beauty of the Christian Faith; for example, he characterized martyrdom as "mere obstinacy."

Christians of noble birth were banished; members of the lower classes were subjected to torture and put to death. St. Polycarp, Bishop of Smyrna, eighty-six years old, was burned on a cross, then stabbed to death. St. Polycarp was a disciple of St. John the Apostle and, as such, represents an important link between the Apostles and the Fathers of the Church.[2] St. Justin Apologist suffered martyrdom at Rome. At Lyons, young and old gave testimony to the Faith that was in them by sacrificing their lives. St. Pothinus, Bishop of Lyons, a man of ninety, and Ponticus, a boy of fifteen, are examples. Blandina, a slave, was gored to death by a savage steer in the arena. There is extant a letter from the Christians in Lyons to the Christians in other churches which is an historical proof of this persecution.

These tragic events were followed by a period of twenty years of comparative peace.

---

[2] The martyrdom of Polycarp took place in 155 A.D., during the reign of Antoninus Pius.

The Fifth and Sixth Persecutions.—The fifth persecution, under Emperor Septimius Severus (193-211), raged chiefly in Egypt and Africa. At Carthage, a noblewoman and young mother named Perpetua deliberately ignored a degree forbidding anyone to be instructed in Christianity. When she was found out, she joyously entered the arena with her slave Felicitas and many other Christians to be gored to death by a furious bull.

The interval between the fifth and sixth persecutions witnessed the erection of churches, and the growth of laxity in faith among the Christians. The sixth persecution, under Emperor Maximinus (235-238), was aimed particularly at Bishops and Priests.

The Seventh Persecution.—The seventh persecution, under Emperor Decius (249-251), was one of the most severe and most deadly in its effects. At this time, about one-third of the population was Christian. The Emperor was determined to annihilate Christianity and yet he did not wish to see so many of his subjects die. Therefore he decreed torture to force submission and the offering of sacrifice to the pagan gods. He wished the persecution to be carried out in every part of the Empire, and therefore threatened with punishment governors who failed to persecute the Christians. Christians were deprived of property, tortured, and banished or put to death when they refused to sacrifice to the pagan gods. There were numerous apostates, for many Christians had become lax in the practice of their faith during the long period of peace. Papyrus documents are preserved that describe the process of apostasy. Yet this persecution has its glorious martyrs and confessors. Among them are Pope St. Fabian, St. Alexander, Bishop of Jerusalem, St. Agatha of Sicily, and St. Apollonia of Alexandria.

The Eighth and Ninth Persecutions.—In the eighth persecution, under Emperor Valerian (253-260), Pope Sixtus was beheaded while celebrating Mass in the Catacombs of Callistus. Six Deacons shared his fate. St. Lawrence, another Deacon present at the ceremony, was detained for three days by the Romans because they hoped to obtain riches supposed to be in his keeping. St. Lawrence requested an opportunity to gather the riches; then he presented himself to the Roman authorities with the poor, the crippled, and the homeless for whom the Church cared. Unmoved by this beautiful act, the Romans condemned St. Lawrence to martyrdom by slowly burning to death on a gridiron.

The ninth persecution was begun at Rome by Aurelian (270-275) but was cut short by this Emperor's death.

The Tenth Persecution.—After a comparatively long interval of peace, Emperor Diocletian (284-305) initiated the tenth persecution, the most cruel and systematic of all. This was intended to put a definite end to Christianity. Diocletian was a cruel but efficient dictator, who administered his vast realm by means of satellite "sub-Emperors," stationed at four widely separated points throughout the Empire. Under this organization, Diocletian persecuted the Christians with a ruthless thoroughness that calls to mind the campaigns against the Church in modern European dictatorships. Churches were demolished, and the Scriptures publicly burned. Soon, Bishops and Priests were cast into prison and subjected to torture. Finally an edict decreed death to all who refused to sacrifice to the pagan gods.

Numerous and noble were the victims. The Theban legion in Switzerland was systematically massacred. Forty martyrs at Sebaste were frozen to death on a lake. Tradition says that 10,000 Christians were crucified on Mount Ararat. St. Catherine of Alexandria suffered martyrdom. St. Sebastian, a prefect of the Praetorian Guard, was pierced with arrows and later clubbed to death. St. Agnes, a noble Roman maiden, was beheaded. St. Lucy, a virgin, died a martyr's death at Syracuse.

Later Martyrs.—One may read the litany of the Roman martyrs in the Canon of the Mass. This is on the lips of millions daily, who faithfully and lovingly recall the saintly deeds of the early heroes of the Church. Every century since has witnessed persecution of some kind, and these later persecutions were also rich in martyrs who loved their Faith with an eternal love. Joseph Dinneen in his book *Pius XII,* written in 1939, says: "Pastors and Priests are made of the same stuff as martyrs." We know that in our own time Priests have suffered ill-treatment, imprisonment and even death, rather than abandon their duties and their Faith.

THE TEN MAIN STAGES OF THE ROMAN PERSECUTION OF THE CHRISTIANS

Number	Persecutor	Time	Place	Characteristics	Illustrious Martyrs
First	Nero	64-68	Rome	Christians accused of burning Rome; vast numbers killed by wild beasts, crucifixion, burning, etc.	St. Peter; St. Paul.
Second	Domitian	95-96	Rome	Aimed at higher classes.	Flavius Clemens, Senator and cousin of Emperor; attempt on St. John.
Third	Trajan	106-117	Provinces	Severe; Christians exposed to wild beasts, burned at stake, and crucified.	St. Ignatius, Bishop of Antioch; Simon, Bishop of Jerusalem; Clement, fourth Pope.
Fourth	Marcus Aurelius	161-180	Lyons	Christians of noble birth banished; those of lower classes put to death.	St. Justin Apologist, at Rome; St. Pothinus, Bishop of Lyons.
Fifth	Septimius Severus	202-211	Egypt, Carthage	19,000 men, women, children perished in general massacre.	Irenaeus, Bishop of Lyons, Apologist; St. Perpetua; St. Felicitas.

Sixth	Maximinus	235-238	Rome	Aimed especially at Bishops and Priests.	St. Cecilia; Valerian, a patrician.
Seventh	Decius	249-251	Rome, Africa, Near East	Systematic campaign to destroy Church; more widespread and better organized than earlier persecutions.	Pope Fabian; St. Agatha in Sicily.
Eighth	Valerian	257-260	Rome	Christians at this time very numerous; apostates in Africa and Asia.	St. Sixtus (Pope Sixtus II); St. Lawrence; St. Cyprian.
Ninth	Aurelian	274-275	Rome	Begun to please Senate and Roman mob; stopped by death of Emperor.	Pope Felix; Dionysius, Bishop of Paris.
Tenth	Diocletian	303-311	Rome, Provinces	Most cruel and systematic of all persecutions.	Sebastian of Roman legion; Lucy; Agatha; Catherine of Alexandria; Anastasia.

PRACTICES OF THE EARLY CHURCH

The Catacombs.—Many Romans cremated their dead and pre served the ashes in urns, but the Jews followed the practice of burial. This Jewish custom was adopted by the early Christians. Some of the Christian cemeteries were much like modern cemeteries, but others were subterranean (*i.e.*, located far beneath the surface). One of the first subterranean Christian cemeteries was situated in a low hollow spot near the Church of San Sebastian in Rome. This cemetery became known as the Catacombs from the Greek *catacumbas,* meaning "lowlands." Gradually the name Catacombs came to be applied to all Christian subterranean burial places. The Catacombs, like all other cemeteries within the Roman Empire, were originally protected by law against molestation. It was not until the later systematic persecutions of the Christians that secrecy became a necessity. Then the Christians protected the Catacombs by filling up the old entrances, which previously had not been concealed, and by constructing new entrances. There are about fifty Catacombs around Rome. If placed end to end in a straight line, these would extend the full length of Italy!

In Rome the surface of the earth is composed of three layers: *pozzolana,* a substance like cement, then *tufa,* a softer substance, and finally stone. The Catacombs are in the tufa layer. They lie thirty to fifty feet below the ground and are reached by stairways. Some Catacombs have three or four stories, all connected by stairways. The roof of each gallery is from thirteen to fifteen feet high. The passageways are narrow and dark, with enclosures on both sides, one above the other. The niches are closed by a marble slab or stone masonry. In the writings of St. Jerome, he records that as a young student at Rome in the fourth century, he and his companions visited the Catacombs on Sundays. He describes how air was admitted from above by holes, how dark the galleries were, and how cautiously people stepped along.

During periods of severe persecution, many Popes were buried in the Catacombs. Often religious services were conducted here, since secret assemblies were forbidden by edicts. The use of the Catacombs ceased in 410 A.D., when the Goths invaded Rome and destroyed a great number of them. In the eighth and ninth centuries, Popes began to transfer bodies from the Catacombs to the churches in the cities. At one time, there were fully 2 million graves in the Catacombs.

Excavation of the Catacombs.—In 1578, a Catacomb was accidentally discovered. Since that time, extensive investigations have been made, and in recent years these subterranean chambers have been carefully excavated in order to obtain relics of the early Christians and historical information concerning their lives and practices. The paintings, sarcophagi, small articles, and inscriptions which have been found prove that the early Christians were one with Catholics today in venerating the truths and mysteries of Faith contained in the Apostles' Creed. Foremost in their thoughts were respect for the Holy Eucharist, prayers for the dead, and belief in a final resurrection. Symbols were used to represent these beliefs, such as, the fish, the peacock, and the dove.

Erection of the Churches.—The first Church building recorded in history was erected in the city of Edessa in Syria,[3] in

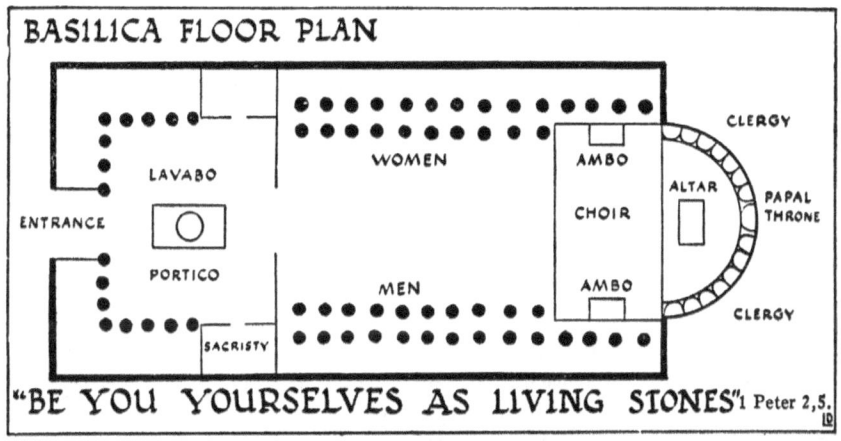

201 A.D. After the third century, longer periods of peace and comparative prosperity made it possible for the Christians to provide many special buildings for religious services. Most of these structures, known as *basilicas*, were extremely modest in their dimen-

---

[3] The Syrian emperors were tolerant of all religions, and the Christians in Syria were recognized as a legal corporation and were free to own property and to erect churches.

sions and decorations. They were oblong in shape, with a large central aisle, known as a *nave*. Here most of the worshippers were seated, with separate places for men and women. The catechumens (those not yet baptized and receiving religious instruction) and persons doing public penance were restricted to the vestibule. At one end of the nave was a semi-circular space known as the *apse*. This was set aside as the sanctuary, and only Bishops and other clergy were admitted to it. The altar was sometimes in the center of the sanctuary; the clergy had seats around the altar, and the Bishop's throne was behind it.

Services were conducted regularly on Sundays, and also at Easter and Pentecost. In the third century, a daily celebration of the Mass was begun in some churches. At first, the Eucharistic services were held in the evening, but in the second century it was made a morning service, preceded by fasting.

THE TRIUMPH OF CHRISTIANITY

The Edict of Milan.—The Roman persecutions of the Christians were ended by the Edict of Milan, issued by the Emperor Constantine in the year 313. Constantine was chosen as Emperor by the army, but he had to subdue a strong rival claimant before he could ascend the throne. As Constantine was approaching Rome from the Alps, on the eve of the decisive battle, he saw a cross of light in the sky above the sun surrounded by the words: *In hoc signo vinces* ("In this sign you shall conquer"). Constantine ordered a military standard (*labarum*) to be made of gold and precious jewels, and with this he went forth to victory at the battle of the Milvian Bridge (312).

Constantine expressed his gratitude for this by conferring many favors upon the Christians. In the first place, his Edict of Milan granted toleration to all religions, and thus brought the blessings of enduring peace to the Church. The death penalty by crucifixion was prohibited, out of respect for Christ the crucified, and the murderous games of the arena were forbidden. Christians could now receive legacies and were made eligible for appointment to public office. The generosity of Constantine and of his mother, St. Helena, made possible the erection of churches at Jerusalem, Bethlehem and Rome. He gave the Lateran Palace

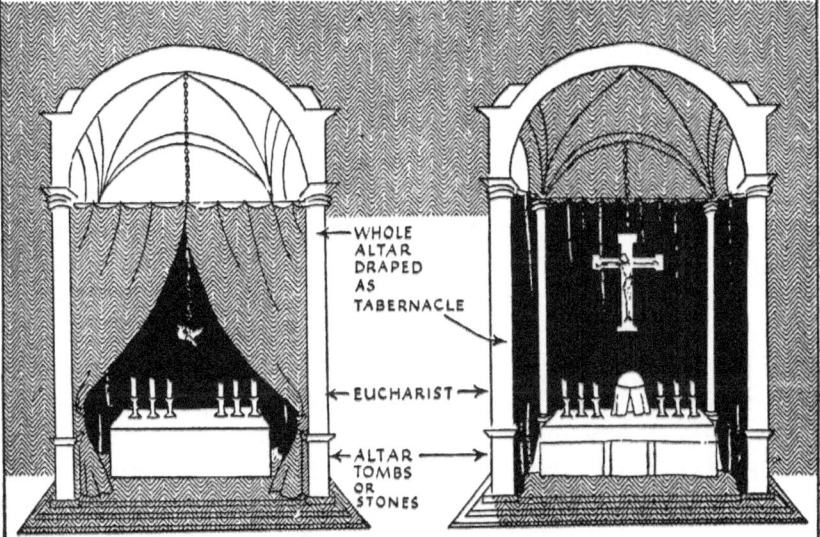

at Rome to the Pope, and made possible the First General Council at Nicaea in 325 (page 44). When Licinius, Emperor in the East failed to observe the Edict of Milan, Constantine twice defeated him in battle, thus definitely ending persecution of the Christians by Roman authority. This established genuine religious toleration for the first time in history.

Before Constantine died in 337, he formally embraced Christianity and was baptized. To honor the memory of this great man, the Roman Senate and people erected an arch, which is still standing. His name is preserved, also, in the city of Constantinople, which he built and established as his capital. Much of Roman culture and civilization was preserved at Constantinople, when Rome was overrun by barbarians some time later. This made easier the growth of spiritual power at Rome.

The Church Triumphant.—After three centuries of struggle with extremely powerful forces (physical, moral and intellectual), Christianity came forth completely triumphant. In spite of the overwhelming forces at their disposal, the persecutors had been unable to crush a divine institution; the blood of innumerable martyrs was the seed of the Church.

The pure lives of the Christians, based upon the Ten Commandments and the Beatitudes, overcame the low moral standards of the Romans. The Christian code challenged the Roman institutions under which a large part of the population were slaves, deprived of all the inalienable rights of man. Christianity taught that every slave possessed an immortal soul, bought by the redeeming blood of Christ and destined to return to Christ. Therefore, it was sinful to treat human beings as slaves—as mere items of property over whom a master exercised the right of life and death. Christianity also acted as a powerful force to improve the lot of women, whom the Romans had placed in a position of the lowest degradation. Mary, the Mother of God, was held up as a model to women. Women were now protected by the marriage bond, for marriage was a sacrament, binding both parties until the death of one of them.

The rationalistic attack on Christianity, an insidious enemy, called into action the early Doctors and Fathers of the Church. They produced many historical documents which explained the doctrines of Christ, described the religious practices of the early Christians, and are of inestimable value to us today.

Growth of the Church.—The first congregation on Pentecost, the birthday of the Church, numbered 3000. After three centuries of the most unrelenting persecution, 4 million Christians testified to the Faith in every portion of the known world, even beyond the Roman Empire. Every city had its Bishop and Priests, and its body of laymen. Altogether, there were about 1500 Episcopal Sees in the world. In the year 197, Tertullian wrote: "We

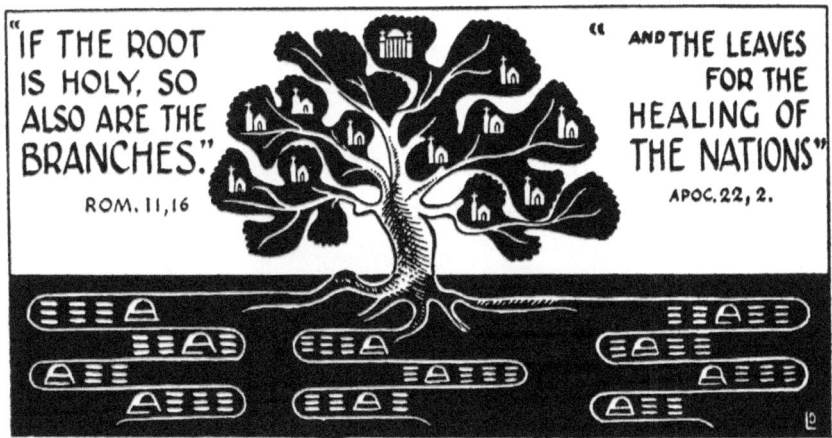

are but of yesterday, yet we have filled all your places of resort—cities, islands, fortresses, towns, councils, the palace, the senate and the forum. We constitute the majority in every city. We have left to you only the temples of your gods."

Reasons for Growth.—There are several reasons for this remarkable growth of the Church. The basic reason, of course, was the Divine Founder's promise of everlasting assistance. Christ had said: "Behold I am with you all days even to the consummation of the world."

The fulfillment of this promise revealed itself in many circumstances which were favorable to the growth of the Church. (1) The sublime doctrines of the Gospels appealed to a Roman world weary of the unsatisfying pagan religion, with its degrading moral code. (2) The promise of eternal life with God was a consolation which attracted vast numbers of slaves and poor people.

(3) The idea of a Universal Catholic Church was easily intelligible to a people who had lived under the Roman Empire, which was a highly centralized world power, with representatives even in the farthest provinces. (4) The Apostolic teachers were aided by the gift of miracles. (5) The Greek language and, to a lesser extent, the Latin language, were mediums of expression by which Christian missionaries could make themselves understood to all men. (6) The great Roman roads made it possible for missionaries to travel all over the known world. (7) Many Roman soldiers became zealous Christians and, since they were sent all over the Empire, they were able to carry the seed of Faith far and wide.

In all these factors which led to the growth of the Church, the finger of God is plainly evident.

CHRONOLOGICAL TABLE OF PRINCIPAL EVENTS IN CHURCH HISTORY

Year (A.D.)	Event
33	Foundation of the Church by Christ
33	Resurrection of Christ
33	Pentecost
33	Death of Stephen by martyrdom
34	Conversion of Saul, later St. Paul
48	First missionary journey of St. Paul to Paphos, Antioch, Lystra, Derbe
52	First Council at Jerusalem
52	Second missionary journey of St. Paul to Philippi, Athens Corinth
56	Third missionary journey of St. Paul to Ephesus, Corinth Jerusalem
58	Arrival of St. Paul at Jerusalem
62	Martyrdom of Apostle James, Bishop of Jerusalem
64-68	First Roman persecution, instigated by Nero
67	Martyrdom at Rome of Peter and Paul
70	Fall of Jerusalem, conquered by Romans
95-96	Second Roman persecution, under Domitian
100	Death at Ephesus of St. John, last Apostle

SUPPLEMENTARY MATERIAL FOR UNIT I

YEAR (A.D.)	EVENT
106-117	Third Roman persecution, under Trajan; death of Ignatius of Antioch
161-180	Fourth Roman persecution, under Marcus Aurelius
201	Erection of first Church building at Edessa, Syria
202-211	Fifth Roman persecution, under Septimius Severus
235-238	Sixth Roman persecution, under Maximin; martyrdom of Cecilia
249-251	Seventh Roman persecution, under Decius
257-260	Eighth Roman persecution, under Valerian
274-275	Ninth Roman persecution, under Aurelian
303-311	Tenth Roman persecution, under Diocletian
312	Battle of Milvian Bridge, won by Constantine
313	Edict of Milan, establishing religious toleration for Christianity and all other religions

REFERENCES

CURRAN, E. L., *Great Moments in Catholic History*, pp. 1-17
DREHER, T., *Outlines of Church History*, pp. 1-28
EUGENE, BROTHER, *Bible and Church History*, pp. 217-245
FORNER, B. N., *The Story of the Church*, pp. 1-36
JOHNSON, G. W., HANNAN, J. D., DOMINICA, SR., *Story of the Church*, pp. 1-85
LAUX, J., *Church History*, pp. 1-90
LORTZ, J., KAISER, E. G., *History of the Church*, pp. 1-43
RAEMER, S. A., *Church History*, pp. 1-85
SPALDING, B. J., *Bible and Church History*, pp. 231-244
Catholic Encyclopedia, "Agaunum," "Catacombs," "Church"
New Testament

QUESTIONS

1. Explain clearly the following terms: (*a*) the *charter* of the Church; (*b*) the *constitution* of the Church; (*c*) the *corner stone* of the Church.

2. (*a*) What is meant by a "perfect society"? (*b*) Why is the Church considered a "perfect society"? (*c*) Give another example of such a society.

3. (*a*) Who were the Apostles? Give their names. (*b*) The Apostles were poor, unlettered men. Why is this an argument for the divine origin of Christianity?

4. (*a*) With what three great cultures of ancient times did Christianity come in contact? (*b*) Did Christianity destroy or ignore these cultures? Explain.

5. (*a*) How many Christians were there on the first Pentecost? How many were there in the year 313? Approximately how many are there today? (*b*) How do you explain this growth?

6. Discuss the life and work of St. Paul. Why is he called the "Apostle of the Gentiles"?

7. (*a*) Explain the dispute which led to the calling of the Council of Jerusalem. (*b*) When and where was it held? (*c*) Name two notable figures who attended the Council. (*d*) What did the Council decide?

8. (*a*) Explain how Christianity was introduced to Rome. (*b*) How do you explain the fact that the Romans at first regarded the Christians as a sect of Jews?

9. (*a*) Explain fully the reasons for the Roman persecution of the Christians. (*b*) How many major phases or stages of the persecution were there? (*c*) Which were the most severe?

10. (*a*) When and how did the Roman persecutions of the Christians come to an end? (*b*) What was the condition of the Church at the close of the persecutions? (*c*) How do you explain the fact that the Roman Empire, with its tremendous material power, was not able to crush Christianity, as it wished to do?

11. Discuss the Catacombs, explaining (*a*) their purpose; (*b*) the reasons for their use; (*c*) their appearance; and (*d*) their importance as a source of historical information.

12. (*a*) Discuss the circumstances which led Emperor Constantine to become a Christian. (*b*) What great service did Emperor Constantine perform for the Church?

SUPPLEMENTARY MATERIAL FOR UNIT I

13. (*a*) When and where was the first known Church building erected? (*b*) Describe the appearance of the early Church buildings.

14. (*a*) Explain fully why the Christians were opposed to the Roman institution of human slavery. (*b*) Were slaves allowed to become Christians?

15. (*a*) Name five martyrs of the Roman persecutions. (*b*) How do Christians now recall the saintly deeds of the early martyrs? (*c*) Were there any martyrs in the centuries after the Roman persecutions? (*d*) Have there been any martyrs in our own times?

MATCHING TEST

In the parenthesis before each item in Column A, write the number of the item in Column B which is most closely associated with it.

A	B
( ) St. Peter	1. Birthday of the Church
( ) St. Paul	2. Roman conqueror of Palestine
( ) Pentecost	3. First martyr
( ) St. Stephen	4. Apostle who died a natural death
( ) Pompey	5. Betrayed Christ
( ) Judas Iscariot	6. Roman philosophers
( ) Constantine	7. Edict of Milan
( ) St. John	8. Apostle of the Gentiles
( ) Cornelius	9. Christian love feast
( ) Catechumens	10. Unbaptized converts
	11. First Pope
	12. First Roman convert

SELECTION TEST

In each of the following groups, select the one name that does **not** *apply.*

1. *Twelve Apostles:* Peter, Andrew, James, John, Philip, Paul, Bartholomew, Thomas, Matthew, James, Jude, Simon, Judas.

2. *Roman Persecutors:* Nero, Septimus Severus, Diocletian, Constantine, Decius.

3. *Attended the Council of Jerusalem:* Peter, Cornelius, James, Paul.

4. *Roman Martyrs:* Sebastian, Cecilia, Paul, John, Ignatius.

5. *Deacons of the Church:* Stephen, Lawrence, Jude, Philip.

COMPLETION TEST

Complete each of the following statements by supplying the correct word or phrase in the blank space.

1. The Church was founded by ....
2. The Apostle who is always named first and is considered to have primacy among the twelve is ....
3. The first Apostle to suffer martyrdom was ....
4. The people to whom Christ preached Christianity were all ....
5. In the liturgy of the Church, the two Apostles ...... and ...... are always honored together.
6. The highest feast in the Church is the Feast of the ......; the second highest is ....
7. The *Apocalypse* was written by ....
8. When Peter preached his first sermon at Pentecost, he and his hearers were favored by the "gift of ...."
9. Ever since St. Peter, the Pope has been Bishop of ....
10. The Apostle ...... was chosen to replace Judas Iscariot.
11. The *Acts of the Apostles* was written by St. ....
12. The early Church buildings were known as .... The large central aisle of such a building was called the .... At one end was a semi-circular space called the ....
13. The last and most cruel of the persecutions was directed by Emperor ....
14. A Roman Senator who was martyred during the second persecution was ....
15. The perfect prayer is the .... This is contained in a sermon delivered by our Lord, known as the ....
16. The Gospel which dwells on the Priesthood of Christ is that of ....
17. St. Mark's Gospel is symbolized by a ....

SUPPLEMENTARY MATERIAL FOR UNIT I

18. The Gospel which exceeds all the others in loftiness of thought and love is that of ....

19. The two Evangelists who were also among Christ's Apostles are ...... and ....

20. The Gospel which gives the most complete account of the passion and death of Christ is that of ....

CHRONOLOGY TEST

Number the items in each of the following groups in their proper chronological order.

A

( ) Conversion of Saul
( ) Resurrection
( ) Martyrdom of Stephen
( ) Pentecost

B

( ) Martyrdom of Ignatius
( ) Persecution under Diocletian
( ) Martyrdom of Cecilia
( ) Persecution under Nero

C

( ) First Roman Persecution
( ) Council of Jerusalem
( ) Paul's first missionary journey
( ) Conquest of Jerusalem by Romans

D

( ) Edict of Milan
( ) Victory of Constantine over rival claimant to throne
( ) Erection of the first Basilica
( ) Baptism of Constantine

UNIT II

THE GROWTH OF CHRISTIANITY (315-590)

PREVIEW

IN this Unit, we are going to study the history of the Church during the fourth, fifth and sixth centuries—a period regarded as the beginning of the Middle Ages. At this stage "... the Church is no longer a tiny seed but has grown to a mighty, though not a fully developed organism." Naturally, new historical forces and problems appear, and the Church must adopt somewhat different instruments and methods to fulfill its divine mission. We shall consider particularly three movements or developments which had far-reaching effects upon the history of the Church: (1) the rise of heresies, and the steps which were taken to crush them; (2) the barbarian invasions of the Roman Empire; and (3) the influence of Christianity upon the barbarian invaders.

Heresies constituted one of the most deadly enemies of the Church. These false doctrines emphasized "now one, then another element of Revelation to the prejudice of the rest of revealed truths." Heresies were valiantly and successfully opposed by the Fathers and Doctors of the Church, brilliant and saintly men, whose glorious writings provided a clear, scientific formulation of dogmas. The first five Ecumenical Councils of the Church guarded the deposit of Faith from the taint of error. The Nicene Creed, used in the Mass almost daily, was written, containing the twelve articles of the Apostles' Creed, with additional statements explaining the doctrines questioned by the heretics. In the decisions of the Councils, Greek culture "instead of becoming a rival to Christian faith was made its servant."

The barbarian invasions of the Roman Empire were a vast population movement, directed in general from northeastern to southwestern Europe. Like a raging mountain torrent, this great migration spread death and destruction in its path; at the same time, it brought new vitality to the decaying Roman Empire. The cruel, unlettered barbarians became the strong, virtuous, Christian founders of the nations of Europe.

This transformation of the barbarians made possible the re-establishment of social and political order, and saved Europe from complete chaos. The credit for this great accomplishment must go to pious, energetic Popes, and to their equally devoted Bishops, missionaries and monks. Zealous missionaries, molded to holiness in the monasteries of the East and West, implanted the seeds of Christian faith in the hearts of the barbarians. During the darkest days of the invasions, the culture of ancient Greece and Rome was preserved only in the monasteries, where accomplished monks copied literary treasures by hand and lavished unlimited patience and talent in adorning the pages of manuscripts. The Christianization of the German tribes resulted in a new civilization, based upon the Graeco-Roman heritage but rich in its own creative genius, which was to blossom forth in the Middle Ages.

CHAPTER 3

THE TRIUMPH OVER HERESIES

Seeing, therefore, that men who agree not among themselves have all alike conspired against the Church of God, I shall call those whom I shall have to answer by the common name of heretics. For heresy, like some hydra of fable, hath waxed great from its wounds, and, being ofttimes lopped short, hath grown afresh, being appointed to find meet destruction in flames of fire.—St. Ambrose ("De Fide," 1, 6, 46)

THE NATURE AND CAUSES OF HERESY

Nature of Heresy.—St. Thomas Aquinas, the prince of philosophers and theologians (page 125) defines heresy as a "species of infidelity in men who, having professed the faith of Christ, corrupt its dogmas."[1] A heretic restricts his belief to certain points of Christianity, selected and fashioned at his own pleasure. A Catholic, on the other hand, believes the sum total of truths revealed in Scripture and Tradition, as presented to him by the Church. A heretic accepts only such parts of these truths as commend themselves to his approval. This is the private judgment claimed by Protestants, all of whom are technically heretics.

Heresy differs from *apostasy*. An apostate abandons *wholly* his faith in Christ, while an heretic retains something of this faith. We must also distinguish heresy from *schism*. A schismatic (such as a member of the Greek Orthodox Church) separates himself from the unity of the Church and refuses to acknowledge the Pope as head of the Church, but he does not deny truths of religion at his own discretion.

The existence of heresy is foretold in the Scriptures. Our Lord stated that there would be wheat and cockles in God's Kingdom until the last harvest (Matt. 13); St. Paul said that heresies must come (1 Cor. 11, 19). We read, also, that "it is not for men, but

---

[1] *Catholic Encyclopedia*, "Heresy."

for Him who searcheth the reins and heart, to sit in judgment on the guilt which attaches to an heretical conscience." [2]

Causes of Heresy.—What are the causes of this perversion of the mind which we call heresy? One of the most common causes is excessive intellectual curiosity, which leads people to think that they can comprehend fully all the truths of faith. The human intellect can understand a great deal about the truths of religion, but it is none the less finite and limited; there are many truths

of religion which, while they are not contrary to reason, can never be fully grasped by reason. A man depending on reason alone to guide him in religious matters is like a traveler in a dense forest who carries only a tiny candle or lantern. Such a traveler will see something, but not everything, and he will inevitably go astray.

In many cases, heresy is caused by pride of intellect. This sin reveals itself commonly when the heretic assumes that he has some superior knowledge or virtue which places him above the doctrines of the Church. It is obstinate pride of this type that

---

[2] *Catholic Encyclopedia*, "Heresy."

leads some persons to read books which the Church has placed on the *Index* [3] as being harmful to faith and morals.

A person may also fall into heresy as a result of being born among heretics and associating with them constantly. Such a person is the victim of invincible ignorance. The Church teaches that an heretic of this type who has been baptized may save his soul, provided he acts according to his beliefs and in good faith.

Why Heresy Spreads.—There are three conditions or circumstances which are favorable to the spread of a heresy. (1) The heretical movement may be led by some forceful character. This individual need not be a man of intellect or learning, but he must have the power to move people and make them follow him. (2) The heretical doctrine may be in harmony with contemporary philosophical ideas, or with social and political conditions. (3) The movement may have the support of powerful secular rulers.

The heresies of the first three centuries died out without causing a great deal of danger because, in general, the favorable conditions noted above did not exist.

Action against Heresy.—The Church acts with promptness and severity against heretical movements. When such a movement grows and threatens to disrupt the Church, Bishops assemble in councils—provincial, metropolitan, national, or ecumenical (*i.e.,* general). These Bishops, acting in conjunction with the Pope, and guided by the Holy Ghost, sit as judges in matters of faith and morals. Christ said: "... but if he refuse to hear even the Church, let him be to thee as the heathen and the publican" (Matt. 18, 17). In accordance with this injunction, the heretic is excommunicated and denied the sacraments and the rites of the Church, unless he acknowledges his errors and repents.

The Church during the period we are considering did not impose any temporal punishment on heretics, except separation from their brethren. However, temporal rulers, Christian Emperors, did adopt rigorous measures against the persons and the goods of heretics. From 313 to 424, penal laws were enacted by Emperors which declared that heretics were guilty of crimes

---

[3] The *Index* is a list of objectionable books which the Church forbids Catholics to read.

against the state. We see this in the Justinian and Theodosian Codes. Various were the penalties, including even the death sentence. Heretical books were burned. After the barbarian invaders overthrew the Roman Empire, the laws against heretics remained in force. Heretics were first burned at the stake in the eleventh century, but always by the secular power.

Today the penalties imposed on heretics are of the spiritual order only. Those who, without the authorization of the Holy See, knowingly read or retain books of heretics which propagate or defend heresy, incur excommunication. They are then denied the sacraments and rites of the Church. Furthermore, no Catholic may marry an heretic unless his own Bishop grants a dispensation.

The Church is severe and intolerant toward heretics, and justly so. We are all intolerant of destructive elements within our physical organism; for example, we try to destroy disease germs without any hesitation. Heresy is a destructive element within the spiritual organism and, as such, must be eliminated. Cruelty can be charged only when the punishment imposed on the heretic exceeds the requirements of the case. Christ said: "Do not think I came to send peace upon the earth; I have come to bring a sword, not peace" (Matt. 10, 34-35).

THE SUCCESSFUL STRUGGLE AGAINST HERESY

Arianism.—One of the earliest and most important of heresies was that of Arianism.

1. *Definition and Origin.*—The heresy of Arianism, which arose in the fourth century, denied the divinity of Jesus Christ. The heresy derives its name from Arius, a Priest of Alexandria. Arius denied that the Son is equal in all perfections to God the Father, and that He is co-eternal with the Father. He taught that the Son was created by God the Father, as the first and chief among His creatures.

2. *Rise and Spread.*—Arius began to preach his false doctrines in Alexandria in the year 318. He was in charge of the Church of Baucalis, one of the largest in the city. This important position helped him to gain many listeners, and because of his impressive, austere appearance, his eloquence his skill in argumentation, and

his reputation for sanctity, he succeeded in leading large numbers of Christians astray.

Alexander, the Bishop of Alexandria, called a conference of his Priests. At this conference, Arius was requested to retract his erroneous opinions about the Trinity. Wounded in his sinful pride, he refused to do so. From this time on, the heresy spread like wildfire. Arius sought support among the Bishops of Greece and Asia Minor, who had been trained, like himself, in the school of theology and Holy Scripture at Antioch by Lucian. Among the Churchmen of this school was Eusebius, Bishop of Nicomedia, and a relative of the Emperor Constantine. This Eusebius agreed with Arius and won support for him. Meanwhile, Arius had been excommunicated by his own Bishop, and had gone from Egypt to Palestine, and thence to Nicomedia. He propagated his false teachings in these places in a book called *Thalia,* and by hymns and songs written for the common folk.

3. *The Council of Nicaea.*—These events led to the calling of the First General or Ecumenical Council, the *Council of Nicaea,* in the year 325. As we have seen (page 30), this Council was called under the authority of Emperor Constantine, and also with the approval of Pope Sylvester (314-337). St. Ambrose in his work, *De Fide,* tells us that 318 Bishops attended. In addition, many brilliant men and profound scholars were present in various capacities. Among these was a young Deacon named Athanasius, secretary of the aged Alexander, Bishop of Alexandria. Athanasius entered into a formal debate with Arius. After long deliberation, the Council adopted the *Nicene Creed,* which is the Apostles' Creed, with additional explanations in the first seven articles. All the Bishops present were asked to subscribe to this Creed, which, of course, rejected the heretical doctrines of Arius. At first, thirteen of the 318 Bishops dissented, then only seven; finally, all but two signed the Creed. These two dissenting Bishops, together with Arius himself, were exiled to Illyria by the Emperor.

4. *The Fall of Arianism.*—Even after the Council of Nicaea, Arianism continued to spread, aided by various Emperors, and by members of the royal courts. By means of political influence, Arius got control of important Bishoprics. An Emperor forced Arianism upon the Goths, and from them it spread to other barbarian hordes. At one stage, it threatened to infest the entire

Empire. Arianism was undoubtedly the greatest internal evil which the Church had to face during this period. However, many conflicts within the movement weakened it and paved the way for its ultimate downfall. Arius himself died a revolting death in 336, on the eve of receiving Holy Communion.

St. Athanasius.—We have referred above to Athanasius, the brilliant young Churchman who debated with Arius at the Council of Nicaea. When still a boy, Athanasius' remarkable talents had brought him to the attention of Alexander, Bishop of Alexandria, and the Bishop gave personal attention to his education. Athanasius proved himself fully worthy of these special favors. He became a profound theologian, an eloquent orator, and a dauntless champion of the truth.

When Athanasius accompanied Bishop Alexander to the Council of Nicaea, the latter was aged and crippled, as a result of having been tortured on the rack during the persecution of Galerius. Therefore, he chose Athanasius to speak for him in answer to the sinful but clever Arius. This duty Athanasius carried out very effectively. After the death of Alexander, Athanasius became Bishop of Alexandria. For the remainder of his life, he defended the Church and its doctrines with great learning, courage, and indefatigable zeal. He was sent into exile five times under four Emperors—twice to the West (to Rome and Treves), and three times to Egypt. In spite of this, he continued his holy work until his death in 373. Athanasius is rightly honored as one of four great Doctors of the Oriental Church.

Pope Liberius.—Pope Liberius occupied the Papal throne from 352 to 366, during the period of the later struggles over Arianism. In 355, the Emperor Constantius made an attempt to have the Arians admitted into the Church. In particular, there was one group of Arians who wished to have the word *homoousios* ("same substance") in the Nicene Creed changed to *homoiousios* ("similar substance"). This, in effect, represented a somewhat modified and concealed version of Arianism (sometimes called "semi-Arianism").

The Catholic Bishops, led by Athanasius, protested vehemently against any such compromise. However, a great deal of pressure was applied to the aged Pope Liberius. He was threatened with banishment to Thrace, and even his life appeared to be in danger. Finally, the Pope yielded and agreed to make the desired change, but he promptly repented and continued to uphold the Nicene Creed.

This action of Liberius is no argument against the doctrine of Papal Infallibility; Liberius in agreeing to make this change in the Nicene Creed imposed no belief on Christians. "Besides, if the Pope is to teach *ex cathedra,* common sense requires that he should be free. Liberius, on the other hand, subscribed to the semi-Arian formula while he was separated from his friends and counselors, and in terror of death." [4]

St. Basil.—St. Basil was one of the three Cappadocian champions of the Faith raised up by God to continue the good work of Athanasius. He was a Greek Doctor who, by his eloquence and his powerful pen, consistently resisted the heresiarch, Arius. Basil was born of an old, distinguished Christian family, and enjoyed every opportunity to acquire the best education which the schools of the day offered to those of unusual mentality. His sister, Macrina, influenced him to devote his talents to the study of the Scriptures, rather than to pagan rhetoric. About 360, he left his school of rhetoric, already famous throughout the Near East, and began to lead the life of a monk; it was during this period that he wrote the Rule which formed the basis of the monastic life in the East.

Soon afterward, Basil was summoned to Caesarea, his native city, to combat Arianism. He was consecrated Bishop in 370, and for nine years labored as only a valiant Bishop can. He aided all classes of people in his diocese, and balked the efforts of the Emperor Valens to reinstate Arians. St. Gregory of Nazianzus wrote an account of St. Basil's dramatic interview with the Pretorian Prefect Modestus, the emissary of Valens. Modestus tried to bribe Basil, and then threatened him with confiscation, torture and death. "As for confiscation, Basil replied that he owned nothing but a cloak and a few books; as for torture, Modestus had threatened to tear out his liver, and Basil said that there was nothing gave him more trouble; as for death, he would gladly welcome it." [5] Modestus was won over.

---

[4] Raemer, S. A., *Church History.*   [5] Laux, J., *Church History.*

St. Basil's writings have been preserved. Among them, is a powerful anti-Arian treatise called *Against Eunomius.*

St. Gregory of Nazianzus.—The second of the Cappadocian Doctors who carried on the work of Athanasius was St. Gregory of Nazianzus, a life-long friend of St. Basil. St. Gregory was more fortunate than St. Basil, in that he had two good Catholic Emperors, Gratian and Theodosius, with whom to work against the Arians. He became Bishop of Constantinople and, in this capacity, he preached continually for two years on the doctrine of the Holy Trinity. He presided at the Council of Constantinople in 381 (see below). His writings are voluminous, including some 18,000 lines of poetry. Toward the end of his life, he resigned his Bishopric and devoted himself to prayer and study. He died in 391.

The Council of Constantinople.—The Council of Constantinople (the Second Ecumenical or General Council) was held in the year 381, under the sponsorship of the Emperors Theodosius and Gratian. Its purpose was to put a definite end to Arianism as a spiritual force.

One hundred and fifty Bishops of the East were present at this Council. At first Meletius of Antioch presided; after his death, his place was taken by Gregory of Nazianzus. It is to be noted that, in contrast to other General Councils, the Bishops of the whole world were not summoned to this meeting; nor did the Papal Legates preside, as is usual. None the less, the Council of Constantinople is recognized as a General Council because Pope Damasus approved its acts, and because its doctrinal definitions were accepted throughout the Church and were reaffirmed by later General Councils.

The Council of Constantinople condemned a new phase of Arianism, which denied the God-head of the Holy Ghost. Macedonius, a semi-Arian Bishop of Constantinople, was the leader of this error. Eusebius' explanations were added to the last five articles of the Apostles' Creed. (Thus, the Nicene Creed contains the doctrinal definitions of the first two General Councils.) The Council also issued certain disciplinary decrees regarding the duties and powers of Bishops.

During the years that followed the Council of Constantinople, there was a temporary cessation of heresy in the Empire, although Arianism was still active among the barbarian nations.

Donatism.—Donatism was a false teaching which held that the validity of sacraments depends upon the moral character of the person conferring them. The Donatist doctrine became prevalent in Africa during the fourth century. The leader of the schism was Donatus, an African Bishop. Donatus and his followers refused to recognize the consecration of a faithful Catholic as Bishop of Carthage, for they wished to see one of their own members in this important post. However, their attempts to invalidate the appointment were unavailing. The refusal of the fanatical Donatists to submit to proper authority caused the Emperor Constantine and his successors to take drastic steps

against them. Their property was confiscated and they were deprived of their churches. The Donatists organized slaves and peasants to resist the Emperor, but the schismatic forces were defeated by a Roman army. The strength of the movement was finally broken when Augustine, Bishop of Hippo, called a special council of Catholic and Donatist Bishops to consider the entire problem. This council, which met at Carthage in 412, decided against the Donatists on all points. After this, the Donatist doctrines soon died out, and harmony was restored to the Church of Africa.

Pelagianism.—This heresy denied original sin and erred on the necessity of grace. It was first taught in Africa and later carried to Jerusalem. Pelagius, an English monk lacking in moderation and too severe in dealing with souls, taught that man is born good;

that he does not inherit original sin; and that he can attain supernatural life without the aid of grace, and by his natural powers alone. St. Augustine, Bishop of Hippo in Africa, made short work of Pelagianism. He wrote against it and called the Council of Carthage, which excommunicated Pelagius (412). Pope Innocent I confirmed the decisions of the Council of Carthage. The Emperor Honorius banished Pelagius and his friends from the Western Empire; they went to Nestorius, the Patriarch of Constantinople, for refuge.

Manichaeism.—This was a religion founded by Manes, a Persian who lived in the third century. It was a synthesis of all the religious systems then known, its principal doctrine being that there are two basic and eternal powers, Light and Darkness. God was the source of Good; Satan was the source of Evil. Man was not responsible for the physical and moral evil in the world. This teaching spread to Africa, Spain, France, North Italy, and the Balkans, where it persisted for a thousand years. It flourished in Mesopotamia, Babylonia, India, and China. St. Augustine for nine years was a Manichaean. His penetrating mind discovered its weakness and shallow teaching, and he refuted it with his powerful pen. He exposed its immorality and its tendency to lead to degeneracy.

St. Augustine.—We have referred to the work of St. Augustine, Bishop of Hippo, in combating Donatism, Pelagianism, and Manichaeism. This genius, the greatest of the Latin Doctors, or the Doctors of the West, was an African, born of a pagan father and a Christian mother, Monica. His mother taught him the religion of Christ in his early childhood and he always loved it, although he went through many experiences before his baptism. Literary studies in Carthage, an intellectual center at the time, prepared his brilliant intellect for the profession of teacher of rhetoric. He taught in Africa and later at Milan. He dabbled in Manichaeism, but while in Milan he met St. Ambrose the Bishop. The worldly Augustine was touched by the sermons of St. Ambrose and he devoted himself to a deep study of Christianity. He was baptized, and later chosen Bishop of Hippo by the voice of the people. The thirty-five years he spent as a Bishop were rich in virtuous accomplishments. He was the outstanding figure of the Catholic Church in Africa, and was known throughout the entire world of his day. Indeed, he is considered one of the greatest personalities in all Church history. "The whole course of the centuries has not dimmed the lustre of his greatness nor lessened the charm of his character." [6]

In his writings, St. Augustine preserved the most worthy elements of Graeco-Roman culture, and added to them all the knowledge and wisdom which the Church had accumulated up to his day. This combination he enriched with the touch of his own creative and saintly personality. His writings are especially notable for their marvelous psychological penetration—that is, their insight into the workings of the human mind and spirit. "He scaled the heights and probed the depths of human nature." [7] One can see this quality with particular clarity in his *Confessions* (really his autobiography), which is considered one of the great treasures of world literature. Another great work of Augustine's is his *De Civitate Dei* ("City of God"). This book was written shortly after the capture of the city of Rome by the barbarian Alaric in 410. Analyzing this event, Augustine showed with matchless eloquence and learning that the "Eternal City" was not a material city of walls, but rather the spiritual force of Christianity.

St. Augustine died in 430, as the Vandals were storming his city.

Nestorianism.—Nestorius was a Syrian who became Patriarch of Constantinople in the fifth century. At that time, there were two centers of theological study, Antioch and Alexandria. One of the principal subjects of theological speculation was the two natures in Christ, the human and the divine. As a member of the school of Antioch, Nestorius taught that there were actually two persons in Christ, and that since Mary was the Mother only of the human person, she could not rightly be called the "Mother of God." The Church, of course, teaches that there is only one person in Christ, although there are two *natures*—the human and the divine. Since the two natures are united in one person, Mary is truly the Mother of God. St. Cyril of Alexandria protested the heretical ideas advanced by Nestorius and brought them to the attention of the Pope, Celestine I, who condemned Nestorius at a synod of Roman Bishops. The heresiarch was asked to retract,

---
[6] Lortz, J. and Kaiser, E. G., *History of the Church.*
[7] *Ibid.*

but he refused to do so, evidently thinking he could depend on the aid of the Emperor, Theodosius II.

To deal with this problem, Theodosius called a General Council, which met at Ephesus in 431. The Holy Father appointed two Papal Legates to preside, and about 200 Bishops attended. Both St. Cyril and Nestorius were summoned, but Nestorius refused to appear. He was excommunicated, deposed and later exiled by the Emperor. He died in Egypt about 450. His heresy however never fully died out; it reached its peak in the fourteenth century, and exists even today, in Persia.

Eutychianism (Monophysitism).—The heresy known as Eutychianism or Monophysitism was founded by Eutyches, an aged, fanatical, proud arch-Abbot of a monastery near Constantinople. Eutyches set himself the task of refuting Nestorianism, but in attempting to do this he went to the opposite extreme; he declared that there was only one nature in Christ—the divine nature. This heresy derives its name (*monophysitism*) from two Greek words: *mono* meaning "one," and *physis* meaning "nature."

Eutyches was supported in his erroneous teachings by Dioscorus, Bishop of Alexandria. A Provincial Council was called at Constantinople, at which Eutyches was excommunicated. He appealed his case to Dioscorus, to the Emperor, Theodosius II, and to the Pope, St. Leo. Flavian, the Patriarch of Constantinople, sent detailed information regarding the case to the Pope. The Pope replied with an Epistle, in which he gave full instructions to Flavian. While this was going on, Dioscorus prevailed upon the Emperor to call a council at Ephesus (449).

Dioscorus assumed control of this council and refused to allow the Epistle of Pope Leo to be read. Flavian, the Papal Legate, was insulted, and died three days later as a result of his mistreatment. The 135 Bishops present were forced, at the point of the sword, to sign the infamous documents which reinstated Eutyches and acquitted him of heresy. When Pope Leo received a report of this council, he called it the "Robber Synod."

The Council of Chalcedon.—The Council of Chalcedon, the Fourth General Council, was convoked in 451. It was attended by 630 Bishops, under the presidency of four Papal Legates. At this great meeting, the Epistle of Pope Leo was finally enunciated, and the true Catholic doctrine explained. The twin heresies of

HERESIES OF THE FOURTH, FIFTH AND SIXTH CENTURIES

Principal Heresiarch	Error of Heresy	Outstanding Catholic Opponents	Condemnation
Arius	Denied the divinity of Christ.	St. Athanasius, St. Basil, St. Gregory Nazianzus, St. Gregory of Nyssa.	Council of Nicaea, 325.
Donatus	Validity of the sacraments depends on the moral qualities of the person administering them.	St. Augustine.	Council of Carthage, 412.
Pelagius	Denied original sin and the necessity of grace for salvation.	St. Augustine.	Council of Carthage (412) and Council of Ephesus (431). Condemnation later confirmed by Pope Innocent I.
Manes	Taught that there are two eternal powers, God and Satan. (A synthesis of all religions existing to that time.)	St. Augustine.	Council of Lateran, 1139 (Pope Innocent II).
Nestorius	There are two persons in Christ; Mary is not the Mother of God.	St. Cyril of Alexandria.	Council of Ephesus, 431.
Eutyches	There is only one nature in Christ—the divine.	Flavian, Patriarch of Constantinople.	Council of Chalcedon, 451 (Pope Leo the Great).

Nestorianism and Monophysitism were refuted; Dioscorus and Eutyches were deposed and excommunicated; and the acts of the "Robber Synod" were revoked.

These decisions of the Council of Chalcedon were received with joy in the West, but in the East they were misrepresented and bitterly opposed. The controversy continued for a century and led to a schism of those Eastern peoples who speak languages other than Greek.

The Fifth and Sixth General Councils.—The Fifth General Council was called at Constantinople in 553 in an attempt to settle doctrinal disputes in the East. The Emperor Justinian had been trying to induce Pope Vigilius to condemn a document known as the *Three Chapters,* which dealt with certain classes of Nestorians. If the Pope had condemned this document, he would have won the favor of pro-Nestorian groups in Egypt and elsewhere. For three years, however, Vigilius refused to approve the condemnation of the *Three Chapters.* Finally, under duress, he did so, but soon afterward retracted his approval.

The Emperor and Pope then agreed to call the Fifth General Council at Constantinople, but the Pope refused to be present personally, and he was sent into exile. Later, to avoid the appointment of an anti-Pope, Vigilius gave his sanction to the acts of the Council. His successor, Pelagius I, did the same. This action won over the Egyptians for awhile, but the conciliation was not general, and a Sixth General Council had to meet at Constantinople in 680 before the doctrinal disputes in the East were finally settled.

The Doctors of the Church.—The fourth, fifth and sixth centuries, during which the above-mentioned struggles against heresy took place, produced a wealth of Christian literature. In particular, there were eight intellectual giants, whose writings against the heretics, and on other moral and doctrinal subjects, were of inestimable value. Upon these brilliant and devoted men the Church has conferred the title of "Doctor of the Church." The four *Greek Doctors* are St. Athanasius, St. Basil, St. Gregory Nazianzus, and St. John Chrysostom; the four *Latin Doctors* are St. Ambrose, St. Jerome, St. Augustine, and St. Gregory the Great. Since 1568, twenty-one men have been proclaimed "Doctors of the Church." Of these, six lived during the

THE GENERAL OR ECUMENICAL COUNCILS OF THE CHURCH

Council	Date	Attendance	Accomplishments	Popes Giving Approval
1. First Council of Nicaea..	325	318 Bishops, Emperor Constantine	Condemned heresy of Arius; promulgated Nicene Creed.	Sylvester I
2. First Council of Constantinople	381	150 Bishops, Emperor Theodosius I	Condemned heresy of Macedonius.	Damasus I
3. Council of Ephesus	431	200 Bishops, Emperor Theodosius II	Condemned heresy of Nestorius.	Celestine I
4. Council of Chalcedon	451	603 Bishops, Emperor Marcian, Papal Legates	Condemned Eutyches and Dioscorus; acknowledged Papal supremacy.	Pope Leo Great
5. Second Council of Constantinople	553	165 Bishops, Emperor Justinian I	Condemned *Three Chapters*; renewed Nestorian condemnation	Vigilius
6. Third Council of Constantinople	680-681	170 Bishops	Condemned Monothelitism.	Agatho (died) Leo II
7. Second Council of Nicaea, ended at Constantinople	787	367 Bishops	Condemned Iconoclasts.	Adrian I
8. Fourth Council of Constantinople	869-870	102 Bishops	Condemned errors of Photius and deposed him; reinstated Ignatius in See of Constantinople.	Adrian II
9. First Council of Lateran (at Rome)	1123	300 Bishops, 600 mitred Abbots	Regulated rights of Church and Roman Emperor in election of Bishops and Abbots.	Calixtus II
10. Second Council of Lateran (at Rome)	1139	1000 Bishops, Pope presiding	Condemned Albigenses; repressed schism of Peter Leo.	Innocent II
11. Third Council of Lateran (at Rome)	1179	300 Bishops	Condemned Waldenses; regulated election of Pope and Bishops	Alexander III

#	Council	Date	Attendance	Actions	Pope
12.	Fourth Council of Lateran (at Rome)	1215	412 Bishops, 800 Abbots and Friars, sovereigns and princes	Annual Confession and Holy Communion during Easter time made obligatory; authorized a Crusade to Holy Land.	Innocent III
13.	First Council of Lyons	1245	140 Bishops, Emperor Baldwin of Constantinople	Excommunicated and deposed Emperor Frederick II.	Innocent IV
14.	Second Council of Lyons	1274	500 Bishops, 70 Abbots, 100 minor Prelates	Attempted to unite Greek Schismatics to Church	Gregory X
15.	Council of Vienne (France)	1311-1312	300 Bishops, many Prelates	Suppressed Knights Templars; condemned Beguards and Beguines.	Clement V
16.	Council of Constance	1414-1418	200 Bishops, Prelates	Condemned schism created by three candidates for Pope; recognized Martin V as lawful Pope.	Martin V
17.	Council of Florence	1438	200 Bishops, Greek Emperor John Palaeologus	Declared supremacy of Pope over whole Church; received submission of Eastern and Russian schismatic Bishops.	Eugenius IV
18.	Fifth Council of Lateran (at Rome)	1512-1517	120 Bishops, representatives of kings and princes	Abolished Pragmatic Sanction (France); dogma of immortality of soul defined; condemned Council of Pisa (1511).	Julius II, Leo X
19.	Council of Trent	1545-1563	200 Bishops, 7 Abbots, 7 generals of Religious Orders, representatives of Catholic kings and princes	Explained Catholic doctrines; condemned contrary errors; reformed discipline.	Paul III, Julius III, Pius IV
20.	Council of Vatican	1869	704 Patriarchs, Bishops, superiors of Religious Orders	Defined supremacy of St. Peter and successors; defined Pope's Infallibility; regulated discipline	Pius IX

period we have been discussing in this chapter: ST. HILARY of Poitiers, ST. EPHREM the Syrian, ST. CYRIL of Jerusalem, ST. CYRIL of Alexandria, ST. PETER CHRYSOLOGUS, and ST. LEO the Great. In our universities today, the writings of all these men are studied, both in translation and in the languages in which they were written—Medieval Latin and Greek. These writings, in poetry and prose, mirror the social, economic, and political life of the people of those days.

We should all be familiar with the lives and achievements of the eight Greek and Latin Doctors who stand out so gloriously in the early history of the Church. Four of these men have already been discussed in our summary of the struggle against heresy. Gregory the Great will be considered in Chapter 5. Following are brief sketches of the other three figures (St. John Chrysostom, St. Ambrose, and St. Jerome).

St. John Chrysostom.—St. John Chrysostom is famed as one of the greatest orators in the history of the Church. In his youth, he sought a career in the forum, the theatre and the halls of learning. Under the influence of his mother, however, he abandoned these pursuits and devoted himself to sacred eloquence; by preaching the truths of the Faith, he became the "Glory of the Christian Pulpit."

John's golden eloquence made him a great favorite in Constantinople, and the people sought him for their Bishop. Because of his reputation as a speaker, he was invited to speak at court, but he was not satisfied merely to impress the Empress Eudoxia and the court Bishops with his fine oratory; with unflinching courage, he insisted on speaking out unpalatable truths about the questionable conduct of the Empress and her followers. Finally, he offended the Empress by comparing her to Herodias demanding the head of John the Baptist. The Emperor exiled him to the Black Sea region, but he died on the journey there in the year 407, at the age of sixty-three.

St. Ambrose.—This Latin Doctor of the Church first drew the attention of the people of Milan to himself when, as governor, he presented himself to restore order at the election of a Bishop. A child in the mob cried out, "Ambrose Bishop," and the inspiration was gladly received. Ambrose protested in vain that he was not worthy of this honor. After eight days of preparation, he

was raised to the dignity of a Bishop, although he had been merely a catechumen up to that time. Ambrose was born and trained to lead people. His father had been a Roman prefect of Gaul, and he himself had occupied important posts as a Roman official.

Ambrose's deeds as a Bishop were glorious. The Empress Justina demanded the surrender of a church for the Arians; Ambrose refused the request. He took refuge in the cathedral when an attempt was made to exile him, and the people guarded him night and day. He spent his time while thus confined composing hymns and teaching the people to sing them. By his sweet preaching and singing, Ambrose attracted the great St. Augustine to the beauties of Christianity. Later in life, he influenced the Emperor Theodosius to do public penance. Theodosius had ordered the massacre of thousands of people at Thessalonica in retribution for the murder of an unpopular governor; Ambrose refused him admission to the cathedral until he had done penance for this horrible deed.

Ambrose was a man of deeds, rather than a man of words. Nevertheless, his writings are many and portray a character of strength and beauty. He died in 397.

St. Jerome.—This fiery, energetic character was the most profound of the Latin Doctors. He was born about 342 of a wealthy Christian family of Stridon in Dalmatia. In Rome, he obtained a fine classical education, mastering Greek and Hebrew thoroughly. As one might expect, he was a brilliant Latinist; he modelled his style upon the writings of Cicero.

At the invitation of Pope Damasus, Jerome translated the entire Bible into Latin from the original Hebrew and Greek. This translation, known as the *Vulgate,* is the version sanctioned by the Catholic Church even today. The monumental work was accomplished in Bethlehem, where Jerome lived the life of a hermit, practicing the virtues of mortification and humility. He was also a Priest, and devoted some time to the spiritual direction of a monastery of wealthy women who desired to live a life of Christian virtue. Among these women was Paula, a noble Roman matron, and her daughter Eustochium. Jerome's other writings are among the finest treasures of the Church. Jerome was not slow to be provoked to anger, a trait which helped to make him a formidable controversialist against such people as Rufinus, the historian and translator of Origen. The Catholic Church honors St. Jerome as the Doctor of Sacred Scripture.

THE ORGANIZATION OF THE PRIMITIVE CHURCH

The Hierarchy.—The governing officials of the Church are the Pope, who is also Bishop of Rome, the other Bishops, the Priests, and the Deacons. The Bishop of Rome, the successor of St. Peter, is the supreme head of the Church, to whom all others owe obedience in spiritual matters. This primacy has been established ever since all the Apostles recognized St. Peter as head of the Church. As the numbers of Christians increased, the Apostles appointed Bishops in the larger centers; these Bishops were given the power to ordain Priests and Deacons, who were to assist the Bishops. Priests, Deacons and sub-Deacons are said to have *major orders,* but there are also four *minor orders* within the clergy: Acolytes, Exorcists, Lectors and Porters. Titles such as *Cardinal* and *Archbishop* do not signify an increase in power or authority; they merely confer honor and the right of precedence on outstanding characters who are more directly in contact with the Pope. These officials keep the Pope informed of the condition and needs of the Church in their localities.

The Papacy.—The Apostolic succession of all the Bishops of the Catholic world has been maintained by the unbroken succession of the Bishops of Rome. In every other See established by the Apostles, there has been a break in the succession; that is, heretical Bishops have occupied the Sees at one time or another.

The first Popes did not exercise all their power and authority. Means of transportation and communication were very limited; generally persecutions hindered free intercourse between Popes and Bishops. None the less, the fact that all but one of the first thirty Popes were martyrs gives some indication of the importance attached to the Papacy by those who were trying to destroy the Church. Even while St. John was living, the fourth Pope, St. Clement, wrote a letter to the Corinthians in which he spoke of the authority of the Pope as binding everyone. There are many historical examples of the early Bishops appealing to Rome to settle disputes. During the struggles with the heresies, even the heretical Bishops appealed to Rome to support their claims. The decrees of the General Councils derived the force of law from the fact that they were approved and ratified by the Popes. Besides, we have seen that these Councils were presided over by Papal Legates. No one exercises all his powers unless a definite occasion calls for it. Thus it was with the Popes; they always possessed full powers, but exercised them only as the need arose.

Bishops.—In Rome, until the fourth century, the Bishop was the one who celebrated Mass and consecrated the Sacred Species, which were then distributed to the various churches by the Priests and Deacons. The Bishop administered the sacraments, while the Priests and Deacons prepared the people for the reception of the sacraments. With the expansion of the Church and the great increase in the number of Christians, it became imperative for Bishops to share their powers and duties with Priests. Today the chief duties of the Bishops are to administer Holy Orders and Confirmation, and to appoint Priests to their parish duties. In the beginning, the Bishops were elected by the people and the clergy; later the people's share in the election became merely a matter of form. After being elected, a new Bishop was approved by the other Bishops of the province, and was then consecrated by three Bishops.

Parishes.—A local congregation committed to one Pastor or Priest is called a *parish*. The Priest celebrates the Mass and administers the sacraments, except Holy Orders and Confirmation, and he preaches the Gospel to the people. There were a few such parishes in the third century in the country districts, but in general they did not begin to exist until the end of the fifth century. Pastors are appointed by the local Bishop, and they exercise their powers and perform their duties only with the authorization of the Bishop.

The parishioners in the early days of the Church were divided into the *faithful* and the *catechumens*. The faithful were those who had been baptized. The catechumens were persons being instructed for baptism. The course of instructions lasted two or three years, and often individuals did not receive baptism until late in life. These catechumens were permitted to attend only the first part of the Mass. The faithful, in turn, comprised several distinct groups—*confessors, widows* and *virgins* Confessors were those who had been imprisoned or tortured for the Faith. *Widows* were pious women who devoted themselves to the service of the Church. *Virgins* were women especially dedicated to the service of God. By the end of the fourth century, virgins wore a special garb and lived in convents, much like those we have today.

The Liturgical Year.—The liturgy refers to public acts of worship. (The Mass, of course, is the public act of worship for all Catholics.) The liturgical year is the ecclesiastical year, beginning with the Sunday nearest the feast of St. Andrew, November 30. A certain portion of the Mass is changed daily, and the prayers honor a particular feast of Our Lord, His Blessed Mother, or the saint of the day.

The primitive Church observed the feasts of Easter, Pentecost, and the Sunday of each week. The feast of the Epiphany was celebrated in the East as early as the second century, but it was not observed in the West until the fourth century. The celebration of Christmas began in the third century. Starting in the second century, each particular church observed the day of the death of its martyrs. The celebration of daily Mass was initiated in all churches in the fourth century. The forty days' fast before Easter began to be observed in the fourth century.

At first, the Bishop and the clergy did not wear special vestments. Gradually, however, the ordinary dress was modified and ornamented for the divine services, until it became distinctive, much as we know it today.

Basilicas.—During the third century, the Christians began to erect separate buildings for divine services. These buildings, known as basilicas, were oblong in shape. A basilica, as we have noted above (page 27), consisted of a long central aisle or *nave;* on either side of the nave, and separated from it by pillars, was a side aisle. The ceiling over these side aisles was somewhat lower than that over the nave. The nave terminated in a semi-circular *apse,* which was occupied by the clergy only. The altar was usually placed in front of the apse, although sometimes it appeared in the center of the apse. The laity occupied the nave and aisles of the church, different sections being reserved for men and women. Nearest the apse, were special places for the consecrated virgins, the widows, and aged women. The interior of the basilica was decorated with frescoes and mosaics portraying scenes from the life of Christ; symbols were employed for decorative purposes. Statues were not used, as there was still fear of pagan worship of "graven images." In the sixth century, the East developed a circular type of church architecture called *Byzantine*.

Constantine erected four great basilicas in Rome: *St. John Lateran, SS. Peter and Paul, St. Paul Outside the Walls,* and *St. Lawrence Outside the Walls*. The same Emperor also built basilicas in Constantinople and Palestine. In the fourth century, Pope Liberius constructed a notable basilica in Rome called *St. Mary Major*.

CHAPTER 4

THE MIGRATIONS OF THE NATIONS
THE RISE OF MONASTICISM

> "The Roman Empire, without the Barbarians, was an abyss of servitude and corruption. The Barbarians, without the monks, were chaos. The Barbarians and the monks united re-created a world which was to be called Christendom."
> —COUNT DE MONTALEMBERT ("The Monks of the West")

THE BARBARIAN INVASIONS

Introduction.—The *migrations of the nations* is an historical term to designate the invasions of Germanic tribes into the Roman Empire during the period from 375 until 568. The general movement was from northeastern to southwestern Europe, and also extended into northern Africa, by way of Spain. The Western Empire bore the brunt of this invasion, and disintegrated in the process, but the Eastern Empire, except for the Balkan peninsula, was scarcely touched. Rome finally fell in 476, when Odoacer deposed the last Emperor, Romulus Augustulus. Amidst the Roman ruins, the Church stood firm. Like a loving mother, she united her children, the Romans and the barbarians, in a European medieval civilization that was to endure over a thousand years.

The Germanic Barbarians.—Roman historians, such as Julius Caesar and Tacitus, introduced the Germanic tribes into the pages of recorded history. We learn from these writers that the German barbarians were a tall, blond, blue-eyed people, of great bodily strength. They were fierce, hard-fighting and hard-drinking. They could neither read nor write, and had only the simplest industries and crafts. Their principal occupation was agriculture, although the men spent much of their time in hunting, fishing, and fighting. The Germans lived in crude huts, which were usually grouped together in small villages. Every tribe had its chief or king, who was really a military commander. These people were independent and liberty-loving, and they were skillful and courageous fighters.

The Romans fought many campaigns against the Germanic tribes, but even under such great leaders as Julius Caesar, they were unable to subdue the barbarians completely. The Germans often raided the frontier, and considerable numbers of them filtered into the Empire and settled there. The main body of the Germans, however, was held in check until the year 376.

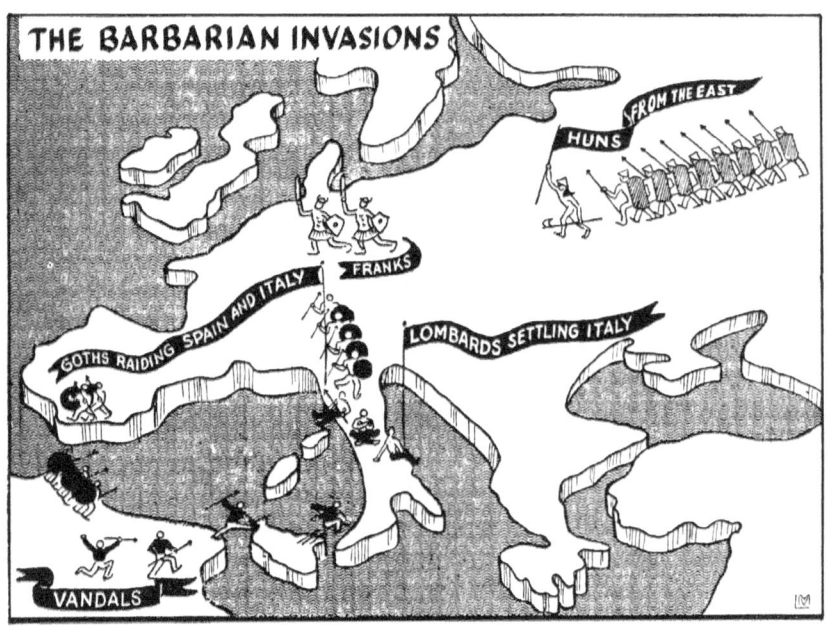

To understand what happened in 376, we must know something of the history of the *Huns*. These were not Germans but fierce nomads from central Asia. They were "fleet and indefatigable horsemen, low in stature, wild in features and appearance, and ruthless in conduct; they carried devastation wherever they went." About 375, they swept into western Europe.

The Visigoths.—A German tribe known as the Visigoths attempted to resist the Huns but they were completely defeated. The Visigoths fled in terror, and soon came to the Danube River, which separated their lands from the Roman Empire. They implored the Emperor, Valens, for permission to cross the river and take refuge within the Empire. This permission was granted, and 200,000 Visigoths settled within Roman territory.

Mistreatment by Roman officials soon caused the Visigoths to revolt. Under their leader, Alaric, they defeated the Romans at the battle of Adrianople, and raided westward into Greece and Italy. Finally, in 410, they entered the city of Rome as conquerers. They pillaged and plundered the city, but spared the public buildings and the Christian churches. For two years, the Visigoth forces remained in southern Italy, where Alaric died. His followers settled in southern Gaul and northern Spain. They were Arians until a later date.

The Vandals.—Simultaneously with the migration of the Visigoths under Alaric, other Germanic tribes invaded the Empire, wreaking havoc with sword and fire. In 406, three tribes, the *Vandals,* the *Sueves,* and the *Asiatic Alans* swarmed through Gaul, Italy and Spain. The Roman Emperor granted northern Spain to the Sueves, Portugal and central Spain to the Alans, and southern Spain to the Vandals. Shortly afterward, a conflict arose between the Visigoths on one side and the Vandals and Alans on the other. The Vandals, 80,000 men, women and children under the leadership of Genseric, crossed the straits of Gibraltar into northern Africa. Genseric captured Carthage in 439, and then, with a large fleet, sailed to Italy. His armies overcame all opposition, and he soon arrived at Rome. There, he was met by Pope Leo I, who prevailed upon the fierce conqueror not to slaughter or torture the people. Genseric, however, did occupy Rome and took away many of the art treasures which the Visigoths had spared in 410. Genseric died in Africa in 477, and the Vandal kingdom lasted until 534, when it fell to Roman power.

The Huns.—We have already seen how the Huns, fierce marauders from central Asia, drove the Visigoths across the Danube River late in the fourth century. After this, the Huns continued their career of conquest. Under the leadership of the shrewd and ruthless Attila, who became known as the "Scourge of God," they spread death and destruction throughout western Europe. The barbarians and Romans united to meet the Huns and, in 451, defeated them in a great battle on the Catalaunian Fields (*Châlons*). This victory thrust back a most formidable threat to Christianity. Some time later, Attila reorganized his forces and drove into northern Italy. There he was met by Pope Leo I, who overawed the "Scourge of God" by his impressive words and appearance. Attila died in 453, and the Huns later disappeared from Europe.

The Ostrogoths.—The Ostrogoths (or East Goths) were Germanic tribes who settled in regions around the Black Sea. When the Visigoths fled before the Huns into the Roman Empire, the Ostrogoths came to occupy the lands which they had vacated. In 380, many Ostrogoths moved into a Roman province. At different times they acted as allies of both the Visigoths and the Romans. In the year 476 [1] the Visigoth chieftain, Odoacer, entered Rome and deposed the last of the Roman Emperors in the West. Odoacer then ruled in Italy as King. The Eastern Emperor, naturally, was disturbed by this triumph of the barbarians, and he finally ordered Theodoric, leader of the Ostrogoths, to expel the Visigoths from Rome. Theodoric discharged the commission in 489; then he settled in Italy with his followers and ruled there, from his capital at Ravenna, until his death in 526. It is to be noted, however, that Theodoric recognized the supremacy of the Eastern Emperor. The Ostrogoths finally migrated to Hungary and Turkey.

An interesting story is told of a prominent Ostrogoth named Totila, who went to visit St. Benedict in 543. St. Benedict told him that he would die in ten years. Totila did die in 552, in accordance with St. Benedict's prophecy.

The Lombards.—Northern Italy was settled by the Lombards in the sixth century. They were even a worse scourge than the earlier barbarians, for they established permanent settlements, while the others had not usually remained long in the same place. Pope Gregory the Great (590-604) met the Lombards and kept them from pillaging Rome by paying an annual tribute. This Germanic tribe lacked a forceful leader. As a result, there was much fighting between jealous Lombard chieftains. After about a century, they were crushed by the Franks under Pepin (page 82).

---

[1] This year is usually taken as the date of the fall of the Roman Empire.

The Franks.—The Germanic Franks settled in northern France. They were heathens but, unlike other Germanic tribes, they were unspoiled by the taint of Arianism. In 493, the Frankish King, Clovis, was converted to Catholicity with 3000 of his warriors. On Christmas day, 496, they were baptized at Rheims by the Bishop. The whole nation became Catholic, and France is called the "eldest daughter" of the Church in Europe. The Franks were to be the first feudal state to emerge from the disorders of the barbaric invasions, and they were destined to dominate the new civilization of the Middle Ages.

The Burgundians.—Southeastern France became the home of the Arian Burgundians. They united with the Franks, who conquered them. Clotilda, the Catholic wife of Clovis, was a Burgundian princess born of Arian parents.

Results of the Barbarian Invasions.—The barbarian invasions and settlements were not an unmixed evil. The immediate effects were disorder and the destruction of Roman civilization. Terrible losses were inflicted upon the Church; her churches and monasteries were destroyed and many of her clergy were killed. But the barbarians, a vigorous, unspoiled people, rid the world of the moral decay of the ancient pagans.

The Church had to begin anew to convert these barbarians. The approach was entirely different than it had been when the Romans were being won over to the Faith. The Romans had been a decadent people, corrupt with wealth, and haughty with intellectual achievements and political power. The barbarians, on the other hand, were simple and vital; they were anxious to find spiritual guidance and to absorb the rudiments of civilization. Conscious of this need, Popes, Bishops and missionaries (especially Benedictines) went forth to meet the barbarians. The barbarians were Christianized and a new civilization sprang up. The German element blended with the Roman and, under the influence of Christianity, the noble medieval culture developed.

MONASTICISM AND MONASTERIES

The Beginnings of Monasticism.—The Church is a divine institution and Divine Providence is ever present to meet each crisis. When the Church seemed on the verge of collapse, about to be crushed by heresy in the East and the barbarians in the West, the institution of monasticism acted as an effectual counter-influence. Monasticism, the way of life chosen by monks and nuns, appeared early in the history of Christianity. Gradually it was subjected to the discipline of the Church. St. Basil wrote the Rule accepted by monasteries in the East; St. Benedict prepared the Rule for the monks in the West.

Monasticism as an institution began in the fourth century in the East. Early in this century, thousands of Christians fled pagan corruption and sought salvation in the deserts of Asia Minor, Arabia and Egypt by living a life of self-denial and prayer. One of the hermits of Egypt was St. Anthony. Other hermits began to gather around this great and good man, seeking his constant guidance. He assembled the hermits periodically for prayers and instructions, but he did not develop a definite plan of organization.

Early Monasteries in the East.—The hermits in upper Egypt wished to join together into a permanent organization. Thus, originated monasticism, a common life of holy men accepting a clearly defined discipline. The first monastery was established on the banks of the Nile in 318. Nine more were established under the leadership of St. Pachomius. According to the rule of Pachomius, the monks divided their time between manual labor, chiefly in the fields, and prayer. They ate the same food and had all things in common. St. Basil, who had traveled and studied the system of Pachomius, saw its value and adopted it. Basil's Rule, however, added a provision for study. This Rule became the basis of monastic life in the East.

Early Monasteries in the West.—About the same time, many eminent men in the West endeavored to lead the lives of hermits. St. Jerome, St. Ambrose, St. Augustine and St. Athanasius all wrote in praise of monasticism. The barbarians, however, devastated practically all the monasteries of the West, except those of Ireland.

The rebirth of monasticism in the West is associated with St. Martin of Tours, St. Columban and, above all, with St. Benedict.

St. Benedict.—Benedict was born late in the fifth century, and was educated in Rome. The vices of the day horrified the youth, and he went into Subiaco to live the life of a hermit in penance and prayer. In a few years, others were attracted to him. He established a monastery at Monte Cassino, Italy, in 529. This was the cradle of the Benedictine Order. Benedict wrote a Rule of Life which went into minute detail on every phase of the monk's life. Benedict's Rule embodied a wholesome balance between prayer and piety on the one hand, and practical work on the other.

The Benedictine monasteries were the main bulwark of the Church during the conversion of the barbarians in Europe. From their foundation in Italy, the Benedictines spread out to Sicily, France, England and Germany. Wherever they went, they drained the marshes, cleared the forests, tilled the barren lands, and built a monastery with its church and school.

The Benedictine Order at one time included 37,000 monasteries and colleges. "The Order of St. Benedict numbers 24 Popes, 200 Cardinals, over 4000 Bishops, 1500 canonized Saints and 15,000 authors," wrote a historian about fifty years ago.[2]

St. Benedict's sister was St. Scholastica, a nun.

Plan of a Monastery.—The architectural plan of a typical monastery was that of an ancient Roman villa. The peristyle became the cloisters; the atrium became the community room; the magnificent Roman garden, with its fountain and statuary, was replaced by the cemetery with its great central crucifix.

The monastery contained workshops for every trade. The monks also raised sheep, whose wool was woven into cloth, and whose skin furnished parchment for books. Most monasteries contained well-stocked libraries. Rheims, for example, had 6000 hand-written volumes. The volumes were ornamented with beautiful designs wrought in gold and other colors. In the monastery school, all who wished instruction received it without charge. The poor and the sick of the neighboring region were cared for in the monastery.

---

[2] Dreher, T., *Outlines of Church History*.

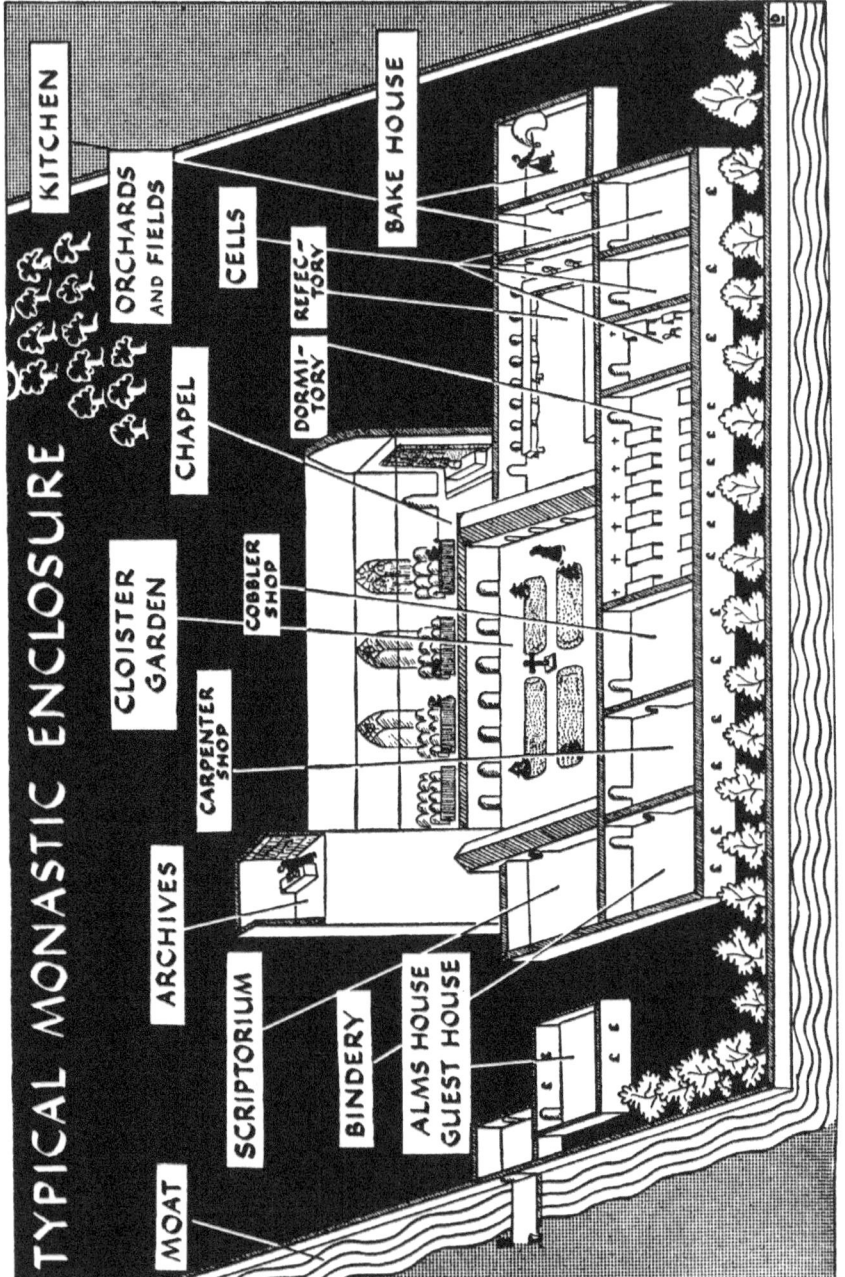

St. Patrick in Ireland.

—Ireland, the "Isle of Saints and Scholars," escaped the social and political upheavals of Europe during the first few centuries of the Christian era. The Roman proconsul and tax gatherer did not drain her resources; nor was she influenced by Roman civilization and corruption.

These circumstances help us to understand the rapidity and intensity with which the Irish people embraced Christianity when the Faith was carried to them. In 431, Pope Celestine sent Palladius, a Roman, to be the first Bishop of the Irish. Palladius remained only one year in Erin, and founded three small churches. This was no more than a small beginning, but the work was carried on by a truly great man, St. Patrick.

St. Patrick was born about the year 389. His exact birthplace is disputed by historians. He came of a pious Christian family and received a good education; in his seventeenth year, however, he was captured by Irish marauders and was carried off to Ireland as a slave. He remained in bondage for some years, tending sheep and holding converse with God. Finally, he escaped to Gaul, where he was received by some kinsfolk and was educated to be a missionary to the Irish. In 432, he returned to Ireland, a consecrated Bishop. Several Priests accompanied him, and for twenty-nine years he and his assistants propagated the Faith in Ireland. Patrick appealed first to the chieftains, then to the poets and lawyers, and finally to the common people. These methods proved highly successful. Patrick died in Ireland in 461.

The monasteries of Ireland during the sixth century became world-famous and were cradles of learning and holiness from which missionaries went forth to evangelize almost every nation of Europe. The most important monastery was Clonard in Meath, founded by St. Finnian in 527. At times, several thousand students were in residence there.

CHRONOLOGICAL TABLE OF PRINCIPAL EVENTS IN CHURCH HISTORY

YEAR	EVENT
318	First monastery founded by Pachomius on the Nile in Egypt
325	First Ecumenical Council, at Nicaea, condemned the heresy of Arius, promulgated the Nicene Creed
376	Visigoths (Germanic barbarians) crossed Danube into Roman Empire
378	Battle of Adrianople, at which Visigoths defeated Romans
379	St. Gregory of Nazianzus became Bishop of Constantinople
381	Second Ecumenical Council, at Constantinople, condemned the heresy of Macedonius, added to the Nicene Creed
390	St. Ambrose, Bishop of Milan, commanded Emperor Theodosius to do public penance
406	Vandals migrated to Africa
420	St. Jerome died at Bethlehem, after finishing the Vulgate version of Bible
430	Death of St. Augustine, Bishop of Hippo
431	Third Ecumenical Council, at Ephesus, condemned heresy of Nestorius and that of Pelagius
432	St. Patrick consecrated Bishop of Ireland
449	The "Robber Synod" of Ephesus
451	Fourth Ecumenical Council, at Chalcedon, condemned heresies of Eutyches and Dioscorus
451	Huns, under Attila, defeated at battle of Châlons
452	Attila persuaded by Pope Leo I not to attack Rome
476	Fall of Rome to barbarians, led by Odoacer
496	Baptism of Clovis and 3000 Franks
529	Foundation of the Benedictines
553	Fifth Ecumenical Council (the second at Constantinople) condemned the *Three Chapters,* confirmed the condemnation of Nestorianism
568	Lombards migrated into Italy
587	Conversion of Spain
590	St. Gregory the Great became Pope

SUPPLEMENTARY MATERIAL FOR UNIT II

REFERENCES

Curran, E. L., *Great Moments in Catholic History*, pp. 18-25
Dreher, T., *Outlines of Churchc History*, pp. 28-42
Eugene, Brother, *Bible and Church History*, pp. 245-260
Forner, B. N., *The Story of the Church*, pp. 36-95
Johnson, G. W., Hannan, J. D., Dominica, Sr., *Story of the Church*, pp. 87-154
Just, Sister Mary, *The Immortal Fire*, pp. 1-29
Laux, J., *Church History*, pp. 104-189
Lortz, J., Kaiser, E. G., *History of the Church*, pp. 86-142
Raemer, S. A., *Church History*, pp. 89-152
Spalding, B. J., *Bible and Church History*, pp. 246-267
Catholic Encyclopedia, "Arianism," "Arius," "Eutychianism," "Heresy," "Hierarchy," "Hierarchy of the Early Church," "Manichaeism," "Monophysites," "Nestorianism"

QUESTIONS

1. (a) Distinguish between *heresy, apostasy* and *schism.* (b) Give an example of each.

2. (a) Explain fully how a person may fall into heresy. (b) Is there any type of heretic who may save his soul? Explain.

3. (a) Explain why the Church must be severe and intolerant toward heretics. (b) What measures did the Church take against heretics in the fourth, fifth and sixth centuries? What measures did temporal rulers take during this period? (c) What measures does the Church take against heretics today?

4. (a) Explain the false teachings of the Arian heresy. (b) Which Ecumenical Council condemned this heresy? (c) Which Creed did this Council adopt?

5. Mention two heresies in addition to Arianism. Give the following information for each: (a) the erroneous doctrines; (b) the time and place at which it was taught; (c) the Council at which it was condemned; (d) the names of outstanding men who opposed it.

6. Discuss the career of St. Augustine, mentioning: (a) his early life; (b) the circumstances that led to his conversion; (c) his services to the Church; (d) his spiritual and intellectual qualities; and (e) the names and subjects of two of his great books.

7. (a) Name the four Greek Doctors of the Church. (b) Name the four Latin Doctors of the Church. (c) Has the Church conferred the title of "Doctor of the Church" on any men besides these eight persons?

8. (a) Name the major and minor orders. (b) What powers are conferred on a Priest by ordination? (c) What authorization does he need to use these powers? (d) Name the ranks of the Catholic Hierarchy.

9. (a) How did the *faithful* in the early days of the Church differ from the *catechumens?* (b) Name the distinct groups into which the faithful were divided.

10. (a) Describe a basilica of the third century. (b) Name four great basilicas at Rome.

11. (a) What is an *Ecumenical Council?* (b) How many Ecumenical Councils were held during the fourth, fifth and sixth centuries? (c) Describe in detail the work of two of these Councils.

12. (a) Name five tribes of Germanic barbarians who invaded the Roman Empire. (b) Explain how the Church was able to derive good from these invasions. (c) Explain how Pope Leo I and Pope Gregory the Great protected the people of Italy against the barbarians.

13. (a) What is *monasticism?* (b) Who wrote the Rule accepted by monasteries in the East? (c) Who wrote the Rule accepted by monasteries in the West?

14. (a) Describe the architectural plan of a typical monastery. (b) Describe the activities carried on in such a monastery.

15. (a) Was Christianity adopted rapidly or slowly in Ireland? How do you explain this? (b) Discuss the services of St. Patrick to the Church.

SELECTION TEST

In each of the following groups, select the one name that does not apply:

1. *Founders of monasteries:* Pachomius, St. Finnian, St. Benedict, Eutyches.

2. *Heretics:* Arius, Genseric, Nestorius, Eutyches, Pelagius, Manes.

3. *Barbarian chieftains:* Constantine, Clovis, Attila, Genseric, Odoacer, Alaric, Theodoric.

4. *Greek Doctors of the Church:* St. Athanasius, St. Basil, St. Jerome, St. Gregory Nazianzus, St. John Chrysostom

5. *Members of the Hierarchy:* Bishops, Confessors, Priests, Deacons.

SUPPLEMENTARY MATERIAL FOR UNIT II 75

MATCHING TEST

In the parenthesis next to each name in Column A, write the number of the item in Column B which is most closely associated with it.

A	B
( ) St. Athanasius	1. Translated the Bible into Latin
( ) St. Augustine	2. Bishop of Hippo
( ) St. Jerome	3. King of the Franks
( ) St. Ambrose	4. Chief opponent of Arius at Council of Nicaea
( ) St. John Chrysostom	5. Apostle of Ireland
( ) Arius	6. "Glory of the Christian pulpit"
( ) Nestorius	7. "Robber Synod"
( ) Attila	8. Denied that Mary was Mother of God
( ) Clovis	9. Donatism
( ) St. Patrick	10. Chieftain of the Huns
	11. Denied the Divinity of Christ
	12. Disciplined Theodosius the Emperor

CHRONOLOGY TEST

Number the items in each of the following groups in their proper chronological order.

A
( ) Battle of Adrianople
( ) Battle of Châlons
( ) Attila persuaded by Leo the Great not to attack Rome
( ) Lombards enter Italy
( ) Visigoths enter Roman Empire

B
( ) Council of Ephesus
( ) Council of Chalcedon
( ) Second Council of Constantinople
( ) Council of Nicaea
( ) First Council of Constantinople

C
( ) Foundation of the Benedictine Order
( ) Writing of the Vulgate
( ) Nicene Creed
( ) First Monastery
( ) Fall of Rome

D
( ) Arian Heresy
( ) Nestorian Heresy
( ) Conversion of Ireland
( ) Conversion of Spain
( ) Conversion of Franks

COMPLETION TEST

Complete each of the following statements by supplying the correct word or phrase in the blank space.

1. The first monasteries in the East were established under the leadership of St. ....
2. The rule established by the saint mentioned in 1 was later supplemented by St. ....
3. The leader of the Vandal invaders of Italy was ....
4. Pope ...... persuaded this Vandal leader not to slaughter the people of Rome.
5. The Lombards were prevented from pillaging Rome by Pope ....
6. A saint who lived the life of a hermit in Egypt before the development of monasticism was ....
7. St. Scholastica was the sister of ....
8. The Bible was translated into Latin from the original Hebrew and Greek by .... This version of the Bible is known as the ....
9. The so-called "semi-Arians" wished to have the word *homoousios* ("same substance") in the Nicene Creed changed to ....
10. The First Ecumenical Council, which met at ...... in the year ......, condemned ....
11. The Second Ecumenical Council, which met at ...... in the year ......, condemned ....
12. The heresy which taught that there are two basic and eternal powers — Light and Darkness — was .... A noted saint and theologian who refuted this heresy was ....
13. The heresy which taught that there is only one nature in Christ was ....
14. The Monastic Order which played the leading part in the conversion of the German barbarians was ....
15. The most important of the early monasteries in Ireland was ....
16. St. ...... is known as the "Doctor of Sacred Scripture."
17. The two outstanding centers of theological study in the fifth century were ...... and ....
18. An Ecumenical Council is usually presided over by ....
19. The council which condemned the Donatist heresy was called by St. ....
20. The barbarian chieftain ...... became known as the "Scourge of God."

UNIT III

THE AGES OF FAITH (590-1274)

PREVIEW

IN this Unit, we shall consider the history of the Church during most of the period which is commonly called the Middle Ages. Historians use the expression "Middle Ages" to designate a period of approximately 1000 years which constitutes a great bridge between Ancient and Modern times. The dates assigned to these periods are by no means definite or universally accepted. The Early Middle Ages, however, are usually regarded as extending from the seventh to the thirteenth centuries; the Later Middle Ages lasted until the end of the fourteenth century.

Renaissance writers and Protestant Reformists employed the term "Dark Ages" to describe a large part of the Early Middle Ages. Historical facts indicate, however, that the use of this term is entirely unwarranted. During the Ages of Faith, the destinies of men were guided by great personalities, such as the Gregories, Charlemagne, Francis of Assisi, Dominic, Thomas Aquinas and Dante. The fusion of the Roman and the Teuton led to a new type of society—feudalism. Feudal lords facing the Mohammedans foreshadowed the Crusades. It is true that there was much violence, suffering and ignorance during this period, but these darker sides of human life are not peculiar to any one age. Moreover during the years which we are about to study, the flame of Christianity burned more brightly than ever before, leading to marvelous achievements in many fields of human endeavor.

During this period, the Faith was propagated by magnificent missionary activity throughout Europe, but the Church had many trials and difficulties with which to contend. The Greek Schism cut off large numbers of souls from communion with Rome. Traces of heresy appeared; this was opposed by the foundation of the Mendicant Orders. The Popes engaged in a bitter struggle with the Emperors over the abuse of lay investiture. These problems and others led to the calling of nine Ecumenical Councils; there was at least one such Council in each of the centuries of this period, except for the tenth and eleventh centuries.

The Church triumphed over all these trials and, in the thirteenth century, she attained her golden age. During this "greatest of centuries," as it has been called, Europe was entirely Christian. The Church founded the first universities, fostered the most perfect type of architecture, the Gothic, and inspired one of the masterpieces of literature, Dante's *Divine Comedy*. These and many other fruits of a truly great civilization sprang from a people united by the bonds of Christian faith.

CHAPTER 5

FROM GREGORY THE GREAT TO THE ELEVENTH CENTURY

"The more closely we examine the question, the less ground we shall find for the conception of the Middle Ages as a long sleep followed by a sudden awakening. Rather we should consider that ancient Greece was the root, and ancient Rome the stem and branches of our life; that the Dark Ages, as we call them, represent the flower; and the modern world of science and political freedom the slowly matured fruit."
—BERNARD BOSANQUET ("The Civilization of Christendom")

INTRODUCTION

The Transition Period.—By the beginning of the seventh century, men no longer spoke of Europe as the *res publica,* that is, "republic" or "commonwealth." The reason for this is that the political unity imposed by the Roman Empire had broken down. It is true that there were still two nominal centers of authority, Rome in the West and Constantinople in the East. But in the West, there was no longer a real central government. Society came to be organized on a *feudal* basis. This meant that, with few exceptions, all effective governmental authority was purely local. A powerful feudal lord could control only the people living on his own lands, which were always limited in their extent (page 100).

From the eighth to the middle of the eleventh century, European civilization went through a most critical period and barely managed to survive. There was much fighting between rival feudal chieftains. Moreover, Christian Europe had to face three serious military threats: (1) the Mohammedans; (2) the Scandinavian pirates (*e.g.*, the Danes in England); and (3) the pagans advancing over the north German plain, up the Danube River. Because of the almost constant fighting and the crude methods of production and transportation, the life of the common people was extremely hard. Illiteracy was widespread.

We must understand, however, that there was another side to the picture. In spite of the political disorganization, there was *religious* unity. The Church provided a common principle of life, which all men accepted. The language of the Church, Latin, was used by educated men everywhere. The Pope and Bishops exercised their spiritual authority over all Europe, and by their influence in civil life did much to overcome some of the deficiencies of the local feudal system. No new arts were created during this period, but the old arts were guarded and cherished in the monasteries. Roads were kept in repair, even though few new roads were built. There were also a few original achievements, such as the development of the legend as a literary form, and the invention of books with pages to supplant the manuscript rolls.

Were the "Dark Ages" Really "Dark"?—Historians who accept the viewpoint of the Protestant Reformation and of the Renaissance have labelled the period from the eighth to the middle of the eleventh century the "Dark Ages." [1] We can see from the above discussion that it is not a just characterization. It is true that during this period there were many undesirable conditions, such as widespread illiteracy, but an illiterate person does not necessarily lack intelligence or understanding.

Far from being completely "dark," the profoundly religious character of the Early Middle Ages entitles it to be called the "Ages of Faith." And this period served as the forerunner of the Later Middle Ages, which may justly be called the "Glorious Ages of Faith."

In other words, there are both good and bad things to be said for the period we are now considering. The same may be said of every stage of human history, including our own.

GREGORY THE GREAT

Early Life of Gregory the Great.—Gregory the Great, the sixty-sixth Pontiff, was both Bishop and secular ruler of Rome for fourteen years (from 590 to 604). Gregory was born to wealth, but it was his extraordinary talents and his piety which won him the love and respect of his fellow citizens. In young manhood, he used his inheritance to found seven monasteries, six in Sicily and one in Rome. He chose the life of a monk, but he was

---

[1] This period is sometimes called the "Iron Age," because of the almost incessant fighting which was going on.

selected by Pope Pelagius II to represent the Holy See in Constantinople. In 585 he returned to the Cloisters in Rome, but he was elected Pope by the clergy and the people in 590.

The "Paymaster of the Lombards."—In his own writings, Gregory describes the deplorable conditions then existing in Rome, mostly because of the depredations of the Lombards. The Papacy, however, received large amounts of foodstuffs and other products from domains in Sicily, Sardinia, Corsica and the provinces. (These domains were called the "Patrimony of Peter.") Gregory used these products to buy off the savage Lombards, and thus to protect the people. For this reason, Gregory called himself the "Paymaster of the Lombards." Gregory also distributed the products he received to many needy people. He raised troops, repaired the walls of the city, regulated justice, and performed many other necessary functions. For all this, he was reproached and insulted by Constantinople, but deeply loved by the grateful Romans.

Missionary Activity.—Gregory also sponsored far-reaching missionary activities. His outstanding accomplishment in this field was the conversion of England. (This will be discussed further on page 90).

Writings of Gregory.—As we have seen, Gregory is one of the four Latin Doctors of the Church (page 53). Outstanding among his brilliant writings is the *Liber Regulae Pastoralis* ("The Pastoral Rule"). This book for centuries helped to regulate the life and manners of the clergy. There are extant 840 of Gregory's letters that prove his devotion and his courage in caring for the welfare of the whole Church. It was Gregory the Great who first used the title of Christ-like humility, "Servant of the Servants of God." Every Pope since has so signed his letters to the faithful.

RELATIONS OF THE CHURCH WITH THE FRANKISH MONARCHS

The Kingdom of the Franks.—We have already seen (page 67) how the Frankish Kingdom was founded by Clovis, who became a Christian late in the fifth century. During the Early Middle Ages, the Frankish Kingdom was the most powerful temporal state in Western Europe. The relations of the Church with this state were most harmonious, and were productive of much good for all of Christendom.

The successors of Clovis soon became degenerate. They had neither the desire nor the ability to attend to the affairs of state, and therefore appointed an official known as the *mayor of the palace* to administer the government. Gradually the mayors of the palace took over most of the real power, while the kings became mere puppets. One of the greatest of the mayors of the palace was Charles Martel, who commanded the Frankish army when it engaged the Mohammedan hosts in the all-important battle of Tours in 732 (page 90).

Pepin's Donation.—Pepin, son of Charles Martel, also became mayor of the palace. In 751, however, Pepin deposed the last of the "do-nothing kings," and ascended the throne himself. In this step, he had the approval of Pope Zachary, the Frankish leaders, and the people. Later, Pope Stephen personally anointed him king. This recognition by the Pope added greatly to Pepin's prestige among his own people. In 754 and in 756, Pope Stephen II appealed to Pepin to assist Rome against the Lombards. Twice Pepin led his army over the Alps and conquered the Lombards. The territory he won, consisting of twenty-two reconquered towns in regions known as the Exarchate and the Pentapolis, was donated to the Pope, even though the Emperor at Constantinople objected to this. In 774 and 781, Charlemagne (son of Pepin) confirmed these donations and made additions to them. These territories came to be known as the *Papal States,* and remained under the Pope's control until 1870. Thus, the Pontiff became a temporal ruler not through motives of ambition, but through necessity, and as a result of voluntary endowments.

This situation led to a 300-year struggle between the lay nobility of Rome and the ecclesiastical power.

Charlemagne.—Charlemagne became King of the Franks in 771. Charles the Great was great as a conqueror, as a ruler, and as a patron of learning. On Christmas Day, 800, the Pope crowned him in Rome not merely King of the Franks, but Emperor of the Roman Empire of the West,[2] and in 812 he was even acknowledged as such by the Emperor of the East. Charle-

---

[2] This title was later changed to Holy Roman Emperor. The office lasted until the nineteenth century.

magne conquered the Lombards in Italy, as his father had done before him. He added lands to his already vast realm by subduing the Bohemians, Avars, Slavs and Bavarians. His most formidable opponents were the Saxons, with whom he fought for thirty years. Finally, he crushed their resistance.

As a ruler, Charlemagne was friendly to the Church. He supported the Popes; he built a splendid church where he worshipped every day; he founded monasteries; and he encouraged all of his subjects to become Christians. He gave great sums for charity to the poor.

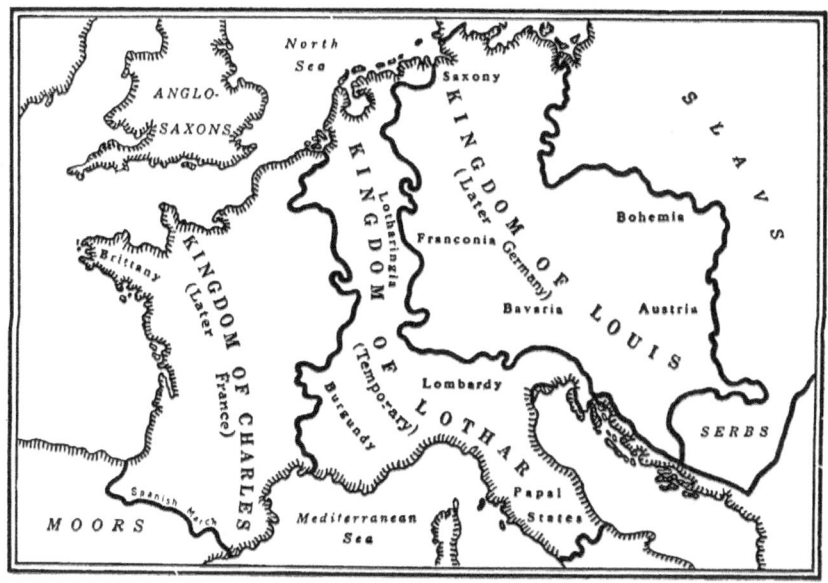

How the Kingdom of Charlemagne Was Divided Among His Three Grandsons

As a patron of learning, Charlemagne gathered about him the best intellects of Europe. The most famous of these intellectuals was Alcuin, the theologian and Latin scholar from England. Alcuin spent fifteen years (781 to 796) with Charlemagne, establishing schools and libraries, and creating a love for learning. Until his death in 804, Alcuin was the intimate friend of Charlemagne, who gave him the Abbey of St. Martin of Tours in which to spend his declining years. Charlemagne himself was a student of languages and literature and did much to improve the German language. After ruling for forty-seven years, he died in 814, the greatest man of his epoch.

After his death, the Frankish Kingdom was divided among his three grandsons and soon disintegrated.

SORROWS OF THE CHURCH

During the period we are considering, the Church was attacked by hostile forces which caused her much sorrow. The most important of these forces were heresy, the Greek Schism, and the rise of Mohammedanism.

The Monothelite Heresy.—The Monothelites were Eastern heretics who fostered a false teaching that grew out of Monophysitism (page 51). They taught, specifically, that Christ had only one will; thus, like the Monophysites, they denied the existence of two natures in the Savior.

Sergius, Patriarch of Constantinople, supported Monothelitism, hoping that it would satisfy the Syrians and Egyptians, and thus induce them to give up their heresy. Sophronius, a learned, saintly man, opposed the Monothelite heresy, first as a monk, and later as Patriarch of Jerusalem. Sergius wrote to Pope Honorius I (625-638) in defense of the error, but he did not state the case clearly. In his reply, Honorius said that the expressions "one-willed" and "two-willed" should be avoided as mere grammatical subtleties. In 680, however, the Sixth Ecumenical Council at Constantinople condemned the heresy, and this decision received the approval of several Popes.

In failing to condemn Monothelitism, Honorius was negligent and allowed himself to be duped, but he was not a Monothelite. His failure to grasp the importance and consequences of the issue cannot be advanced as an argument against Papal Infallibility, for he did not teach the matter *ex cathedra*.

The Iconoclasts.—During the eighth century, there was death and destruction in the East, caused by the iconoclasts ("image-breakers"). St. John Damascene wrote three discourses on images, in which he explained the Church's teaching on the subject. St. John says: "Images are for the unlearned what books are for those who can read; they are to sight what words are to the ear."

During the seventh and eighth centuries, certain abuses over the use of images had appeared in the East. Leo the Isaurian, Emperor in the East, decided to correct these abuses. However, he went to the opposite extreme, for in 726 he forbade all veneration of images. He ordered the destruction of all images in the churches, and even wished to smash the celebrated image of Christ over the bronze door of the palace. There was an uproar among the people. The servile Bishop sided with the arrogant Emperor, but the monks resisted nobly. Monasteries were razed to the ground and monks became martyrs. Leo then decided to

go to Rome, in order to destroy the image of St. Peter there and to capture the Holy Father. His fleet was destroyed on the journey. When Leo died in 780, his wife, the Empress Irene, tried to renew the veneration of the images.

The Seventh Ecumenical Council, held at Nicaea in 787, and the Eighth Ecumenical Council, held at Constantinople in 869, defined the Church's teaching concerning images; the *proper* use of images was approved. Images are intended to elevate our thoughts and to inspire us. They are *not* objects of adoration.

Causes of the Greek Schism.—The iconoclastic controversy foreshadowed a conflict which was to last for centuries and ultimately resulted in the complete separation of the Greek Church from unity with Rome. This estrangement arose basically over matters of Church government, rather than over articles of faith. The more important causes were as follows.

1. Ill feeling and jealousy existed between the East and the West since the Council of Nicaea in 325. The East had been the cradle of heresies condemned by Rome. Byzantine Bishops banded together in opposition to Rome, and gradual estrangement resulted.

2. The East never abandoned pagan conceptions of the secular power. There was widespread acceptance of the doctrine of Caesaro-Papism, which holds that the Emperor is supreme in spiritual as well as temporal affairs. The Bishops of Constantinople were servile to the Emperor, and their powers decreased while those of the Papacy increased. Many Easterners, with their exaggerated reverence for the Emperor, felt that the Pope should also reside in Constantinople.

3. There was a difference between Church discipline in the East and that in the West. The East was stagnant, too conservative, rigid in adherence to forms of the past; the West was a vital, growing organism, developing its liturgy. This also led to estrangement.

4. The East protested one point of Catholic doctrine. The word *filioque* (meaning "and from the Son") had been added to the Nicene Creed, but the East refused to accept this. The word added no new doctrine; it merely clarified the Church's doctrine regarding the Blessed Trinity and the procession of the Holy Ghost from the Father and from the Son.

5. The alliance of the Papacy with Pepin, and later the coronation of Charlemagne as Roman Emperor (page 82), increased the animosity of East and West.

6. The iconoclastic controversy (see above) widened the breach.

7. Both Rome and Constantinople claimed jurisdiction over Bulgaria, which had recently become Christian. The Bulgarian Prince, Bogoris (page 96), complicated matters by his vacillating conduct.

The Separation from Rome.—All the above-mentioned factors caused bad feeling between the East and the West. Matters came to a head in the middle of the ninth century. Ignatius, a virtuous

POPE RECEIVES EMPEROR'S HOMAGE.

EMPEROR RECEIVES BISHOPS' HOMAGE.

ROMAN AUTHORITIES CONDEMN.

GREEK AUTHORITIES ARE CONDEMNED.

PATRIARCH ?

IGNATIUS, SENT BY POPE.

OR PHOTIUS, FRIEND OF EMPEROR.

 ACTIVE

 RIGID

ROMAN | **GREEK**

CAUSES OF THE GREEK SCHISM

and fearless man had been appointed Patriarch of Constantinople by Pope Nicholas I at the request of Theodora, regent Empress of the Byzantine Empire. Ignatius protested the immoral conduct of Bardas, Theodora's brother and the tutor of her son, Emperor Michael III. In 857, Ignatius publicly refused to give Bardas Holy Communion. Also he refused to force Theodora and her daughters to enter a convent, as Bardas desired for political reasons. Ignatius was illegally deposed and Photius, a learned and ambitious layman, was uncanonically made Patriarch. Photius enjoyed a short triumph until 867, when the Emperor was murdered. Then the Eighth Ecumenical Council deposed Photius and reinstated Ignatius. In 877, Ignatius died. Photius came forth again and by diplomacy obtained the Patriarch's throne. The Pope, acting mercifully, rehabilitated Photius, although in provisional terms. In 886, Emperor Leo VI, motivated by unworthy personal considerations, deposed him, and he died in exile in 891. Recent research defends Photius as a learned statesman, in contrast to Saint Ignatius, an unworldly simple character. St. Ignatius seems to have been the Mindszenty of his century, a period of sharp conflict between East and West.

Mohammedanism.—The seventh century witnessed the rise of *Mohammedanism* or *Islam*, a political and religious power that was to reduce the number of Christians in the East and to harass the entire Christian world for practically a thousand years.

1. *Origin.*—Mohammed was born about 570 in Mecca, a city in Arabia. He became an orphan at an early age, and worked as a shepherd, and also as a camel-driver. When he was twenty-five years of age he married a wealthy woman, who was captivated by his business ability and winning personality. Mohammed was afflicted with epilepsy and was a religious fanatic. At the age of forty he proclaimed that he had beheld visions sent to him by the Angel Gabriel. This divine revelation, he asserted, had revealed to him the word of *Allah* (God), and he set about organizing a new religion.

2. *The Koran.*—The utterances of Mohammed, which he believed were the word of God, were set down in a book called the *Koran*. This is the Mohammedan Bible. It contains religious principles derived from three sources: (*a*) the paganism of Arabia, that honored 360 false gods; (*b*) the practices of Judaism; and (*c*) the beliefs of Christianity imbibed from a Nestorian sect.

The Koran teaches that there is one God and that Mohammed is His prophet. Virtue lies in submission to the will of God. (*Islam,* which is often used as the name of the grossly sensual Mohammedan religion, means "submission.") The Koran imposes four duties on every Mohammedan: (*a*) prayer five times a day; (*b*) the giving of alms, to the extent of from 5% to 20% of one's income; (*c*) fasting during a certain sacred month each year; (*d*) a pilgrimage to the city of Mecca, at least once during the person's lifetime. The Koran teaches that those who follow these precepts will live forever after death in Paradise, a garden of sensual delights.

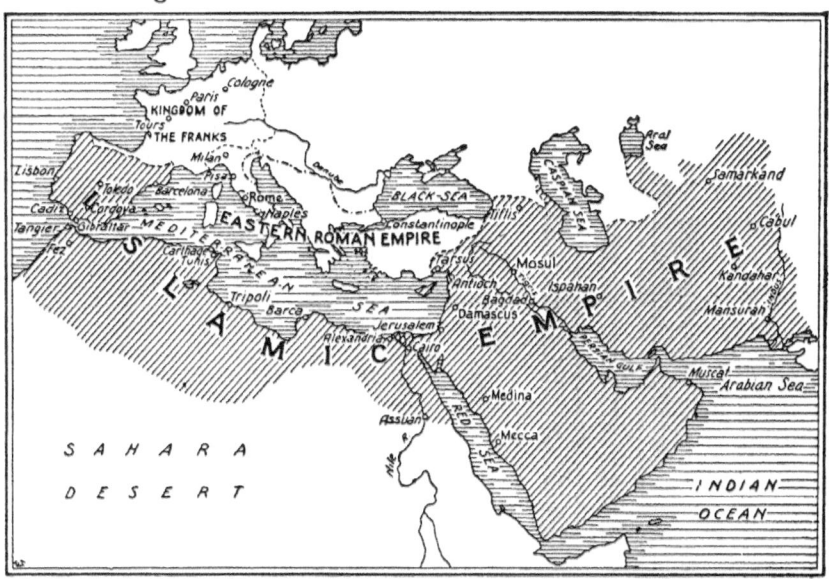

The Islamic Empire at the Time of Its Greatest Extent

3. *The Spread of Mohammedanism.*—When Mohammed began to preach his new religion, he gained a small body of converts. However, most of the inhabitants of Mecca did not believe him and he was forced to flee to the city of Medina. This *Hegira,* or flight, took place in 622, and is celebrated as the year 1 in the Mohammedan calendar.

The people of Medina accepted Mohammed as a true prophet, and from then on the religion grew with astonishing speed.

Mohammed taught that his doctrines should be spread by the sword, if necessary, and in his own lifetime all Arabia was conquered and converted. After his death, his leadership was taken over by the *Caliphs* (kings), and Islam was spread over Syria, Palestine, Persia and North Africa. The seemingly irresistible Mohammedans crossed into Spain and drove north into France.

4. *The Battle of Tours.*—All Europe seemed threatened by the Mohammedans. But Christian France, under the leadership of Charles Martel [3] ("Charles the Hammer") checked their savage advance at the Battle of Tours (732). This battle, one of the most important in world history, lasted for several days. On one side was the Cross, the symbol of Christian salvation; on the other side, the Crescent, the symbol of Mohammedan cruelty and slavery. When Charles Martel and his brave warriors won, Europe was saved for Christianity. The Mohammedans retired to Spain, never to return to France. But the Christian world had to fight them again and again, as we shall see in the later chapters of this book.

PROPAGATION OF THE FAITH IN THE EARLY MIDDLE AGES

In the Early Middle Ages, the extent of Christendom was greatly increased. The Faith was carried to the far corners of Europe by valiant missionaries.

Propagation of the Faith in England.—Roman Britain had been Christian, but the invasion of the Angles [4] and other Germanic tribes in the fifth century caused the island to revert to paganism. We have previously mentioned that it was Pope Gregory the Great who sent the first missionaries to England. His interest was first aroused in Rome, where he saw some remarkably handsome youths being offered for sale as slaves. When he learned that they were Angles, he was immediately inspired to carry the tidings of Christianity to that far-off people, so that they might gain the company of the angels in eternity.

---

[3] We have already learned that Charles Martel occupied the office of "mayor of the palace" of the Frankish Kingdom. He was the father of Pepin and the grandfather of Charlemagne.

[4] The name *England* is derived from the *Angles*.

Distribution of Principal Religions About 1100

Gregory sent to England forty monks from St. Andrew's Monastery in Rome. They were led by St. Augustine (or Austin). These holy men were kindly received by Ethelbert, King of Kent and Overlord of England, whose wife, Bertha, was a Christian. In a few months the ruler and 10,000 Kentish men were baptized. Soon the See of Canterbury was founded, with a Benedictine monastery not far off. London and Rochester were granted Bishops. More missionaries were dispatched by Gregory, and books were sent to form the first English library.

In the northern part of the island, Celtic monks led by St. Aidan founded the monastery of Lindisfarne, with the coöperation of St. Oswold, King of Northumbria. Gradually the Faith spread to the east and then to the very heart of the island. Monks went about the country preaching, and many monasteries were built. In 688, a Greek monk, Theodore, became Archbishop of Canterbury. Theodore was a great organizer; he divided the country into bishoprics, and established parishes entrusted to pastors. Monastic schools were opened. In these schools England produced great scholars, such as Venerable Bede (673-735) and Alcuin (735-804). Venerable Bede wrote the *Ecclesiastical History of England,* and it is believed that he wrote over forty other books. Alcuin brilliantly carried Christian learning to the renowned schools of Charlemagne's realms in France. Caedmon, a poet-monk, wrote the first poem on English soil; the subject of his poem was the Creation. Within a century, Christianity was spread over all of England, and the missionaries met with no persecutions from the Anglo-Saxons.

At about the same time, Irish missionaries, guided by St. Columba, were successfully evangelizing Scotland.

Propagation of the Faith in Germany.—The conversion of the Germans beyond the Roman provinces was a most difficult task. Missionaries from Ireland, Scotland and France worked simultaneously, and encountered innumerable dangers and obstacles. The true Apostle of Germany was the Anglo-Saxon, St. Boniface. This "propagator, purifier, and organizer" of the Church in Germany was born about 680 of noble Anglo-Saxon parents. Boniface (known in his youth as Winifred) became a Benedictine Monk. In 719, Pope Gregory II [5] sent Boniface from Rome to

---
[5] It was Pope Gregory II who gave this Saint the name of Boniface.

Germany as a missionary. This was the start of a missionary career that was to last for thirty-five years. As Priest and Bishop in Germany, Boniface destroyed pagan temples and sanctuaries and built churches and oratories in their places to shelter multitudes of Christians. Boniface was aided by prayers, books, altar linens, and money from England.

An incident is related which shows the courage and fortitude of Boniface. The German heathens venerated an oak called the

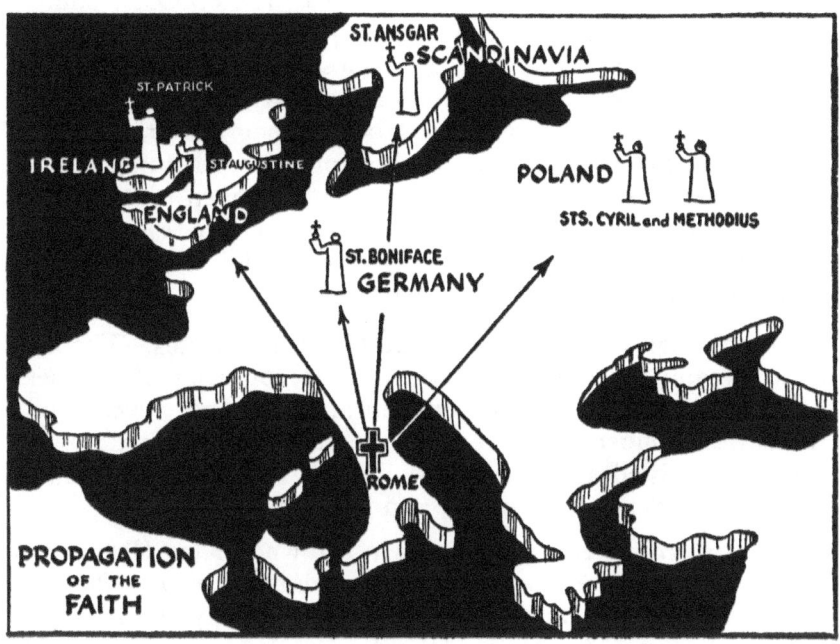

"Tree of Thor." They boasted that this tree had supernatural powers, and finally Boniface, with his own hand, felled the tree in their presence. From the wood he built an oratory dedicated to St. Peter. The heathens were baptized in great numbers after they had beheld the impotency of Thor and the fearlessness of Boniface.

Gregory III made Boniface an Archbishop in 731. After this, Boniface invited other holy men and women from England to assist him. These men and women founded monasteries that became famous centers of learning and holiness. *Fulda,* founded in 744, was the chief monastery. During the lifetime of its founder, Fulda had over 400 Benedictine Monks. During its first century, twenty-two of the pupils of this monastery became Archbishops and fourteen became Abbots. Boniface's cousin, Lioba, founded monasteries for women, and these were no small help in evangelizing Germany. By 738, Boniface had converted about 100,000 pagans.

Still more strenuous work remained for the now aged Boniface. He was assigned to the task of reorganizing the Frankish Church, among whose clergy there were many serious abuses. This he did with great success, renewing the close bond of union between Rome and the Frankish Church. The last days of his fruitful life were spent in purely missionary labors among the Frisians, who martyred him with fifty-two of his followers in June, 754. A sword pierced his head. Battle-axes opened heaven to his followers. Historians consider that the work of Boniface was as important to the development of the German people as that of any other character, political or ecclesiastical.

Propagation of the Faith in the North Countries.—The Germans became ardent missionaries in the countries of northern and central Europe. During the ninth, tenth, and eleventh centuries vast numbers of converts were added to the Church among the Danes, Swedes, Norwegians, Poles, Moravians, Bohemians, Hungarians, Serbs, Bulgarians, and Russians.

1. *Denmark* accepted the Faith in 826 when King Harold and 400 of his royal suite were baptized. Ansgar, a young Benedictine Monk, labored among these people for forty years, but his holy labors were largely undone by the Viking raids. In 948 the Christianizing of Denmark was renewed successfully, and the final triumph was reached in 1014-1035 under King Canute the Great.

2. *Sweden's* reception of the Faith was slow and painful. In 829, St. Ansgar made a missionary tour there and sowed the good seed by his preaching. After more than a century had passed, English missionaries again did fruitful work in part of Sweden. Many martyrdoms took place, but by 1078 Christianity was firmly founded. It was not until 1163, however, that the last pagan stronghold was replaced by a Christian church.

3. *Norway* was converted by Olaf Tryggvasen, an adventurous companion of the Vikings, who plundered the shores of Europe during the tenth century. A missionary converted Olaf, who, in turn, invited missionaries from England and Germany to Norway. Bishoprics and schools were established, and the royal leaders were converted, but the Faith did not flourish here until a later date. Olaf II (1016-1029) completed the work begun by his predecessor. These Christian rulers of the North countries were *sometimes more zealous than prudent. On occasions, they forced their people to accept the Faith, and such forced conversions were* not always enduring.

Many of the Norwegians settled in northern France, which received the name of *Normandy*. The greatest warrior in Normandy was the picturesque Rollo, who was converted to Christianity in 992, after thirty-six years of raiding, plundering, and terrorizing in France. Rollo was baptized Robert and took a French bride, Gisela. His followers imitated his example and great prosperity came to the country he settled.

4. At the end of the tenth century, Christianity was introduced to *Iceland* and *Greenland,* the neighbors of the Scandinavian countries. There were thousands of Christians, and hundreds of churches and Priests, monasteries and schools. In the fourteenth century the population was largely destroyed by the plague, and the Eskimos scattered the rest.

Propagation among the Poles, Slavs and Hungarians.— These people, living in central, eastern and southeastern Europe, made up the larger part of the total population of the continent. They first received the Faith from French and German missionaries and from Eastern Monks. Two Greek brothers, St. Cyril and St. Methodius, both of whom were Monks and Bishops, labored long and fruitfully in southeastern Europe during the latter half of the ninth century. Cyril spent five years in this work, during which he devised the Slavic alphabet. He died in 869 in Rome, but Methodius labored for twenty-five years more. He was successful where other missionaries from the West had failed, because he knew the language of the people and he used their own tongue in the liturgy of the Church, with the approval of the Pope.

Cyril and Methodius traveled from one tribe to another, carry-

96 VISUALIZED CHURCH HISTORY

ing the truths of Christianity. They started originally from Constantinople, and worked in southern Russia among the Chazari. The neighboring Bulgarians invited the missionaries to visit them. The invitation was extended through the sister of Prince Bogoris, who was a Christian. Prince Bogoris was chiefly influenced by a picture which he had requested St. Methodius to paint. Methodius chose to depict the Last Judgment as an awe-inspiring theme. Bogoris was greatly impressed and asked for baptism for himself and his subjects. Moravia was also the scene of many conversions. In the Moravian court, at a banquet, a Bohemian Duke, Borzivoy, was won over by the gentle kindness of Methodius. His whole family accepted the Faith; the Duke's grandson was St. Wenceslas. There was a struggle here between Christians and heathens but after forty years of missionary zeal, heathenism was vanquished.

Bohemians carried the Faith to the Poles. In 972 the Hungarian sovereigns became Christian and their son Stephen left an entirely Catholic kingdom at his death in 1038.

Thus by the middle of the eleventh century Europe was Catholic from Spain to Russia, and from Greenland to Greece and Italy.

MONASTICISM IN THE EARLY MIDDLE AGES

The Monastic Orders.—Monasticism, introduced in the fourth century (page 68), has ever since been a characteristic feature of the Catholic Church. To understand the Middle Ages from a social and economic viewpoint, one must be familiar with monasticism during that period. It is important to appreciate clearly the distinction between the *Monastic Orders* and the *Religious Orders*. Monastic Orders were widespread during the early Middle Ages, whereas Religious Orders (*i.e.*, the Mendicant Orders) were first founded in the thirteenth century. Monasticism was essentially an institution to promote the contemplative life, with active life as an accidental feature. The Mendicant Religious Orders were intended primarily to promote the active life, with the contemplative life as a basis of apostolic preaching.

Services of the Monasteries.—Monks have two great aims in life: personal holiness, and service to their neighbors. Personal holiness is made more certain by the observance of the vows of *poverty, chastity* and *obedience*. In the Early Middle Ages, the monks not only impressed and ennobled mankind by their holiness, but also performed many valuable services. These are summarized below.

1. *Promotion of Agriculture and Commerce.*—Agriculture in Europe owes much to the work of the monks who lived in the midst of the barbarians and taught them, by example, the nobility of labor. Monks cleared primeval forests, especially in Germany. In France they transformed vast tracts from barren wastes into beautiful gardens. Swamps in England became fertile fields as a result of drainage, fertilization, rotation of crops and careful selection of seeds. Monks built bridges and roads in order to convey their products from monastery to monastery. They promoted fairs to exchange the products of the earth for the other necessities of life. Gradually these fairs developed into commercial centers to continue trade during the entire year. Thus towns originated.

2. *Preservation of Literature.*—The monks copied manuscripts. This was essential, since printing was not discovered until the fifteenth century. There was a time during the Early Middle Ages when the monasteries alone preserved the Sacred Scriptures and the pagan masterpieces of literature. This literature is priceless to Western civilization. In the *scriptorium,* found in every monastery, gifted monks spent hours each day copying books. These books were illuminated—that is, artistically decorated in colors. Illuminated manuscripts today are rare, and are considered great treasures. An excellent example of such a manuscript is the *Book of Kells,* in the library of Trinity College, Dublin. This was produced by Irish monks.

3. *Education.*—Monks were the educators of the Middle Ages. Monastic control of education existed from the time of Charlemagne until the foundation of the Mendicant Orders. Every monastery had its school, open to clerics, to the sons of the nobility, and to the youth of the countryside. Those being educated were required to live in the monastery, separated from their families and living a holy life. Today we hear much about vocational schools. The monastery schools taught not only the intellectual branches of learning but also the trades and crafts. And what marvelous craftsmen they produced! The stained glass windows

of the Middle Ages are an object of wonder today; the bells wrought so many centuries ago are still calling men to prayer; the great cathedrals stand like the mountains, immune to the passage of time.

4. *Architecture and Other Arts and Sciences.*—The monks did much to produce one of the greatest glories of the Middle Ages, *Gothic architecture.* This is perhaps the most perfect type of architecture ever developed. Certainly, it is without any superiors. Our American skyscrapers employ some of the basic principles and features of Gothic architecture, such as lofty lines, much window space, and balancing of stresses and strains. (See page 126 for a further discussion of Gothic architecture.)

Besides architecture, other arts and sciences were cherished and developed by the monks. These include sculpture, hand carving in wood and bronze, music, and the physical sciences.

5. *Historical Records.*—The monks kept extensive historical and patristic records. This has proved of inestimable value to the historians of later generations.

6. *Missionary Work.*—Last, but not least, the monks were the missionaries, the great Apostles of the nations. The bond of unity in Europe for 1000 years was the Catholic Faith. This gift of God, as we have seen, was carried from nation to nation by the monks, and with the Faith came civilization.

Famous Monasteries.—During the seventh, eighth, and ninth centuries the famous monasteries were Benedictine. Monte Cassino in Italy (page 69) sent forth missionaries, who founded monasteries in France, England and Germany. From these great institutions came Popes, Bishops, and Abbots, to carry on the work of God.

1. *Cluny.*—During the ninth and tenth centuries, worldliness crept into the Benedictine monasteries, largely because the Abbots were vassals of kings. This dependence on a temporal ruler was not likely to increase spirituality. Rich gifts to monasteries led to a weakening of the spirit of poverty, and to an impairment of true learning. Some monks and nuns, however, were true to the rule and the spirit of the founders. One of these holy monks, St. Berno, was invited by the rulers of France to found a monastery in Cluny, a wondrously beautiful wooded valley. In 910 this Benedictine foundation became a center of fervor

for the revival of monasticism. A change in government was developed here. Before this time, the position of an Abbot had been like that of a father, controlling a monastic family; at Cluny, the Abbot became more like a general commanding an army. Cluny established dependent houses throughout Europe, but the control of the entire organization remained centralized in the mother house. Before the middle of the eleventh century, 300 Benedictine monasteries dotted Europe; Cluny was a power for good, second only to the Papacy. At the commencement of the twelfth century, 2000 monasteries had been reformed.

The Location of the Leading Monasteries of Western Europe

2. *Grand Chartreuse.*—This monastery was founded in 1084 by St. Bruno. Bruno had been a teacher in a Cathedral school in Rheims, France. One of his pupils here was a future Pope, Urban II. Bruno left the school and, with six companions, went to a deserted wilderness in the Alps, where he established his monastery. Grand Chartreuse became the mother house of fifty monasteries. The life in this Monastic Order was most severe, and reform was never needed.

3. *Cîteaux.*—This monastery was founded in 1098 in France by St. Robert of Molesme. The white-robed Cistercian monks developed new institutions of government. A yearly *Chapter* or Assembly was held, at which each dependent monastery had representatives. The Abbot of Cîteaux visited the monasteries each year and checked up on disciplinary matters. This fostered a revival of fervor.

The most famous Cistercian monk was Bernard of Clairvaux. He founded the monastery of Clairvaux, which became the mother house of seventy monasteries. St. Bernard was not only a mystic, but also a highly influential man in the political affairs of his century. He was a most successful diplomat, representing the Pope in dealings with kings and princes. By the year 1300 there were 700 Cistercian monasteries, mostly in northern Europe.

FEUDALISM

Nature of Feudalism.—We have already pointed out that the social and governmental institutions prevailing during the Middle Ages are known as feudalism. Feudalism resulted from the breakdown of the Roman Empire, and the intermingling of the Teutonic invaders with the older population. Its origins may be traced to certain conditions and practices existing among both the Romans and Germans. Feudalism formed the basis of European civilization for more than a thousand years.

Feudalism was basically a system of landholding. The importance of this becomes apparent when we realize that almost all people during the Early Middle Ages made their living by working the soil. During the chaotic period that followed the collapse of Roman authority, emperors, kings and other rulers found that they could not effectively control all the lands they were supposed to govern. Therefore, it became customary for rulers to grant certain lands to their warlords or leading supporters. The recipients of this land, known as *vassals,* promised to render military service to the ruler, and also to help him in other ways. The estate which the vassal held was called a *fief.*

A vassal might *sub-infeudate* part of his holdings—that is, assign it to a sub-vassal. In practice, the structure of feudalism was very complicated. One person might be a vassal or sub-vassal to several lords and, at the same time, the lord of many vassals.

At the very bottom of the feudal system of society was the *serf*, the ordinary agricultural laborer, who made up by far the most numerous class of the population. The serf was not a slave, for his lord could not sell or transfer him to another lord. On the other hand, the serf was not free, as we understand the term, for he was bound to the land; he was not free to leave if he desired to go somewhere else. Moreover, if the land changed hands, the serf's obligations were transferred with it.

There were usually many serfs working in a single *manor* or agricultural community. Each serf cultivated certain strips of land, which the lord assigned to him. In return, the serf worked on the lord's own lands for one or more days each week, and he also gave the lord a stipulated part of the crops which he raised. All the serfs used certain facilities which the lord provided for them, such as an oven, mill, winepress, etc.

The Church, of course, was very much involved in the feudal system. In the first place, this system determined the general conditions of life under which the Church functioned. Second, as a result of gifts, the Church became one of the largest landholders. The Church owned probably about one-third of the land. Bishops and Abbots were among the richest feudal lords, and they also acted as vassals and sub-vassals.

Advantages of Feudalism.—Feudalism benefited the Church in some ways. It made possible an orderly and settled life, even though there was no longer a powerful central government as in the days of the Roman Empire. Although each lord was practically supreme on his own domains, this was certainly better for the Church, and for society as a whole, than complete disorganization. The fixed relations between lord and vassal, and between lord and serf, inculcated a sense of responsibility, as well as a respect for law. Although it is true that the feudal system was undemocratic and unjust in many ways, it emphasized the fact that a lord had definite obligations to everyone below him, even the lowliest serf.

Disadvantages of Feudalism.—On the whole, however, feudalism did more harm than good to the Church. Bishops and other members of the clergy, as we have seen, were among the great feudal lords, and their absorption in these civil affairs sometimes interfered with their spiritual duties. Moreover, Churchmen often became vassals, and this status obliged them to perform feudal services and court duties. These included clerical functions, acting as advisers and ministers to kings and other great lords, and caring for the poor, the sick, homeless children, and other types of dependents. These services were well rendered, but in time various abuses resulted, such as lay investiture, simony and interference by lords in the election of Bishops (page 104). Another great disadvantage of feudalism was the almost incessant petty warfare between rival lords. Moreover, many rapacious lords ground down their serfs, and did not hesitate to seize harmless persons and hold them for ransom.

The Influence of the Church on Feudalism.—The Church strove nobly and effectively to remedy the abuses of feudalism. Popes and Ecumenical Councils curbed the intrusion of laymen into Church matters. Overbearing and unjust feudal lords were often rebuked and controlled by the Church. The Church was much concerned, also, over the continual fighting that was taking place. To protect women, children, clergy and other non-combatants, the so-called *Peace of God* was instituted. Later, came the *Truce of God* (originated in France at the beginning of the eleventh century), which forbade fighting during Lent and Advent, and during the rest of the year from each Wednesday night until the following Monday morning. This insured about 240 days of peace each year. Those who were admonished three times for violating the Truce were subject to excommunication.

The Truce of God became the general law of the Church in the Canons of the Ninth Ecumenical Council (1123), the Tenth Ecumenical Council (1139), and the Eleventh Ecumenical Council (1179).

CHAPTER 6

THE GOLDEN AGE OF THE CHURCH

"Is it any wonder, then, that we should call the generations that gave us the cathedrals, the universities, the great technical schools that were organized by the trade guilds, the great national literatures that lie at the basis of all our modern literature, the beginnings of sculpture and art carried to such heights that artistic principles were revealed for all time, and, finally, the great men and women of this century—for more than any other it glories in names that were born not to die...the period which...saw the foundation of modern law and liberty,...the greatest in human history?"

—J. J. WALSH ("The Thirteenth, Greatest of Centuries")

TWO GREAT POPES—GREGORY VII AND INNOCENT III

Gregory VII.—Gregory VII (also known as Hildebrand), who served as the Vicar of Christ from 1073 to 1085, was a Tuscan of humble birth. He was trained by the Benedictine Monks in Rome and, after completing his studies, spent some years in the monastery at Cluny. His remarkable talents soon brought him to the attention of his superiors, and several Popes used his services in various important capacities. Indeed, for about twenty-five years before his elevation to the Papacy, he was the leading figure in the Papal government.

During the early years of Gregory's career, while Nicholas II was Pope (1058-1060), legislation was passed to regulate the elections of future Popes. The legislation provided that the Pope was to be nominated and elected by the Cardinals. After this election, the Emperor, the clergy and the Roman people were to have the privilege of expressing their consent.

Gregory was elected Pope, in accordance with this legislation, in 1073. His Pontificate of twelve years was the culmination of a saintly life, and was rich in good for the Universal Church. He combated fearlessly and effectively the three great evils that afflicted the Church in the eleventh century—simony, lay investiture, and the marriage of the clergy. He also raised an army of 50,000 men to fight the Mohammedans. The monks and the common people loved Gregory and gave him their steadfast support, but the Holy Roman Emperor, the married clergy, and some Bishops opposed him bitterly. But Gregory refused to be swayed, and when he died in exile in 1085, he had carried out great reforms, and had securely established his reputation as one of the greatest Popes. Indeed, many consider him the very greatest of the Bishops of Rome.

The Struggle over Lay Investiture.—Lay investiture refers to the practice by which a *temporal ruler* bestowed a bishopric or abbey on a candidate for the office. In other words, the layman took it upon himself to appoint a high Church officer, and transferred to him the ring and crozier, the symbols of his authority. Obviously, lay investiture is a serious abuse, opposed to the teachings and ideals of the Church.

Lay investiture was first practiced in the Frankish kingdom. In the tenth and eleventh centuries, the abuse became very common throughout all Christendom. It was often associated with *simony*, that is, the practice of selling Church offices. The prince or king sold a bishopric; the petty lord sold a parish. The inevitable result of this was unworthy Bishops, Abbots and Priests.

When the great-hearted Gregory VII became Pope, he determined to uproot the evil. At a Roman synod held in 1075, he issued a decree which abolished the right of lay investiture. "Lay investiture makes all appointments null and void; whoever receives a spiritual office at the hands of a layman, whether he be baron, duke, king, or emperor, is to be deposed, and a layman who dares to confer a spiritual office, is to be excommunicated."

Gregory's fearless action instantly precipitated a struggle between him and the young Emperor Henry IV. Henry was talented, but dishonest, immoral and despotic. He refused to obey the Pope's decree, even though Gregory solemnly warned him that if he failed to do so, he would suffer excommunication and the loss of the allegiance of his subjects. Henry was defiant in word and in act, and insultingly refused to answer the Pope's summons to appear in Rome. When Gregory excommunicated Henry, the German people and many German Bishops sided with the Pope. The German princes decided that Henry would have to face the Pope at Augsburg and settle the issue. Henry, however, feared a public trial and sagaciously avoided it. In 1077, with his wife, child, and one friend, he traveled over the Alps in the dead of a severe winter to a castle at *Canossa* in Tuscany, where the Pope was being shown hospitality by a Countess Matilda. In lowly garb, barefooted in the snow, Henry did penance here for three days. Gregory finally recognized Henry as a repentant sinner, gave him absolution and Holy Communion, and released him from excommunication after solemn promises on Henry's part.

The Final Solution of the Investiture Problem.—Henry, however, violated his promises not to engage in investiture, and was again excommunicated and deposed. A civil war followed, in which much damage was done. Gregory died in the midst of the quarrel in 1085. Other Popes continued the struggle with Henry IV and his successor, Henry V. France and England also offered some resistance to the Papal decrees, but the most serious trouble continued to be with Germany.

The dispute was finally settled by the *Concordat of Worms,* entered into in 1122 by Emperor Henry V and Pope Calixtus II. The Pope agreed that elections of Bishops and Abbots might take place in the presence of the Emperor, and also that the Emperor might invest the Bishop with the scepter, a symbol of temporal power. The Emperor agreed to give up investiture with the ring and crozier, to allow free elections by the Church authorities, and to aid in the restoration of Church property which had been confiscated in the struggle. The Concordat of Worms was sanctioned by the Ninth Ecumenical Council in 1123.

The historical importance of the Concordat of Worms is that it confirmed the independence of the Church from the State, and the supremacy of the Church in her own sphere. The German Church was acknowledged to be not an instrument of the Emperors, but rather an integral part of the Universal Church. Bishops became truly independent of the secular power. Thus, feudalism no longer endangered the Church by giving her unworthy Bishops and Abbots.

Frederick Barbarossa.—Frederick Barbarossa, who reigned as Emperor from 1152 to 1190, tried to impose his rule on the cities of northern Italy. These city-states (notably Milan) formed an alliance known as the *Lombard League* to resist him. In this they were encouraged by the Papacy, which was keenly aware of the dangers of Frederick's imperialist policies. (The Emperor's supporters were known as *Ghibellines;* the followers of the Lombard League and the Papal party, as *Guelfs.*) In 1176, the Lombard League crushed Frederick's forces in a great battle at Legnano.

Innocent III.—Innocent III, who was Pope from 1198 to 1216, was descended from a noble Italian family. He received his early education at Rome, then studied theology and philosophy at Paris, and later law at Bologna. After this intensive training, he returned to Rome and entered upon the career of an ecclesiastical diplomat. He soon demonstrated his remarkable talents, and at the age of thirty-seven was elevated to the Papacy.

Innocent was a brilliant and pure-hearted man who defended and advanced the interests of the Faith with great skill and tenacity. Some of the outstanding triumphs of his Pontificate are as follows.

1. Innocent enlarged the Papal States and brought them to the greatest extension they have ever reached. He broke the political bond between Germany and southern Italy; Sicily recognized Papal suzerainty.

2. During Innocent's Pontificate, there was a serious dispute regarding the succession to the office of Holy Roman Emperor. While two claimants for this throne fought each other, Innocent protected the rightful heir, a member of the Hohenstaufen family. This Hohenstaufen was elected Emperor by the German princes, and Innocent induced King Philip Augustus of France to aid in placing him on the throne. Philip did so, and the man whom Innocent had protected became Emperor Frederick II.

3. Innocent forced Philip Augustus of France to respect the sanctity of marriage by giving up Agnes, his second wife, and taking back Ingeborg, his rightful spouse. For nine months France was under interdict before Philip would yield. Innocent also defended the unity, indissolubility and sanctity of marriage in the cases of Petro II of Aragon and Alfonso IX of Leon.

4. From 1205 to 1213, Innocent III struggled with King John of England over the recognition of Stephen Langton, the rightful Archbishop of Canterbury. In the end, John acknowledged himself to be a vassal of the Pope and agreed to the appointment of Langton.

The temporal authority of the Papacy reached its highest point under Innocent III. Innocent is glorious, however, not only for the power he gained for the Papacy, but also for the manner in which he exercised this power. He had an unwavering faith, a keen sense of responsibility, and a burning desire to restore the Church to perfect purity. This is evidenced in the complete program of religious reform which he carried through. Like Gregory VII, Innocent III represents the Papal power at its best. The splendor of his Pontificate was crowned by the demonstration of the extent of his powers at the Fourth Lateran Council (page 128).

HERESIES DURING THE TWELFTH AND THIRTEENTH CENTURIES

The Golden Age of the Catholic Church, like so many other periods, was disturbed and saddened by heresies. There were a number of minor sects, such as the *Berengarians*, who taught false doctrines regarding the Holy Eucharist, and the *Petrobrusians*. The two most important bodies of heretics, however, were the *Waldenses* and the *Albigenses*.

The Waldenses.—The Waldensian heresy was started in the twelfth century by Peter Waldes, a merchant banker of Lyons, France. The death of a dear friend turned Waldes to preoccupation with religious matters. Like many others, he was scandalized by the wealth and power of the Catholic clergy. Waldes had the four Gospels and some of the writings of the Fathers translated into French by Priests. He read these writings eagerly in search of Apostolic perfection. In 1176, he distributed his wealth and adopted a life of extreme poverty. His first followers were from the lower and uneducated classes. With no authorization, they began to go about, two by two, and preach. Their doctrines included a belief in the necessity of extreme poverty in order to attain salvation; a denial of purgatory and of the efficacy of prayers for the dead; a refusal to take oaths; and a condemnation of warfare. They also forbade marriage. There were two classes among them: the "Perfect" (Bishops, Priests and Deacons) who did no manual labor, and "Friends" or ordinary laymen.

The Waldenses spread to Lombardy in Italy, where they were more radical than in France, and then to Spain. At first, an attempt was made to win them back to the Faith by persuasion, and some did return. Ultimately, however, it became necessary to

108   VISUALIZED CHURCH HISTORY

use more drastic means: in 1184, the Waldenses were excommunicated; in 1192, many of them were put into chains and imprisoned; in 1194, King Alfonso II banished them from Spain; in 1197, the penalty of death by burning was authorized. In France, there was generally less severity than elsewhere, but even so seven French Waldenses suffered the death penalty in 1214.

All attempts at converting these heretics (such as that of St. Vincent Ferrer in the fourteenth century) did not succeed. The activities of the Inquisition also were of no avail. The Waldenses finally affiliated with Protestant sects, but they retained their own identity. There are today over 20,000 of them living in the Alps. They have their center at Turin, Italy. This sect also has representatives in the United States, in Texas, North Carolina, and Missouri. At present, the Waldenses use two sacraments—the Eucharist and baptism.

The Albigenses.—The Albigenses were a sect of anti-clerical heretics, who arose in the twelfth century. They represent the last group of Manichaeism, the false doctrine of the fourth century (page 49), which subsequently appeared in many different countries under various names.

The Albigenses derived their name from the town of Albi in the Province of Languedoc, in southern France. The city of Toulouse, however, was the center of their activities. The heresy spread quickly and soon more than a thousand towns and villages in Languedoc were infected. Many circumstances favored the rise of Albigensianism in this region: the fascination of the easily understood doctrine of dualism (see below); the contempt for the Catholic clergy caused by the ignorance and the too often worldly and scandalous lives of these Churchmen; the protection which the nobles afforded or promised to Albigenses; the remnants of Mohammedan doctrines which existed as a result of the proximity of Mohammedan centers in Spain; and the connection between the heretical religion and local patriotic aspirations.

1. *The Albigensian Doctrines.*—The most distinctive Albigensian doctrine was the teaching that there are two basic principles in the universe—good and evil. This doctrine, as we have already learned, is known as *dualism*. The Albigenses condemned all war and capital punishment. They believed in the transmigration of souls.

Some of the moral principles of the Albigenses were destructive not only of Christianity but of human society altogether. For example, they commended suicide, since it freed the soul from its "prison," the body. They preferred concubinage to marriage, since the former relationship is less permanent. The Albigenses liked to be known as the *Cathari*, meaning the "Pure," but we can see from the above summary what a mockery this name was. The heresy was condemned by the Tenth Ecumenical Council (1139).

2. *The Crushing of the Albigensian Heresy.*—Popes and Bishops tried every possible means to convert the Albigenses. Pope Innocent III, in particular, was determined to win these heretics back to the Faith, and he sent St. Dominic to preach to them. In Languedoc, Dominic founded his famous Mendicant Order, and he and his followers strove nobly to convert the Albigenses. The Dominicans were trained preachers with university educations, but they were not content to appeal to the heretics only with persuasive words; they used example as well. St. Dominic rejected the excessive outward display which had characterized previous Catholic preachers, and adopted instead true Apostolic simplicity and austerity. His Friars, dressed in a white habit and black cappa, preached during the day and did penance at night. Dominic himself often spent the entire night in prayer. God blessed these holy men with the power of miracles. In 1206, Dominic established a convent for women, hoping thus to increase his influence among the Albigenses, since they made much use of women as propagators of their heretical ideas.

These efforts were only partially successful. Finally, Innocent III ordered the Cistercians (page 99) to preach a crusade against the heretics. The loyal Catholic nobles of France, led by Simon de Montfort, marched into Languedoc. For twenty years (from 1209 to 1229) a terrible war raged, which caused much suffering and destruction. Finally, the Albigenses were defeated. Even this did not wipe out the heresy. In 1233, the Dominicans were empowered by Pope Gregory IX to employ the Inquisition to eliminate Albigensianism, and toward the end of the fourteenth century the heresy disappeared entirely.

The Inquisition.—The Inquisition was a tribunal for the discovery, trial and punishment of heretics. An Episcopal Inquisition was first set up by the Council of Verona in 1184. The

Twelfth Ecumenical Council of 1215 gave explicit instructions for the procedure to be followed. However, it was not until 1229 that the Episcopal Inquisition was definitely organized at Toulouse. As we have seen, Pope Gregory IX, in 1233, sent the Dominicans to Languedoc to perform the duties of Inquisitors against the Albigensians. The Pope did this because he feared that if the local Bishops were authorized to try the heretics, they would favor their friends.

The Inquisition was *not* a pontifical court. The Inquisitors were theologians who examined the suspects and, if they found them guilty, prescribed spiritual penances. Then the heretics were handed over to a civil court for physical punishment, such as imprisonment, torture, or death. Later, the rigors of the

Inquisition were modified somewhat. The Inquisition was used not only in Languedoc, but in the whole of France, Spain, Italy, Germany, Poland and England.

The above description applies to the Inquisition established and supervised by the Church. However, there was a *national* Inquisition established in Spain in 1479 which lasted for three centuries and was responsible for hundreds of deaths annually. This was directed particularly against the Moors and Jews. Some biased historians attribute the notorious Spanish Inquisition to the Church, but this is confusing and unfair. Even so, the Spanish Inquisition was not so bad as the bloody conflicts introduced into Europe by Protestantism. Historians such as Gibbon and De Maistre attest to this fact.

THE CRUSADES

What Were the Crusades?—The Crusades were a series of combined religious wars and pilgrimages which took place during the eleventh, twelfth and thirteenth centuries. They constitute one of the most remarkable and fascinating chapters in all history.

The Crusades were directed against the Mohammedans, and the chief battleground was the Holy Land, including the city of Jerusalem. For many centuries, Christian pilgrims had been accustomed to visit Jerusalem to express their devotion to Christ. They were free to do this because the Holy Land was controlled by the Eastern Emperor. In the eleventh century, however, the Seljuk Turks became the masters of Jerusalem. They soon began to molest the pilgrims and to desecrate the splendid basilicas which had been built by Christian piety.

These outrages were made known to Pope Gregory VII, and he resolved to organize a great military expedition which not only would regain the Holy Land for Christendom, but would also end the Greek Schism. Gregory died before he could execute his plans, but the good work was carried on by his successor, Urban II.

In 1095, Urban summoned the *Council of Clermont,* at which he sent out an appeal to all Christendom to join in a united effort to drive the infidel Turks from the scenes of Christ's life on this earth. Great preachers, notably Peter the Hermit, went out to carry the Pope's message to the people. With the cry "God wills it," they responded in vast numbers. The First Crusade [1] set forth in 1096. This was only the beginning; within approximately the next 180 years, seven other great expeditions were organized to reconquer the Holy Land for Christendom.

The chief motive which impelled the great majority of the Crusaders was pure Christian faith. Of course, there were some who went because of love of adventure, hope of gaining wealth, a desire to escape the conditions of feudal life, and other less worthy reasons, but this does not in any way diminish the glory

---

[1] The word *Crusade* is derived from the cross which the Crusaders wore on their breast and right shoulder.

THE CRUSADES

Crusade	Date	Leaders	Description of Events	Results
1. *Knights' Crusade* (Preacher: *Peter the Hermit*)	1096-99	Godfrey of Bouillon, Raymond of Toulouse, Bohemond	Group of religious enthusiasts, led by Peter, was destroyed by Turks. Main expedition, led by feudal nobles, defeated Turks, and established several "Latin Kingdoms" in Holy Land. These Kingdoms lasted for about a half century.	Jerusalem taken; "Latin Kingdoms" established.
2. *St. Bernard's Crusade* .... (Preacher: *St. Bernard*)	1147-49	Conrad III of Germany, Louis VII of France, Baldwin III	Aimed to retake Edessa, which had been conquered in First Crusade, and later reconquered by Turks. This expedition was hampered by poor generalship, dissensions among Crusaders, treachery of Greeks.	Failure.
3. *Kings' Crusade* (Preacher: *William, Archbishop of Tyre*)	1189-93	Frederick Barbarossa, Philip II of France, Richard the Lion-Hearted of England	This Crusade was better organized than others. Only soldiers went to the Holy Land, while people at home contributed money. Frederick was drowned in Cilicia in 1190, Philip returned to France. Richard fought well in Holy Land; signed a three years' truce with Saladin, leader of Turks.	Ascalon and Acre taken; Turks checked.
4. *Pseudo-Crusade* (Preacher: *Fulk of Neuilly*)	1202-04	Baldwin of Flanders, Boniface of Montferrat	Venetian traders induced Crusaders to attack Constantinople, instead of Holy Land. Constantinople was captured and looted. No action against Turks.	Latin Empire of Constantinople founded; this lasted 57 years.

Children's Crusade	1212	—	Thousands of children, led by a false monk, traveled toward the Holy Land. Large numbers perished from hunger and fatigue. Survivors were captured by Saracens and sold into slavery.	—
5. Hungarian Crusade	1217-21	Andrew II of Hungary, John of Brienne	Andrew defeated at Mount Thabor; returned home. John of Brienne led expedition to Egypt, and took Damietta after two years' siege. He soon gave up Damietta to Sultan to obtain passage home for troops.	Failure.
6. German Crusade (Preacher: Pope Honorius III)	1228-30	Frederick II of Germany	Frederick arranged a shameful peace by bribing the Sultan. He promised the Sultan to allow the Mohammedans freedom of worship in Jerusalem.	Jerusalem, Bethlehem, Nazareth, Tyre, Sidon, surrendered to Christians.
7. Louis IX's Crusade .... (Preacher: Innocent IV)	1248-54	Louis IX (St. Louis) of France, Charles of Anjou	Louis took Damietta. Later, he was defeated at Cairo. He stayed four years in Palestine.	Damietta taken.
8. Louis IX's Second Crusade	1270-74	Louis IX of France	Louis transported an army of 60,000 men to Tunis in Africa. Half his army was destroyed by pestilence and lack of provisions. Louis himself died of a fever. Twenty years later, the Mohammedans retook Jerusalem, the last Christian possession in the Holy Land.	Louis died; final failure of attempts to regain Holy Land.

of the Crusades. Moreover, it is to be noted that it was the Pope, rather than the Emperor, who played the leading part in organizing the great pilgrimages. This is further evidence that when the Crusades were undertaken, Europe was inspired by an ardent faith. Only faith could have united so many thousands of people, differing widely in language, customs, education, wealth, social position, and in every other imaginable respect, except religion. Only faith could have impelled them to undertake the indescribable hardships and dangers of a 2000-mile journey, at the end of which lay a cruel and powerful foe.

Leading Events of the Crusades.—The leading events of the eight Crusades are presented in the chart on pages 112-113. This, of course, is merely an outline. Doubtless, you will want to become more familiar with this glorious chapter of Christian history. Many splendid books have been written on this subject. A few are suggested in the bibliography at the end of this unit.

Why the Crusades Failed to Achieve Their Objectives.—It is evident from the summary on pages 112-113 that the Crusades failed to achieve their primary objectives. In spite of many great victories, after almost two centuries of fighting, the Christian warriors were completely expelled from the Holy Land.

Why did this happen? The problem is not a simple one. Indeed, Hilaire Belloc, quoting Gibbon, has called the Crusades the "World's Debate"—the question of debate being the reason for the failure. It may be said, however, that the basic reason was the almost insuperable difficulties of reinforcing and supplying large forces at a distance of 2000 miles from their homeland. It must be remembered that, in those days, means of transportation were very primitive; in many places, even crude roads did not exist. Another reason for the failure was the lack of wholehearted and sustained coöperation among the Christian leaders. They did work together nobly on many occasions, but in time, rivalries and jealousies usually appeared and weakened their joint efforts against the Mohammedans.

Results of the Crusades.—It must not be supposed that, because the Crusades did not achieve their primary objectives, they did no good at all. Indeed, the Crusades were one of the most fruitful and beneficial of all the events of the Middle Ages. The most important of these beneficial results were as follows.

1. The Crusades renewed Christian faith, charity and fervor.

2. They strengthened the influence of the Church and the Popes.

3. They promoted Christian knighthood.

4. The wars of the Crusades provided a constructive outlet for the energies of petty princes and chieftains, who previously had spent their time fighting among themselves, to the great detriment of the people as a whole.

5. These great expeditions brought together the political leaders of Europe and promoted a spirit of unity.

6. Europe became familiar with products of the East, such as silks, rugs and spices. Eastern industrial processes were introduced, *e.g.*, paper-making and silk-weaving.

7. Commerce and navigation developed. New sea routes were sought, an activity which led to the discovery of America.

8. Untold thousands of serfs left the manors. Many feudal lords were killed in battle. As a result, the entire feudal system was greatly weakened. The spirit of individual freedom began to emerge.

9. Europeans adopted Arabic numerals (*i.e.*, the numerals we still use today) to replace the unwieldy Roman numerals. This was a great advantage in science and business.

10. The Crusades held the Turks in check for 200 years, thus preventing them from weakening or destroying Western civilization while Europe was developing its social and political institutions.

Military Orders.—We have referred above to the fact that the Crusades served to promote Christian knighthood. Even before the Crusades the rules and ideals of knighthood or *chivalry* had begun to develop. The knight was a mounted, armored warrior, who was sworn to lead a valiant and honorable life, to protect the weak, and to defend the Faith. He was the Christian gentleman of Medieval Europe.

A boy who wished to become a knight was trained in the arts of warfare as a squire from the age of fourteen until twenty-one. When he reached this age, he was required to spend a night's vigil in church, with his armor and sword at the foot of the altar. In the morning, he received Holy Communion, and his sword was blessed and dedicated to the service of widows, orphans and the Church.

Knights played an all-important part in the military activities of the Crusades. They were the "shock troops" of Christendom. In order to serve the cause more effectively, the knights joined together in great organizations or *orders,* whose members vowed to fight the Turk, to protect pilgrims, and to care for the sick and wounded. There were three such orders.

1. *The Knights of St. John.*—This was the oldest of the three orders. It originated during the First Crusade. The Knights of St. John wore a black cloak with a white cross. They are sometimes called the *Knights Hospitalers* because they built a hospital in the Holy Land and ministered to the sick and wounded.

In 1291, the order settled on the island of Rhodes in the Mediterranean. When this was captured by the Turks in 1523, Emperor Charles V gave the Knights the island of Malta. Napoleon expelled them from here in 1798, but the Knights of Malta, as they came to be known, are still in existence.

2. *The Knights Templars.*—This order was originated by nine French knights in 1118. The order had its first quarters in the palace of Baldwin at Jerusalem, on the site of the Temple of Solomon. St. Bernard wrote a rule for the Knights Templars, and the Pope gave his approval to the organization in 1128. During the Crusades, they fought most valiantly. When Acre fell in 1291, they returned to Europe. King Philip the Fair of France, who coveted their wealth, accused them falsely of heresy, and persuaded Pope Clement V to suppress them. In 1314, their last Grand Master, with fifty-four members, was burned at the stake. They were the most numerous and the most powerful of the three orders. They wore a white cloak with a red cross.

3. *The Teutonic Knights.*—This order of German knights was founded at Jerusalem during the Third Crusade. Like the Knights of St. John, they established a hospital. They resided at

THE GOLDEN AGE OF THE CHURCH

Acre until its fall, but even in 1226 went to aid Hungary and Prussia in their wars with the heathen Slavs and Tartars. They tried to convert these barbarians by force, rather than by persuasion, as the great missionaries had done.

The Teutonic Knights served well during the later Crusades. However, the religious fervor of the organization degenerated sadly. In the sixteenth century, the Grand Master joined the cause of Luther.

"THE GREATEST OF CENTURIES"

The thirteenth has well been called "the greatest of centuries." In this century, under the inspired leadership of Innocent III and other Popes, the Church reached the height of her power. The influence of the Catholic religion, purified and triumphant, pervaded every field of human endeavor and led to magnificent achievements which have been the wonder of mankind ever

118 VISUALIZED CHURCH HISTORY

since. No other century has ever witnessed such an unfolding of true spiritual fervor and creative genius.

We shall now consider briefly some of the achievements of Christendom in the thirteenth century.

The Mendicant Orders.—By the thirteenth century, the older monasteries had grown wealthy, and many of the monks were somewhat lax in discipline and deficient in religious fervor. The Mendicant Orders of Friars arose as an instrument of Divine Providence to do the great missionary work which was then so

HERMITS —	MONKS —	FRIARS
LIVE IN SOLITUDE LIKE ST. ANTHONY	LIVE TOGETHER IN ENCLOSURES LIKE BENEDICTINES	TRAVEL TO PREACH AND TEACH LIKE DOMINICANS

badly needed, especially in towns and cities where the clergy were silent while the people lived in ignorance and sin. This neglect on the part of the clergy produced a reaction among the people; lay preaching became widespread, and abuses and heresies soon crept in. This was the situation in which the Mendicant Orders made their appearance. The Second Council of Lyons (1274) recognized four great Mendicant Orders: the *Dominicans,* the *Franciscans,* the *Carmelites* and the *Augustinians.* Of these, the first two are the most important. The *Servites,* founded in 1233, are a fifth Mendicant Order that later gained approval and still serves the Church.

The Friars, who first appeared in the thirteenth century, are distinctly different from the Monks who originated in the fourth century. The Monk sought peaceful retirement and solitude in the country; the Friar assumed a public ministry in a busy, crowded city. Mendicant Friars, unlike Monks, are not bound by a vow of stability to *one* house; the Friars are sent out, two by two, as Apostolic missionaries. They exercise the duties of the sacred ministry within a province, but with the permission of their General, they may be sent all over the world. The organization of the Order is democratic; the superiors are not elected for life, and are subject to the General Chapters. Poverty is characteristic of the Mendicant Friar, who originally was to live on the voluntary offerings of the faithful. Since the Council of Trent, Mendicants (except for the Friars Minor and the Capuchins) may enjoy corporate possession.

1. *The Franciscans.*—The founder of the Franciscans, St. Francis of Assisi (1182-1226), was the son of a wealthy cloth merchant. His youth was that of a cultured, carefree gentleman. In his early twenties, he had a prolonged illness that afforded him much time to think about religious matters. He became devout and charitable. His charity led to a dispute with his father over money matters. Francis decided to embrace absolute poverty, and he started in a dramatic fashion by stripping off his costly attire in the presence of his father and the Bishop, and putting on the garb of the poor peasant, a coarse, brown robe girded with a knotted cord. His first spiritual followers were some of the townsmen of Assisi. Francis was gifted as a preacher and prepared himself for a Deacon's orders so that he might preach penance to the poor with the approval of the Church. He went to Rome, and Pope Honorius III expressed his full approval of the aims and organization of the Order.

St. Francis had an intense love of poverty, both as an end in itself and as a means of advancing the spiritual welfare of the common people, including the heretics. All his followers, therefore, were sworn to rigorous poverty. They went about preaching penance, explaining the Gospels, exhorting the people to live as true Christians, and helping the sick, the poor, and other unfortunates. St. Francis himself set a wonderful example for his Friars.

Never has there been a nobler spirit, a heart more filled with love for the Church and for all mankind. The splendor and purity of his personality shine through the centuries as an inspiration to all Christians. The people called him *il Poverello* ("the little poor man"), which well expresses their affectionate regard for him.

Within fifty years, the Order had thirty-three provinces, 8000 monasteries, and 200,000 members throughout Europe and Asia. As you know, the importance of the Order has increased, rather than diminished, with the passage of time. The Franciscans are known officially as *Friars Minors (Ordo Fratrum Minorum,* abbreviated *O.F.M.).* There are other branches of Franciscans: the *Capuchins (O.M.Cap)* and the *Coventuals (O.M.C.).*

Many of the greatest figures of Church history have been Franciscans. St. Bonaventure was a brilliant philosopher and theologian, who became a Cardinal. Duns Scotus and Roger Bacon were eminent thinkers and holy men. St. Louis (King Louis IX of France), who organized the last Crusades, was a Franciscan Tertiary. So was St. Elizabeth, Queen of Hungary, who labored heroically for the Church.

2. *The Dominicans.*—St. Dominic was born of noble blood in 1170, in Castille, Spain. He was a brilliant university student, and became a Priest. He accompanied his Bishop to Rome, where, in 1204, Innocent III appointed him to preach to the Albigensian heretics in southern France. Dominic's preaching was to be doctrinal, rather than moral, as St. Francis's preaching was. In other words, Dominic was to preach the truths of Faith, not just penance. This required great learning and intellectual ability. "One need not be very learned to preach morality to the poor and the peasant, but the case is otherwise when one is concerned with the defense of the whole economy of Catholic dogma against the attacks of heretical pastors and apostate doctors." [2]

For ten years, Dominic with a few companions labored among the heretics of Languedoc. The Albigensians had criticized the wealth and luxury of certain clergy. Dominic realized that to appeal to these heretics, his Friars would have to be trained, eloquent preachers who lived a life of austerity and poverty, thus preaching by example as well as by word. For this reason, young Dominicans were sent to the universities, where they were trained in philosophy and theology; the discipline was strict and poverty was required of the Friars.

---
[2] Townsend, A. M., *Dominican Spirituality.*

In Languedoc, Dominic and his companions carried on their missionary work with great zeal and ability. One of Dominic's spiritual weapons in his attempts to win back the heretics was the Devotion to the Rosary. This devotion is dear to the heart of every Catholic. In 1206, Dominic with his companions founded a convent at Prouille in the Pyrenees Mountains, to educate girls and women whom he had converted from Albigensianism. Nine noble women were the first Dominican Nuns.

After laboring for ten years in Languedoc, Dominic decided to organize his preachers into a body which would combat heresy throughout the world. His Order was the first to receive Papal approval as a worldwide organization (1216). Immediately Dominic dispersed his brethren and the Dominican Order spread rapidly all over Europe. By the time of Dominic's death in 1221, there were sixty religious houses in eight provinces. The influence of the Order was tremendous, and there were great Dominican teachers in all the leading universities. One of the very greatest Dominicans was St. Thomas Aquinas, the prince of theologians and scholars (page 125). Four Popes have been Dominicans. There are fifteen canonized Dominican Saints and 296 beatified Dominicans.

Perhaps the greatest of Dominican Tertiaries was St. Catherine of Siena, who lived in the latter part of the fourteenth century. At the age of twenty-seven, she displayed rare heroism in caring for the sick during a terrible plague, and thus won the love of the people. In 1377, she saw Pope Gregory XI return to Rome after the Popes had lived for seventy years in Avignon, France (page 145). Gregory's return was largely the result of the influence of Catherine. When she died at the age of thirty-three, she left 400 *Letters,* addressed to Popes, Cardinals, Bishops, and Kings. These letters, together with her other writings, give her a place in Italian literature beside the immortal Dante.

Any Catholic youth of eighteen years of age, who loves his Faith sufficiently, can become a Dominican or Franciscan Tertiary, and aspire to follow in the footsteps of these great characters of Church history.

3. *The Carmelites.*—The Carmelites were founded in 1156 by Berthold of Calabria, a Crusader, who settled with ten companions near the cave of Elias on Mount Carmel in the Holy

Land. In the thirteenth century, the Carmelites moved to Europe and were ranked as a Mendicant Order. Simon Stock was their first Master General in Europe. To them we owe the Devotion to the Scapular as a preservative against unprovided death. Today, they do unmeasured good in the field of education.

4. *The Augustinians.*—The Augustinians were organized as a Mendicant Order in 1256. The Augustinians of the thirteenth century were Italians, but since then the Order has spread widely.

Universities.—"Intellectually the thirteenth century in western Europe is marked by three closely connected phenomena: the growth of universities, the discovery and appropriation of Aristotle, and the activities of Dominicans and Franciscans." [3] This statement gives us some conception of the tremendous importance of the universities in Medieval civilization.

The modern university is definitely a product of the Middle Ages. There was nothing like it in ancient Greece or Rome. In the Early Middle Ages, higher education could be had only in a monastery, usually located in some secluded spot, far from any city. In time, however, groups of students began to gather in large cities. At Bologna, they organized as "corporations" and engaged teachers or professors to instruct them. (The Latin word *universitas* means "corporation.") At Paris, the professors organized; at other institutions, both students and professors organized. At first the universities did not even have special buildings. On more than one occasion, an entire body of students and professors migrated from one city to another, as from Bologna to Vincenza in 1204. In time, however, the universities acquired regular quarters, although they were usually not very elaborate or impressive. In any event, buildings and other property were not an essential attribute of the Medieval university. All that was needed was a corporation of masters and students, with authorized privileges, a fixed curriculum, and definite standards of accomplishment.

1. *Famous Universities.*—The oldest of the universities was at *Bologna,* in Italy; this became famous particularly for the study of law. The *University of Salerno,* also in Italy, was outstanding as a center of medical study. The greatest university during the twelfth and thirteenth centuries was the *University of Paris,*

---

[3] Taylor, H. O., *The Medieval Mind.*

which was noted for philosophy and theology. There were two famous universities in England, at *Oxford* and at *Cambridge*.

2. *Organization of the Universities.*—Most universities had a charter; this was obtained from the Pope, a civil ruler, or both. Of the eighty-one universities founded before the Protestant Revolt, thirty-three had Papal charters; twenty had both Papal and Imperial charters; fifteen had only civil charters; and thirteen had no charter at all. A university with a Papal charter

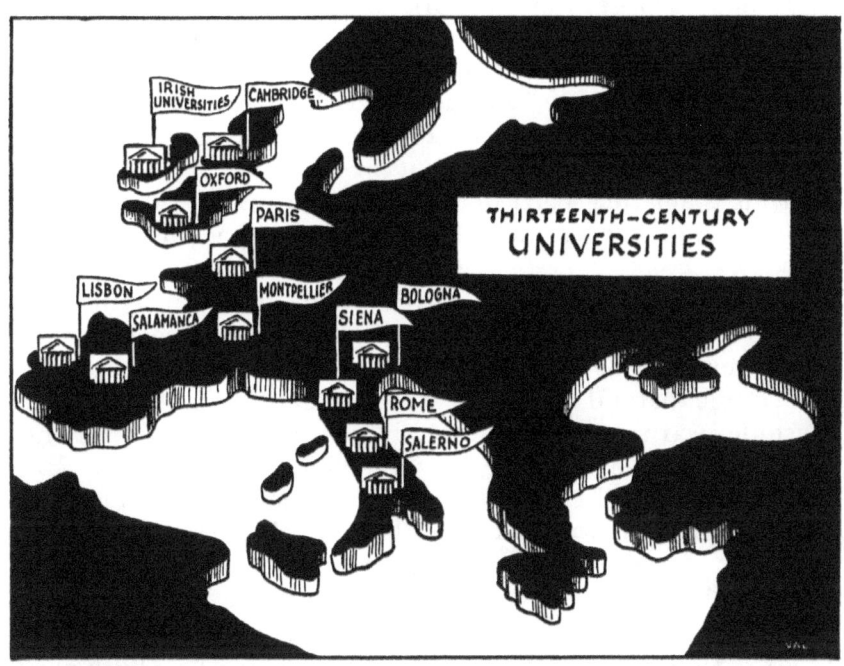

granted its graduates the right to teach anywhere in the world; a university with a king's charter could grant this right only within the monarch's realms. The administrative head of a university was the *rector,* elected by both students and professors. In universities with Papal charters, the Pope was represented by a *chancellor,* who usually had more authority than even the rector. The university was divided into *colleges,* each of which specialized in a particular subject or course of study, or had some other distinctive feature. The University of Paris had sixty colleges; Oxford had eleven colleges; Cambridge had thirteen.

3. *Students at the Medieval University.*—The Medieval university did not accept women as students. The students were a most cosmopolitan group. In most cases, they came from all over Europe. For this reason, it was customary to divide the student body into "nations." A document prepared in 1249 lists four nations at the University of Paris: French, Normans, Picards and English. The "English nation" comprised all students from the British Isles and northern Europe, including Germany.

It may surprise you to learn that the universities of the thirteenth century had more students than all but a few of the largest universities today. According to some authorities, Paris had from 20,000 to 40,000 students, Bologna about 10,000, and Oxford 30,000. Other authorities believe the enrollment was somewhat smaller than this, but in any case the number of students is amazing, particularly when we consider that the total population of Europe was then only a small fraction of what it is today.

All instruction, of course, was in Latin. The course of study consisted of grammar, rhetoric, logic, arithmetic, geometry, and astronomy, as well as theology and philosophy. (Philosophy included the natural sciences.) The ancient Greek philosopher, Aristotle, was studied very intensively. At first, the universities used a Latin translation of Aristotle which was tainted by false Arabic doctrines. In 1263, however, Thomas Aquinas remedied this by having a Dominican, William of Moerbeke, prepare an authentic Latin translation of Aristotle from the original Greek. Other good Latin translations were made.

The lowest degree granted by the university was the *Bachelor of Arts,* which carried with it the right to teach. The highest degree was the *Doctorate,* which was not granted to anyone below the age of thirty-five. The candidate for this degree had to qualify by carrying on a lengthy disputation with learned professors. In some cases, these disputations lasted from six in the morning until six in the evening, with only a brief respite during the lunch hour.

The students in the Medieval universities were high-spirited and sometimes got into trouble with the local authorities. On the whole, however, they were filled with a great passion for learning, and applied themselves enthusiastically to their difficult studies. As a result, these institutions produced large numbers of learned and pious men who went forth all over Europe to instruct the people in the truths of the Faith, and to serve them in many other ways.

4. *Professors of the Medieval Universities.*—At first, as we have seen, professors were hired by the students and were paid by them directly. Later, the university itself engaged the teachers and paid them regular salaries. The term *faculty* was first applied to the teachers of a university by Pope Honorius III in 1219; Gregory IX, in 1231, recognized separate faculties for different subjects. The word *university* in its original usage referred only to the students, but eventually its meaning was extended to include both professors and students. Professors, as well as students, were classed as clerics, and they were subject to trial only by the ecclesiastical courts, not by the civil courts.

The chief pride of a Medieval university was not a beautiful campus or a huge football stadium, but rather its great professors. Students often traveled from one university to another in order to listen to the lectures of the most famous and learned teachers.

Scholasticism.—The word *scholasticism* is applied to the method of investigation which was developed by the great theologians of the Middle Ages. We have already remarked that one of the most important intellectual events of the Middle Ages was the rediscovery of the works of Aristotle, the great philosopher of the ancient Greeks. The Scholastics or Schoolmen, as they were known, found in Aristotle's works a wonderful tool of logical analysis. Their use of this tool did not involve new matter, but rather a systematic presentation and development of familiar matter. The syllogism was the form used.

The greatest of the Scholastics was St. Thomas Aquinas, called the "Angelic Doctor," and the Patron Saint of all Catholic schools. His masterwork, *Summa Theologica*, is considered second in importance only to the Bible. Thomas was an Italian of noble birth, being related to Popes and Holy Roman Emperors. As we have seen, he became a Dominican Friar, and spent his religious life as a university professor and writer. Many times, he was summoned to Rome so that the Popes might benefit from his powerful mind. On one occasion, as he knelt in prayer before the crucifix, Our Lord greeted him, saying, "Thomas, thou hast written well of Me. What reward wilt thou have?" Thomas answered, "None other than Thyself, O Lord." In addition to his epoch-making theological treatise, Thomas wrote the beautiful Mass for the feast of Corpus Christi, and the poetic hymn always sung at the Benediction of the Blessed Sacrament. Thomas died in 1274, when he was not quite fifty years of age, while traveling to the Council of Lyons.

Other outstanding Schoolmen were St. Albert the Great, a German noble; Roger Bacon, an Englishman; Duns Scotus, a native of Scotland; Abelard, a French monk; and St. Bonaventure, an Italian.

Art in the Middle Ages.—During the Middle Ages, the arts, such as architecture, sculpture, painting and poetry, were a great instrument of popular education. In this respect, they resemble the newspaper, radio and moving pictures in our own time. These features of modern civilization do a great deal of good, but they also do much harm because they are not properly controlled. The arts of the Middle Ages, in contrast, served to ennoble and enrich the lives of the people, without harming them in any way.

Gothic Architecture and Sculpture.—The typical architectural form of the Middle Ages, as we have learned, was the Gothic cathedral. These cathedrals, both as works of art and as engineering achievements, rank among the mightiest triumphs of human genius. Most of the greatest cathedrals were built or completed during the thirteenth century. There were eighty cathedrals in France alone, among them *St. Denis* in the north, *Sainte Chapelle* and *Notre Dame* at Paris, *Rouen, Chartres,* and *Amiens.* England had twenty cathedrals, among them *Lincoln* and *Salisbury.* The greatest cathedral in Germany was at *Cologne.*

Gothic architecture is characterized by great poise, point, and height, combined with wonderful delicacy and precision. Wall space is almost entirely occupied by magnificent stained glass windows. The great *rose window,* over the main entrance, is often about forty feet in diameter. The vaulted or domed ceiling is supported by "ribs" of stone. The outward thrust or push of these ribs is balanced by beautiful *flying buttresses.* All arches are pointed, which enhances the grandeur and dignity of the structure.

The exterior of the cathedral is as impressive as the interior. In some cases, spires rise as high as 500 feet. Innumerable statues are found everywhere, particularly above the main entrance. They represent Christ and the Saints, as well as scenes from the everyday life of the times. The same is true of the stained glass windows. When we examine these products of inspired craftsmanship, we can understand why the cathedrals are called "books in stone."

The cathedrals were not the product of a few skilled engineers and an army of slaves. Whole populations worked on them, rich and poor, old and young, skilled and unskilled. They labored with joy and enthusiasm, because they were building not merely a structure of stone, but a monument to the faith that filled their hearts.

Painting.—The greatest painter of the period we are studying was Giotto (1266-1336). Giotto was a native of the city of Florence in Italy. He was only a poor shepherd boy, drawing on stone with a pebble, when an artist of the day named Cimabue took an interest in him. Cimabue became the master of Giotto, and the pupil soon excelled his teacher.

Painting before the time of Giotto was cold, formalized and inexpressive. Giotto broke with the past and made his figures natural, and throbbing with life and movement. His great pictures, which represent scenes from the life of Christ and of St. Francis, indicate that the artist possessed not only marvelous technical skill and poetic insight, but also the faith of a true Christian.

Many critics consider Giotto to be the most influential single figure in the history of painting. In any case, there can be no doubt that he was a great pioneer and laid a solid foundation for the famous painters who came later, such as Michelangelo, Leonardo da Vinci, and Raphael.

Poetry.—The Middle Ages gave us the greatest Christian poet, Dante (1265-1321), who wrote the *Divine Comedy* in the Italian language. The only other poets of all time who may be compared with him are Homer and Shakespeare. Dante's poem is the story of a soul who makes a journey through hell, purgatory and heaven. On the journey, he meets various outstanding characters, from the beginning of time down to the thirteenth century. *The Divine Comedy* is often called "Thomas Aquinas in poetry." It has been translated into many languages. There is an excellent poetic translation in English by Longfellow.

Other poetic types reached perfection during this period. Latin hymns still in use today were composed. These include the *Dies Irae,* the *Tantum Ergo,* and the *Stabat Mater.*

The Fourth Lateran Council.—The most important ecclesiastical assembly of the Middle Ages was the Twelfth Ecumenical Council, also called the Fourth Lateran Council, which was held in 1215. This Council marks the zenith of ecclesiastical life and Papal power. It was convoked by Innocent III. In the letter of convocation, sent out in 1212, the Pope wrote:

> Two things lie particularly near my heart: the regaining of the Holy Land and the reform of the whole Church.... I have decided after the manner of the ancient fathers to convoke a general council by means of which evils may be uprooted, virtues implanted, mistakes corrected, morals reformed, heresies extirpated, the Faith strengthened, disputes adjusted, peace established, liberty protected, Christian princes and people induced to aid the Holy Land, and salutary decrees enacted for the higher and lower clergy.

The Council was attended by the Patriarchs of Constantinople and Jerusalem, 412 Bishops, 800 Abbots and Priors, and other dignitaries, such as St. Dominic. Emperor Frederick II and kings of many countries also were present. The Council enacted seventy canons, the first of which was directed against the Albigenses and Waldenses. Most of the other canons were concerned with regulation of discipline and with the organization of a new Crusade.

SUPPLEMENTARY MATERIAL FOR UNIT III

CHRONOLOGICAL TABLE OF PRINCIPAL EVENTS IN CHURCH HISTORY

YEAR	EVENT
590	Gregory the Great elected Pope
597	St. Augustine arrived in England as Missionary
622	Mohammed's flight (*Hegira*) from Mecca
680	Sixth Ecumenical Council (Third Council of Constantinople) condemned Monothelites
732	Charles Martel defeated Saracens at Tours
751	Pepin anointed King of Franks by St. Boniface
755	Martyrdom of St. Boniface, Apostle of Germany
756	Pepin's gift to Pope Stephen II established temporal power of Popes
787	Seventh Ecumenical Council (Second Council of Nicaea) condemned Iconoclasm
800	Pope Leo III crowned Charlemagne Emperor of the West
826	St. Ansgar began conversion of Norway, Denmark, Sweden
857	Photius, leader of Greek Schism, uncanonically replaced Ignatius, Patriarch of Constantinople
863	St. Methodius and St. Cyril began missionary work in southeastern Europe
869	Eighth Ecumenical Council (Fourth Council of Constantinople) condemned Photius
957	Conversion of Russia
972	Conversion of Hungary
1000	Christianity introduced into Iceland
1017	Olaf II established Faith in Norway
1054	Greek Schism completed by Michael Cerularius
1059	Election of Popes by Cardinals decreed by Pope Nicholas II
1073	Hildebrand elected Pope (Gregory VII)
1082	Carthusian Order founded by St. Bruno
1095	Pope Urban II promoted first Crusade, preached by Peter the Hermit
1099	Jerusalem taken from the Turks; Knights of St. John founded
1120	Order of Premonstratensians founded by St. Norbert

Year	Event
1122	Concordat of Worms
1123	Ninth Ecumenical Council (First Lateran Council) confirmed Concordat of Worms
1139	Tenth Ecumenical Council (Second Lateran Council) held
1156	Carmelites founded
1179	Eleventh Ecumenical Council (Third Lateran Council) held
1209	Simon de Montfort led a crusade in France against Albigenses; Franciscan Order founded (fully approved by Honorius III in 1222)
1215	Dominican Order founded (fully approved by Pope Honorius III in 1216); Twelfth Ecumenical Council (Fourth Lateran Council) condemned Albigenses, Waldenses and issued Seventy Canons on discipline
1228	Sixth Crusade begun
1230	Peace established between Pope and Emperor; Franciscans at University of Paris; Raymond of Pennafort, a Dominican, codified Canon Law
1245	Thirteenth Ecumenical Council at Lyons excommunicated Frederick II
1270	Eighth Crusade begun
1274	Death of St. Thomas Aquinas and of St. Bonaventure; Fourteenth Ecumenical Council (Second Council of Lyons) held
1294	Pope Boniface VIII elected

REFERENCES

BELLOC, H., *The Crusades   Europe and the Faith*
CURRAN, E. L., *Great Moments in Catholic History*, pp. 26-55
DESMOND, H. J., *Mooted Questions in History*
DREHER, T., *Outlines of Church History*, pp. 43-77
DVORNIK, F., *The Photian Schism*
EUGENE, BROTHER, *Bible and Church History*, pp. 261-270
FLETCHER, SIR BANISTER, *History of Architecture*
FORNER, B. N., *Story of the Church*, pp. 96-188
JOHNSON, G. W., HANNAN, J. D., DOMINICA, SR., *Story of the Church*, pp. 155-268
JUST, SISTER MARY, *The Immortal Fire*
LAUX, J., *Church History*, pp. 190-389

LORTZ, J., KAISER, E. G., *History of the Church*, pp. 143-256
NOVICES, *Dominican Saints*
RAEMER, S. A., *Church History*, pp. 153-302
SPALDING, B. J., *Bible and Church History*, pp. 268-284
WALSH, J. J., *The Thirteenth, Greatest of Centuries*
WHITE, H. C., *Not Built with Hands*
———, *A Watch in the Night*
Catholic Encyclopedia, "Albigenses," "Investiture," "Monasticism," "Universities," "Waldenses"

QUESTIONS

1. (*a*) What was *lay investiture?* (*b*) With what other abuses was it associated? (*c*) Explain the dispute of Pope Gregory VII with Emperor Henry IV over this abuse. (*d*) How was the investiture problem solved?

2. Innocent III is considered one of the greatest of all the Popes. Explain three accomplishments of Innocent's reign which justify this judgment.

3. (*a*) Mention two important heresies that appeared during the Early Middle Ages. (*b*) State briefly the false teachings of one of these heresies. (*c*) Explain in detail how the Church combated one of these heresies.

4. In regard to the Episcopal Inquisition, give the following information: (*a*) its purpose; (*b*) when and where it was used; (*c*) its relation to the civil courts; (*d*) how it differed from the Spanish Inquisition.

5. (*a*) Discuss the circumstances that led to the calling of the first Crusade. (*b*) Name the Pope who called this Crusade, and two leaders of the expeditions to the Holy Land. (*c*) What were the motives which impelled large numbers of Christians to go on this Crusade? (*d*) What were the achievements of this Crusade? (*e*) Give the same points of information for one of the other Crusades.

6. (*a*) How many Crusades were there? (*b*) Between what years did they take place? (*c*) Did the Crusades succeed in their primary objectives? Explain fully. (*d*) State five beneficial results of the Crusades.

7. (*a*) To what period has the term "Dark Ages" been applied? (*b*) Do you think that this term is historically sound? Explain.

8. (*a*) Define *feudalism,* and state its principal features. (*b*) State three advantages and three disadvantages of feudalism. (*c*) Explain how the Church exerted a beneficial influence on the feudal system.

9. (a) Distinguish between the *Monastic Orders* and the *Mendicant Orders*. (b) Explain the services which the monasteries performed for society during the Early Middle Ages. (c) Name three famous monasteries of this period. (d) Name one outstanding personality connected with the Monastic Orders.

10. (a) State five causes of the Greek Schism. (b) At which Ecumenical Council did ill-feeling between the East and the West first appear? (c) When did the Greek Church formally break with Rome? (d) Does this Schism still exist?

11. Explain briefly how the Faith was propagated during the early Middle Ages in (a) England, (b) Germany, (c) Scandinavia, and (d) Russia. Name at least one outstanding personality connected with the missionary work in each of these countries.

12. The thirteenth century has been called the "greatest of centuries." Explain fully the reasons for this evaluation.

13. (a) When did the Mendicant Orders arise? (b) Why were they badly needed at this time? (c) Name the four great Mendicant Orders. (d) Which two of these were the most important? (e) Discuss their services to the Church. (f) Discuss the personality and the work of either St. Francis or St. Dominic.

14. (a) How did universities come into existence during the Early Middle Ages? (b) Which was the greatest of these universities? Name two other important universities. (c) What subjects were studied at these institutions? (d) Name two degrees which were conferred. Which was the higher? (e) Discuss the services rendered to society by the universities of the Early Middle Ages.

15. (a) What is *scholasticism*? (b) Who was the greatest of the Scholastics? (c) What great book is his masterwork?

CHRONOLOGY TEST

Number the items in each of the following groups in their proper chronological order.

A	B
( ) Pope Innocent III	( ) Augustine of Canterbury
( ) Pope Gregory VII	( ) Cyril and Methodius
( ) Pope Honorius III	( ) Dante
( ) Pope Leo III	( ) Alcuin
( ) Pope Urban II	( ) Bede

SUPPLEMENTARY MATERIAL FOR UNIT III

C	D
( ) Pepin	( ) Greek Schism
( ) Charlemagne	( ) Concordat of Worms
( ) Henry IV	( ) Henry IV at Canossa
( ) Frederick Barbarossa	( ) First Crusade
( ) Louis IX	( ) Crowning of Charlemagne

MATCHING TEST

In the parenthesis next to each name in Column A, write the number of the item in Column B which is most closely connected with it.

A	B
( ) Gregory the Great	1. *Divine Comedy*
( ) Charles Martel	2. Koran
( ) Greatest King of the Franks	3. Canossa
( ) St. Dominic	4. Charlemagne
( ) St. Francis	5. Leo the Isaurian
( ) St. Louis	6. Preacher to the Albigenses
( ) Gregory VII	7. Founder of the Friars Minors
( ) Dante	8. Leader of the Third Crusade
( ) Giotto	9. Defeated Mohammedans at Tours
( ) Frederick Barbarossa	10. Leader of the seventh and eighth Crusades
	11. "Paymaster of the Lombards"
	12. Great painter

SELECTION TEST

In each of the following groups, select the one term that does not apply:

1. *Mendicant Orders:* Franciscans, Dominicans, Cistercians, Carmelites, Augustinians.
2. *Military Orders:* Knights of St. John, Teutonic Knights, Crusaders, Knights Templars.
3. *Heretics:* Albigenses, Waldenses, Monothelites, Iconoclasts, Servites.
4. *Universities:* Paris, Bologna, Oxford, Fulda, Salerno, Cambridge.
5. *Monasteries:* Cluny, Clairvaux, Rheims, Cîteaux, Grand Chartreuse.

COMPLETION TEST

Complete each of the following statements by supplying the correct word or phrase in the blank space.

1. The book *Liber Regulae Pastoralis,* designed to help regulate the life of the clergy, was written by ....
2. The Frankish King ...... made a donation of lands in Italy to the Papacy.
3. The son of the King mentioned in question 2 was ....
4. On Christmas day, 800, ... was crowned "Emperor of the West" by the Pope.
5. The Eastern Church in the Early Middle Ages refused to accept the addition of the word ...... to the Nicene Creed.
6. Mohammed's flight from Mecca to Medina is called the ....
7. An early Christian scholar in England who wrote the *Ecclesiastical History* was .... Another English scholar of this period was ....
8. The chief monastery founded by St. Boniface in Germany was ....
9. To attain personal holiness, monks take vows of (a) ......, (b) ...... and (c) ....
10. The typical architectural style of the Middle Ages is called ...... Architecture. Three great examples of this style of architecture are (a) ......, (b) ...... and (c) ....
11. The great monastery at Cluny was founded by St. ....
12. The most famous and influential of the Cistercian monks was ....
13. Under the feudal system, a person who received a grant of land in exchange for a promise to render military service was called a(n) .... The estate which such a person held was called a (n) ....
14. An agricultural community under the feudal system was known as a (n) .... The agricultural laborer was called a (n) ....
15. To curb the almost incessant fighting during the Early Middle Ages, the Church instituted the ....
16. The investiture dispute was finally settled by an agreement known as the ....
17. The Crusade against the Albigensians was led by a Catholic nobleman named ......
18. The kingdoms established in the Holy Land as a result of the first Crusade were called the "...... Kingdoms."
19. The nickname *il Poverello* was applied to ....
20. The greatest ecclesiastical assembly of the Middle Ages was the ...... Council.

UNIT IV

THE LATER MIDDLE AGES AND THE RENAISSANCE

PREVIEW

IN this Unit, we shall consider the history of the Church during the fourteenth and fifteenth centuries. This period is usually regarded as marking the transition from the Middle Ages to Modern Times. The pattern of events is very complex, and the rate of change in different fields is most uneven, but the general trend is unmistakable. Historians call the new era the *Renaissance*. This is a French word, meaning "rebirth," and refers to the revival of literature, art and science that took place at this time. It must be understood, however, that the Renaissance marks not only a "rebirth," but also the fulfillment of Medieval promise. The Later Middle Ages, covering most of the fourteenth century, blended almost imperceptibly into the Renaissance.

During this period, the stability which had characterized European society during the Middle Ages gave way to a spirit of change. The Church, of course, was profoundly affected by these changes. The political authority which had resided in the Pope and the Holy Roman Emperor was taken over by absolute national monarchs. France, as a leading national power in Europe, needed money to build up and unify the country, and taxed the Catholic clergy illegally. The struggles that ensued weakened the Papacy, until the Pope came to be looked upon as one of several princes or rulers, all of whom had temporal powers equal to those of the Vicar of Christ. Pope Boniface VIII struggled valiantly with Philip the Fair of France, but Philip triumphed and the Pontiff died, the victim of violent and irreverent treatment at the hands of the French. Then followed the "Babylonian Captivity," during which a succession of seven Popes resided at Avignon in France. Some of these Popes were worthy of their exalted office, but others were merely weak tools of the French throne.

The Popes finally returned to Rome, but this happy event was soon followed by the Great Schism, caused by rivalry between Italian and French interests over the Papal throne. The Schism was ended after forty years by the Council of Constance, and all Christendom again recognized a single spiritual head. Shortly after the Council of Constance, Nicholas V became Pope (1447). He was the first of a series of ten Pontiffs, known as the "Renaissance Popes," who fostered and encouraged the Renaissance movement. The actions of some of these Popes leave us silent in sorrowful amazement; but others were talented men who sought to act as true Catholics in assimilating, purifying and consecrating all that was good in the artistic and intellectual activities of the day. Many great artists and writers, such as Petrarch, Michelangelo, Raphael and Leonardo da Vinci, were encouraged by the Renaissance Popes.

Toward the end of this period, Spain began to emerge as the leading European power. It was under the sponsorship of the Spanish monarchs that Columbus sailed forth to find a new all-water route to the East, and instead of this discovered America. With Columbus went missionaries, who carried Christianity to the New World. In the same year in which Columbus landed in America, the Spaniards completed the conquest of the Mohammedan Moors in the Iberian Peninsula.

CHAPTER 7

THE LATER MIDDLE AGES

"I see the flower-de-luce Alagna enter,
And Christ in His own Vicar captive made.
I see Him yet another time derided;
I see renewed the vinegar and gall.
And between living thieves I see Him slain.
I see the modern Pilate so relentless . . ."

—Dante ("Purgatorio")

INTRODUCTION

Character of the Later Middle Ages.—In this chapter, we shall consider the history of the fourteenth century, which marks the beginning of the Renaissance and the end of the Middle Ages. The one word that expresses the keynote of the spirit of this era is *change*. This change had varied economic, social, political, and cultural aspects. Economically, the development of industry, the expansion of trade and commerce, and the widespread use of coined money heralded the emergence of a capitalist society, which was gradually to replace the declining feudal system. The secluded nobleman's castle and the imposing Bishop's palace yielded place to the crowded, industrious cathedral and university towns as centers of social activity. Politically, the era saw an increase in the powers of the national governments. Kings acquired sovereign or absolute power, whereas formerly they had been suzerains. State taxes began to take the place of feudal dues, but for a long time powerful nobles continued to exact feudal dues and to enjoy feudal privileges at the expense of the helpless peasantry. State taxes were used to pay government officials, who enforced the laws and administered justice. National standing armies replaced the old feudal levies.

Cultural Achievements.—Culturally, the period is noted for the great development of the national (vernacular) languages, which began to replace Latin as the language of educated laymen.

As we shall see in Chapter 8, two great Florentines, Petrarch and Boccaccio, made outstanding contributions to literature, writing in their native Italian tongue. In the fields of painting, sculpture, architecture, and other arts, the foundations were laid for the great achievements of the fifteenth and sixteenth centuries. Notable progress was made, also, in the field of science, largely as a result of the rediscovery of the thought of the ancient world. This was reflected in the epoch-making voyages of discovery which took place in the next centuries.

THE REIGN OF BONIFACE VIII

The Character of Boniface VIII.—The last of the Medieval Popes was Boniface VIII (1294-1303). He was born in 1235, a member of the well-known Gaetani family. Boniface was a courageous and high-minded man, determined to protect the interests of the Church against any forces that might threaten it. He had, moreover, a brilliant mind and was highly skilled in both canon and civil law. One of his less attractive characteristics was a rather sharp temper. Cardinal Wiseman says that he was stern and inflexible, but not cruel or revengeful.

Philip the Fair of France and Taxation of the Clergy.—Upon ascending the throne of St. Peter in 1294, Boniface resolved to seek an end to the war which was then in progress between Philip IV (Philip the Fair) of France and Edward I of England. The Pope planned to organize another Crusade to the Holy Land when peace was restored.

The war which Boniface sought to terminate had been brought about by Philip the Fair. This ruler, a grandson of Louis IX (St. Louis), was an able but unscrupulous man, whose supreme ambition was to unify the French nation and to extend its national boundaries. Philip was a poor financier and soon found himself in desperate need of revenues. He saw an opportunity to replenish his coffers by acquiring several rich feudal estates in southwestern France, which were then in the possession of the English crown. Edward I resisted Philip's efforts to appropriate these estates, and war resulted.

It soon became clear that Philip intended to obtain the money he needed to carry on the war by taxing the French clergy and ecclesiastical property. This was in direct violation of the traditional Church legislation that the clergy might not be taxed without the consent of the Pope. The doctrine had been reaffirmed in 1215 by the Fourth Lateran Council (page 128).

The *Clericis Laicos*.—In 1296, the French clergy appealed to Boniface to protect them against the illegal taxes levied by Philip. Boniface responded with his famous Bull, *Clericis laicos*. In this Bull, the Pontiff threatened with excommunication all rulers who sought to levy taxes upon the clergy without Papal sanction, and all clerics who paid such taxes to laymen. Philip interpreted this Bull as a direct challenge to his royal authority and countered by prohibiting the exportation of all gold and silver from the country. Since France was then the predominant power in Europe, this was a severe blow, cutting off the chief source of Papal revenue. Boniface then issued a new Bull, *Ineffabilis*, in which he asserted that Philip's counselors had misinterpreted the *Clericis laicos*. Philip accordingly suspended his counter-measures, but retained the power of taxation over the French clergy.

The Peace of Amiens.—In 1298, the French and English monarchs agreed to let Boniface arbitrate their dispute in the capacity of a private individual. The resulting truce led to the Peace of Amiens, which was signed in 1303. Both monarchs agreed to restore all territories which had been conquered during the conflict and consented to the intermarriage of their families.

Effect of the *Clericis Laicos* in England.—In England, the *Clericis laicos* helped to establish the democratic principle of "no taxation without representation." In 1297, an English Archbishop named Winchelsey refused to grant money to King Edward I; he based his position on the Papal Bull. He was joined in this refusal by the English barons, who were already heavily burdened by taxation. The barons refused to participate in the war against France until the King recognized the right of Parliament to pass upon royal requests for taxes. The assent of King Edward to this demand was incorporated in a number of articles called the *Confirmation of the Charters*. These articles helped to strengthen limitations upon the authority of the monarch which had been established by the famous *Magna Carta* (1215). Nearly five centuries later, the principle of "no taxation without representation" was to play an important part in the struggle of the American colonies for independence.

Boniface Asserts Papal Supremacy.—Boniface VIII and Philip IV did not long remain on good terms. Philip ordered the Papal Legate in France seized, had him robbed of his official papers, tried him for treason, and imprisoned him. Boniface protested with the Bull *Ausculta, fili* ("Listen, my son"), written in 1301. It was delivered in 1302, but the French Count of Artois snatched the document from the Papal Legate and thrust it into a fire. A new document, written in insulting language, was forged by an agent of the French King named Peter Flotte, who also wrote Philip's reply to the purported Bull. The contents of both documents were then announced to the French people in order to arouse patriotic feeling and to incite popular anger against the Pope.

Philip then summoned the Estates General [1] to meet in Paris. At this assembly, the representatives of the common people for the first time sat together with the clergy and the nobility. Making use of the document forged by Peter Flotte, Philip induced the nobles and the commons to side with him in his controversy with Boniface. The clergy, although hesitant at first, finally agreed with the King and wrote to the Pope asking him to reconsider his policy toward the French monarch.

Boniface, intrepid and unflinching, answered the French Estates General with the Bull *Unam sanctam*. In this Bull, the Pontiff reiterated the Christian principle, upheld by the Church from its earliest days, that there is a distinction between spiritual and temporal power, and that, of the two, spiritual power is superior. The Bull was, in fact, an assertion of Papal supremacy over all temporal rulers.

The Great Jubilee of 1300.—This event was the one joyous interlude in the troubled reign of Boniface VIII. The Jubilee was proclaimed by the Pope in February, 1300. All repentant sinners who received the sacrament of penance and visited the basilicas of St. Peter and St. Paul in Rome a specified number of times, were granted an indulgence. Romans were required to

---

[1] The Estates General was, in theory, a representative legislative body, similar to the English Parliament. In actuality, however, it was little more than a "debating society." without real powers.

make thirty visits; all others, fifteen. According to one contemporary writer, 200,000 pilgrims flocked to Rome to attend the Jubilee. A scene of splendor was enacted on Christmas Eve, 1300, as the Pope, standing in the loggia of the Lateran and surrounded by Cardinals and his court, imparted his blessing *urbi et orbi* ("on the city and on the world"). This inspiring scene was preserved for posterity in a painting by Giotto. Dante wrote of the Jubilee in his *Divine Comedy*, describing the coming and going of the pilgrims across the bridge of St. Angelo. But the period of gladness was soon to be followed by a tragedy.

The Tragedy of Anagni.—Peter Flotte, Philip's notorious agent, was killed at the battle of Courtrai, in which the Flemings won their independence from France. A Frenchman named Nogaret took over Flotte's villainous work. Philip falsely accused Boniface of heresy and ordered Nogaret to seize him. In connivance with the Colonnas, the Italian enemies of Boniface, Nogaret sent an armed band to do Philip's bidding. The sacrilege was consummated in the Papal palace at Anagni, the Pontiff's birthplace. By sheer brute force, the armed band broke into the palace and seized the Pope, who met his captors in full Pontifical vestments. After three days of mistreatment at the hands of his captors, he was rescued by the townsmen of Anagni. Boniface was then escorted back to Rome by Italian noblemen. He died one month later (October, 1303), as a result of the abusive treatment which he suffered while in captivity. Dante commemorated the evil deed in his *Divine Comedy,* Purgatorio XX, 86-90 (See the quotation on page 137.)

THE "BABYLONIAN CAPTIVITY"

Benedict XI (1303-1304).—Pope Benedict XI, who succeeded Boniface, was conciliatory, and tried to make peace with Philip by granting him numerous concessions. But mild as he was Benedict excommunicated Nogaret and Sciarra Colonna for their parts in the outrageous sacrilege against Boniface. Philip attempted to throw the blame for the affair on Boniface, repeating his false charge that the Pontiff had been a heretic. Benedict rejected Philip's contention. The Pope died after a reign of only nine months; he was believed by many to have been poisoned because of his opposition to Philip.

Clement V (1305-1314).—Philip's far-reaching influence enabled him to secure the election of a French Bishop as the successor of Benedict. The election of this Pontiff, Clement V, marked the beginning of a period which Italian writers called the "Babylonian Captivity." [2] For the next seventy years the seven Popes who ascended the throne of St. Peter were all Frenchmen, and resided at Avignon, a town near the Italian border.

Clement V was crowned in 1305 at Lyons, France, rather than in Rome, and took up residence in a Dominican monastery at Avignon. This town was nominally free, but was actually French in character and sympathies. One of Clement's first acts was to appoint nine new French Cardinals. During the nine years of his reign, Clement revealed many instances of weakness and granted numerous favors to Philip. However, he manifested a strong missionary zeal, taking an active part in missionary work in China. At the instance of the French monarch, Clement called the Fifteenth Ecumenical Council at Vienne, France, in 1311. This Council conducted an investigation into the life of Boniface VIII and cleared his name of the many unjust charges brought against him by Philip's followers. But the greedy Philip prevailed upon Clement and the Council to suppress the Knights Templars (page 116), whose vast wealth he regarded with envy. Philip had fifty-four Knights charged with heresy and burned at the stake. The King then seized their wealth.

---

[2] The term "Babylonian Captivity" is derived from an episode in the history of the Hebrews, in which they were carried off by the Babylonians and held in captivity from 586 to 539 B.C.

John XXII (1316-1334).—After a vacancy of two years following the death of Clement V, another Frenchman, John XXII, was elected to the Papacy. John was an able administrator who issued more than 60,000 documents during the eighteen years of his Pontificate. Immediately after assuming the tiara, he appointed seven new French Cardinals.

John engaged in a struggle with the Holy Roman Emperor, Louis of Bavaria, to enforce the Papal privilege of deciding all controversial elections to the office of Emperor. There were two claimants to the Imperial throne, Louis of Bavaria and Frederick of Austria. The former refused to await a Papal decision, and attempted to force the issue by engaging in civil war against his opponent. Louis defeated Frederick at the battle of Muldorf in 1322, and at once declared himself Emperor. For this unauthorized act, the Pope excommunicated him and placed his country under an interdict. Louis then gathered about him several allies, including Sciarra Colonna and a group of heretical or schismatic Franciscans known as the *Fraticelli*. He set out for Italy, where he was crowned King of Italy by excommunicated Bishops and by Sciarra Colonna. The assembly which elected Louis then brought the Pope to trial, deposed him, and elected an anti-Pope, a Franciscan, who took the name Nicholas V. However, the Italian people soon rose in anger and forced Louis to flee back to Germany. The anti-Pope then surrendered to John XXII, who treated him mercifully.

Benedict XII (1334-1342).—This gentle Pope, whose reign saw the beginning of the Hundred Years' War between France and England (page 166), decided to return to Rome, but was opposed in this desire by the French Cardinals. Benedict thereupon began the erection of a great Papal palace at Avignon.

The reign of Benedict XII is remembered for the *Decision of Rense*, issued by the Electors of the Holy Roman Empire, at the city of Rense in Germany. This Decision was of great importance because it held that the authority of the state was actually independent of the Pope. Specifically, it denied the right of the Pope to approve or reject an elected ruler of Germany.[3] The Decision

---

[3] Although the Decision of Rense was confirmed by the Council of Constance (1414), it never received the approval of the Pope. Martin V did confirm several of the decrees of the Council of Constance, but not the one relating to the Decision of Rense.

also advanced the *conciliar theory*, which stated that all Bishops, including the Pope, have equal power, and that supreme ecclesiastical power is vested in the General Council under the control of the temporal power, rather than in the Pope. The Decision of Rense definitely ended Medieval Papal supremacy, and the theories which it embodied were responsible for the appearance of evils in the Church in the following century. Despite the concessions granted by Benedict, the Holy Roman Emperor (Louis the Bavarian) continued to defy the Pope.

Clement VI (1342-1352).—Clement was a generous and charitable Pope. In the year 1348, a great plague, known as the Black Death, swept across all of Europe, causing terrible loss of life. It has been estimated that fully one-third of the entire population of Europe, or 25,000,000 persons, died in this plague. During these trying times, the Pope distinguished himself by innumerable acts of charity. He also did much to protect the Jews against the distraught populace, who unjustly accused them of causing the plague by poisoning the wells. It is now believed that the Black Death was an epidemic of a disease known as the bubonic plague. People at that time, of course, knew very little about the natural causes of disease; this ignorance was the reason for the fantastic charges against the Jews.

Clement displayed magnificent splendor on the Pontifical throne but had to impose heavy taxes to maintain the luxurious court life demanded by the French Cardinals. He purchased the site of the Papal palace from Queen Ivanna of Naples. In 1346, the Pope induced the German princes to elect a new Emperor, Charles IV, Prince of Bohemia. Louis of Bavaria prepared to resist Charles' election, but died the following year. All Germany then recognized Charles as Emperor.

Innocent VI (1352-1362).—Innocent VI made possible a reduction of burdensome taxes by exercising rigid economy in the Papal palace. He curbed the extravagance of the Cardinals both in legislative matters and in their personal expenditures. Innocent also took an interest in the political affairs in Italy and in Rome. He reëstablished the Papal authority in Rome after it had been tyrannically usurped by Italian nobles.

Urban V (1362-1370).—This Pope led a life of exemplary virtue, and demanded similar conduct from all in the Papal court. He was a patron of learning and a friend of the poor. A new Crusade which he undertook against the Turks in the East resulted in the capture of Alexandria, but the Crusade failed because of lack of support from Europe. In 1367, with the support of Emperor Charles IV, Urban decided to return to Rome from Avignon. The French Cardinals objected to the transfer, but only three failed to follow the Pope to Rome. However, the turmoil which at that time existed in Rome and throughout all Italy soon induced Urban to return to the quiet of Avignon, where he died after three months. (Urban's death fulfilled the prophecy of St. Bridget of Sweden.) Pope Urban V was beatified by the Church.

Gregory XI (1370-1378).—Gregory XI, who was a nephew of Clement VI, put an end to the Babylonian Captivity and returned the Papacy to Rome. The honor of bringing about this important event belongs chiefly to St. Catherine of Siena. The city of Florence had openly rebelled against the Papal States in Italy. To combat the rebellion, the Pope placed the city under an interdict, crippling its commerce. Florentine officials appointed Catherine of Siena as their ambassadress to the Pope at Avignon. By writing numerous letters of reconciliation and by making a personal appeal to the Holy Father, she induced Gregory to return to Rome. Accompanied by all but six of the Cardinals, Gregory arrived in Rome in January, 1377, and was joyously acclaimed by the populace. But during the long absence of the Popes, Rome had been reduced to a sad state. Most of the 414 basilicas were in ruins, commerce was paralyzed, and the population had fallen to a mere 30,000. Despite Gregory's return to Rome, turmoil continued. However, before his death in 1378, Florence finally consented to open negotiations for peace.

Missionary Activity in the Far East.—The one great achievement of the Avignon period is the missionary activities carried on in India, Central Asia and China. This missionary work in foreign lands indicated inspiration by a truly divine Christian spirit. Bishops were sent abroad, carrying with them spiritual and material aid; converts were baptized in large numbers. Unfortunately, in 1368 the Ming Dynasty of China destroyed much of the good work accomplished by the servants of the Church of Christ.

THE GREAT SCHISM (1378-1418)

Nature of the Great Schism.—After the seventy years of the Babylonian Captivity, the Church had to weather still another storm. The Great Schism of the West, as this dispute has been called, lasted for forty years, from 1378 to 1418, and embraced the Pontificates of four true Popes: Urban VI, Boniface IX, Innocent VII and Gregory XII. During this period there were anti-Popes at Avignon: Clement VII and Benedict XIII; and anti-Popes at Pisa: Alexander V and John XXIII. At times, as many as three candidates simultaneously claimed the throne of St. Peter, each denying the authority of the others. The result was that no individual was recognized as Pope by all of western Europe. Rulers and people were honestly confused as to whom allegiance was rightly due. Even saints were divided in their allegiance. Thus, St. Vincent Ferrer supported the anti-Pope in France,[4] while St. Catherine of Siena and St. Bridget swore obedience to Urban in Rome. The Christian world was sorely distracted by this unhappy state of affairs, but the Divine Protector was always present, as He had promised the Apostles.

Origin of the Great Schism.—Immediately after the death of Gregory XI in 1378, the Cardinals in conclave at Rome elected Urban VI, an Italian. The absent Cardinals at Avignon gave their consent in writing to Urban's election, attended his coronation and rendered homage to him. However, Urban showed poor diplomacy when, soon after the election, he strongly reproached the French Cardinals for their worldly lives. Three months later these Cardinals left Rome, using the oppressively hot weather as a pretext. They soon met together and elected an anti-Pope, who assumed the title of Clement VII. The French Cardinals justified their action by the claim that the election of Urban VI had not been free. This claim was false, for historical facts show irrefutably that the election was free. Nonetheless, all the nations of western Europe soon took sides on the issue and Christendom was actually divided into two camps.

---

[4] The anti-Pope whom St. Vincent supported was Pedro de Luna, who assumed the title of Benedict XIII. Vincent, however, finally recognized the anti-Pope for what he was, and denounced him forthrightly before a vast audience. This sermon cost de Luna his last adherents.

Many solutions of the problem were suggested, but chaotic conditions prevailed, especially in Italy and France. Meanwhile, Urban VI created a new College of twenty-nine Cardinals at Rome. Finally, a Council was called at Pisa in 1409. This Council was not summoned or approved by the Pope and cannot therefore be considered one of the Ecumenical Councils. The Council of Pisa was schismatic and only complicated matters by electing a third claimant to the Papal throne, who took the title of Alexander V. (He was soon succeeded by John XXIII.) As a result, there were now three contending factions: at Rome, at Avignon and at Pisa.

Council of Constance (1414-1418).—Pope Gregory XII, successor to Urban VI, was the prime mover in inducing Emperor

Sigismund to convoke a council at Constance (Germany), with the object of putting an end to the Great Schism. Gregory sent Cardinal John Dominic, O.P. to Sigismund, secretly asking him to call a council. The result was the Council of Constance (the Sixteenth Ecumenical Council), which lasted from November,

1414 to April, 1418. It soon became clear that the cause of John XXIII of the Pisa faction was hopeless, and he was forced to renounce his claim. Pope Gregory XII then canonically convoked the Council through the agency of Blessed John Dominic, the Papal Legate, who dramatically appeared at the fourteenth session and announced Gregory's resignation of his right to the Papacy in the interest of reëstablishing unity. Benedict XIII (Pedro de Luna), the claimant of the Avignon faction, remained firm in his refusal to renounce his claim. He was finally deposed by the Council in July, 1417.

After the Papacy had been vacant for two years, the election of a new Pope was arranged. In order to give greater authority to the selection of the Council, it was decided that six delegates from each nation (Italy, France, Germany, England and Spain) should be associated with the Cardinals from these nations, and that a two-thirds vote of each of the five national groups should be required to elect the Pope. In addition, the successful candidate was required to receive a two-thirds vote of the twenty-three Cardinals. It was felt that a Pope elected by such an overwhelming and representative majority would command the undivided allegiance of the Catholic world. After three days, on November 11, 1417, the Council elected a new Pope, Martin V. On April 22, 1418, Martin dissolved the Sixteenth Ecumenical Council. The Great Schism of the West ended with Martin's election.

HERESIES OF THE FOURTEENTH CENTURY

Wycliffe.—John Wycliffe (1324-1384) was an English scholar and Priest. As a professor at Oxford University, he sided with King Edward III in opposing the authority of the Papacy. Later, in his sermons he advocated that the Church surrender its property to the government in order that clergymen might be free to perform their religious duties. Wycliffe believed that everybody should study the Bible for himself. To make this possible for the common people, who understood no Latin, he translated the Bible into English. He also taught that no ecclesiastical or secular officer possessed any rightful authority unless he was himself free from sin. This heresy served to undermine all authority, temporal as well as spiritual. Wycliffe was condemned by the

Council of London in 1382, and deprived of his Oxford professorship. His followers (known as *Lollards*) were persecuted and suppressed by the English government. However, Wycliffe's ideas crept into Bohemia, which was closely associated with England in those days.

Hus.—John Hus (1373-1415), a Bohemian clergyman and professor at the University of Prague, was affected by Wycliffe's teachings and began to preach similar heretical doctrines. Hus translated the *Trialogus* of Wycliffe into Czech and circulated the heresy, even after ecclesiastical authority had condemned it. In 1411, he was excommunicated, but continued his propagation of error and incited his countrymen to revolt. He was ordered to recant by the Council of Constance and, when he refused, was burned at the stake, July 6, 1415. The Hussites successfully resisted the military forces sent against them by the Emperor Sigismund for more than ten years. However, in 1431, the more conservative Hussites made peace with the Church and the radicals were sternly suppressed.

The Council of Basle-Florence (1431-1439).—The Council of Basle-Florence, the Seventeenth Ecumenical Council, was sanctioned by Pope Eugenius IV, the successor of Martin V, and met in Basle in July, 1431. The business of the Council dealt with the reconciliation of the Hussite heretics, the reunion of the Greek and Roman Churches, and the enactment of Church reforms.

The Council was a stormy one, opening with a struggle between the Bishops and the Pope over the question of conciliar supremacy (page 144). Then followed a dispute over union with the Greek Church. Eugenius finally ordered the Council dissolved and summoned the fathers to Ferrara, where he opened a new synod. The outbreak of a pestilence later compelled him to transfer the synod to Florence.

In Florence, Eugenius succeeded in effecting a temporary union between the Roman and the Greek Churches (July 6, 1439). But the Council at Basle, although abandoned by most of its members, remained in existence and maintained that it was the only canonical Ecumenical Council. It proceeded to depose Eugenius (July 25, 1439) despite the opposition of most of the European powers, and elected an anti-Pope, who took the name Felix V.

The schism which thus resulted lasted for ten years, although almost all of Europe remained loyal to Eugenius. Finally, in 1449, the anti-Pope abdicated, and the fathers of Basle returned their support to Nicholas V, the rightful Pope, who had ascended the throne upon the death of Eugenius in 1447. The theory of the supremacy of the Council had been defeated, and the Papacy emerged triumphant. Thus ended the last Church schism.

CHAPTER 8

THE BEGINNINGS OF MODERN TIMES

"Renaissance signifies the cultural achievements of European society between 1300 and 1600 which mark the passage from the Middle Ages to the modern world. These include not only such higher accomplishments as art, literature, music and science, but also far-reaching changes in the economic bases of life, the structure of society, and the organization of states."—H. S. Lucas ("Renaissance and Reformation")

INTRODUCTION

Characteristics of the Renaissance.—We have already emphasized that the chief characteristic of the Renaissance period was *changeableness*. From the viewpoint of the Church, the basic change was from the sublime spirit of glorious faith to a very worldly spirit. This worldly spirit is discernible in every human activity, such as those mentioned in the above quotation from Lucas. In the sphere of politics, for example, the guidance of religion was set aside in favor of individualism. Absolute monarchs, imitators of the Roman Emperors, guided the destinies of national states; attempts by Popes to arbitrate differences between the states were frowned upon. In this chapter, we shall consider chiefly cultural changes, since cultural changes are a reflection of the spiritual forces that determine the character of an age.

To the characteristics of the Renaissance already mentioned (*i.e.*, changeableness and a worldly attitude) we may add a third —imitation. The Renaissance frankly imitated nature, as well as Greek and Roman antiquity. The spirit of imitation is in striking contrast to the creative originality of the Middle Ages. For example, we do not find a new type of architecture in the Renaissance, but rather a development of the Gothic, with classical influences also evident. In these buildings, ornamentation is used for the sake of ornamentation, rather than as a functional part of the structure.

SPIRIT OF THE RENAISSANCE
CHANGE

THE BEGINNINGS OF MODERN TIMES

Achievements in Art and Science.—In painting, conventionalism gave way to naturalism in line and color. The great painters and sculptors of the period studied anatomy intensively, and the figures in their masterpieces seem almost to speak and move. In music, the organ added sensual warmth to melodious sound. The invention of gunpowder and the improvement of firearms transformed the art of warfare. The known limits of the earth were extended as a result of the work of navigators and astronomers. The invention of printing made possible a far greater diffusion of books and of the knowledge contained in books. The Church recognized much good in all this seething activity and tried to guide and Christianize it. But the Church also recognized powerful forces of decay at work which threatened the very moral foundations of the worldly minded Renaissance generations.

THE RENAISSANCE POPES

The Papacy during the Renaissance.—The ten Popes who ruled from 1447 to 1521 are usually known as the "Renaissance Popes" (sometimes, also, as the "political Popes"). The first of them, Nicholas V, was the 210th Pope; the last, Leo X, was the 219th Pope. To keep the Church free from the control of kings and princes, the Popes were compelled to strengthen their temporal power by means similar to those which secular rulers employed. For example, they sought to protect the Papacy from its political enemies in Italy by practicing nepotism—that is, appointing relatives to important Church offices. The Popes usually felt that they could depend on their close relatives, while outsiders might be won over by the secular rulers. As a result of this practice, the College of Cardinals came to include ignoble men, who finally elected to the Papacy Alexander VI, a member of the notorious Borgia family.

As patrons of art and literature, the Renaissance Popes performed a great service, for which they merit the everlasting gratitude of the world. The Popes of this period encouraged and rewarded scholars and artists, who otherwise might not have been able to do their immortal work. They built the Vatican, the art-center of the world, and St. Peter's, whose grandeur is an inspiration to all Christianity.

Nicholas V (1447-1455).—Nicholas V, the first of the Renaissance Popes, was one of the three great humanists [1] among them. (The others are Pius II and Leo X.) He founded the Vatican library of 5000 volumes, among which he had 824 Latin and 352 Greek manuscripts. It was during the Pontificate of Nicholas V that Constantinople fell to the Turks. This event, and the two Ecumenical Councils a few years previously, drew many educated Byzantines to Rome and Italy. These savants brought with them numerous Greek manuscripts, while European libraries yielded a rich harvest of Latin authors. Nicholas employed Fra Angelico to paint his study in the Vatican Palace. He invited to his court poets and scholars upon whom he conferred rich rewards.

Pius II (1458-1464).—This Pope, born Aeneas Silvius Piccolomini, was a typical character of the Renaissance. He was born near Siena in 1405, the oldest of eighteen children. He was educated at the parish school by the pastor, and was also instructed by his father. At the age of eighteen, he went to Siena and lived with his uncle, who sent him to the University of Siena, noted for its law faculty. At his own initiative, he studied the Latin classics; later his relatives sent him to Florence, where he met renowned classical scholars, as Filelfo, the Greek master.

In 1431, a Cardinal passing through Siena to the Council of Basle took Aeneas for his secretary. Aeneas became the secretary of one Cardinal after another on the anti-Papal side. During this period, he wrote a history of the Council of Basle, and then a history of Bohemia, into which he introduced the humanism of the period. Later he found employment in the court of Frederick III of Germany, thus carrying the torch of humanism to Germany. In 1446, he was ordained a Priest. During the Pontificate of Nicholas V, he represented Frederick III at Rome. During all these years, he was also writing material similar to the unwholesome stories of Boccaccio (page 160); in later life, Aeneas sincerely regretted these unworthy writings. In 1450, he wrote a treatise on education for Ladislaus, Duke of Bohemia; it is interesting because it gives us a contemporary description of a Renais-

---

[1] The *humanists* in the Renaissance era were those who admired, and promoted the study of, the ancient classics. As we shall see, there were conservative or Christian humanists, who used the classics constructively; and radical humanists, who sought to paganize art and thought.

sance education. In 1453, Aeneas was made Cardinal of Siena. At the age of fifty-two, he was elected Pope, and assumed the name of Pius II. He reigned for six years and acted as a genuine patron of the arts. In addition, he had other interests, such as the crusade against the Turks.

Sixtus IV (1471-1484).—Sixtus IV, originally a Franciscan Friar, is not one of the three great humanist Popes but he was friendly towards the Renaissance. He toiled to beautify Rome by straightening, widening and paving streets, and by building bridges, walls, gates, churches, and other structures. He was a collector of museum objects, many of which he housed in a museum built by his predecessor, Paul II. Sixtus was especially active as a patron of painting. He employed Forli to paint a fresco in the Vatican library. In this fresco, Sixtus is represented seated, surrounded by his four nephews, who are standing; Platina, the librarian, kneels before him.

Sixtus built the Sistine Chapel in which he had twelve marvelous frescoes painted by the master artists of the day. Six portray the life of Moses; six picture Christ's mission on earth. The greatest is Perugino's picture of Christ giving the keys to St. Peter. These twelve masterpieces adorn the side walls. A later Pope was to have the ceilings decorated by the immortal Michelangelo.

Alexander VI (1492-1503).—Alexander VI, a member of the Borgia family, completely secularized the Papacy. He was primarily a politician, and his chief interest was to strengthen the power of the Papal States. He was an extremely worldly person and, although a highly gifted man, brought dishonor to the Papacy. However, he was a patron of the arts and gave much attention to architecture and painting. He improved many buildings in and around the Vatican. During his Pontificate, Bramante built the first Roman church of the Renaissance type. In justice to Alexander, it must be said that although he misused his Pontifical power, he never compromised either faith or morals in any of the numerous official documents issued by him.

Julius II (1503-1513).—This warrior-Pope was a striking contrast to his immediate predecessors. When Michelangelo portrayed him in sculpture, Julius chose to be represented with a sword rather than a book in his hands. With this sword, he saved the Papal territories and drove the French from Italy. He was very just and waged war only for the independence of the Church; no family clique profited by his conquests. He is rightly called the "Liberator of Italy," and the "Savior of the Church."

Julius' great achievements as a soldier and statesman do not overshadow his services as a munificent and discerning patron of the arts. The greatest architect of the Renaissance, Bramante, designed St. Peter's Cathedral for him. Michelangelo, the supreme artist, decorated the ceiling of the Sistine Chapel at his invitation. This truly great Pontiff was also an outstanding spiritual leader. This is indicated by the fact that he convoked the Eighteenth Ecumenical Council (Fifth Lateran Council) for the purpose of reform (1512-1517). He strove to protect future Papal elections from simony and to awaken the Cardinals to a sense of their responsibility.

Leo X (1513-1521).—Leo X, a member of the de Medici family, was the last of the Renaissance Popes. He continued all the projects of his predecessors—the Ecumenical Council, the construction of St. Peter's, the support of great artists. To these activities, Leo added a great love and a profound knowledge of classical literature. A brilliant group of Latin and Greek scholars came to Rome. Many books were added to the Vatican library, and Leo proved himself a most generous and discriminating patron.

Leo also sponsored great artists, including Bramante, Michelangelo and Raphael. In one of Raphael's famous frescoes, which represents Leo I halting the advance of the Huns under Attila (page 66), the face of this early Pope is actually a portrait of Leo X. When Bramante died in 1514, Raphael was appointed to continue the construction of St. Peter's.

The achievements of Leo X must not blind us to the fact that he was a worldly Pope. His reign was to witness the revolt of Luther, a revolt brought on partially by the secularism and paganism of the Renaissance period.

THE ART OF THE RENAISSANCE

Character of Renaissance Art.—Most of the sculpture and painting of the Renaissance dealt with religious subjects. However, the purely religious value of this art has often been exaggerated. This is well expressed in the following passage: [2]

> The great peril here lies not in the fact that the masters of the Renaissance painted profane and mythological themes in addition to religious ones, but in the spirit motivating their work. Even in many of Raphael's madonnas, to cite an example, the spirit is the triumph of human motherhood, of richness and depth of feeling, but it is not really religious. His *Disputa,* a really theological theme, is simply overwhelming, an incomparable miracle of drawing and composition, but it is not a work of piety. . . . The entrance of the earthly spirit, the craving for a glamorous and indulgent life, into the spirit of sacred building is objectionable. . . . Michelangelo's very grandeur is a source of danger to religion in his influence on others, whose subjectivity meets with secularistic tendencies with which the world is filled.

Today, there is a movement among Catholic artists to abandon imitation of the Renaissance period, and to produce an art that will be more original and spiritual, and will not appeal so strongly to sense appreciation. The true Catholic artist of today wishes his art to influence by the spiritual thought portrayed, rather than by the natural form in which the thought is robed.

Let us now consider a few of the greatest Renaissance artists.

Fra Angelico (1387-1455).—So far as religious spirit is concerned, Fra Angelico is the greatest of the Renaissance painters. A native of Florence, he became a Dominican and led a saintly life. From 1436 to 1445 he lived at the church of San Marco in Florence, where many of his great frescoes were painted. Perhaps the most famous of these is his *Annunciation,* which is unique for the spirituality of expression in the countenances, and the reverence of the postures. His coloring is pure and gem-like in its clearness. He has never been surpassed in depicting the seraphic. Fra Angelico's angels are just human enough to be comprehensible, but not so human that their spiritual nature is

---

[2] Lortz, J. and Kaiser, E. G., *History of the Church.*

veiled. The Dominican convent in Florence is now a national museum in which some of Fra Angelico's paintings are preserved. He painted in Rome at the Vatican under Eugenius IV and Nicholas V. The latter Pope offered Fra Angelico the Archbishopric of Florence, but the noble and modest painter referred him to St. Antoninus, as more worthy of the post.

Leonardo da Vinci (1452-1519).—This great painter was a versatile genius, who excelled in sculpture, painting, architecture, engineering and science. *The Last Supper,* his masterpiece, was painted at Milan for a Milanese ambassador, Lodovico; the fresco may still be seen in the refectory of a Dominican monastery adjoining the church of Santa Maria della Grazie. The painting portrays the emotions of the twelve Apostles at the moment when Christ said, "One of you shall betray Me." Da Vinci was the great pioneer in the true representation of the human figure. He was the first painter to make records of the internal structure of the body; his drawings of this were not excelled in accuracy for centuries. Another of Leonardo's most famous paintings is the *Mona Lisa,* which hangs in the Louvre in Paris. We cannot consider his achievements in the other fields mentioned above, but it may be said that in any one of them he could have won immortality.

As a child, Leonardo was deprived of parental love; he lived a rather lonely life, and in maturity he was strange in appearance and in manner of living. He died in exile in France, regretting that he had not painted more.

Raphael (1483-1530).—This Renaissance artist is regarded by some critics as the greatest painter of all time. Most of his world-famous pictures, such as the *Disputa,* have religious themes; others, as the *School of Athens,* deal with classical subjects. Raphael is particularly noted for his representations of the Virgin Mary. He painted the Madonna with a placid, oval face, reminiscent of the earlier paintings of Perugino. Raphael also shows the influence of Leonardo in his drawings of the Christ Child and in his triangular compositions. One of the greatest of Raphael's paintings of the Virgin is the *Sistine Madonna,* now in the gallery at Dresden. Raphael also tried to imitate Michelangelo, but with less success. He died comparatively young, at the very height of his powers.

THE BEGINNINGS OF MODERN TIMES

Michelangelo (1475-1564).—Michelangelo was probably the greatest sculptor of all time. The mighty figure of *Moses,* which he made for the tomb of Pope Julius II, is unsurpassed. He is also immortal for his work as a painter. His outstanding achievement in this field is the ceiling of the Sistine Chapel in the Vatican. Michelangelo painted this at an advanced age over a period of four years. The ceiling, which covers 6000 feet, is decorated with 149 pictures, containing 394 figures, some of which are ten feet high. Michelangelo's paintings, like his sculptures, are tremendously powerful. They portray the energy and strength of muscular men, in imitation, it would seem, of Greek gods and heroes. Michelangelo also did outstanding work as an architect. He designed the dome of St. Peter's, one of the architectural wonders of the world.

Leonardo da Vinci did not like Michelangelo's work; Raphael gave him the highest praise, imitation. But Michelangelo, an irascible genius, was unaffected by either, and surpassed both in certain lines. These three giants have never been equalled in the naturalism of their work, but Fra Angelico excelled them all in the quality of spirituality.

Renaissance Literature.—Renaissance literature brought forth two groups, the conservatives and the radicals. The conservatives were humanistic in style but Christian in thought. The radicals imitated not only the style of the ancients, but also their pagan immorality. The leaders of the conservative Christian humanists were Petrarch, Cardinal Cusa, Thomas More, Cardinal Fisher, John Colet, and Linacre. To them, the classics were only a means of embellishing and dramatizing the teachings of Christ. The most prominent of the radical humanists were such men as Boccaccio, Filelfo, Ariosto, and Erasmus; they were so infatuated with the pagan way of life that they practically worshipped the ancients, and eventually they all became like the objects of their idolatry.

The center of literary activity, as of all forms of art, during the Renaissance was Italy. Paris, however, remained the center of scholasticism, which never seemed to take firm roots in Italy. It must be understood that the Renaissance at its best was not a rejection of scholasticism but rather a natural outgrowth of Medieval intellectuality.

Petrarch (1304-1347).—Petrarch was the son of a Florentine family living in exile. He attended the University of Montpellier in southern France. His father intended him to study law, but he soon acquired a profound admiration for Virgil and Cicero, and determined to become a writer and scholar. At the age of twenty-three, he fell in love with a lady named Laura. She was unresponsive to his admiration, but none the less became the inspiration of his world-famous lyric poetry. These lyrics, pure and lofty in sentiment, were written in Petrarch's native Tuscan Italian, in the sonnet form, which he perfected for future generations. "The secularism or this-worldliness of the new age, built on the foundations of the new economic, social and political life, was first and best revealed by the songs of Petrarch."[3] He wrote of human love, human nature, and the natural beauty of Italy, but always with a sublime reverence for God and holy things. He was a typical Renaissance character, with many-sided interests that caused him to travel through Germany, France, Italy and Spain. Everywhere he was recognized and honored as a poet and as a great classical scholar who had collected invaluable Latin and Greek manuscripts.

Boccaccio (1313-1375).—As Petrarch is the most eminent representative of the conservative school of Renaissance literature, so Boccaccio, his friend, is a typical example of the radical, thoroughly pagan Renaissance man of letters. An Italian, Boccaccio was born in Paris. His father sent him to Naples to serve as an apprentice in a banking business, but his sensitive, poetic nature found a stimulating environment in the French court of Naples. He soon abandoned banking in favor of literature. Boccaccio, too, was inspired by a woman, Fiammetta, who for ten years was the theme of his lyrics. In 1341, he returned to Florence, where he wrote his greatest work, the *Decameron*. The plot of this book is that, at the time of the Black Death in 1348, seven young women and three young men retired to a villa near Naples, where they hoped to be safe from the plague. To while away the time, they told stories. The *Decameron* is a collection of 100 of these tales, arranged in groups of ten. The lucid prose is artistically perfect, but it is debased by a jaunty irreverence

---

[3] Lucas, H. S., *Renaissance and Reformation*.

which "treats holy things with cynical familiarity, spiced by the author's libertinism." [4]

Boccaccio, like Petrarch, loved to collect Greek and Latin manuscripts; he is particularly noted for having recovered a copy of Tacitus' *Histories* and *Annals*. These two men had many enthusiastic pupils. As a result of their activities, many Greek scholars came to Italy, carrying Greek manuscripts of rare value.

Cardinal Nicholas of Cusa (1401-1464).—This great scholar brought a large number of Greek manuscripts from Constantinople. He was an astronomer and mathematician, and is renowned as one of the first men to proclaim and defend the theory that the earth moves around the sun.

Thomas More (1478-1535) and Erasmus (1466-1536).— Thomas More, an Englishman, and Erasmus, a Hollander, were fellow students of Greek at Exeter College, Oxford. They became the most eminent humanists in their native lands, but More remained a saintly Christian, while Erasmus became a radical humanist, who did far more harm than good by his superb scholarship. We shall have more to say of these two humanists in our discussion of the Protestant Revolt.

One of the best known of Thomas More's writings is a book called *Utopia,* which described an imaginary island whose inhab-

[4] *Ibid.*

itants lived under ideal social and economic institutions. This brilliant book has had many imitators and has greatly influenced all subsequent thought regarding the reform of government and society. Thomas More coined the word *Utopia,* taking it from two Greek words meaning "nowhere." As we use the term *utopian* today, it means "ideally perfect," and also "visionary and impractical."

Invention of Printing.—The mechanical art of printing was the most important invention of the Renaissance. John Gutenberg, the inventor (1400-1467), set up the first printing press in 1445 at Mainz in western Germany. Shortly before this, Europe had adopted the Chinese process of paper-making. The rapid and cheap multiplication of books which this made possible greatly promoted the diffusion of thought and literature. At this time, there was already a large number of cultivated townsmen who were eager for the writings of the period.

Important as this invention was, Gutenberg profited very little from it personally because lack of funds prevented him from developing it on a commercial scale. The first book of importance he printed was the Latin Bible. The invention soon spread from Germany to other countries. John Caxton, an Englishman, set up a press in London in 1476. A printing press was established in Paris in 1470. Hungary had a printing press in 1473, Denmark in 1482, and Constantinople in 1490. Before the end of the century, Spain had more than thirty printing firms; Italy had 190 in Rome, and 100 outside Rome. Frankfort-on-Main in Germany was the center of the world's book trade. Bibles were printed in German, as well as in Latin; and Thomas More testifies that he saw Bibles printed in English "fair and old." During the first fifty years of the printing press, 38,000 books were printed, of which only 2592 may be attributed to the humanists. Nearly half of the total number, in contrast, came from the pens of Dominicans and Franciscans. The volumes printed included the Bible, the writings of the Greek and Latin fathers, books of devotion, the Greek and Latin classics, and the works of the humanists. All this, it is to be noted, took place before the Protestant Revolt.

The earliest specimens of printing, called *incunabula,* are the invaluable treasures of fortunate libraries and museums. These early specimens show a high quality of workmanship that commands admiration. The Library of Congress in Washington, D. C., has amost 5000 incunabula, ranking twelfth among the libraries of the world in this type of collection. Of these 5000 books, 607 were written by Dominicans.

The Church cherished the invention of printing as a means of furthering the work of salvation, and accorded generous favor and protection to it, especially in the monasteries. At Florence, in Italy, the Dominicans had the largest monastic printing establishment in Europe before 1520. As early as 1476, a group of two Dominican Friars and twenty-five Dominican Sisters began to publish books. The Sisters were the type-setters and the Priests or lay brothers ran the press and acted as business managers.

The Church and Galileo.—Some scientists and writers who lack a knowledge of Church History point to the career of Galileo to prove that there is a conflict between faith and science. However, since the Scriptures and the teachings of the Church are truth, they cannot conflict with scientific ideas, insofar as these ideas are also true. The facts in the case of Galileo have been distorted by many writers, and this has led to widespread misunderstandings. To appreciate the real issues involved, we must know something about the history of the science of astronomy.

A Graeco-Egyptian astronomer named Ptolemy, who lived in the second century A.D., formulated a theory in which he held that the earth is the fixed center of the universe, and that the sun and all the planets revolve around it. This so-called "Ptolemaic system" was generally accepted throughout the civilized world for more than a thousand years. In the sixteenth century, however, a Polish astronomer named Copernicus wrote a book in which he held that the earth revolves around the sun. In accordance with Copernicus' own wishes, his book was not published until he was on his deathbed. Soon afterward, an Italian scientist, Galileo, adopted the Copernican theory, and advanced some additional evidence in favor of it. This evidence was not sufficiently convincing to warrant the discarding of a theory which had so long been supported by the scholars of the world.

Controversy arose; exponents of both the Ptolemaic theory and the Copernican theory quoted the Bible to support their arguments. Galileo was among the most active of these disputants. The Church authorities did nothing to deter him so long as he acted purely as a scientist. Galileo, however, "was not satisfied to present a scientific astronomical system, but insisted on binding it up with an intrusion into the realm of Theology." [5] In other words, an individual scientist was attempting to interpret the Bible, a right which is reserved for the Catholic Church alone. Accordingly, one of the Roman Congregations condemned Galileo twice (in 1616 and in 1632). In the first decree, his name was not mentioned, and he was released without any penalty, after promising to refrain from dabbling in Scripture in his arguments. He broke this promise, and the second condemnation, in 1632, declared him suspect of heresy, demanded that he abjure his teaching and condemned his book. The penalty he suffered was mild; he was confined to a pleasant villa in Italy, where he was paid a life pension by the Pope and enjoyed the privilege of carrying on scientific research undisturbed. He was never tortured, ill-treated or condemned by any Pope.

The theory of Copernicus and Galileo that the earth revolves around the sun was not scientifically proven until late in the seventeenth century, when Sir Isaac Newton worked out the concept of universal gravitation. It is true that a mistake was made by the Roman Congregation, but Catholics do not claim infallibility for such a body. Infallibility is claimed only for the Pope, when he speaks *ex cathedra,* on matters of faith and morals. Thus the case of Galileo does not show a contradiction between faith and science, nor does it disprove the infallibility of the Pope.

POLITICAL EVENTS OF THE RENAISSANCE

Savonarola the Reformer.—One of the outstanding personalities of the Renaissance era was Girolamo Savonarola (1452-1498), who sought to utilize his religious fervor in the cause of social and political reform. As a young man, Savonarola was ordained a Priest and joined the Dominican Order. He became Prior of the Dominican Church of San Marco in Florence. From the pulpit of this Church, he raised an eloquent voice against the evils permitted and sponsored by the Medici, the ruling family of Florence. He also criticized the Roman Curia, and Pope Alexander VI.

---

[5] Lortz, J. and Kaiser, E. G., *History of the Church.*

Savonarola attracted a large following and became one of the most powerful men in Florence. When King Charles VIII of France invaded Italy, the Medici were exiled from Italy. Savonarola utilized this opportunity to establish a Republic in Florence. This change was very popular with the people. For political reasons, however, Savonarola was silenced as a preacher by the Pope. After numerous protests, Savonarola was allowed to resume his preaching, but he was soon silenced again. This time he refused to obey, believing that the Pope was misinformed and was influenced by political bias. He wished to appeal to a General Council and was supported by the French King, by the University of Paris, and by the Republic of Florence, which he had truly reformed. However, he had incurred the enmity not only of the Pope, but also of the Franciscans and the powerful Medici family. Finally, the Franciscans demanded that he prove that he was a prophet of God, as he claimed, by submitting to an ordeal by fire. An ordeal by fire was forbidden by canon law, and the Pope disapproved. The people of Florence, however, still believed in the efficacy of this ancient custom and looked forward to the event with great excitement. After much arguing and delay, a date was set for the ordeal, but on the appointed date Savonarola refused personally to go through with the trial. The people of Florence were disappointed because the ordeal had not taken place. A mob assaulted the Monastery of San Marco and, with the aid of the officials of Florence, arrested Savonarola and condemned him for heresy. Savonarola and two other Dominicans were hanged and their bodies were reduced to ashes. This sad event took place in 1498.

Savonarola's writings were examined by Rome and pronounced free from doctrinal error. He was a holy man, who represented the best spirit of the Renaissance; but he was perhaps overzealous in his participation in the politics of Florence. This was the cause of his tragic end. He loved Florence, but he lamented the worldliness of the Renaissance. He burned with an ardent desire to eliminate these abuses and to restore and preserve a deep religious spirit in his countrymen. He spoke and wrote to the people in the vernacular, rather than in Latin, which shows how well he understood the spirit of the age and could adapt himself to it.

166 VISUALIZED CHURCH HISTORY

The Hundred Years' War.—The greatest military conflict of the era we are now studying was the Hundred Years' War between England and France. This began in 1337 and continued, with long intervals of peace until 1453.

1. Causes.—The basic cause of the Hundred Years' War was the fact that the English Kings had large feudal holdings in southwestern France. The English wished to consolidate and enlarge these holdings; the French wished to get rid of their English vassals. Another cause of the conflict was commercial rivalry in Flanders. The prosperous Flemish weavers were an important market for English wool. However, the Count of Flanders was a vassal of the French King and the latter often interfered, or threatened to interfere, with the English-Flemish trade. There was also bad blood between France and England because France had aided the Scots in 1314 in their successful revolt against the English.

All these rivalries came to a head in a bitter dynastic dispute. The direct male line of the French dynasty had died out, and Edward III of England claimed the throne on the ground that his mother was a daughter of Philip the Fair. Philip IV, the new French King, refused to admit the validity of this claim, and Edward declared war in 1337.

2. English Victories.—For many years, the fighting was overwhelmingly in favor of the English. They won great victories at *Crécy* (1346), *Poitiers* (1356), and *Agincourt* (1415). A combined British and Flemish fleet won a notable naval triumph at *Sluys*. In the battles of Crécy and Poitiers, the English archers established their superiority over the heavily armored French knights. This marked the end of feudal methods of warfare. After Agincourt, the English and their allies pressed steadily southward, and all of France seemed doomed. The country was saved by the appearance of one of the most remarkable personalities in all history, Joan of Arc.

3. Joan of Arc.—Joan of Arc was a peasant girl born in Domremy in 1413. When a young girl, she was favored with visions and she heard "voices" of St. Michael, St. Catherine, and St. Margaret, bidding her to go to the aid of the French King. Two or three times a week for three years she heard these voices. At the age of seventeen, after she had undergone many examinations by ecclesiastical and civil authorities, she asked for an audience with the King. The King consented, but to test Joan he had her introduced into his presence while he stood among his courtiers, dressed in simple attire. Although Joan had never seen him before, she instantly recognized him. She further convinced the King of her divine inspiration by revealing to him secrets which he had thought were known to him alone.

Joan was given command of the French army. She dressed in a coat of mail, carried a sword, and actually led the soldiers into battle. Under her inspired leadership, the French troops were victorious at Orleans in 1429. In July, 1429, after overcoming much opposition caused by jealousy and intrigue, the "Maid of Orleans," as Joan came to be known, witnessed the coronation of Charles VII as King of France at the Cathedral of Rheims.

The English, however, still held much territory in France, and hard fighting continued. In 1430, the treacherous Burgundians captured Joan in a battle and sold her to the English for $110,000. Joan was taken to Rouen, where she was tried for heresy, found guilty, and condemned to be burned at the stake. On May 30, 1431, she suffered this terrible penalty. Charles VII, for whom she had done so much, made no attempt to help her. However, some years after her martyrdom, he demanded a revision of the trial, and her innocence was admitted and acknowledged. The Catholic Church canonized her May 16, 1920. Joan of Arc is the noblest woman in French history.

4. *Results of the Hundred Years' War.*—By 1453, the French had regained complete possession of their native land, with the exception of the port of Calais, which remained in English hands for about another century. Henceforth, both the French and English people were free to proceed with the unification and strengthening of their respective lands, without outside interference. Although the long war had caused terrible suffering and destruction, France and England soon emerged as the most powerful and stable of the new national states.

The War of the Roses.—The War of the Roses was an English civil war which lasted from 1455 to 1485. The issue in the war was the succession to the throne of England. The contestants were the House of Lancaster, which had most of its support in the northern part of the country, and the House of York, which had its largest following in the south. The war derived its name from the fact that the Lancastrian party used a red rose as an insignia or emblem, while the followers of the Duke of York wore a white rose.

After much loss of life, cruelty, revolting crime and intrigue, the House of Lancaster won and placed Henry VII, a member of

Summarize the Achievements of Each of these Three Great Women.

the Tudor family, on the throne. The Tudors were absolute monarchs who lessened the powers of Parliament and played a large part in converting Merrie Catholic England into Protestant England.

Ferdinand and Isabella of Spain.—While France was struggling with England, Spain was establishing national unity after eight centuries of warfare. The two most important kingdoms in Spain were joined when Isabella of Castile married Ferdinand of Aragon in 1469. This laid the foundation for the magnificent national government that was destined soon to overshadow every other European monarchy.

Ferdinand actually continued to rule Aragon after his marriage, and Isabella continued to rule Castile, but both pursued the same policies and used the disinterested assistance of Cardinal Ximenes (1436-1517) as chancellor of Castile and counsellor of

THE BEGINNINGS OF MODERN TIMES 169

Aragon. The united efforts of these three made it possible for the Spaniards to push back the Moors, who had once dominated the entire Iberian Peninsula. Finally, in 1492, the Moors were forced to abandon their last stronghold, the city of Granada. Spain was redeemed for Christianity! All Europe rejoiced in this re-conquest, which was regarded as some consolation for the fall of Constantinople to the Turks in 1453. In the same fateful year, 1492, the generosity of Isabella made it possible for Columbus to set forth on his epoch-making voyage of geographical discovery. The importance of the discoveries of Columbus and his successors to the world and to the Church can scarcely be overestimated.

CHRONOLOGICAL TABLE OF PRINCIPAL EVENTS IN CHURCH HISTORY

Year	Event
1294	Beginning of quarrel between Pope Boniface VIII and Philip IV (the Fair) of France over taxation of clergy
1296	Boniface issued *Clericis laicos;* Philip retaliated by forbidding exportation of gold and silver from France
1297	English nobles used *Clericis laicos* to force King to accept principle of "no taxation without representation"
1298	France and England accepted arbitration by Pope (as private individual, not as Pope)
1300	Great Jubilee held
1302	Papal Bull *Ausculta, fili* rejected by Philip IV; Boniface issued intrepid answer, *Unam sanctam*
1303	Philip's agents seized Boniface, their mistreatment causing his death ("Tragedy of Anagni")
1304	Birth of Petrarch, leader of Italian literary Renaissance (died in 1374)
1309-1377	"Babylonian Captivity," during which seven French Popes resided at Avignon; many French Cardinals created; Papal prestige weakened
1311	Fifteenth Ecumenical Council held at Vienne; Knights Templars condemned as heretics; Philip the Fair seized their wealth
1313	Birth of Boccaccio, prominent figure of Italian literary Renaissance (died in 1375)

Year	Event
1314	Death of Philip the Fair, enemy of the Pope
1316-1334	Struggle of Pope John XXII with Emperor Louis the Bavarian over Papal right to confirm election of Emperor
1337-1453	Hundred Years' War between France and England, won eventually by France
1346	English victory over French at Crécy signalized end of feudal methods of warfare
1347	Calais captured by English
1348	"Black Death," terrible epidemic, swept away third of population of Europe
1356	English victory over French at Poitiers
1377	Pope Gregory XI, influenced by Catherine of Siena, returned to Rome from Avignon
1378-1418	Great Schism of the West, caused by rivalry of French and Italian Cardinals; four valid Popes at Rome; two anti-Popes at Avignon; two more anti-Popes at Pisa
1387	Birth of Fra Angelico, most spiritual of artists (died in 1455)
1414-1418	Sixteenth Ecumenical Council at Constance; end of Great Schism
1455-1485	War of Roses, English civil war; ended with ascension of Tudors to throne
1469	Birth of Machiavelli, noted political writer (died in 1527)
1475	Birth of Michelangelo, great painter and sculptor (died in 1564)
1483	Birth of Raphael, great painter (died in 1530); also birth of Guicciardini, greatest Italian historian of Renaissance (died in 1540)
1489	Savonarola came to Florence and began career of reform as Prior of Dominican Church of San Marco
1492	Moors finally expelled from Spain by Isabella and Ferdinand; Columbus, financed by Spanish monarchs, discovered America
1498	Savonarola executed at Florence as a heretic
1512-1517	Seventeenth Ecumenical Council (Fifth Lateran Council) convoked by Julius II, the warrior-Pope; abolished Pragmatic Sanction of 1438
1517	Death of Cardinal Ximenes, who was largely responsible for the unification of Spain and its establishment as strongest nation in Europe

SUPPLEMENTARY MATERIAL FOR UNIT IV

REFERENCES

CURRAN, E. L., *Great Moments in Catholic History*, pp. 55-63
DREHER, T., *Outlines of Church History*, pp. 80-83
FORNER, B. N., *Story of the Church*, pp. 147-151, 189-200
GUGGENBERGER, A., *A General History of the Christian Era*, Vol. I, pp. 422-439; Vol. II, pp. 1-139
JOHNSON, G. W., HANNAN, J. D., DOMINICA, SR., *Story of the Church*, pp. 268-301
LAUX, J., *Church History*, pp. 391-418
LORTZ, J., KAISER, E. G., *History of the Church*, pp. 256-338
LUCAS, H. S., *Renaissance and Reformation*, pp. 1-416
NELSON, BRO. J. S., *Aeneae Silvii de Liberorum Educatione*
RAEMER, S. A., *Church History*, pp. 303-338
ROEDER, R., *Man of the Renaissance*
SISTERS OF NOTRE DAME, *Compendium of Church History*, pp. 109-116
SPALDING, B. J., *Church History*, pp. 472-559
VALLENTIN, A., *Leonardo da Vinci*
WEBER, N. A., *The Christian Era*, A.D. 1-1517, pp. 223-331
Catholic Encyclopedia, "Renaissance"
Christian Social Art Quarterly

QUESTIONS

1. (*a*) Explain fully the circumstances surrounding the issuance of the Papal Bull *Clericis laicos*. (*b*) Summarize the content of this Bull. (*c*) What effect did this Bull have on the development of constitutional government in England?

2. Discuss the "Babylonian Captivity" of the Church, including the following: (*a*) the circumstances which led to it; (*b*) the principal events of the "Captivity"; (*c*) the effects on the authority of the Papacy.

3. (*a*) Which Pope put an end to the "Babylonian Captivity"? (*b*) Discuss the role played by St. Catherine of Siena in inducing the Pope to return to Rome.

4. (*a*) What was the underlying cause of the Great Schism of the West? When did it take place? (*b*) How many contending factions laid claim to the Papacy during this period? Name them. (*c*) How was the issue finally settled? (*d*) Who became the new legitimately elected Pope?

5. (a) Describe the heretical doctrines which were preached by Wycliffe and Hus. (b) What effect did these doctrines have on temporal and spiritual authority? (c) What measures did the Church take against these heresies?

6. (a) What was the *Renaissance?* Where and when did it originate? (b) Discuss three general characteristics of the Renaissance period.

7. (a) Define *nepotism*. (b) Why were the Renaissance Popes sometimes compelled to practice nepotism? (c) What evil sometimes resulted from this?

8. Name the three great humanist Popes of the Renaissance period and discuss their achievements.

9. Describe the contributions of each of the following great men to Renaissance art and literature: (a) Fra Angelico, (b) Leonardo da Vinci, (c) Raphael, (d) Michelangelo, (e) Petrarch, (f) Boccaccio.

10. (a) What was *humanism?* (b) Distinguish between the conservative or Christian humanists and the radical humanists. Name two representatives of each group.

11. (a) Why is the invention of printing from movable type considered the most important invention made during the Renaissance? (b) Who was the inventor? (c) What was the earliest book printed from movable type? (d) Discuss the attitude of the Church toward the new invention.

12. Summarize the life of Savonarola the Reformer.

13. (a) What were the causes of the Hundred Years' War between France and England? (b) Discuss the achievements of St. Joan of Arc during the Hundred Years' War. Why is she considered the noblest woman in French history?

14. (a) Who were the contenders in the War of the Roses? (b) What issue was involved? (c) Discuss the outcome of the War of the Roses.

15. Trace the process of the national unification of Spain in the fifteenth century.

SELECTION TEST

In each of the following groups, select the name that does not apply.

1. *Christian Humanists:* Thomas More, Petrarch, Boccaccio, Cardinal Nicholas Cusa, Cardinal Fisher.

2. *Pagan Humanists:* Filelfo, Ariosto, Erasmus, Boccaccio, Linacre.

3. *Renaissance Popes:* Nicholas V, Pius II, Julius II, Boniface VIII, Leo X.

SUPPLEMENTARY MATERIAL FOR UNIT IV

4. *Great Artists of the Renaissance Period:* Michelangelo, Leonardo da Vinci, Raphael, Fra Angelico, Giotto.

5. *French Popes at Avignon:* Clement V, John XXII, Benedict XII, Julius II, Gregory XI.

CHRONOLOGY TEST

Number the items in each of the following groups in their proper chronological order.

A
( ) Great Schism
( ) "Babylonian Captivity"
( ) Council of Constance
( ) *Clericis laicos*
( ) Tragedy of Anagni

B
( ) Start of War of Roses
( ) Start of Hundred Years' War
( ) Coronation of Charles VII of France at Rheims
( ) Henry VII becomes King of England
( ) Battle of Agincourt

C
( ) Execution of St. Joan of Arc
( ) Capture of Constantinople
( ) Invention of printing
( ) Final expulsion of Moors from Spain
( ) Execution of Savonarola

D
( ) Pope Leo X
( ) Pope Boniface VIII
( ) Pope John XXII
( ) Pope Julius II
( ) Pope Gregory XI

MATCHING TEST

In the parenthesis next to each item in column **A,** *write the number of the name in column* **B** *which is most closely associated with it.*

A
( ) *Disputa*
( ) Designed Dome of St. Peter's
( ) *The Last Supper*
( ) *Annunciation*
( ) Christian humanist
( ) Designed St. Peter's Cathedral
( ) *Decameron*
( ) "Maid of Orleans"
( ) Member of Borgia family
( ) Last of Renaissance Popes

B
1. Pope Leo X
2. Leonardo da Vinci
3. St. Joan of Arc
4. Bramante
5. Petrarch
6. Boccaccio
7. Fra Angelico
8. Pope Julius II
9. Michelangelo
10. Raphael
11. Erasmus
12. Pope Alexander VI

COMPLETION TEST

Complete each of the following sentences by supplying the correct word or phrase.

1. The French king who quarreled with Pope Boniface VIII over taxation of the clergy was ....

2. The first Pontiff to occupy the throne of St. Peter during the "Babylonian Captivity" was ....

3. The Decision of Rense was issued during the reign of Pope ....

4. The followers of the English heretic Wycliffe were known as ....

5. The book *Utopia* was written by ....

6. Pope ...... is known as the "Liberator of Italy" and the "Savior of the Church."

7. The Renaissance painter who excelled in the representation of spiritual subjects was ....

8. The greatest sculptor of the Renaissance period was ....

9. When Philip the Fair of France seized and imprisoned the Papal Legate, Boniface VIII protested in the Bull entitled ....

10. The French, led by St. Joan of Arc, won a great victory at the Battle of ....

11. The Decision of Rense advanced the conciliar theory, which holds that supreme ecclesiastical authority is vested in ....

12. A joyous event during the reign of Boniface VIII was ....

UNIT V

PROTESTANTISM AND THE COUNTER-REFORMATION

PREVIEW

THE events which we are to consider in this Unit are among the most momentous and most absorbing in the entire history of the Christian Church. They are events which caused great sorrows to the Church, and also resulted in sublime joys. Religious unity in Europe was definitely destroyed by the Protestant Revolt, which began in Germany with the activities of Martin Luther. The Revolt spread rapidly to other lands. England's participation in this tragic movement was the deciding factor which made complete restoration of Catholicity an impossibility. Among the individuals who played prominent roles in these events in England are such diverse historical characters as Henry VIII, Queen Elizabeth, St. Thomas More and Cardinal Fisher.

Like all the other great trials of the Church, the era of the Protestant Revolt is rich in heroes and martyrs. Vast numbers died, rather than renounce their religion. In Ireland and Spain, the Revolt was resisted successfully. The Irish people suffered grievously in the years that followed, and many of them fled to the New World, bringing the Faith with them.

Spain, at that time the most powerful nation in Europe, led the Counter-Reformation. A dynamic, many-sided campaign was undertaken to stem the Revolt by eliminating the abuses which had appeared within the Church and by explaining the errors of Protestantism to the people. In this campaign, the most effective instrument was the Order of the Jesuits, led by St. Ignatius Loyola. Great Popes also played a prominent part in the Counter-Reformation, notably Paul III, who called the epoch-making Council of Trent, and Pius V, who enforced the decrees of this Council. This period of struggle also has a brilliant galaxy of Saints, such as Saint Charles Borromeo and St. Theresa of Avila. Among these Saints were dauntless spirits who carried the Faith to the furthest corners of the globe, including America, India and China.

In the field of temporal government, the outstanding movement of this period was the growth of the doctrine of absolutism. Absolutism, as we shall see, conflicted with the teachings of Christianity and was vigorously opposed by the Church.

CHAPTER 9

THE PROTESTANT REVOLT IN EUROPE

"Pride and avarice caused the reformation in Germany, lawless love in England, and love of novelty in France."—Frederick the Great

INTRODUCTION

Importance of the Protestant Revolt.—The Protestant Revolt is one of the most important events in the history of the Catholic Church because it was responsible for a great transformation of human society and altered the entire course of history. The Revolt, which began in Germany in 1517 and spread through northern Europe, resulted in the disruption of Christian unity and was accompanied by terrible civil strife and bloodshed. Not since the days of the Arian heresy, early in Church history, had any European movement caused so much havoc. But, while vast numbers of Europeans were turning away from the Catholic Church, zealous Catholic missionaries, with the assistance of Divine Providence, were successfully winning millions of new converts to the Faith in the Americas, India and China.

Causes of the Protestant Revolt.—Several important factors contributed to the outbreak of the Protestant Revolt.

1. The radical school of the Renaissance, with its strong element of paganism, caused confusion and helped to undermine the authority of the Church by attacking the philosophy and theology of the Middle Ages and by condemning monasticism.

2. The bonds of Catholic unity had been weakened during the two preceding centuries by the opposition of national monarchs (*e.g.,* Philip the Fair of France and Emperor Louis the Bavarian) to the authority of the Papacy. The "Babylonian Captivity" and the Great Schism had further impaired the Papal authority.

3. Many unworthy Bishops had been nominated to high Church offices by secular authorities. These Bishops introduced laxity and worldliness among the clergy and into the monasteries.

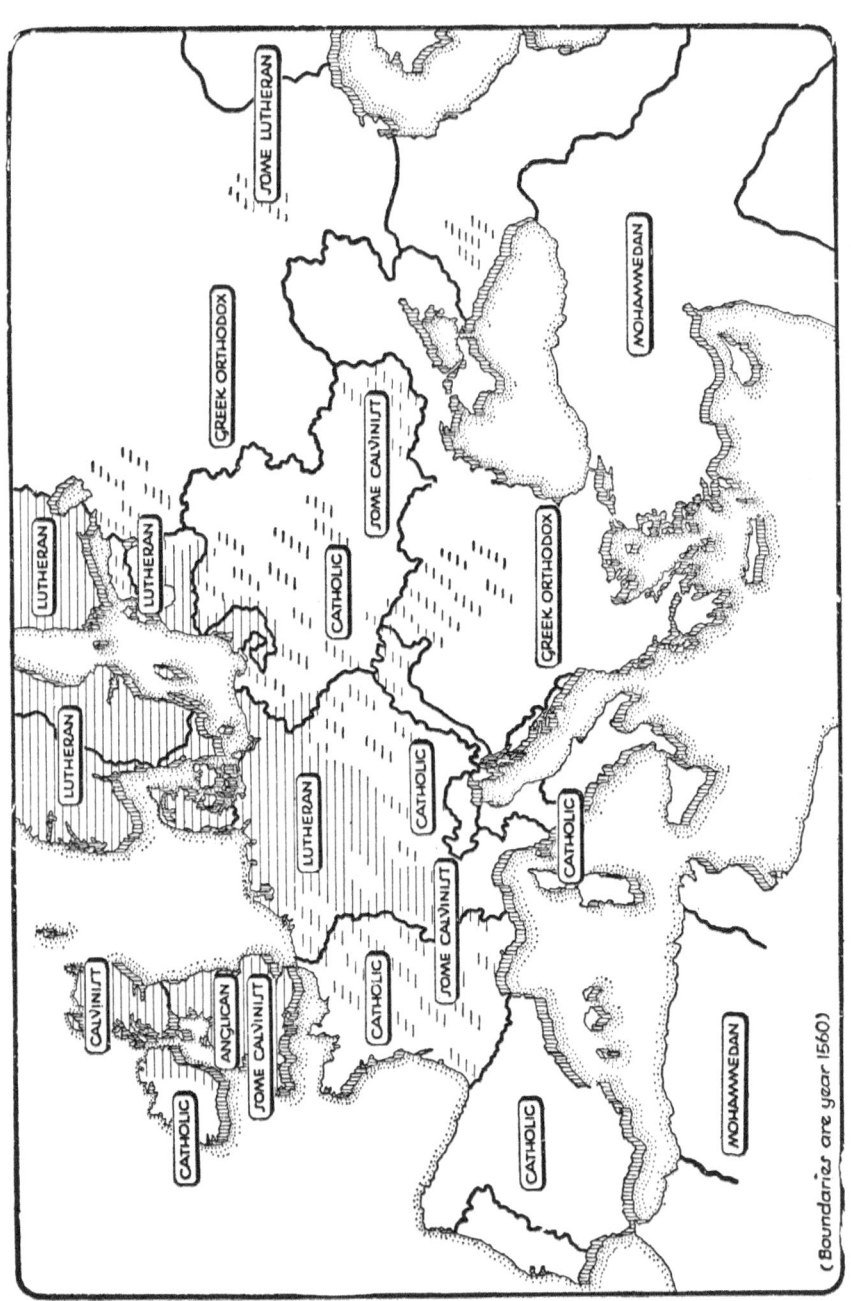

Distribution of Religions in Europe after the Protestant Revolt

4. Many German princes, Gallicans, Bishops and others objected to the primacy of the Pope. They favored the supremacy of the General Council, convoked by the secular authority.

5. Selfish kings and princes were envious of Church lands and other properties, and sought to secularize them under the pretext of reform.

6. The rulers of the new national states laid claim to absolute authority over all the affairs of their subjects.

7. The growth of the spirit of nationalism among the peoples of Europe was inimical to the welfare of the Universal Church.

THE REVOLT IN GERMANY

The Background.—In the fifteenth century, the Church held about one-third of the property in Germany. It must be borne in mind that the Church maintained many institutions and performed numerous services which in modern times are financed by the state or by private agencies. In any event, powerful princes coveted the property of the Church, and, for this reason, sought to undermine ecclesiastical authority. Laxity had infected the clergy, many of whom thus forfeited the respect and esteem of the people. Finally, discontent became widespread among the peasantry and among the oppressed laboring classes in the cities, and manifested itself in opposition to the Church. It was in this setting that Martin Luther, leader of the Protestant Revolt in Germany, made his appearance.

Martin Luther (1483-1546).—Perhaps more than any other individual, Martin Luther was responsible for the Protestant Revolt. Luther's childhood was an unhappy one, having been spent in a home where excessive parental discipline increased the suffering of poverty. By working as an itinerant chorister, Luther managed to obtain sufficient funds to complete his education at the University of Erfurt. In early manhood, he narrowly escaped death, when a bolt of lightning struck a companion who was standing nearby. This incident seemed to have a marked effect on Luther's personality, inducing a fear of sudden death. In 1505, this melancholy and often bitter young man entered the Augustinian Monastery at Erfurt, and in 1507 he was ordained a Priest.

Luther's conduct in the Priesthood was most erratic. For weeks he would neglect obligatory prayers, and then for an equally long time he would perform various penances of his own choosing. Finally, he came to the conclusion that good works were of no avail and that faith alone was sufficient for salvation. When he became a professor of theology at the University of Wittenberg in 1515, he began to preach this unsound doctrine openly.

Indulgences and Luther's Ninety-Five Theses.—The immediate cause of the outbreak of the Protestant Revolt was a dispute over *indulgences*. An indulgence is a partial or complete remission of the temporal punishment which would otherwise be inflicted upon a person in Purgatory, after his sins had been pardoned. An indulgence is never granted until after the sinner has repented sincerely and has undertaken the performance of some good works, such as giving alms to the poor, or contributing to a Church fund.

In 1517, a Dominican Friar, John Tetzel, was sent by the Pope to preach an indulgence that would be granted to persons who made a contribution toward the construction of St. Peter's Basilica in Rome; persons who lacked funds could obtain the indulgence by performing some other good work. When the Friar came to Wittenberg, Luther wrote a document containing ninety-five theses or propositions, in which he expressed his opposition to indulgences; he then nailed this paper to the church door. The theses attacked several real abuses which existed in Germany at that time, but Luther went on to attack the entire doctrine of indulgences as taught by the Catholic Church. Under normal conditions, the posting of the ninety-five theses would have produced a debate and the question would have been settled amicably. Unfortunately, the times were not normal. Luther's action was the spark that ignited the flame of the Protestant Revolt.

Luther soon became the central figure in the struggle of all the discontented elements in Germany against the Papacy. The theses were translated from Latin into German and circulated throughout the country. Letters of encouragement soon began to pour in on the proud, audacious Luther. It is true that many of his supporters sincerely desired much-needed reforms; but the radical humanists of the day and various anti-clerical elements, including the avaricious princes, saw in this dispute an opportunity to enrich themselves at the expense of the Church. In order to retain the support of these princes, Luther made many concessions, and soon was forced to compromise nearly every principle of religion.

Condemnation by the Papacy.—Luther not only attacked the Church doctrine of indulgences and the efficacy of good works in relation to salvation, but soon denied the value or efficacy of the Sacraments, and condemned monasticism as well as celibacy of the clergy. In a famous debate with John Eck in the year 1519, Luther openly expressed all these views and rejected the authority of the Pope.

From 1517 to 1520, the Church patiently urged Luther to retract his heretical writings, but he continued to defy both the Pope and Emperor Charles V. (Forty-one of Luther's ninety-five theses had been judged heretical.) On June 15, 1520, he was condemned by Pope Leo X in the Bull *Exsurge Domine*, and was granted sixty days in which to retract his heresies and return to the Church. Luther remained defiant. In December, 1520, he gathered his university students about him and, in their presence, thrust the Papal Bull into a bonfire. On January 3, 1521, the Pope solemnly excommunicated Luther and requested Charles V, the newly elected Holy Roman Emperor, who was a devout Catholic, to enforce the Bull of Excommunication.

The Diet of Worms.—Charles summoned Luther to appear for examination before the Diet of Worms, guaranteeing him an imperial safe-conduct. At the diet, Luther brazenly admitted authorship of several heretical pamphlets, and remained adamant in his defiance of the Pope. Matters dragged on in this way until Luther had only twenty-one more days of guaranteed safety, after which he could have been condemned to death as a heretic. At this juncture, Luther was rescued by his powerful friend, Frederick, the Elector of Saxony. He was given refuge in the castle of the Wartburg, near Eisenach, Germany. Emperor Charles was powerless to intercede, as he was already fully engaged in wars against the French and the Ottoman Turks. While at this castle (1521-1522), Luther continued his attacks on the Church. He also translated the Bible into German and composed a number of Protestant hymns.

The Peasants' War (1524-1525).—The Protestant Revolt not only caused the secession of Germany from the Catholic Church, but also was the signal for the outbreak of a general political and economic revolution. Civil wars raged throughout the land, lasting from 1522 to 1555

The most destructive of these civil conflicts, which began in south Germany in 1524, is known as the *Peasants' War*. It was instigated by a group of extremist reformers known as *Anabaptists* (so-called because they denied the validity of infant baptism). The Anabaptists supported revolutionary doctrines in politics as well as religion. Although the peasants of south Germany rose originally against feudal oppression, their struggle, under the leadership of the Anabaptists, soon developed into a war against all authority and an attempt to establish an ideal equalitarian state, in which all goods would be held in common. Luther, however, did not intend his religious revolt to develop into a sweeping program of economic and social reform, and called upon the princes who supported him to crush the uprising. The peasants were poorly organized and lacked leadership, and their uprising was soon savagely suppressed. Before this was accomplished, however, there was widespread destruction, and terrible cruelties were committed on both sides. More than 1000 castles and monasteries lay in ruins, hundreds of villages were burned to the ground, and about 130,000 persons were slain.

Some good, however, resulted from all this misery and bloodshed. The south German peasants were won back to the Faith, and this region (Bavaria) remains predominantly Catholic to this day. The same is true of the German-speaking inhabitants of Austria.

The Diet of Spires.—In 1529, at the Diet of Spires, Emperor Charles V agreed to tolerate Lutheran doctrines wherever they had already been generally accepted. However, the introduction of Lutheran beliefs into new territories was forbidden, and Catholics everywhere were to be permitted freedom to practice their religion. This decision was *protested* by six Lutheran princes and fourteen Lutheran cities. Thereafter, Lutherans and, in time, all Christians who had broken away from the Catholic Church, came to be known as *Protestants*.

The Confession of Augsburg.—A summary of the Lutheran doctrines was presented to the Diet of Augsburg in 1530, in the form of a document which is now known as the *Confession of*

Augsburg. This document, which was drawn up by Philip Melanchthon, one of Luther's associates, embodied the principles of the Protestant faith which are observed by the Lutheran churches today.

The Peace of Augsburg.—Between 1530 and 1555, the Lutheran princes, who had formed the *Protestant League of Schmalkald,* engaged in warfare against Emperor Charles V. They were occasionally joined in this fight by French forces, and the Emperor was aided by many princes from southern and central Germany, who remained loyal to the Catholic Church. The Catholic forces won various important battles but Charles was still involved in other conflicts and therefore was unable to make the Protestants accede to his terms. Finally, in 1555, he decided to bring the long conflict to a close and agreed to the *Peace of Augsburg.* The principal provision of this treaty was that the prince or ruler of each state was to determine whether the religion of his subjects should be Catholicity or Lutheranism. A subject had no voice in the matter; if he objected to his ruler's choice, his only recourse was to emigrate. This principle, often referred to as *cujus regio, illius religio,* did not receive the approval of the Pope.

Luther did not survive to witness the Peace of Augsburg, but he did live long enough to regret many of his actions and to admit the great harm he had done.

THE SPREAD OF PROTESTANTISM TO SCANDINAVIA AND SWITZERLAND

Protestantism in Scandinavia.—From northern Germany, Protestantism swept into Norway, Denmark and Sweden. The great majority of the populations of these countries remained devoted to Catholicity, but the Kings saw in the new religion an opportunity to increase their powers, and forced it upon their unwilling subjects. Catholicity was outlawed, the property of the Church was seized, and many Bishops who tried to defend their loyal followers paid for their heroism with their lives. In Norway and Denmark, Lutheranism was made the state religion in 1537. By 1593, it had also become the established religion of Sweden.

The Revolt in Switzerland.—At the same time that Luther's religious ideas were spreading throughout Germany and Scandinavia, two reformers appeared on the scene in Switzerland.

1. Zwingli (1484-1531).—Zwingli was a German Priest who was born in Switzerland. He was a great lover of the classics and an admirer of Erasmus, whose influence led him to read Luther's heretical pamphlets. When this fact became known to his parishioners, Zwingli was deprived of his pastorship and banished. He then went to the city of Zurich, where he won over the city council by his eloquent preaching. In addition to preaching Luther's errors, Zwingli taught a denial of the Divine Presence in the Holy Eucharist. His preaching led to the outbreak of violence against Catholics, to the plundering of churches and to other outrages. Eventually, seven of Switzerland's thirteen cantons united in opposition to Zwingli's Protestant followers. A decisive battle was fought at Cappel in 1531, in which the Catholic forces were victorious and Zwingli was killed. A short time later, however, a new preacher, John Calvin, assumed the leadership of the Protestant movement.

2. John Calvin (1509-1564).—Calvin was a native of France, where he received an excellent education and became a practitioner of law. Calvin lost his faith after being influenced by the writings of Luther and Erasmus. Since heretics were not tolerated in France at that time, he sought refuge in Switzerland. There, in 1536, he wrote and published a summary of his beliefs called *Institutes of the Christian Religion*. This book was responsible for the spread of Calvinism to non-Lutheran countries, such as France and Scotland. It was originally written in Latin, but was later translated into French.

Calvin adopted some of Luther's teachings, but added the theory of *predestination*. He taught that man did not have a free will and was predestined (that is, destined even before birth) to eternity in Heaven or Hell. Calvin's religious ceremonies were simple and austere, and centered about the preaching of a sermon. There was no Mass, no music, no singing. Church organization was also very simple. Like Zwingli, Calvin denied the Real Presence.

At first, the Swiss people rejected Calvin's cold, bare religion, but with the aid of a preacher of kindred spirit named Farel,

THE PROTESTANT REVOLT IN EUROPE 189

Calvin soon became very influential. In 1541, he settled in Geneva. Taking advantage of the religious and political turmoil which existed in the city, he soon established a personal dictatorship. From 1546 until his death in 1564, Calvin remained in absolute control. During his dictatorship, dissent on religious matters was not tolerated; fifty-eight persons were executed on religious grounds, seventy-three were banished and more than 900 were thrown into prison.

PROTESTANTISM IN FRANCE

The Huguenots.—Calvinist doctrines were introduced into France by many preachers who had been trained in the Calvinist Academy at Geneva. Frenchmen who accepted the Calvinist doctrines (known as *Huguenots*) were most numerous in southern and western France and were recruited chiefly from the lesser nobility and the wealthy middle class of the cities. The French monarchs of the period, Francis I, Henry II, Francis II and Charles IX, consistently sought to suppress the dissemination of Protestant doctrines by the Huguenots. After destructive civil wars, which lasted intermittently from 1562 to 1598, the Huguenots were finally granted freedom of worship by the Edict of Nantes.

The St. Bartholomew's Day Massacre.—The most widely remembered event of the French civil wars was the terrible massacre of St. Bartholomew's Day, August 24, 1572. The real power behind the French throne during this period was the Queen mother, Catherine di Medici. Three of her sons sat on the throne of France. Catherine maintained her power by her influence over her sons, and also by shrewd diplomatic maneuvers, in which she played the two most powerful noble families of the day (the Catholic Guises and the Protestant Bourbons) against each other.

In 1572, Catherine planned to assassinate the leader of the Huguenots, Admiral de Coligny, who had been attempting to influence her son, Charles IX. Her hired assassin, however, failed to carry out his mission, although his intended victim was wounded in the arm. The enraged Huguenots threatened revenge. In fear of her life, Catherine decided to arrange for a massacre of Huguenots, thousands of whom were then assembled in Paris for a royal wedding. Before dawn on St. Bartholomew's Day, Coligny and some 2000 of his followers were slain in cold blood by Catherine's troops. Within a few days, another thousand were killed near Paris.

Catherine's foul deed was not motivated by a love of Catholicity but by personal fear and ambition, for she had previously sided with the Huguenots when political conditions made it expedient for her to do so. Pope Gregory XIII deeply deplored this bloody event.

Conversion of Henry IV (1593).—Henry III, who was assassinated in 1589, had no children. His two nearest relatives were Henry, the Catholic Duke of Guise and Henry of Navarre, head of the Protestant house of Bourbon. The Duke of Guise was murdered in 1588, and Henry of Navarre ascended the throne as Henry IV (1589-1610). The laws of Catholic France, however, forbade a Protestant ruler. Henry thereupon took instructions and freely became a Catholic (1593). Until he was assassinated in 1610, Henry remained outwardly a Catholic, but his life was far from exemplary and he gave much assistance to Protestant England and Protestant Germany. However, he was an able organizer and did much to develop his realm and increase the prosperity of the people. Henry IV was the founder of the Bourbon dynasty, which was to rule France continuously for more than two centuries.

The Edict of Nantes (1598).—One of the most notable events in the career of Henry IV was the issuance of the *Edict of Nantes*. The purpose of this ruling was to put an end to the religious wars in France and to insure the loyalty of the Huguenots. Under the Edict of Nantes, Protestants were granted freedom of worship wherever they had been established prior to 1597, and were allowed civic privileges. They were also permitted to retain and fortify their military strongholds, the most important of which was at the city of La Rochelle.[1]

Nearly a century later, in 1685, Louis XIV revoked the Edict of Nantes because he felt that religious disunity tended to bring

---

[1] This right was revoked in 1629 after the Huguenots, who had become a powerful political group, were defeated in battle by the forces of Cardinal Richelieu.

on political discord. As a result of Louis' action, thousands of Huguenots migrated to England, Holland and America rather than accept Catholicity. All France was then reunited by the bond of Catholic faith.

PROTESTANTISM IN THE NETHERLANDS

Protestantism and the Struggle against Spain.—In the sixteenth century, the Netherlands were under the control of Spain. The Netherlands then consisted of what later became the kingdoms of Holland and Belgium, as well as a portion of northern France. All of this territory was divided into seventeen provinces. Protestantism was introduced into the country by foreign merchants, by the Swiss and German soldiers of Emperor Charles V (who was also King of Spain), and by the English Protestants who had fled the harsh treatment of Queen Mary (Mary Tudor). Charles' rule over the Netherlands was benevolent, and he checked the spread of Protestantism by exercising moderation and discretion. However, when Charles abdicated in 1556, the Netherlands passed into possession of his son, King Philip II of Spain. Philip, in contrast to his father, was despotic and intolerant; he adopted harsh and repressive measures against the Protestants in the Netherlands. Edicts called *Placards* were issued and enforced against both Calvinists and Lutherans. Both sects were found principally in the northern provinces—Calvinists in the west, Lutherans in the east. Philip attempted to curtail the rights of the cities and of the nobility, and enacted various tyrannical laws. These measures finally aroused the whole people against him. The various anti-Spanish factions formed an alliance called the *Compromise of Breda* (1565). The Calvinists took the lead in this organized opposition to Spanish domination, and in their religious zeal, attacked and pillaged Catholic churches and monasteries throughout the land. More than 400 churches were destroyed in Flanders alone.

The Dutch Gain Their Independence.—Philip II commissioned the Duke of Alva as governor of the Netherlands and ordered him to crush the uprising. Alva adopted brutal repressive measures, including wholesale executions and confiscation of property. More than 100,000 Protestants were forced to emigrate.

The military forces of the Netherlands were led by William the Silent, head of the House of Orange. William was a courageous and capable military leader, whose resourcefulness and patriotic fervor helped the Dutch to hold out against an overwhelmingly superior foe.

The ten southern provinces (modern Belgium), which had remained largely Catholic, finally made peace with Alva's successor, Alexander Farnese. The seven northern provinces (modern Holland) continued the struggle against Spain and, in 1579, bound themselves together by the *Union of Utrecht*. In 1584, William was assassinated by Philip's agents. Despite the loss of their leader, the Dutch continued the desperate struggle for many years. A truce was signed in 1609, but it was not until 1648 that the Spanish government, by the Treaty of Westphalia (page 197), finally recognized the independence of Holland. To this day, Holland is predominantly Calvinist, while Belgium is Catholic.

As a result of this long, destructive war, many wealthy Netherlands traders emigrated to Asia and founded the colonies now known as the Dutch East Indies. Others sailed westward and founded the colony of New Amsterdam (New York) in the New World.

The Martyrs of Gorkum.—Gorkum is a little town on the Meuse River which was the scene of Catholic martyrdom during the struggle between Spain and the Netherlands. For twenty years, St. John of Cologne, a German Dominican, had been Pastor of the village of Hoornaer, which was near Gorkum. In the summer of 1572, he learned that several Priests in Gorkum had been thrown into prison because they refused to renounce their Faith. The Dominican Priest went to Gorkum and attempted to secure the release of his imprisoned brothers. Meanwhile, he strove to care for the needs of their Parishes as best he could. A few days later, while on his way to baptize an infant, he too was seized and thrown into prison. For ten days the Calvinists, under the leadership of Brant, tortured and mutilated the seventeen Priests and two Lay Brothers whom they held captive. Despite their inhuman treatment, all steadfastly refused to deny their belief in the Real Presence and in Papal supremacy. In the middle of the night of July 9, 1572, St. John and his brother Priests were taken to a stable and hanged. Many miracles bore witness to their sanctity and they are revered in Holland today. In 1865, they were canonized by Pope Pius IX.

PROTESTANTISM IN SCOTLAND

John Knox and Presbyterianism.—Protestantism was propagated in Scotland by John Knox (1505-1572), an apostate Catholic Priest, who had embraced the Calvinist doctrines. Calvinism in Scotland became known as *Presbyterianism*. Laxity in the monasteries made the Church an easy target for the greed of the Scottish nobles and facilitated the spread of the new religion.

The Tragedy of Mary Queen of Scots.—In 1525, the Scottish King, James V, and his Parliament temporarily checked the spread of Presbyterianism. In 1541, James died and left an infant daughter, Mary Queen of Scots, who was taken to France and reared as a devout Catholic. She became the wife of King Francis II of France.

In 1561, after the death of her royal husband, Mary returned to Scotland. She found that Protestantism, under the leadership of John Knox, had made such headway that in the preceding year the Scottish Parliament had proclaimed it as the state religion. Catholic worship was abolished and death or banishment was decreed for Catholics. Even as Queen of the land, Mary found it extremely difficult to secure permission for the celebration of Mass in her private chapel. In 1568, the young Queen was forced to abdicate and was thrown into prison by her English cousin, the Protestant Queen Elizabeth. Elizabeth feared the existence of plots which were aimed at placing the Catholic Queen of Scotland on the throne of England (page 193). In 1587, after nineteen years in prison, Mary was condemned to death. She died bravely, under the axe, remaining a loyal Catholic to the very end.

A prominent historian [2] writes of Mary Queen of Scots:

> If it can be truly said that the matrimonial entanglements of her checkered career sullied the purity of her name, it can no less be truly asserted that the holy death which she suffered so nobly and so courageously expiated that stain in the sight of God and man.

---

[2] Weber, N. A., *The Christian Era*.

PROTESTANTISM IN ENGLAND

Henry VIII and the Church.—Although the outbreak of the religious revolt in Europe naturally affected England, the type of Protestantism which was adopted there was not the result of Lutheran or Calvinist agitation. It is true that Calvinism had gained some converts among the middle-class merchants and town artisans, but the English break with the Papacy was pre-

cipitated not by any doctrinal dispute, but by the matrimonial troubles of the English monarch, Henry VIII. For the two preceding centuries, English Kings had shown signs of hostility toward the Papacy. For example, in 1279, a decree was published prohibiting the willing of property to the Church without the consent of the King. In the fourteenth century, the *Statute of Provisors* prohibited the appointment of foreigners to English Church offices, and the *Statute of Praemunire* denied the right of appeal from English courts to any foreign courts (including Papal courts).

THE PROTESTANT REVOLT IN EUROPE 191

Henry VIII became King of a Catholic England of 4,000,000 souls in 1509. Henry was an accomplished scholar, and in 1521 Pope Leo X granted him the title of *Defender of the Faith* because he had publicly burned the writings of Luther and written a *Defense of the Seven Sacraments,* against Luther. In 1509, Henry married Catherine of Aragon, an aunt of Emperor Charles V. A daughter, Mary, was born in 1516, but the King was sorely disappointed because his marriage was not blessed with a son and heir. In the meantime, Henry had fallen in love with a court attendant named Anne Boleyn. Because of this infatuation, as well as his desire for a son to insure the succession of the crown, Henry sought to have his marriage declared invalid so that he would be free to marry Anne Boleyn. The grounds which he advanced were mere pretexts, and Pope Clement VII refused to annul the marriage.

The Break with the Church.—Enraged at his failure to obtain an annulment, Henry retaliated by openly denying the Papal authority. With the help of a man named Thomas Cromwell, he dissolved the monasteries and confiscated the wealth of the Church, transferring it to the crown. The break became complete in 1534, when Parliament passed the *Act of Supremacy,* which declared Henry to be the supreme head of the Church of England. (This became known as the *Anglican* or *Episcopal* Church.) Many prominent persons, including Sir Thomas More, Bishop John Fisher, and several Bishops, Priests, Abbots and Monks, refused to take the oath acknowledging the royal supremacy over the Church. For their loyalty to their religion, they were put to death. Bishop Fisher and Sir Thomas More were canonized by Pope Pius XI in 1935.

In 1538, King Henry VIII was excommunicated by Pope Paul III. His outrageous conduct fully merited this punishment. As stated above, he was a man of intellect, who understood the truths of religion. He did not bring about the break with the Church because of doctrinal confusions, but solely because of his uncontrollable ambitions and desires. As a matter of fact, Henry disliked Protestant doctrines. This is shown by his execution of several leaders who advocated the adoption of such doctrines for the Church of England. Henry's defection from the Universal Church was particularly tragic because, it is believed by many historians, if England had remained loyal to Rome, the Protestant Revolt probably would have ended in failure and all Christian nations would now be united under a single spiritual leadership.

Henry's Later Marriages.—When Henry failed to secure a Papal annulment of his marriage, the brilliant Cardinal Wolsey, who had been the King's chief adviser, passed from favor. Thomas Cranmer took his place as the most powerful Churchman of England. He was appointed Archbishop of Canterbury, and declared null and void Henry's marriage to Catherine, although the latter refused to admit the legality of these proceedings until her death (1536). Notwithstanding, Henry married Anne Boleyn in 1533. Anne gave birth to a daughter, who was to become Queen Elizabeth, but she did not provide Henry with a male heir. In 1536, she was condemned to death on a charge of immoral conduct, and beheaded.

Four other wives followed before Henry's matrimonial ventures came to an end. Jane Seymour, whom he married in 1536, died the following year, but before her death she gave birth to a male heir, Edward VI. The King then married Anne of Cleves for political reasons, but divorced her when she proved personally distasteful and the marriage unnecessary. (For advocating this marriage, Henry had his minister, Thomas Cromwell, beheaded.) His next wife, Catherine Howard, was also beheaded in 1542. Catherine Parr, his final wife, survived him, when he died in January, 1547.

Edward VI (1547-1553).—Henry's son, Edward VI, was only a boy of eleven when he ascended the throne in 1547. During his brief reign, England moved toward the type of Protestantism which existed on the Continent. Mass was abolished, Latin gave way to English in the religious ceremonies, and many Protestant professors were placed in the universities. These changes were brought about largely through the efforts of the Regent, the Duke of Somerset, and Archbishop Cranmer. Edward died in 1553 and was succeeded by Mary Tudor, the daughter of Henry VIII and Catherine of Aragon.

Mary Tudor (1553-1558).—Under Mary's five-year reign, England returned to Catholicity. But Mary was too zealous in her efforts to stamp out Protestantism. Over 200 prominent Eng-

THE PROTESTANT REVOLT IN EUROPE 193

lishmen, such as Cranmer, Hooper, Latimer, Ridley and several Bishops, were convicted of heresy and burned at the stake. Many refugees fled the country. Mary made another serious mistake when she married Philip II of Spain, whom the English people feared. She soon lost the confidence of her people and her influence rapidly declined. Upon her death, she was succeeded by Elizabeth, the daughter of Henry VIII and Anne Boleyn.

Elizabeth (1558-1603).—When Elizabeth was proclaimed Queen in 1558, she took an oath to uphold the Catholic Faith. Elizabeth knew, however, that her Catholic subjects did not regard her as the legitimate heir to the throne because the Catholic Church had never recognized the marriage of her parents. She therefore felt insecure, fearing Catholic attempts to dethrone her. She was soon persuaded by William Cecil, a wealthy landowner, to support the Protestant Anglican Church. After her coronation, Parliament repassed the Act of Supremacy making Elizabeth the head of the Church, and enacted another law compelling all persons to attend Protestant services. It also adopted the *Thirty-Nine Articles,* which defined the beliefs of the Anglican Church.

Only one of the sixteen Catholic Bishops of England submitted to these heresies. The others were exiled or cast into prison, where twelve of them died. One thousand Priests resigned or were deprived of their office. In 1570, Pope Pius V excommunicated Queen Elizabeth. This act marked the beginning of an era of violent persecution of English Catholics, during which many of the faithful suffered martyrdom. The terrors and suffering which Catholics endured during Elizabeth's long reign have been described in many historical novels and biographies of the times. (Among the more recent of these are *Late Harvest,* a novel by Olive B. White, and a new biography of Queen Elizabeth by Theodore Maynard.) A study of the Elizabethan period has persuaded many a prominent Englishman to return to Catholicity.

One of the reasons why Elizabeth succeeded in establishing the Anglican Church is that, throughout a large part of her reign, England was menaced by Philip II of Spain. This danger, naturally, tended to arouse the patriotism of the people and to rally them behind their Queen. Finally, in 1588, Philip sent a huge

Armada (fleet) to invade England. The English seamen, aided by the elements, completely defeated the Spaniards in one of the decisive battles of history.

James I (1603-1625).—Elizabeth's death in 1603 brought to an end the reign of the Tudors, since Elizabeth had never married. Her cousin, James VI of Scotland (the only son of Mary Queen of Scots), ascended the throne as James I of England. He was the first monarch of the Stuart dynasty. The new King was disliked by the people because of his extravagance, his overbearing manner and his open insistence on the *Divine Right of Kings*. (According to this doctrine, the King was God's lieutenant on earth and was not responsible to the people or Parliament, but to God alone.)

Resentment against King James was intensified because he severely persecuted all religious dissenters. Although the Anglican Church was the established church of England, there were numerous other religious sects. In addition to the Catholics, who constituted about one-twentieth of the population, there were Puritans (Calvinists), Presbyterians, and Independents (Congregationalists). The Puritans wished to eliminate all Catholic practices from the Anglican Church, but did not advocate separation from it. The Presbyterians favored the religious system adopted in Scotland. The Independents insisted upon self-government for individual congregations.

On November 5, 1605, an attempt was made to assassinate the King and some members of Parliament. The "Gunpowder Plot," as this attempt was called, was led by five radical Catholics, but was supported by all the dissenting Protestant sects. The plot was exposed in time and no harm was done, but all the blame for the conspiracy was placed upon the Catholics. As a result, further restrictive measures were enacted against them.

Charles I (1625-1649).—James I was succeeded by his son Charles I, who continued his father's policies. The new ruler was even more intolerant of religious dissenters than his father had been. He utilized two special tribunals to deal with dissenters, particularly Puritans—the *Star Chamber* and the *Court of High Commission*. These tribunals were conducted by the Anglican Archbishop Laud. During this period, thousands of Puritans were forced to flee the country, among them the Pilgrims, who established a colony in New England.

Charles' insistence upon maintaining a personal rule, his constant quarreling with Parliament over taxation, and his persecution of the politically powerful Puritans, finally precipitated a civil war. In this conflict, the Catholics, the Anglicans, the nobility and the country gentry sided with the monarch, while the Parliamentary forces were supported by the Puritans, the Presbyterians, the commercial classes and the small farmers. The King's followers were known as *Cavaliers,* the supporters of Parliament as *Roundheads.* The Parliamentary forces, led by Oliver Cromwell, were victorious. In 1646, Charles surrendered himself to the Puritan army. He was executed for treason in 1649.

Oliver Cromwell.—From 1649 until 1658, England was a military dictatorship ruled by one man, Oliver Cromwell. During this period, all religious beliefs except Puritanism were suppressed. However, the dictatorship of Cromwell did not long survive his death in 1658. His son Richard assumed control of the government, but he lacked the support of the army and was forced to abdicate in 1660. A freely elected Parliament then voted to restore the monarchy, and invited Charles II to return to England from exile in Holland.

Charles II (1660-1685).—When Charles II ascended the throne, the Anglican Church, as it had existed before the Puritan Revolution, was reëstablished. The public reaction against Puritanism led to the enactment of several laws aimed at suppression of all dissenting Protestant sects, as well as the Catholics. In later years, the King, who had secretly become a Catholic, attempted unsuccessfully to secure religious toleration for Catholics and Protestant dissenters. But the lot of Catholics in England became worse than ever.

The reign of Charles II witnessed the last execution of a Catholic for his faith. In 1681, Titus Oates, an unprincipled adventurer, who asserted that he had been converted from Catholicity to Protestantism, fabricated a ridiculous tale of a so-called "Popish plot" to kill Charles II. Oliver Plunket, the Catholic Primate of Armagh, was accused of complicity in this "plot," and was condemned and executed. He was beatified in 1920.

James II (1685-1688).—Charles II was succeeded on the throne by his brother, James II. James openly proclaimed his Catholic faith and his intention of restoring Catholicity to England. However, his attempt to appoint Catholic officials and to suspend the various anti-Catholic laws made him unpopular with the Anglican hierarchy.

James had two daughters, Mary and Anne, who had been reared as Protestants. When James' first wife died, he remarried a Catholic princess who, in 1688, gave birth to a son. This greatly alarmed the Anglicans, because it indicated that the royal line would henceforth be Catholic. A group of prominent Englishmen therefore invited James' older daughter Mary and her husband, William of Orange, the ruler of Holland, to ascend the throne of England. James opposed this attempt to dethrone him, but his army deserted him and joined the forces of William and Mary as they landed in England. James was forced to flee to France. A new Parliament then formally declared the throne vacant and offered it to William and Mary. A law was passed barring Catholics from the throne of England and prohibiting the marriage of any English monarch to a Catholic. This episode in English history is known as the "Bloodless Revolution" or the "Glorious Revolution."

The Fate of Ireland.—Politically, Ireland was conquered by the English during the reign of Queen Elizabeth, but the Catholic faith of the Irish people remained untainted despite long years of oppression. Henry VIII, Queen Elizabeth and Oliver Cromwell successively visited destruction on Ireland and attempted to convert the people from Catholicity. The invaders seized the land and other property of the inhabitants, denied them civil and religious rights, and plundered their monasteries. Bishops, Priests and Monks were persecuted and hundreds of them died for their religion. Yet, there were always other faithful to take the places of those who had fallen. In these trying times, the Franciscans and Dominicans were especially active in ministering to the people. Truly, the "Isle of Saints and Scholars" became the "Isle of Martyrs and Confessors."

THE THIRTY YEARS' WAR

Nature of Causes of the Thirty Years' War.—The Peace of Augsburg in 1555 did not permanently end the military conflicts between Catholics and Protestants. A series of bitter religious wars broke out in 1618 and continued intermittently until 1648. The Thirty Years' War, as this struggle is known, was fought principally in Germany. The principal reasons for the prolonged hostilities were as follows: (1) the rivalries among the many small states into which Germany was then divided; (2) the numerous disputes which arose as a result of the confiscation of Church lands; (3) the demands of the Calvinist princes for the same privileges which were accorded to Lutherans under the Peace of Augsburg; and (4) the general hostility between Catholics and Protestants.

At first, the war was fought between the Catholic Hapsburg rulers of Austria and the Protestant Czechs of Bohemia. The latter were defeated by the forces of Emperor Ferdinand II. Between 1625 and 1635, most of the German states and Protestant Denmark and Sweden were drawn into the war. Denmark was defeated by the Emperor's forces led by Wallenstein, but Sweden, under its brilliant soldier-King, Gustavus Adolphus, won two hard-fought battles against the Imperial armies. In the second of these, the battle of Lützen, Gustavus Adolphus was killed, thus depriving the Protestant cause of its most effective leader. The last phase of the war, which began in 1635, saw France arrayed against Austria and Spain. This struggle, obviously, was purely political, for all the main antagonists were Catholic. The conflict was instigated primarily by the astute French minister, Cardinal Richelieu, who sought to enlarge the territories of France at the expense of both Austria and Spain. Under the circumstances, this was nothing less than treason to the Church.

The Treaty of Westphalia.—The French generals Condé and Turenne won important victories, and the Hapsburgs finally agreed to come to terms. The agreement which was negotiated, the Treaty of Westphalia, contained the following terms: (1) Calvinist princes secured rights equal to those of Lutheran and Catholic temporal rulers. (2) Protestant princes retained all ecclesiastical lands which they had seized up to the year 1624; lands seized after that date were to be restored to the Church. (3) The full independence of Holland and Switzerland was recognized. (4) Numerous territorial readjustments were made. France, Sweden and the German state of Brandenburg (Prussia) were the principal gainers.

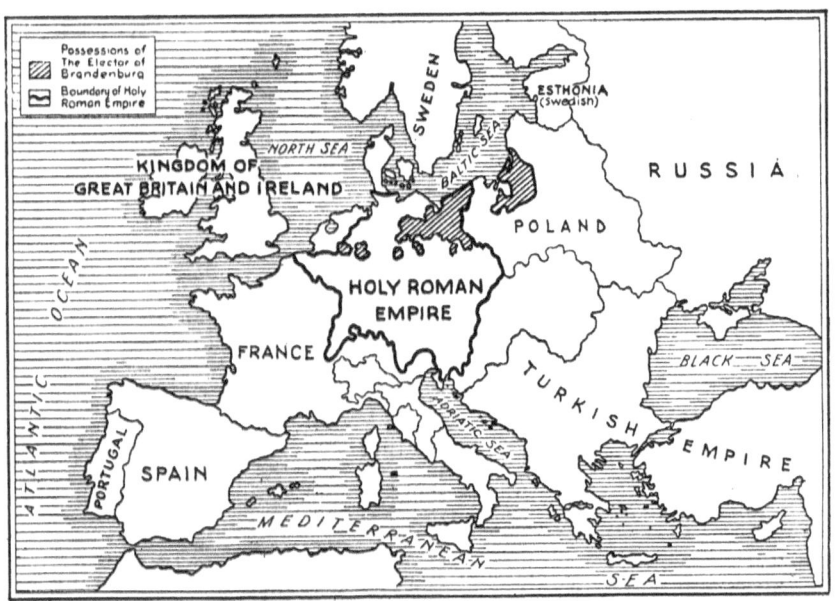

Europe at the Close of the Thirty Years' War.

Germany was so terribly ravaged by the Thirty Years' War that it did not fully recover for many years. The Holy Roman Empire was further weakened, and France emerged as the strongest state on the continent. It was evident after the Treaty of Westphalia that there was no immediate hope of winning back the Protestant countries of Europe to the Universal Church. Such was the result of Cardinal Richelieu's unprincipled attack upon the champions of Catholicity.

Results of Protestantism.—Following are a number of the more important results of the Protestant Revolt.

1. Christian unity was destroyed. Religious wars, often fratricidal in character, resulted in terrible loss of life and property. Poverty and ruin spread throughout Europe.

2. The rejection of ecclesiastical authority logically encouraged the rejection of all authority and the outbreak of lawlessness.

3. Divorce, one of the greatest evils of modern times, was popularized in society.

4. A century of martyrdom renewed the faith of the people, thus revealing again the heaven-sent vitality of the Church.

5. Valiant missionaries carried Christianity to far-off lands, thus following Christ's command to teach all nations.

6. As we shall see in the following chapter, the Council of Trent, which was called by the Catholic Church as an answer to the Protestant Revolt, reëxamined all matters of faith and morals which were under dispute, and defined the teaching of the Catholic Church in terms which have been unmistakably clear to all succeeding generations.

CHAPTER 10

THE CATHOLIC COUNTER-REFORMATION

"It was an evil day for new-born Protestantism when a French artilleryman struck down Ignatius Loyola in the breach of Pampeluna."
—FRANCIS PARKMAN

What Is the Counter-Reformation?—The Counter-Reformation is a movement inaugurated by the Church in order to combat the evil effects of the Protestant Reformation, to eliminate abuses within the Church, and to revive the true spirit of Catholicity. The general objectives and methods of this great program were laid down by the *Council of Trent*. The nation that did the most for the movement was Spain, with her galaxy of saints and her monarchs, sincerely devoted to Christianity. The outstanding individual figure of the entire Counter-Reformation was St. Ignatius Loyola, founder of the Society of Jesus. Of the many exemplary Popes who assisted in this holy work Pius V, a Dominican, was the greatest.

THE COUNCIL OF TRENT

Introduction.—The Council of Trent, the Nineteenth Ecumenical Council, was convoked by Pope Paul III in 1545. It met in the Austrian city of Trent, located in the Alps. The time and place of the meeting had been the subject of jealous diplomatic wrangling. The Council extended over a period of eighteen years. However, it was interrupted twice (once by pestilence and once by political quarrels among the German princes), and was actually in session only in the following years: 1545 to 1549, 1551 to 1552, and 1562 to 1563. A total of twenty-five sessions were held.

Acts of the Council.—During the discussions of the Council of Trent, the Bible and the *Summa* of St. Thomas were always exposed on the altar. This was highly appropriate, for these holy books were the guide and inspiration of the gathering. Papal Legates presided at all times. Noted theologians, including par-

"CLEAN FIRST THE INSIDE...THAT THE OUTSIDE TOO MAY BE CLEAN." MATT. 23,26

ticularly Spaniards, drew up articles dealing with dogmas of faith that Protestantism had questioned. The traditional doctrines and practices of Catholicity, were restated. Great scholars prepared a revised version of the Latin Bible, the *Vulgate,* and issued a uniform catechism. Steps were taken to insure more thorough religious training for the laity. In addition, canons of reform were drawn up, including a set of disciplinary laws, designed to eliminate laxity among the clergy.

There was much stormy debate over the decrees of the Council of Trent. Often it seemed that agreement would never be reached. In the final sessions, however, a great leader and conciliator appeared in the person of St. Charles Borromeo, who was the Archbishop of Milan and the nephew of Pope Pius IV. This noble man has been called the "Soul of the Council of Trent." Largely as a result of his influence, the decrees of the Council were finally signed by 255 Bishops and Generals of Religious Orders. Then, all the decrees were submitted to Pope Pius IV for his rejection or approval. In January, 1564, the Pope gave his formal approval to these decrees. The canons of the Council met with resistance in some parts of the Catholic world, but eventually they were observed and put into effect by Bishops everywhere.

It is interesting to note that the Holy Roman Emperor, Charles V, insisted that certain Protestant Reformers under his control attend the Council. However, they were dissatisfied with the conditions imposed, and it is doubtful whether any good resulted from their attendance.

Effects of the Council of Trent.—The Council of Trent helped mightily to stem the tide of Protestantism by purifying and revitalizing the Church. It is generally regarded as the most important of the twenty Ecumenical Councils.

POPES OF THE COUNTER-REFORMATION

Much of the success of the Council of Trent and of the entire Counter-Reformation was made possible by the zealous Popes who occupied the throne of St. Peter during the sixteenth century.

Paul III (1534-1549).—This Pontiff fought nobly to defend the unity of Christianity. In 1538, he excommunicated King

THE CATHOLIC COUNTER-REFORMATION   203

Henry VIII of England. In 1540, Paul gave official approval to the Jesuit Order page 205). Finally, this Pontiff succeeded in convoking the Council of Trent in 1545.

Pius V (1566-1572).—This great Pope was born in 1504 to a poor, virtuous family in Bosco, Italy. As a boy he entered Italy. As a boy, he earnestly desired to be a Priest, and entered the Dominican Order. For many years, he lived a truly holy life, and was appointed an Inquisitor. The disagreeable but necessary work which he performed in this capacity has caused some historians to misrepresent him. After years of Apostolic labor, he was elected to the throne of St. Peter in 1565. As Pope, he labored successfully to enforce the salutary decrees of the Council of Trent. Political opposition in some European countries made this task an extremely difficult one, but God raised up many saints to aid the Pope in his holy work. In 1570, Pius excommunicated Queen Elizabeth of England, who had done almost irreparable harm to the Church for ten years and had defiantly rejected all the advice and pleadings of the Holy See.

Internal troubles were not the only ones which appeared during the stormy years of Pius' reign. The Turks, who had become masters of the Balkan Peninsula, preyed on the commerce of the Mediterranean Sea. They grew more and more bold, and the situation was rapidly becoming intolerable. Finally, a great fleet composed of Spanish, Venetian and Genoese ships was sent forth under the command of Don Juan of Austria to meet the arrogant Turks. The Catholic fleet prepared well by receiving the sacraments and saying the Rosary on the eve of the battle. On October 7, 1571, Don Juan and his men won a decisive victory at *Lepanto*. This victory was miraculously made known to St. Pius at the very moment it was consummated, while he was reciting the Rosary. This is why the Feast of the Holy Rosary is celebrated on October 7 of each year. Moreover, as a result of the battle of Lepanto, the invocation "Help of Christians" was added to the Litany of the Blessed Virgin.

As Pontiff, Pius V continued to wear his white habit of the Dominican Order. Every Pope since has worn a white cassock, as a tribute to the piety and great achievements of St. Pius V.

Gregory XIII (1572-1585).—The strength and security which the reign of Pius V had brought to the Catholic world made possible the splendor of the Pontificate of Gregory XIII. Gregory founded seminaries and colleges in Rome to educate Priests. To the various Catholic nations, he sent representatives called *nuncios,* whose chief duty was to see that the decrees of the Council of Trent were carried into effect. Gregory revised the calendar which had been used in Europe since the days of Julius Caesar. This so-called Julian calendar was imperfect, and by the sixteenth century had led to an accumulated error of ten days. To correct the error, Gregory ordered October 5, 1582, to be dated October 15. Then he instituted the Gregorian calendar, which avoided future errors by means of the device called "leap year." All countries use this calendar now, although Protestant countries lagged behind Catholic countries in adopting it. Russia was the last to accept it (1901).

Sixtus V (1585-1590).—Sixtus was an ideal Pope, a Franciscan of fearless energy. Sixtus did much to improve conditions within Rome itself. The city at the time was infested by bandit gangs. The Pope effectively checked their evil activities by prescribing the death penalty for all bandits, regardless of their noble birth or political connections. Soon public order was restored. He coped with the situation of unemployment among the poor by promoting the silk and woolen industries. Instead of starting new building projects, he renovated many church properties in Rome, and completed many unfinished projects, such as the Vatican Library, the Lateran Palace, and the dome of St. Peter's. Under Sixtus' sponsorship, a printing establishment was set up at the Vatican. This Pope encouraged scholars such as Cardinal Robert Bellarmine, who was canonized in 1930.

SAINTLY LEADERS OF THE COUNTER-REFORMATION

The sixteenth century was a century of saints. Many of these saints were dominant factors in the Counter-Reformation, and are still influencing the world for good through their writings and the educational institutions and charitable institutions that they founded. Because of limitations of space, we can now consider only a few of these glorious figures of Church History. No doubt, you will want to learn about their many noble co-workers.

THE CATHOLIC COUNTER-REFORMATION

St. Ignatius of Loyola (1491-1556).—Mention of the Protestant Reformation instantly brings to mind the name of Martin Luther; in the same way, the Catholic Counter-Reformation inevitably suggests to us the name of Luther's greatest opponent, St. Ignatius of Loyola.

Ignatius was a member of a noble Spanish family. He became a soldier and was wounded in a war against France in 1521. Up to this stage in his life, Ignatius had not been especially distinguished for his piety, but while he was recovering from his wound, he read the lives of the saints. This inspired him to become a soldier in the service of Christ.

Ignatius prepared himself for the priesthood by studying at Salamanca, Alcala and Paris. While he was at Paris, his pious, manly personality and high-minded ideals attracted seven gifted noblemen, who became his followers. This small group formed the nucleus of the *Society of Jesus*, or *Jesuits*, as they are commonly known. In 1534, the Society of Jesus placed itself at the disposal of the Pope. In 1540, it received the official Papal sanction.

The general purpose of the Society of Jesus was to check Protestantism and to spread and strengthen the Catholic faith in every way possible. The Society's motto *Ad Majorem Dei Gloriam!* ("To the Greater Glory of God!") well expresses its basic aim. Candidates for the Society were required to undergo a long and rigorous training. When they had completed this training and were accepted as full-fledged members, they took the usual monastic vows, and also swore implicit obedience to the Pope. St. Ignatius was a truly great administrator and he organized his followers on a semi-military basis that contributed much to his glorious success. At the head of the Society was a commander-in-chief known as a General. Ignatius, of course, was the first to hold this position. In the various countries, the General had subordinate commanders known as Provincials.

The Jesuits preached in Protestant countries and administered to Catholics there. Often they engaged in this holy work at the risk of their lives. They labored to detect and uproot any signs of heresy in Catholic lands. They engaged in missionary work in far-flung quarters of the globe, including the newly discovered lands in America. They conducted schools which became generally recognized as the best in Christendom. Through all these activities, the Jesuits served as the chief bulwark of the Church in weathering the storms of the Protestant Reformation.

When Ignatius died in 1556, the Jesuits numbered about 1000. Many of these were destined to become canonized saints like their valiant and pious founder. In 1950, the Jesuits numbered 30,000.

St. Francis Xavier (1506-1552).—One of the first companions of St. Ignatius was a young Basque nobleman, who was won over to the cause of the Jesuits while studying at Paris. This man, Francis Xavier, was destined to become the Apostle of India and Japan and one of the greatest of all the missionaries of the Church. He served as Papal Legate to India, where he

labored more than ten years as an Apostolic missionary. In southern India, he baptized hundreds of thousands, trained teachers and founded schools. After this, Francis went to Japan, where he toiled two years and converted 2000 of the most intelligent people of the island. These 2000 were to increase to 30,000 within twenty years. Francis then set out to China, but a tropical fever contracted on the lonely island of Sancian opened eternity to his Apostolic soul. His *Letters* have inspired a vast amount of missionary activity and have helped to make many a saint.

St. Peter Canisius (1521-1597).—This Hollander was the second Apostle of Germany. Luther had propagated his destructive doctrines by means of pamphlets in question-and-answer form. St. Peter Canisius, who had been trained at Rome by St. Ignatius of Loyola, wrote catechisms in German and thus pre-

THE CATHOLIC COUNTER-REFORMATION

served the faith of multitudes and counteracted the terrible influence of the falsehoods propagated by Lutherans. For thirty years this saint devoted himself untiringly to the salvation of Germany, working in Bavaria, the Tyrol, Bohemia and Austria. He was canonized in 1925.

St. Angela Merici (1474-1540).—While still a young woman, this noble daughter of Italy gathered about her twelve other ladies resolved to further the wish of God. By their united efforts, and with the encouragement of St. Charles Borromeo, this group founded the *Ursuline Nuns,* to teach little children and to care for the sick. The Ursuline Nuns were a vital force in the Counter-Reformation in Italy, France, and Germany. They were the first Sisters to come to the New World (1636). In 1727, they founded at New Orleans the first Catholic school taught by Nuns in the United States.

St. Theresa *(1515-1583).*—St. Theresa was a native of the city of Avila in Spain. She grew into an enthusiastic, high-spirited maiden, and entered the Carmelite Convent of her native city. At first, she was very fond of reading romantic literature, but she finally yielded to divine inspiration and devoted her intense love to God alone. She became one of the mystic saints of the Church, and aided the Counter-Reformation by reforming the lax discipline in the Carmelite Convent. Theresa founded thirty-two Carmelite Houses, all of which were models of exemplary living and discipline.

St. Theresa's writings, especially *The Way of Perfection,* are written in a pure classic style and rank with the masterpieces of Spanish literature.

Carmelite Convents today are centers of prayer, especially in large cities. Their holy work brings down spiritual blessings on people who otherwise might deserve the wrath of God because they neglect the duty of prayer. Carmelites pray particularly for Priests and missionaries.

St. Vincent de Paul (1581-1660).—This "Apostle of Organized Charity" was the founder of two religious orders, a reformer of the clergy, and a promoter of missions. He was born a member of a poor French peasant family, but his parents' sacrifices enabled him to become a Priest. Five years after ordination, he was captured by Mohammedan pirates and remained a slave for three years. This event was the turning point of Vincent's life; he converted his master and both returned from Tunis to Paris. As a Parish Priest, Vincent saw the needs of the poor. Twelve other Priests joined him and they founded the Congregation of the Missions, usually called *Vincentians* or *Lazarists*. These Priests gave missions to the poor in the villages of France. St. Vincent organized Parish Societies to care for the needy; he established homes for the aged, where husband and wife would not be separated; he established foundling homes for unwanted babies. Lastly, he founded the Sisters of Charity, who have done valuable work as nurses and teachers the world over. St. Vincent de Paul Societies exist in most well-organized parishes today to care for the poor.

SAINTS OF THE ERA OF THE PROTESTANT REVOLT AND COUNTER-REFORMATION

ENGLAND

Saints	Dates	Outstanding Facts
St. Thomas More............	1480-1535	Refused to take oath acknowledging Henry VIII as head of Church of England; martyred (July 6).
St. John Fisher..............	1459-1535	Cardinal and Bishop of Rochester; like Thomas More, refused to give up allegiance to Pope, and was martyred (June 22).

GERMANY AND LOW COUNTRIES

Saints	Dates	Outstanding Facts
St. Peter Canisius..........	1521-1597	Second Apostle of Germany; wrote catechisms.
St. John of Cologne.........	?—1572	Martyred at Gorkum, Holland with eighteen others who would not deny the primacy of the Pope.
St. Fidelis Sigmaringen.......	1577-1622	Lawyer of the poor; martyred by Calvinists in Switzerland.

THE CATHOLIC COUNTER-REFORMATION

	SPAIN	
St. Francis Xavier............	1506-1552	Missionary to India and Japan; converted hundreds of thousands in twelve years.
St. Ignatius Loyola...........	1491-1556	Founder of the Jesuits; powerful opponent of Lutheranism.
St. Theresa of Avila..........	1515-1583	Reformer of the Carmelite Nuns; mystical writer.
St. Louis Bertrand............	1526-1581	Dominican missionary; baptized 25,000 pagans in eight years in Colombia and Panama.
St. Francis Solanus...........	1549-1610	Franciscan missionary for twenty-seven years among Indians of Peru.
St. Turibius	1538-1606	Archbishop of Lima, Peru; traveled 50,000 miles, baptizing, preaching and confirming natives.
	FRANCE	
St. Vincent de Paul...........	1580-1660	Founder of Congregation of Missions, to preach to poor in villages of France; founder of Sisters of Charity; organized charity in parishes.
St. Francis de Sales..........	1567-1622	Reformer of laymen; great mystical writer; as Bishop of Geneva, converted 70,000 Calvinists.
St. Jane de Chantal...........	1572-1641	Founder of Visitation Order, for visiting and bringing spiritual ministrations to the ill, aged, etc.
St. John Baptist de la Salle...	1651-1719	Founder of Christian Brothers; reformer of popular education for boys.

ITALY		
St. Charles Borromeo.........	1538-1584	Reformer of the clergy; Bishop of Milan; the "Soul of the Council of Trent"; gave First Holy Communion to St. Aloysius Gonzaga, patron of youth.
St. Pius (Pope Pius V).......	1504-1572	Vigorous reformer, who excommunicated Queen Elizabeth of England and enforced decrees of the Council of Trent; formed alliance against Turks.
St. Robert Bellarmine.......	1542-1621	Cardinal; writer of catechisms.
St. Philip Neri..............	1513-1595	Reformer in Rome; founder of Oratory Priests; the "Sunshine of the Reformation."
St. Angela Merici............	1474-1540	Founder of the Ursuline Nuns, first non-cloistered Sisters to teach.

CHAPTER 11

ROYAL ABSOLUTISM

"It is remarkable that the greatest increase of royal power in Europe dates precisely from the commencement of Protestantism.... Was there any hidden connection between Protestantism and the development and definitive establishment of absolutism? I think there was; and I will even add, that, had Catholicism retained an exclusive sway in Europe, the power of the throne would have been gradually diminished—that representative forms would probably not have disappeared altogether—that we should have been much farther advanced in civilization, much better fitted for the enjoyment of true liberty—that this liberty would not be associated in our minds with scenes of horror."

—J. L. BALMES ("European Civilization")

NATURE AND CAUSES OF ABSOLUTISM

Introduction.—After centuries of struggle, the English people finally succeeded in imposing far-reaching limitations on the authority of their Kings; the monarchs on the continent of Europe, however, suffered no such curtailment of power. In the period from the Treaty of Westphalia (1648) until the outbreak of the French Revolution (1789), the authority of these rulers was, for the most part, *absolute*. They could do practically as they wanted, without effective control by the people, the nobility or the Church. Indeed, the Kings dared, in some cases, to interfere in purely ecclesiastical affairs.

The most powerful and representative of the absolute monarchs were Louis XIV of France, Frederick the Great of Prussia and Peter the Great of Russia, all of whom we shall consider in the following pages.

Reasons for the Rise of Absolutism.—What were the reasons for the rise of royal absolutism? The explanation may be found, in part, in such historical processes as the breakdown of the feudal system, the expansion of commerce and industry, and the growth of the middle class. The feudal system, as we have seen, was based on institutions of local government; feudal lords were virtually sovereign within their own realms. Naturally, when truly national states developed, the kings took over most of the powers formerly exercised by the landed aristocracy. The increasingly influential commercial classes supported this change because they hoped that a strong national state would insure peace and order, do away with local tariff barriers, build roads and bridges, and help trade and commerce in various other ways.

This analysis is valid so far as it goes, but it does not really get at the root of the matter. It does not tell us what had happened to the moral ideals and institutions which, in previous centuries, tended to prevent any one man from assuming absolute governmental power. If we approach the problem from this angle, we can see that the real explanation for the rise of absolutism lies in the Protestant Revolt. This idea is well expressed in the quotation from Balmes on page 211, which you should read very carefully. If all of western Europe had retained its allegiance to the Catholic Church, the rulers of France, Prussia and other countries would, in all probability, never have dared to claim absolute powers. Like the great Medieval Emperors, they would have found that the word of God, as interpreted by the Universal Church, set very definite limitations to their authority. In such an atmosphere, the institutions of representative government could have survived and developed without violence or extremism.

If this had happened, as the quotation from Balmes indicates, mankind would have been spared not only the excesses of absolutism, but also the excesses of the revolts against absolutism which occurred in the eighteenth and nineteenth centuries. (This will be discussed in detail in later chapters.) The whole subsequent history of Europe, America and the entire world would have been changed for the better.

THE ABSOLUTE MONARCHIES

France under Louis XIV (1643--1715).—In 1643, Louis XIV ascended the throne of a united, wealthy and powerful France. His personal authority over temporal matters was supreme. He could declare war, make peace, levy taxes, appoint officers and proclaim degrees without having to consult or secure the approval of any authority. During his long reign, Louis attempted to extend and consolidate his power by interfering in religious affairs. In pursuit of this aim, he revoked the Edict of Nantes (page 186), which granted religious toleration to the influential Protestant Huguenots. He also instituted a movement called *Gallicanism,* the object of which was to nationalize the Catholic Church in France.

In his efforts to advance the cause of Gallicanism, Louis continually interfered in the election of Bishops. In 1682, he prevailed upon the nationalistic clergy of France to hold a national council. At this council, Bishop Bossuet presented and condemned a document called the *Declaration of the French Clergy,* which expounded the contentions of Gallicanism. The Declaration maintained:

1. That the Pope has no authority over kings in temporal affairs.

2. That, according to the decrees of the Council of Constance, the Papal powers are limited by the Ecumenical Councils.

3. That, consequently, the exercise of Papal authority is limited by the canons of the Councils and particularly by the customs and practices of the Gallican Church.

4. That the decisions of the Pope become infallible only after they have been accepted by the Church.

This document caused a bitter dispute with the Holy See. The Pope refused to grant canonical confirmation to candidates for Bishoprics who attended the assembly. Thirty-three sees remained without Bishops. In 1687, Louis was excommunicated. When the number of vacant sees reached forty, and three Popes had remained firm against him, Louis yielded. The Declaration of the French Clergy was officially withdrawn in 1693. However, the doctrines of Gallicanism continued to be widely held and died out only very slowly.

Prussia under the Hohenzollerns.—Prussia was originally inhabited by Slavs. They resisted Christianity until the thirteenth century, when it was forced upon them by the Teutonic Knights, who colonized the region. Gradually, the German racial strain became dominant in Prussia. During the sixteenth century,

Lutheranism was introduced, and the Franconian or Protestant branch of the Hohenzollern family became the rulers of Prussia. They reigned as absolute monarchs. Early in the eighteenth century, the Hohenzollern ruler assumed the title of "King of Prussia." However, Rome refused to grant this recognition to him or to any of his successors.

The most famous of the Hohenzollern monarchs was Frederick II, also known as Frederick the Great (1740-1786). Like his predecessors, Frederick was interested above all in personal glory and territorial aggrandizement. To this end, he engaged in long and bloody wars, notably the Seven Years' War (1756-1763). He enjoyed considerable success in these wars, largely because of the incompetence and disunity of his adversaries, and was able to make important additions to his realms.

Frederick governed his country as an absolute tyrant; there were no restraints upon his power. He jeered openly at religion, thus exemplifying the contempt for supernatural principles which was so typical of this epoch. Motivated largely by the belief that religious conflicts tended to weaken the state, he issued a decree of religious toleration for all, including the inhabitants of the lands added to Prussia by conquest. The civil rights of Catholics were restricted, however, for they could hold only minor offices in the Prussian government. It must be emphasized that Frederick's support of religious toleration was born of indifference, skepticism, and selfishness, rather than of any highminded principle.

Frederick introduced various internal reforms, notably a new code for the administration of justice. One of the truly creditable acts of his long reign was his invitation to the Jesuits to come to Prussia. This invitation was extended in 1773, at a time when the Jesuits were being suppressed in Catholic countries.

Austria.—In Austria, royal absolutism was associated with Empress Maria Theresa (1740-1780), and with her son Emperor Joseph II (1765-1790). Joseph pursued an anti-clerical policy, which is sometimes referred to as *Josephism*. He interfered in ancient Church customs, even going so far as to decide how many candles should be used at Mass, and how many Masses might be said at one time in a Church. He also attempted to write sermon plans for his Priests. To satisfy his desire for an all-powerful state,

Joseph aimed to secularize the lands of the Church, and to bring the clergy and Religious Orders under his domination. Pope Pius VI paid the Emperor a personal visit in 1782 in order to dissuade him from this anti-religious program, but Joseph refused to be moved. Eventually, however, Josephism proved to be a complete failure.

Russia.—Russia remained under the sway of the Romanoff dynasty for more than three centuries—from 1613 to 1917. The most famous of the Romanoff Tsars was Peter the Great (1682-1725). When Peter ascended the throne, Russia was a very backward country and was largely Oriental in her mode of life. Peter was greatly interested in Western civilization and decided to introduce Western ideas, methods and customs in order to make Russia a great European power. He did a great deal to modernize his vast realm and to increase its influence among the nations of Europe. Unfortunately, he also used his absolute powers to interfere in religious matters. He suppressed the Patriarchate (a high office in the Greek Orthodox Church), proclaimed himself head of the Church, and appointed a Holy Synod to govern its affairs.

Poland.—In the later Middle Ages, Poland was a large and powerful state and one of the strongholds of the Catholic Faith. More than once, valiant Polish soldiers helped to defend Christian Europe against pagan invaders from the East. As late as 1683, a Polish army headed by John Sobieski played an heroic and all-important part in beating back the Turks from the very gates of Vienna.

In the eighteenth century, however, Poland was seriously weakened by a number of factors. In the first place, the country lacked racial and religious unity. Although the Poles themselves were solidly Catholic, there were four distinct racial minorities which included many members of other religions. Poland's powerful and greedy neighbors (Prussia, Austria and Russia) encouraged the disunity by playing one race against another. In addition, Poland lacked natural boundaries, such as rivers and mountains, and could easily be invaded. The government, moreover, was deplorably weak. The King was elected by the nobles and had little real authority. The nobility governed the country by means of an assembly or diet, but since a unanimous vote was required to pass any law, very little constructive action was taken.

These conditions explain why Poland was unable to resist when her neighbors began to partition her late in the eighteenth century. In 1772, Frederick the Great of Prussia, as well as the

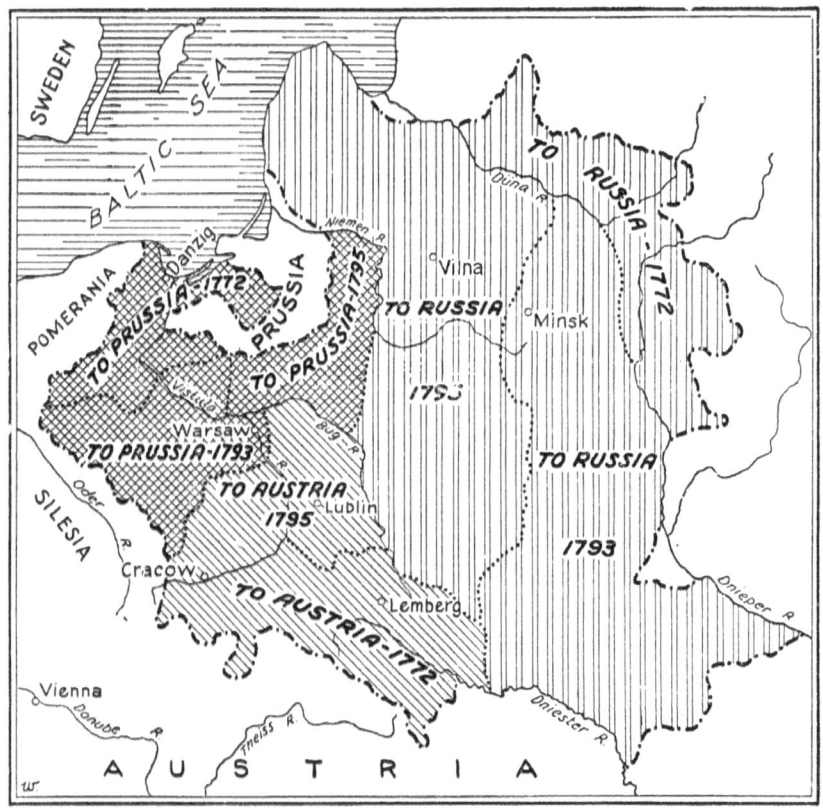

The Three Partitions of Poland.

rulers of Austria and Russia, seized about one-fourth of Poland's territory. In 1793, Prussia and Russia joined in a second partition. Finally, in 1795, the remainder of the country was divided among Austria, Russia and Prussia. Poland ceased to exist as an independent state until revived after the First World War.

Although most of Poland passed under the control of non-Catholic nations, the great majority of the Polish people clung valiantly to their Faith. Like the Irish, they suffered for their religion, and found in it a never-failing source of strength and consolation.

CHRONOLOGICAL TABLE OF PRINCIPAL EVENTS IN CHURCH HISTORY

Date	Event
1517	Martin Luther (1483-1546) began Protestantism in Germany
1519	Zwingli (1484-1531) introduced Luther's doctrines into Switzerland
1519	Charles V became Emperor—a good Catholic who opposed Protestants; ruled until 1556
1520	Luther condemned by Pope Leo X
1521	Diet of Worms (presided over by Emperor Charles V) outlawed Luther
1524	Peasants' Revolt in Germany; vast slaughter and devastation; revolt crushed
1527	Rome sacked by 40,000 Lutherans, Spaniards, Italians
1529	Diet of Spires; the term "Protestant" coined
1530	Diet of Augsburg; *Confession of Augsburg,* summary of Luther's beliefs
1534	Paul III became Pope (convoked Council of Trent in 1545); Act of Supremacy passed in England, leading to open break with Church
1539	Foundation of Ursulines by St. Angela Merici
1540	Society of Jesus received official Papal sanction
1545	Council of Trent convoked
1552	St. Francis Xavier died on island of Sancian
1553	Mary Tudor ascended throne of England; restored Catholicity, dealt harshly with Protestants; ruled until 1558
1555	Peace of Augsburg signed between Emperor Charles V and Protestant princes of Germany
1556	Death of St. Ignatius of Loyola, founder of the Jesuits
1558	Beginning of Elizabeth's reign in England; Anglican Church established; persecution of Catholics initiated
1562	Huguenot wars began in France, continuing intermittently until 1598
1563	End of the Council of Trent

DATE	EVENT
1566	St. Pius became Pope
1571	Battle of Lepanto, defeat of Turks
1572	Gregory XIII became Pope; St. Bartholomew's Day Massacre occurred; Martyrs of Gorkum met glorious deaths
1578	Treaty of Utrecht: Calvinism established in Holland; Belgium saved for Catholicity
1584	Death of St. Charles Borromeo (1538-1584), "Soul of Council of Trent"
1585	Sixtus V became Pope
1586	Jesuits began Paraguay missions
1587	Mary Queen of Scots executed by order of Queen Elizabeth
1588	*Defeat of the Spanish Armada*
1593	Henry IV of France converted, thus saving Catholicity in France
1597	Death of St. Peter Canisius, second Apostle of Germany and author of Catechism
1598	Edict of Nantes granted toleration to Huguenots in France
1603	James I, son of Mary Queen of Scots, became King of England, beginning Stuart dynasty
1618	Beginning of Thirty Years' War in Germany
1635	France, under influence of Cardinal Richelieu, entered Thirty Years' War against Catholic Austria and Spain
1648	Treaty of Westphalia ended Thirty Years' War; Protestantism saved in northern Europe, due largely to Richelieu's treason to Church
1649	Charles I of England executed and Cromwell became dictator
1660	Death of St. Vincent de Paul, Apostle of Organized Charity in Parishes; Stuarts restored to throne of England (Charles II).
1681	Founding of Christian Brothers by St. John Baptist de la Salle
1683	Poles under John Sobieski defeated Turks at gates of Vienna
1685	Louis XIV of France revoked Edict of Nantes
1725	Foundation of Passionist Fathers by St. Paul of the Cross
1732	Foundation of the Redemptorists by St. Alphonsus Liguori
1738	Freemasons condemned by Pope Clement XII
1772	First partition of Poland by Russia, Prussia, and Austria
1773	Jesuit Order suppressed by Clement XIV
1793	Second partition of Poland by Prussia and Russia
1795	Third and final partition of Poland by Prussia, Russia, Austria

SUPPLEMENTARY MATERIAL FOR UNIT V

REFERENCES

BELLOC, H., *Characters of the Reformation*
BENSON, R. H., *Come Rack; Come Rope* (a novel)
BROWNE-OLF, LILLIAN, *Sword of St. Michael* (Pius V)
CURRAN, E. L., *Great Moments in Catholic History*, pp. 64-74
DREHER, T., *Outlines of Church History*, pp. 84-108
FORNER, B. N., *Story of the Church*, pp. 201-270
GUGGENBERGER, A., *A General History of the Christian Era*, Vol. II, pp. 146-465; Vol. III, pp. 1-116
JOHNSON, G. W., HANNAN, J. D., DOMINICA, SR., *Story of the Church*, pp. 302-385
LAUX, J., *Church History*, pp. 420-521
LORTZ, J., KAISER, E. G., *History of the Church*, pp. 339-455
LUCAS, H. S., *Renaissance and Reformation*, pp. 417-765
NOVICES, *Dominican Saints*, "Pius V," "John of Cologne"
RAEMER, S. A., *Church History*, pp. 339-488
SABATINI, R., *Fortune's Fool* (a novel)
———, *Captain Blood* (a novel)
SISTERS OF NOTRE DAME, *Compendium of Church History*, pp. 117-132
SPALDING, B. J., *Church History*, pp. 503-618
WEBER, N. A., *Christian Era*, A.D. 1517 to Present, pp. 1-304
WHITE, O. B., *The King's Good Servant* (a novel about Thomas More)
———, *Late Harvest* (a novel)

QUESTIONS

1. (*a*) State five basic causes of the Protestant Revolt in Europe. (*b*) What conditions existed in Germany in the early sixteenth century which made it a particularly fertile breeding ground for heretical doctrines? (*c*) What was the immediate cause of the outbreak of the Protestant Revolt?

2. (*a*) Describe the early life and character of Martin Luther. (*b*) What was the subject matter of Luther's ninety-five theses? (*c*) Why did Luther gain the support of many princes in his dispute with the Papacy?

3. (*a*) When and by whom was the Diet of Worms convoked? (*b*) Who was summoned to appear before this Diet? (*c*) Discuss the events of the Diet of Worms.

4. (a) What is the origin of the name *Protestant?* (b) What was the *Confession of Augsburg?* (c) What was the principal provision of the *Peace of Augsburg?*

5. Summarize the life of: (a) Zwingli, (b) Calvin. Describe the heretical doctrines preached by each.

6. (a) What classes of the population of France joined the Protestant Revolt? What were these French Protestants called? (b) Describe the events leading up to the St. Bartholomew's Day Massacre of 1572. (c) State the provisions of the *Edict of Nantes*. By whom was it issued? Why? (d) Who revoked the Edict of Nantes? When did this occur? Why was this action taken?

7. (a) Why did the Netherlands revolt against Spanish rule? (b) Describe the struggle of the Netherlands against Spanish domination. (c) When, and in what treaty, did Spain finally recognize the independence of Holland? (d) Relate the story of the martyrs of Gorkum.

8. (a) Were the causes of Protestantism in England the same as on the Continent? Explain fully. (b) Why did Henry VIII seek a divorce from Catherine of Aragon? (c) How did Henry retaliate for his failure to obtain a divorce? (d) Name two famous men who were martyred for refusing to take an oath acknowledging royal supremacy over ecclesiastical matters in England.

9. (a) Describe the religious changes which took place in England during the reigns of Edward VI and Mary Tudor. (b) Why did Queen Elizabeth decide to support the Protestant Anglican Church after she had taken an oath to uphold the Catholic Faith? (c) Describe the fate of Catholics in England during the reign of Queen Elizabeth. (d) Why do historians regard the separation of England from the Church as a particularly momentous event?

10. (a) What was the doctrine of the *divine right of kings?* (b) What was the cause of the civil war which broke out in England during the reign of Charles I? (c) Name the groups which supported each side in this civil war. Who was victorious? (d) What kind of government existed in England after the close of the civil war? Who was the dominant figure in this government?

11. Discuss the life of Mary Queen of Scots. Why is her death considered a glorious one?

12. (a) Describe the nature and causes of the Thirty Years' War. (b) Summarize the principal events of this war. (c) State the provisions of the Treaty of Westphalia.

13. State six important results of the Protestant Revolt.

SUPPLEMENTARY MATERIAL FOR UNIT V

14. (*a*) What was the general purpose of the Council of Trent? (*b*) When and by whom was it convoked? How long did it last? (*c*) What were the accomplishments of the Council of Trent? (*d*) Describe the role of St. Charles Borromeo in the deliberations of the Council. (*e*) What were the effects of the Council of Trent?

15. Name the three great Pontiffs of the Counter-Reformation and state why each is an outstanding figure in the history of the Church.

16. (*a*) Relate the history of the founding of the Society of Jesus by St. Ignatius of Loyola. (*b*) What was the general purpose of this Society? (*c*) Describe the work carried on by this great organization.

17. Describe the work of the following saints of the Counter-Reformation: (*a*) Saint Francis Xavier, (*b*) Saint Angela Merici, (*c*) Saint Peter Canisius, (*d*) Saint Theresa, (*e*) Saint Vincent de Paul.

18. (*a*) What is meant by *royal absolutism*? (*b*) When did it appear in Europe? (*c*) Name three of the best-known absolute rulers. (*d*) Discuss fully the causes for the rise of royal absolutism.

19. (*a*) What was *Gallicanism*? (*b*) Who originated this movement? Why? (*c*) What were the contentions of the *Declaration of the French Clergy*? (*d*) What was the fate of Gallicanism?

20. Poland was partitioned in the eighteenth century and did not regain her independence for more than a century. Yet, the history of Poland during this period is considered a glorious one. How do you explain this?

MATCHING TEST

In the parenthesis next to each item in column **A**, *write the number of the name in column* **B** *which is most closely associated with it.*

A	B
( ) Dictator of Geneva	1. Anabaptists
( ) Issuance of Edict of Nantes	2. St. Charles Borromeo
( ) Missionary to India	3. St. Ignatius Loyola
( ) Peasants' War in Germany	4. Calvin
( ) Council of Trent	5. Henry VIII
( ) Founder of the Jesuits	6. Pope Pius V
( ) Battle of Lepanto	7. Emperor Charles V
( ) Revised Julian calendar	8. Henry IV of France
( ) Act of Supremacy	9. St. Francis Xavier
( ) Gallicanism	10. Thomas Cromwell
	11. Louis XIV
	12. Pope Gregory XIII

CHRONOLOGY TEST

Number the items in each of the following groups in the proper chronological order.

A

( ) Peasants' War
( ) Diet of Worms
( ) Calvin's dictatorship established
( ) Diet of Spires
( ) Martyrdom at Gorkum

B

( ) Peace of Augsburg
( ) Edict of Nantes
( ) Act of Supremacy
( ) Council of Trent
( ) Conversion of Henry IV

C

( ) Pope Gregory XIII
( ) Pope Sixtus V
( ) Pope Pius V
( ) Pope Paul III
( ) Pope Leo X

D

( ) Battle of Lepanto
( ) Founding of Society of Jesus
( ) Union of Utrecht
( ) Beginning of reign of Henry VIII
( ) Issuance of Luther's ninety-five theses

SELECTION TEST

In each of the following groups, select the word or phrase that **does not** apply.

1. *Leaders of Protestant Revolt:* Henry VIII, Luther, Zwingli, Charles V, Calvin.

2. *Popes of the Counter-Reformation:* Pius V, Sixtus V, Gregory XIII, Paul III, Leo X.

3. *Martyrs of the Reformation Period:* Sir Thomas More, Cardinal John Fisher, John of Cologne, John Knox, Oliver Plunket.

4. *Saints of the Reformation Period:* Ignatius of Loyola, Charles Borromeo, Pius V, Theresa of Avila, Joan of Arc, Angela Merici.

5. *Catholic Writers of the Period:* Cardinal Robert Bellarmine, Peter Canisius, Theresa of Avila, Sir Thomas More, Philip Melanchthon.

SUPPLEMENTARY MATERIAL FOR UNIT V

COMPLETION TEST

Complete each of the following sentences by supplying the correct word or phrase.

1. In 1517, a Dominican Friar named ...... came to Wittenberg, Germany, to preach an indulgence.

2. In 1519, Luther openly expressed his opposition to several Church doctrines in a famous debate with ....

3. Luther was excommunicated by Pope ...... in 1521.

4. The Tsar who began the process of modernizing and westernizing Russia was ....

5. The three countries which participated in the partitions of Poland were (a) ......, (b) ...... and (c) .... Of these three powers, only ...... was predominantly Catholic.

6. Calvin summarized his Protestant beliefs in a book called ....

7. The Pope (did, did not) ...... approve of the St. Bartholomew's Day Massacre in France.

8. The region of the Low Countries which became predominantly Protestant is now known as .... The region which remained largely Catholic is now known as ....

9. Calvinism in Scotland became known as .... The most influential leader of this heresy in Scotland was ....

10. For his brilliant defense of the Catholic Faith against Luther's heretical doctrines, Henry VIII was awarded the title ....

11. Queen Elizabeth was the daughter of Henry VIII and ....

12. The doctrines of the Anglican Church were summarized in a document known as ....

13. After the downfall of James II, in the so-called "...... Revolution," the throne of England was given to ....

14. During the Council of Trent, great Catholic scholars prepared a revised version of the Latin Bible called ....

15. The Feast of the Holy Rosary is held on October 7 of each year in commemoration of ....

UNIT VI

FROM THE FRENCH REVOLUTION TO THE PRESENT DAY

PREVIEW

THE eighteenth century witnessed the emergence of the doctrine of *free thought,* which has played a pernicious role in the history of the Church until the present day. Free thought was the logical result of the denial of the authority of the Catholic Church in religious matters. Protestants had rejected authority and demanded *personal* interpretation of the Scriptures. In the eighteenth century, large numbers of misguided individuals went even further; they rejected the Scriptures entirely and, in the place of Christianity, advocated *Deism.* The Deists (or Rationalists) believed in a personal God, whose existence and attributes were to be established by "reason" only; Christian revelation was entirely rejected. Catholic doctrine, in contrast to Deism, teaches us that reason can demonstrate the facts of revelation, and that therefore it is truly reasonable to accept these facts and all that God has told us about Himself.

In England, the Rationalists found support in Freemasonry. In France, these irreligious ideas were expounded and popularized by such brilliant but unprincipled writers as the Encyclopedists, Jean Jacques Rousseau, and Voltaire. This exaggeration of the importance of reason sowed the seeds of the French Revolution, a bloody social upheaval, during which religion became separated from the state.

The opening years of the nineteenth century were marked by the ambitions and achievements of Napoleon. Although this conqueror restored the Catholic Faith in France, the Church suffered severely because of the secularization of its property.

Freemasonry spread from England to France, and from France to the other countries of Europe. The most active and effective opponent of the Rationalists and Freemasons was the Society of Jesus. Although this holy Order had been suppressed in 1773, it was restored in 1814 by a later Pontiff.

The work of the Jesuits was aided by the efforts of gifted defenders of the Faith in all the lands of Christendom. In England, the Oxford Movement brought many brilliant men back to the Church. When the Hierarchy was restored, such figures as Cardinal Newman, Cardinal Manning, and Cardinal Wiseman inspired countless thousands by their lives and writings. Powerful orators, such as Lacordaire, helped to strengthen the Church in France. Germany's von Kettler was a pioneer in Catholic social reform. In Italy, Don Bosco introduced notable reforms in education for boys.

The twentieth century has been a period of storm and stress for the Church. Rapid, far-reaching economic and social changes have released disruptive forces and have introduced a host of new problems. However, twentieth-century Catholics have been inspired by such canonized Saints as the Curé of Ars, Bernadette of Lourdes and Therese of Lisieux, models of virtue and heavenly intercessors. Great Popes, such as Leo XIII and Pius XI, have been effective economic reformers. In recent years, there have been many noble martyrs in Spain, Russia, Germany, Poland and Mexico. Today, the Church is facing a life-and-death struggle with such organized forces of evil as Communism, Nazism and Fascism.

CHAPTER 12

THE FRENCH REVOLUTION

"The strongest and most unbalanced, in fact, the most naïve exaggeration of reason and knowledge is the characteristic feature of this philosophy which culminates in the 'religion' of reason in the French Revolution."—J. LORTZ, E. G. KAISER ("Church History")

THE BACKGROUND OF THE REVOLUTION

Nature of the French Revolution.—The French Revolution of 1789 was a terrible political and social upheaval which has exerted a far-reaching influence on all subsequent history, up to our own day. Although the Revolution was called forth, in part, by serious abuses, it soon assumed a radical character which led to the most appalling horrors and excesses. It was not until 1815, when Napoleon was finally overthrown, that the Revolutionary Era came to an end.

The French Revolution was the first instance in Europe of large-scale resistance to absolutism. Since absolutism itself was in large part the offspring of Protestantism, it can be seen that this cataclysm need never have occurred had it not been for the split in the Universal Church. Protestantism also tended to bring on the Revolution by its denial of religious authority and its emphasis on private interpretation of the Scriptures. This soon led to the undermining of all authority, civil as well as spiritual, and to the false doctrine of rationalism, which tells us that reason is supreme and solely sufficient. All these forces appeared with particular virulence in France. Thus, the Church and the King were spurned, and the rabid revolutionary mobs expressed their fury in bloodshed and destruction. Even after the close of the Revolutionary Era, the influences of rationalism and radicalism remained in France. For a century and a half, religion and authority were sneered at by a large section of the population. As a direct result of these unholy ideas, France underwent a process of internal decay that made her easy prey to Hitler's Nazi hosts in 1949. (We shall consider this further on pages 258-259.)

Causes of the Revolution.—We have mentioned above the basic, underlying cause of the French Revolution. However, there are a number of specific factors which help us to understand why the Revolution took place when and where it did, and why it assumed its peculiar character.

1. *Influence of Thinkers and Writers.*—In the eighteenth century, France produced a number of brilliant but unprincipled writers who exercised a profound influence on the thought and social life of their times. These self-styled "philosophers" sneered at all things sacred, and directed their bitterest attacks against the Catholic Church.

Perhaps the most intellectual and most harmful of these writers was Voltaire (1694-1778). Voltaire was a Deist whose chief aim was to crush the Catholic Church, which he regarded as the greatest barrier to scientific progress.

Jean Jacques Rousseau (1712-1778), one of the most popular and influential members of this radical group, attacked the Church's teachings on education and marriage in his novel *Emile*. His *Social Contract* made a powerful appeal for political reforms which would give the people a voice in the government.

Diderot (1713-1784) was the leader of an influential group of writers known as the *Encyclopedists*. (They were so-called because they collaborated in the preparation of a voluminous Encyclopedia.) The Encyclopedists made a strong appeal to various elements in France and other countries; for example, to society ladies who had an exaggerated regard for the natural sciences and disdain for the spiritual and moral precepts of religion. Diderot is quoted as expressing the hope that "the last king might be strangled with the entrails of the last priest."

All these writers, and many others whom we cannot mention, contributed to the loss of faith and moral ruin of the masses of the people, and thus were a potent cause of the Revolution.

2. *Freemasons.*—Freemasons are a secret society of a religious nature, originally organized in London, England, where their first Grand Lodge was founded in 1717. Freemasonry was introduced into France in 1725 by Lord Derwentwater. The Freemasons were, and are, a numerous and powerful society whose chief aim is the destruction of established religions, particularly the Catholic religion. The French Revolution, and every revolution in Europe in the eighteenth and nineteenth centuries, bear witness to their destructive power. Catholics may not be Freemasons. The society has been condemned by various Pontiffs, among them Clement XII in 1738, Benedict XIV in 1751, and Leo XIII in 1884.

3. *Suppression of the Jesuits.*—Voltaire declared that the destruction of Christianity would be an easy task if the Society of Jesus could first be eliminated. In 1773, the governments of France, Spain, Portugal and Naples urged Pope Clement XIV to suppress the Jesuits. The Pope finally assented, but fear rather than conviction motivated his act; he was afraid that schisms would result if he refused. Portugal had expelled the Jesuits in 1759; France in 1764; Spain in 1767; and Naples and Parma (Spanish dependencies in Italy) in 1768. Austria soon took similar action, but the infidels of Europe would be satisfied with nothing less than complete suppression. In Russia, the order of suppression was not executed; the Jesuits, with the assistance of Catherine II, were able to keep their corporate organization in that land. Frederick II of Prussia also aided them in Silesia. Elsewhere, however, 22,000 Jesuits submitted without a protest. The great majority of Catholic Bishops, Priests and laymen

bowed in grief at this unjust treatment. Their grief was fully justified, for, with the Jesuits out of the way, the destructive forces that were to bring on the Revolution were relieved of one of their most powerful adversaries. Incidentally, it should be pointed out that all the charges brought against the Jesuits at the time of their suppression have been disproved by historians.

4. *Extravagance and Financial Exhaustion.*—From the middle of the seventeenth century until the Revolution, France pursued an aggressive foreign policy that required huge expenditures for military purposes. This policy was initiated by Louis XIV (1643-1715), who fought a series of wars with the sole aim of extending the boundaries of his realms. Louis was also fantastically extravagant in his personal and social life. The "Sun King," as he was known, built a great palace at Versailles, where he lived in extreme luxury, attended by no fewer than 15,000 nobles, including members of the higher clergy. The material splendor and fastidious etiquette that prevailed here were only a cloak for shameful vices. The King and his courtiers were parasites, living in luxury and idleness at the expense of the masses of the people. As a result of Louis' military adventures and personal extravagance, the state was forced to assume huge debts.

The next King, Louis XV (1715-1774), was even worse than his predecessor. His reign was characterized by extreme wastefulness and corruption. There is a tradition that upon one occasion this King remarked "After me, the deluge"; this means that he foresaw the terrible revolutionary upheaval which was to break out in his unhappy land.

Louis XVI (1774-1792) was a good man, but dull and weak. He was not personally extravagant, but he did nothing to reduce expenditures at court, and new debts had to be incurred to meet even ordinary expenses of government.

As a result of these decades of conscienceless waste, the closing years of the eighteenth century found France on the very verge of national bankruptcy and complete economic chaos.

5. *Unfair Taxation of the Third Estate.*—Under the *Old Regime* (as the rule of the pre-Revolutionary Kings came to be known) society was divided into three classes or estates. The clergy constituted the *first estate,* the nobility the *second estate,* and all others (laborers, merchants, peasants, serfs, professional

people, etc.) the *third estate*. The bulk of the crushing taxation which the extravagances of the Kings necessitated fell on the third estate. Among the taxes were the *taille* (a land tax), the *gabelle* (a salt tax), a poll tax, and an income tax. Moreover, the peasants were liable to the *corvée*, forced labor on the roads for a few days each year, with no pay. Besides this, the Church collected its tithe, and the nobles demanded feudal dues. It is estimated that in some districts the common people paid away 80% of their incomes in taxes. The privileged classes, however, were able to avoid most of these taxes. "The system of taxation was oppressive in its nature, unjust in its distribution, and arbitrary in its collection." [1]

It is important to understand that only the *higher* clergy enjoyed the privileges of the first estate. These higher clergy usually came from noble families. The lower clergy, on the other hand, were drawn largely from the common people, and often sympathized with them against their oppressors. They worked indefatigably to help the poorer classes and were so miserably paid by the government that their economic status was usually no better than that of a peasant or laborer. At the time of the Revolution, there were in France 131 Archbishops and Bishops, 60,000 secular Priests, 23,000 Monks and 37,000 Nuns.

6. *Other Injustices.*—Under the absolutism of the Old Regime, there was no freedom of speech and press. The King could arbitrarily suppress any criticism of his rule. By means of sealed orders known as *lettres de cachet,* he could order the imprisonment of any person for an indefinite period without even preferring any charges against him or bringing him to trial.

7. *The American Revolution.*—The successful revolution in America and the establishment of a democratic government was an inspiration to the people of France. It gave them hope that they too might be able to throw off the yoke of oppression. The French were particularly interested in the success of the American Revolution because their government had aided it with men and money. Lafayette, De Grasse and Rochambeau are some of the gallant Frenchmen who helped Washington achieve a final victory.

---

[1] Guggenberger. A., *A General History of the Christian Era.*

THE RISING TIDE OF REVOLUTION

The Calling of the Estates-General and the Formation of the National Assembly.—By 1789, the financial situation in France was desperate. The need for new revenues was so great that the King finally agreed to call the Estates-General, which had not met for nearly two centuries. The assembly which convened in Paris comprised 1214 representatives (285 nobles, 308 clergy, and 621 commons). The third estate was determined to secure financial reforms and the elimination of the other abuses of the Old Regime. However, they immediately ran into a serious obstacle when an attempt was made to arrange matters so that the voting would be by estates, rather than by individuals. In other words, each estate would have one vote, and the two higher estates would thus be able to out-vote the representatives of the masses of the people. When the nobles and higher clergy refused to meet with them, the members of the third estate declared themselves a *National Assembly*. When the King's soldiers barred them from their usual place of assembly, they met at a tennis court at Versailles, and here took the famous "Tennis Court Oath" not to disband until France had a constitution.

This persistence soon had its reward. Within a week the members of the third estate were joined by almost all the clergy and by many of the nobles. The King had no choice but to recognize the National Assembly. Rumors were spread, however, that the King and his advisers were plotting to destroy the Assembly. The people were greatly excited by these reports and on July 14, 1789 a mob attacked and razed the Bastille, a royal prison in Paris. This event was regarded as a symbol of the destruction of the Old Regime, and had repercussions throughout the country. Peasants were emboldened to attack the castles of their lords. Soon the National Assembly passed a series of decrees which abolished feudal dues, serfdom, exemption from taxes, the *corvée,* and many other special privileges and abuses. The Assembly also drew up a document known as the *Declaration of the Rights of Man,* which stated the basic principles of democratic government and guaranteed certain civil liberties, such as freedom of speech and the press. (This was expressed in the

Revolutionary slogan, "Liberty, Equality, Fraternity.") The administration of the government was reorganized, and steps were taken to relieve the financial crisis.

The purpose behind many of these reforms was good, but most of them were rendered ineffective because of mob rule.

Civil Constitution of the Clergy.—In 1790, the infidels who controlled the National Assembly drew up a Civil Constitution for the Catholic Church in France. This infamous law nationalized all Church property. Parish Priests and Bishops were to be elected by the people, and the Bishops were not to seek any confirmation of their appointment from the Pope. Salaries of Churchmen were to be paid by the government. The King, who, with all his faults, was a devout Christian, signed the law under compulsion, hoping in this way to protect his family.

Early in 1791, the Assembly ordered all Bishops and Priests to take an oath to support this Civil Constitution. However, the great majority of the clergy valiantly followed the Pope, who had condemned the Constitution, and refused to obey the command of the Assembly. Of 130 Bishops, only four took the oath; of 70,000 Priests, less than 20,000 did so. The *non-juring clergy*, as those who refused to take the oath were called, exposed themselves to terrible reprisals at the hands of the civil authorities and the mob, but they remained undaunted. Thus a schism was created in France.

The Legislative Assembly.—The National Assembly finally drew up a Constitution which established France as a limited monarchy (1791). The King remained, but his powers were to be shared by a Legislative Assembly, elected by all citizens who possessed certain property qualifications. One of the first acts of this Legislative Assembly was to exile the more than 50,000 non-juring Priests. In September, 1792, there was a massacre of nobles and Priests at Paris. About 1400 were beheaded, including three Bishops and 250 Priests. This horrible crime was repeated on a smaller scale in other cities. The massacre was planned and instigated by the most radical and Godless of all the Revolutionary factions, the so-called *Jacobins*. The leaders of the Jacobins were Danton and Marat.

The Establishment of a Republic.—Many of the French nobles escaped to other countries, where they tried to enlist support for armed intervention in France in order to crush the Revolution. These *émigrés*, as the exiled noblemen were called, joined the armies of Prussia and Austria, which invaded France. The invading armies were defeated by the French forces. The monarchy, however, became more unpopular than ever, for it was widely believed that the King and his wife, Marie Antoinette, had encouraged the foreign sovereigns to form a coalition and make war on the Revolutionary government of France. As a result, the King was deposed in September, 1792, and a Republic was set up. The King was then tried for treason and was guillotined in January, 1793. Later in the same year, Marie Antoinette was also executed. The heir to the throne, an eight-year-old boy, died two years later as a result of mistreatment. His sister, Maria Theresa, was delivered to the Austrians.

The Reign of Terror.—The government of France was now entrusted to a National Convention, but the real power was in the hands of a small group of men who formed the so-called *Committee of Public Safety*. The Committee was dominated by Jacobin extremists, particularly by an atheistic fanatic named Robespierre. Robespierre instituted a Reign of Terror which lasted for several years and is believed to have cost the lives of over one million Frenchmen, who died under the guillotine. The people were led to tolerate these unspeakable outrages because during all these years France was fighting a coalition of foreign nations, and those who were sent to the guillotine were denounced as would-be betrayers of the Republic.

Robespierre's greatest hatred, however, was against the Church. Thousands of Priests were executed, and thousands of others were exiled. Even constitutional Priests (those who recognized the Civil Constitution of the Clergy) were persecuted. In 1793, the National Convention abolished Christianity. The calendar was changed by establishing a ten-day week and by renaming the months of the year; the holy feast days of the Church were replaced by Revolutionary festivals. The supreme sacrilege took place in 1793, when a vile woman, treading on the Crucifix, was borne in a procession to the Cathedral of Notre Dame. There, she was placed upon the main altar and worshipped as the "Goddess of Reason." This detestable "festival of reason" was arranged by extreme Jacobin atheists, such as Hebert and Chammette.

It must not be supposed that these desecrations met with no opposition from the people. Rebellions against Robespierre and the Convention broke out in such cities as Lyons, Marseilles and Bordeaux. The devout Catholic peasants of La Vendée, a region in western France, rose up in defense of their religion. Large armies were sent from Paris to crush this movement but the Vendeans, under such leaders as Stofflet and Charette, fought with desperate courage. Although many thousands of them were killed, the government was finally forced to grant them freedom of worship.

The End of the Reign of Terror.—In the meantime, the Reign of Terror moved on to ever madder license. Not only royalists and clergymen, but even moderate republicans were sent to their deaths. In 1794, Danton, one of the radical leaders of the Revolution, was guillotined because he opposed some of Robespierre's extreme policies. Famine added to the misery of the people, and a number of corrupt Terrorist politicians took advantage of the situation to amass huge fortunes. Finally, the people could stand the horrors of the Terror no longer. In July, 1794, Robespierre himself was sent to the guillotine. His death marked the end of the Reign of Terror.

The Directory.—After Robespierre's death, the National Convention proceeded to draw up still another constitution for France, which went into effect in 1795. This constitution set up a legislature composed of two houses, but executive authority was entrusted to a group of five men called the *Directory*. The Directory was faced by serious internal difficulties and foreign wars. Their inefficiency and corruption in the face of these problems paved the way for the rise of the military dictator, Napoleon Bonaparte, whose career we shall consider in the next chapter.

Pope Pius VI.—During the years of the French Revolution, the throne of St. Peter was occupied by Pius VI (1775-1799). Pius was a valiant and vigilant defender of the Faith. When the Revolution broke out, he realized immediately that it represented a great threat to Christianity. His worst fears were borne out by the anti-clerical measures of the Revolutionary authorities and by their bloody persecution of the clergy. Pius thus became an uncompromising enemy of the Revolution, and his moral influence was a powerful factor in the various coalitions formed to combat the Godless French government.

In 1796, a French army under Napoleon invaded Italy and, in the course of this campaign, fought against the Papal troops. Two years later, French troops actually invaded Rome and proclaimed the Papal States a republic. When Pius bravely refused to renounce his civil authority he was taken prisoner and transported to Valence, in southern France. Here he died in August, 1799. This mistreatment of the Pope was one of the blackest acts committed by the corrupt Directory.

CHAPTER 13

THE NINETEENTH CENTURY—THE CENTURY OF CONCORDATS

"His (Napoleon's) memory resembles a gigantic cliff emerging from the sea of time. The waves of calumny may break against it; the lightning's bolt of hatred may descend upon its brow; the cutting winds of sarcasm and malice may attack its surface; clouds of misunderstanding may conceal it; and even the disintegrating touch of Time may strive to mar its massiveness; but presently the waves are stilled, the tempest disappears, the cliff is there, serene and indestructible."
—J. L. STODDARD ("Lectures")

FRANCE

The Rise of Napoleon Bonaparte.—The dominating figure in Europe during the early years of the nineteenth century was Napoleon Bonaparte. He was born in 1769 of Italian parents on the island of Corsica, a French possession. Napoleon received a good military education, and soon showed that he possessed remarkable talents. He first won public recognition in 1795, when he helped the Directory crush an uprising in Paris. Although still in his twenties, he was placed in command of the French army in northern Italy, where he won brilliant victories. By 1797, he was a national hero. After an unsuccessful campaign in Egypt, he returned to France and succeeded in overthrowing the corrupt Directory (1799). He became head of the government with the title of "First Consul."

In the next few years, Napoleon fought several coalitions of European powers and won tremendous victories—victories which have gained him recognition as perhaps the greatest military genius of all times. In 1804, he assumed the title of Emperor. The French people, dazzled by his feats and weary of the turmoil of the last fifteen years, welcomed this revival of autocratic government.

When Napoleon reached the height of his power, about 1810, he was the lord of continental Europe. Vast areas had been annexed to France. Other states were mere vassals of France

Napoleon's brothers sat on the thrones of three kingdoms, including Spain. Russia, Prussia and Austria, although still independent, were unable to offer effective opposition to the Emperor. England alone remained strong and defiant. As one writer described the situation: "All the world, including his royal brothers, were to be the slaves of military France, and France, the slave of her Emperor." [1]

Napoleon's Marriages.—When Napoleon was still an obscure young officer, he had married a widow named Josephine Beauharnais. This marriage was not blessed by children. When Napoleon became Emperor, he was extremely eager to have an heir to succeed him. For this reason, he heartlessly decided to abandon Josephine, and sought the hand of Maria Louisa, Princess of Austria. Napoleon did not even seek a dissolution of the marriage bond from the Pope, the rightful authority, but forced the pliant Bishops at Paris to grant him one. He ordered the Cardinals to attend his wedding ceremony, and the thirteen who absented themselves were exiled and forbidden to wear their red robes of office. They are known in history as the "Black Cardinals." A son was born to the marriage of Napoleon and Maria Louisa. Although he is usually referred to as Napoleon II, he never ruled France and died in 1832 at the age of twenty-one.

The Concordat of 1801.—Catholicity was still firmly rooted in the hearts of the people of France. Napoleon knew this, and realized that his position would never be really secure until he was able to effect a reconciliation with the Church. Motivated largely by these considerations, he entered into negotiations with Pope Pius VII and arranged an agreement known as the *Concordat of 1801*. This agreement had the following main provisions.

1. The Church and state in France were once more united.
2. The Pope was recognized as head of the Catholic Church.
3. Bishops and other high Church officials were to be nominated by the French government, but were not to take office until their appointments had been confirmed by the Pope.
4. Parish Priests were to be appointed by their Bishops.
5. The state was to pay the salaries of Priests and Bishops.

---
[1] Guggenberger, A., *A General History of the Christian Era.*

This Concordat, which on the whole represented a notable victory for the Church, remained in force until 1905. It served as a model for various other agreements between the Church and European governments during the nineteenth century.

Conflict between the Pope and Napoleon.—The Emperor's dictatorial and unscrupulous temperament soon involved him in conflicts with Pope Pius VII. Napoleon asked the Holy Father to annul the marriage of his brother Jerome to an American (Elizabeth Patterson), so that he might be free to marry into European royalty. This Pius courageously refused to do. Later, Napoleon asked the Pope to exile English and Russian residents in the Papal States, because France at the time was at war with England and Russia. Pius, however, refused flatly to show discrimination against Catholics of any particular race or nation. Enraged at this, Napoleon seized Rome by military force. Finally, Napoleon violated the Concordat by attempting to dominate completely the selection of French Bishops. The Pope had been very patient, but this was too much; he excommunicated Napoleon in 1809. One month later, Napoleon's soldiers seized the Holy Father and held him a prisoner. The valiant Pontiff was subjected to many indignities: he was cut off completely from communication with the Church, and was even deprived of books and writing materials.

For several years Pius was forced to remain at Fontainebleau in France. By this time, however, Napoleon was meeting with military reverses. In 1813, no longer so confident of his power, the Emperor sent the Pope back to Rome. In 1815, at the battle of Waterloo, Napoleon met decisive defeat at the hands of a German and British army. The former master of all Europe was exiled to the tiny island of St. Helena. In his bitterest moment of defeat and humiliation, Napoleon asked to receive the ministrations of a Priest; with true Christian charity, Pope Pius overlooked all that he had suffered at the hands of the Emperor and granted him this favor. Napoleon died on St. Helena in 1821, reconciled with the Catholic religion.

Restoration of the Jesuits.—The above discussion has indicated the sublime courage and faith which Pope Pius VII displayed in the face of Napoleon's persecutions. In 1814, after he had returned to Rome, this Pontiff gave further proof of his sagacity by restoring the Jesuits. The Catholic world, as a whole, rejoiced. Spain, France, Italy and Switzerland eagerly welcomed back the Christian soldiers enrolled under the banner of the Society of Jesus. Some opposition, however, was shown in Portugal and Brazil, where the governmental power was then largely in the hands of Freemasons.

Summary of Napoleon's Accomplishments.—Napoleon's epoch-making career was a strange mixture of good and evil. We

have seen how, because of his boundless ambition, he bathed Europe in blood, deprived nations of their independence, defied the Church, and violated the person of the Holy Father. On the other hand, it is true that he negotiated the Concordat of 1801, which reversed the vicious anti-clericalism of the French Revolution and was to endure for more than a century. Among his other constructive achievements were the following:

1. He carried out important judicial reforms. A revised and improved legal code (the *Code Napoleon*) was put into effect.

To this day, the *Code Napoleon* remains the basis of the legal system of France, of various other nations of western Europe, and of our own State of Louisiana.

2. He set up a centralized system of governmental administration within France, which lasted until the disaster of 1940.

3. He created a sort of national board of education, known as the University of France.

4. Under his guidance, many important public works were carried out. Industry and agriculture were encouraged by the construction of roads, bridges, docks, etc.

5. He established the Legion of Honor, an honorary body to which only Frenchmen who had rendered distinguished service to the nation were to be elected.

The Congress of Vienna (1814-1815).—Even before the final downfall of Napoleon, representatives of the great powers met at Vienna to provide for the reconstruction of Europe. This assembly was dominated by Prince Metternich of Austria and by Tsar Alexander I of Russia. The astute Talleyrand strove, with considerable success, to protect the interests of defeated France.

The general purpose of the Congress of Vienna was to reëstablish the Old Regime. To this end, the rulers of France, Spain, Sardinia, and various other states were restored to their thrones. Many territorial changes were made, and a Confederation of German states was created, with Austria as the most important member. On the whole, the Congress of Vienna was opposed to the spirit of the times, and most of its work was undone in the turbulent era that followed. It did, however, perform a number of constructive acts. One of the most important of these was the restoration of the Papal States to the Church.

France after Napoleon.—The Congress of Vienna restored the Bourbon monarchy to the throne of France in the person of Louis XVIII. Louis' successor, Charles X, was overthrown by revolution in 1830. The Orleans monarchy, which followed, was overthrown in the revolutionary upheavals that swept across Europe in 1848. After this, France became a Republic (the "Second Republic"). Louis Napoleon, nephew of Napoleon Bonaparte, was elected President. But Louis, like his uncle, wished to be an absolute ruler and, in 1852, he succeeded in converting the

Second Republic into the Second Empire. He ascended the throne as Napoleon III. Napoleon ruled until 1870, when a disastrous military defeat at the hands of Prussia overthrew the monarchy. After a period of turmoil, during which the extremely radical Paris Commune was crushed, the Third French Republic was proclaimed. This government ruled France until 1940.

During all these political upheavals, the Concordat of 1801 remained in effect. To this extent, the Church was protected. France continued to suffer, however, from the after-effects of the Revolution. The spirit of skepticism and anti-clericalism was only too widespread. This manifested itself, for example, in the *Ferry Laws* (1881-1886), establishing state primary schools, in which no religious instruction of any kind was allowed and in which clergymen were not permitted to teach. Another symptom was the growth of Godless radicalism among the working class and among certain types of "intellectuals." In spite of these evil forces, Catholic France during the nineteenth century produced many great personalities, both Churchmen and laymen. We shall consider a few outstanding figures.

Louis Pasteur (1822-1895).—Louis Pasteur was undoubtedly one of the greatest biologists of all time and one of the foremost benefactors of the human race. Pasteur formulated the theory that diseases (as well as such processes as fermentation and decay) are caused by minute living things known as "microbes" or "germs." This discovery formed the basis of modern antiseptic surgery and sanitation. Pasteur used his knowledge of microbes to combat a disease which was attacking grapevines in France. In this way, he saved the wine industry, on which thousands of people depended for their livelihood. He performed a similar service for the silk industry by stamping out a disease which was affecting the silkworms. His greatest triumph, however, came when a little shepherd boy named Jupille, who had been bitten by a mad dog, was brought to him for treatment. Up to this time, any person who suffered such a bite almost always contracted the terrible disease known as rabies, or hydrophobia. Pasteur inoculated Jupille with a serum which he had developed, and the lad recovered completely. Today, as a direct result of the Pasteur treatment, rabies is almost unknown.

Pasteur was a true and ardent Christian throughout his entire life. He loved science, mankind, and above all, the Catholic Faith. He has been well called the "Apostle of Health."

Lacordaire (1802-1861).—The greatest pulpit orator of the nineteenth century was a brilliant French Dominican named Jean-Baptiste Lacordaire. His sermons drew people of all classes to Notre Dame Cathedral at Paris, and did much to restore the faith of the laity.

In 1830, Lacordaire collaborated with Robert de Lamennais, a Priest, and Charles de Montalembert, a layman, in founding a paper named *L'Avenir* ("The Future"). This paper expressed certain unsound views regarding civil questions and the relations of Church and state. Lamennais perversely refused to admit his errors, but Lacordaire submitted readily to the decision of Rome. Henceforth, he devoted his great talents solely to the task of combating skepticism and promoting the glory of God. He wrote several books, of which one of the best known is the "Life of Saint Dominic."

The Curé of Ars (1786-1859).—The man who was to win deathless glory as the Curé of Ars was born Jean Marie Vianney, the son of humble peasant parents. These good folk had implanted the Catholic faith in the hearts of their children during the dark days of the French Revolution. When Jean was only eight years old, he did missionary work among the children of his neighborhood, many of whom had been raised in ignorance of Christianity. Although he had considerable difficulty with his studies, he persisted and became a Priest at the age of twenty-nine. He was appointed to serve as *Curé* (Priest) of the village of Ars, where the faith of the people had almost died out. For thirty-eight years, he labored with inspired zeal in this obscure hamlet; his efforts to win back the people to the love of Christ met with splendid success. Although the Curé of Ars did not seek recognition for himself, his fame spread far and wide, and thousands came to hear his simple sermons and to receive the Sacraments from him. Even Lacordaire, the brilliant orator of Paris, came to listen to him and to receive his blessing. The Curé of Ars was a martyr to the confessional, where he often spent twelve hours or more daily. Pope Pius XI canonized him in 1925.

Bernadette of Lourdes.—Bernadette Soubirous was born of humble parentage in the town of Lourdes, in the French Pyrenees. As a girl, she was very devout and was accustomed to spend much time in solitude in a beautiful Grotto near the town. On February 11, 1858, when Bernadette was only fourteen years old, a vision appeared to her in this Grotto. The vision was a beautiful lady, clothed in white, with a blue sash and golden roses on her feet. Bernadette asked the lady who she was, and she replied: "I am the Immaculate Conception." The Holy Virgin appeared to Bernadette in the Grotto no fewer than eighteen times, the last vision occurring on July 16, 1858. On one of these occasions, the Virgin told Bernadette to drink the water of a spring which suddenly appeared at the foot of the Grotto. Now, the water from this spring gushes into a drinking fountain and three pools, to which about 600,000 pilgrims come annually in search of restored health. One wall of the Grotto is completely covered with crutches that have been discarded here. In the basilica above, tablets bear witness to other miracles.

Bernadette became a Sister of Charity in Nevers, France, and died in 1879, Pope Pius XI canonized her in 1933.

St. Therese of Lisieux.—One of the most beautiful characters in the recent history of the Church was St. Therese, who spent her entire life at Lisieux, in southern France. When very young, she entered the Carmelite Order and died in the convent, in 1897, at the age of twenty-four. Her life of unusual piety and sacrifice won the admiration of all who knew her. She is sometimes called the "Little Flower," because she prophesied that she would make a "shower of good deeds" fall to earth like a shower of roses. A large modern basilica has been built to her memory at Lisieux, which is visited by many thousands of pilgrims yearly.

GERMANY

German Concordats.—In the years after the downfall of Napoleon, the Catholic Church negotiated a number of Concordats with German states. (There was no National Catholic Church in Germany because political unification had not yet been achieved.) These four Concordats were: with Bavaria in 1817; with Wurtemberg, Baden and the three Hessias in 1821; with Prussia in 1821, and with Hanover in 1824. These four

Concordats differed in some details but the following basic provisions were common to all of them.

1. The Catholic Church was restored and was to enjoy full toleration.

2. The Papacy was recognized as a sovereign power by all the states concerned.

3. No support was to be given to anti-Papal or Episcopal tendencies within the Church, such as Josephism and Febronianism.

The Catholic Revival in Germany.—In the first part of the nineteenth century, there was a great revival of Catholicity in Germany. There were many outstanding Catholic achievements in literature and in art. Catholic intellectuals, among them Princess Amalie von Gallitzin, Josef von Gorres and Wilhelm Emmanuel von Ketteler, were among the most brilliant figures of the period. Such cities as Cologne, Munster, Mainz, Munich and Vienna were the centers of the movement.

The Catholic intellectuals of this period demonstrated their courage in 1838 when they united to support the Pope's decree with regard to mixed marriages. This decree ruled that when a Catholic married a non-Catholic, both parties would have to enter into a written promise to give all their children a Catholic upbringing. The Prussian government objected to this, insisting that in all such cases, boys should follow the religion of their father, and girls that of their mother. The Archbishop of Cologne resisted the Prussian government on this issue, and was arrested and thrown into prison. Josef von Gorres, a highly gifted writer, took up the cause and wrote a book entitled *Athanasius*, with which he aroused public opinion in favor of the Church. The devotion and courage of the Catholics won the day, and the Papal decree regarding mixed marriages went into effect throughout Germany.

The Unification of Germany.—The outstanding political event in Germany during the nineteenth century was the political unification of the country, under the leadership of Prussia. Previously, Germany had consisted of a large number of independent kingdoms, duchies, principalities, free cities, etc. The tendency toward unity emerged during the era of the French Revolution. Napoleon hastened the process by consolidating many of the smaller states into larger countries. Napoleon also abolished the Holy Roman Empire, which by this time was merely an empty and useless relic of the past. As stated above, the Congress of Vienna set up a German Confederation, under the leadership of Austria, but this was little more than a pretense at union.

In the years that followed the forces for unification grew stronger and stronger. Prussia supplanted Austria as the dominant state in Germany. In 1862, Otto von Bismarck was appointed Chancellor of Prussia and launched a vigorous program designed to join all the German states (except Austria) in one empire. Bismarck's instrument was military power and war. Under the leadership of the "Iron Chancellor," Prussia defeated Denmark (1864), Austria (1866), and France (1870-1871). This last and most important victory was followed by the proclamation of the German Empire at Versailles. William I of Prussia (a member of the Hohenzollern dynasty) became German Emperor. The unification of Germany under Protestant Prussia caused apprehension among many German Catholics. It was not to be long before these apprehensions were fulfilled.

The *Kulturkampf*.—The *Kulturkampf* (literally "struggle for civilization") was a struggle between the German State and the Catholic Church in Germany. In spite of the tremendous material resources of the State, the Church emerged victorious.

The first phase of the *Kulturkampf* developed when a number of German Catholics (later known as "Old Catholics") resisted the dogma of the Infallibility of the Pope, as proclaimed by the Vatican Council in 1869 (page 253). The Old Catholics remained obdurate, and were thereupon excommunicated by the Pope. The German Bishops then demanded that all Old Catholics who were employed as teachers in state educational institutions should be dismissed. This Bismarck refused to do. One of the reasons for his hostility was that he feared the influence of the Center Party, a Catholic political group which had many millions of followers.

Bismarck then adopted a policy of undisguised persecution of Catholics. The Jesuits and members of other Religious Orders were expelled from Germany. Those Bishops who refused to recognize the duty of implicit obedience to all state regulations were to have their emoluments withdrawn. In 1873, the Prussian Legislature enacted the notorious *May Laws,* which sought to give the state control over Catholic education and over the appointment and discipline of the clergy. Other states of the German Empire passed similar laws. Pope Pius IX declared these laws invalid, and the German Bishops valiantly refused to obey them. Falk, the Prussian Minister of Public Worship, resorted to force. Bishops were imprisoned and exiled; indeed, only three German Bishops continued in office throughout this entire period. More than 1700 Priests met the same fate. Other faithful Catholics were driven from their homes.

For once, however, the "Iron Chancellor" had selected an opponent stronger than himself. The Catholics adopted a policy of passive resistance to the oppression which they were suffering. The Center Party operated more vigorously than ever and made important gains under the leadership of such strong characters as Windhorst, Mallinckrodt and Reichesspeiger. Bismarck was particularly alarmed at this because he needed support to combat the Socialists, who were growing in numbers. Finally, in 1878, Bismarck virtually acknowledged his defeat; most of the anti-Catholic legislation was withdrawn, and the persecution of Priests ceased. Gradually, all the obnoxious laws were repealed. In 1890, two years after William II became Emperor, Bismarck was dropped as Chancellor and full toleration for Catholics was insured.

Bishop von Ketteler (1811-1877).—One of the outstanding German Catholics during the period of the *Kulturkampf* was Bishop Wilhelm Emmanuel von Ketteler. He was born to a noble family and obtained a position with the government. He was dissatisfied with this, however, resigned his position, and entered the Priesthood. He rose to the Bishopric of Mainz; in this office, he was the precursor of Pope Leo XIII in supporting social reforms in favor of the poor working people. Bishop Ketteler was one of the most ardent and fearless of the Catholic leaders in the *Kulturkampf*. Although he did not live to witness the great victory over Bismarck in 1878, he deserves much of the credit for this victory. He also led the fight of the Catholic Center Party against the Socialists, supporters of an anti-religious program of economic reform. Bishop Ketteler was one of those who were in opposition to the proclamation of the dogma of Papal Infallibility at the Vatican Council of 1869. When the dogma was officially proclaimed, however, this great Churchman gave it his loyal support.

ITALY

Background of the Roman Question.—During the first part of the nineteenth century, Italy, like Germany, was divided into a number of separate states. Among these was the Papal States. Austria ruled over several million Italians in the provinces of Lombardy and Venetia, and Austrian princes sat on the thrones of Parma, Tuscany and Modena.

The Austrian rule of Italian territory and the disunity were intolerable to Italian patriots, who wished to see their country free, united and strong. This desire was natural and laudable. Unfortunately, in attempting to achieve unity, the political leaders trampled on the rights of the Papacy and caused a bitter quarrel between the Italian government and the Popes which was not settled until 1929. This quarrel is known in history as the "Roman Question."

Early Attempts at Italian Unification.—Italian patriots formed a secret society known as the *Carbonari* ("charcoal burners"). In 1820 and 1830, the *Carbonari* tried to stage revolts against the Austrians, but these uprisings were easily crushed. In 1831, a talented leader named Mazzini organized the Young Italy Society. This organization directed a formidable rebellion against Austria, which broke out in 1848. In the course of this rebellion, a national assembly set up at Rome abolished the temporal authority of the Pontiff and clerical superintendence of the schools; Church property was confiscated. Pope Pius IX fled to Gaeta in the Kingdom of Naples. French, Spanish and Austrian troops soon restored Papal sovereignty and crushed the revolutionists throughout Italy; this foreign intervention, however, created a spirit of tension and resentment that boded ill for the future.

Unification and Conflict with the Church.—After the unsuccessful revolution of 1848, the Kingdom of Sardinia was the dominant Italian state and the center of the nationalist movement. The Sardinian King, Victor Emmanuel II, and his able Prime Minister, Cavour, set about the task of unification determinedly. They formed an alliance with France, and then drove the Austrians out of part of northern Italy. Popular uprisings against the Austrian rulers took place in Parma, Modena and Tuscany. Garibaldi led a military expedition which conquered Naples and Sicily. As a result of these steps, the Kingdom of Italy was proclaimed in 1861, with Victor Emmanuel II as King. In 1866, by joining with Prussia in a victorious war against Austria, Italy gained additional territory in the north.

Although a section of the Papal States had become part of the Italian Kingdom in 1860, Rome itself remained under the control of the Popes. This was made possible by the support of the French Emperor, Napoleon III, who maintained troops in the Holy City. In 1870, however, the Franco-Prussian War broke out, and Napoleon withdrew all his troops from Rome. The soldiers of Victor Emmanuel thereupon took possession of the city. Pope Pius IX refused to surrender his temporal powers. Although he could not resist the Italian Kingdom by physical force, he delivered a powerful moral protest by making himself the "Prisoner of the Vatican." For the remainder of his life, he refused to set foot outside the Vatican. This policy was followed by the successors of Pius IX until 1929 (page 260).

Don Bosco (1815-1888).—One of the most beautiful characters who lived in Italy during the nineteenth century was a simple Priest named Don Bosco. Don Bosco had not only a singularly pure heart but also great practical ability which he devoted to the task of furthering educational opportunities for poor boys. He began this work alone, but was soon joined by other Priests, whom he organized into an Order known as the *Salesian Fathers*. The Salesians were pioneers in modern vocational training. They devoted their labors to the poor, to rural communities, to evening schools for workmen, and to seminaries for those who wished to enter the Priesthood comparatively late in life. They accomplished a vast amount of good throughout the world. Don Bosco was canonized in 1934.

ENGLAND AND IRELAND

Catholic Emancipation in Britain.—For centuries after the establishment of the Church of England (Anglican Church), Catholics were persecuted in Britain and were made to suffer various legal disabilities. It was not until 1792 that Catholics were given the right to vote. Catholics still could not sit in Parliament, however, because all members of Parliament were required to take an oath of fidelity to the Anglican Church.

In spite of this, the Catholics of County Clare in Ireland elected a sturdy champion of Catholic rights, Daniel O'Connell, as their representative in Parliament. O'Connell was not seated in Parliament because he refused to take the outrageous oath required of him. He was reëlected, and this time Parliament did seat him. In 1829, largely as a result of O'Connell's hard fight, the *Catholic Emancipation Act* was passed; this made it possible for Catholics to sit in Parliament without taking an oath of fidelity to the Anglican Church.

Disestablishment of the Anglican Church in Ireland.—The Anglican Church was also the established Church in Ireland, where the overwhelming majority of the population was Catholic. Irish peasants were taxed to support the Anglican Church. In 1838, legislation was passed to relieve the peasants of this utterly unjust tax burden. Landlords, however, continued to pay this tax until 1869, when the Anglican Church in Ireland was disestablished.

The Oxford Movement and Cardinal Newman.—About 1835, a group of students and faculty members at Oxford University began the publication of a series of papers called *Tracts for* *the Times*. These papers dealt with religious and moral questions, and criticized severely the shallow materialist philosophy which was then widely accepted in England. The outstanding member of these Tractarians (as the members of the Oxford Group were called) was a young Episcopalian clergyman and professor named John Henry Newman. He wrote *Tract 90*, the most famous of these papers, in which he expressed some ideas rather disquieting to the authorities of the Church of England. The criticism which he aroused led Newman to a careful consideration of basic issues, and in 1845 he was converted to Catholicity. Soon he had many hundreds of followers. In 1849, he was ordained a Priest and in 1879, after thirty years of noble religious activity, Pope Leo XIII made him a Cardinal.

Cardinal Newman had a great mind and a truly beautiful character. He was a master of English prose and will always be remembered for his inspiring autobiography, *Apologia pro Vita Sua,* and for his noble addresses in *The Idea of a University.* He also wrote splendid poems such as *Dream of Gerontius,* and the well-known hymn *Lead Kindly Light.*

Restoration of the Hierarchy in England.—In 1850, Pope Pius IX decided to reëstablish the Hierarchy in England. He appointed Cardinal Wiseman Archbishop of Westminster, and set up eight Bishoprics with English titles. There was considerable opposition to this restoration among English Protestants, but Cardinal Wiseman, with great dignity and brilliant pen, subdued all unjust protests. Soon, colleges, seminaries, schools, hospitals, and various other charitable and religious institutions were founded. Converts, including many distinguished persons, came back to the Catholic Faith by the hundreds and thousands. Today, the legal and social position of the Catholics in England is one of absolute equality with the rest of the population. All **public offices (except that of King) are open to Catholics. Catholic** converts, including such brilliant writers **as Gilbert K. Chester**ton and Maurice Baring, have established **a new school of litera**ture.

OTHER NATIONS OF EUROPE DURING THE NINETEENTH CENTURY

Holland.—In 1814, Holland adopted a constitution which established religious freedom, but anti-Catholic discrimination continued. In 1853, the Catholic Hierarchy was restored to Holland. For the remainder of the century, Catholics in this country enjoyed full civil and religious rights.

Belgium.—After the final overthrow of Napoleon in 1815, Catholic Belgium was joined to Protestant Holland. This union was extremely distasteful to the Belgians and, in 1830, they set up an independent government. In 1839, the Great Powers recognized the independence of Belgium and signed a covenant which made the country a neutralized state. This meant that they agreed never to make war against Belgium, and never to send troops into Belgian territory.

After the winning of national independence, Freemasons became very active in Belgium. They attacked Catholic educational institutions, and for a time Catholics who wished their children to have a religious education had to pay taxes both for their own schools and for the state schools. In 1884, however, the Catholics gained control of the government, and retained it until 1914. Under this Catholic administration, Belgium revised its constitution and adopted universal manhood suffrage (1893).

Poland.—Throughout the nineteenth century, most of Catholic Poland was under the rule of Russia. The devout Polish people suffered severe persecutions at the hands of the Greek Orthodox Tsars. Attempts at rebellion in 1831, and again in 1863, were suppressed with much savagery.

Spain.—Spain during the nineteenth century continued to be a stronghold of true Catholicity. Freemasons and radicals, however, were active and tried to combat Christianity in various ways.

Austria-Hungary.—The Congress of Vienna, which undertook the reconstruction of Europe after the final defeat of Napoleon, was controlled largely by the Austrian Chancellor, Prince Metternich. For many years thereafter, Austria was the dominant state on the Continent. However, the mixture of races living within the boundaries of this nation was a serious source of weakness.

The Hungarians, in particular, were strongly nationalistic and made several attempts to gain their independence. In 1867, after Austria had suffered a crushing military defeat at the hands of Prussia, Emperor Franz Josef granted the Hungarians a considerable measure of self-government under an arrangement known as the "Dual Monarchy of Austria-Hungary." This Austro-Hungarian Empire lasted until the World War of 1914-1918, when it was broken up into many small fragments.

The Austro-Hungarian Empire was 95% Catholic. Among the many minorities, however, was a good-sized group of Prussian Protestants, who proved most troublesome. In 1855, a Concordat was arranged between Rome and Austria. The influence of the Protestants and other groups rendered the Concordat ineffective, and it was abrogated in 1874. The Catholics then organized politically to protect their religious interests. Under the Dual Monarchy established in 1867, the Catholic Faith flourished in Hungary.

Scandinavia.—There were very few Catholics in the countries of Scandinavia during the nineteenth century. Those who did live there sometimes suffered discrimination of various types.

POPES OF THE NINETEENTH CENTURY

Pius VII (1800-1823).—Pius VII, as we have already seen, was made to suffer severe trials at the hands of the unscrupulous Napoleon. He negotiated the Concordat of 1801 which did much to protect the Catholic people of France in the exercise of their Faith; but even after this, interference with religious education and clerical discipline continued. After the fall of Napoleon, Pius VII resumed his rule over the Papal States, which were restored to the Church by the Congress of Vienna (1815). The Pope became extremely active in negotiating other Concordats designed to undo the damage caused by the Napoleonic wars and by Freemasonry. This Pontiff also is noted for the encouragement and help he gave to Religious Orders engaged in teaching.

Leo XII (1823-1829).—Leo XII also negotiated Concordats advantageous to the Papacy. During his reign, he reduced taxes and instituted various financial reforms.

THE CENTURY OF CONCORDATS

Pius VIII (1829-1830).—During his short reign, Pius VIII directed his attention to the problem of the education of children of mixed marriages in Germany. This matter was carried to a successful conclusion by his successor, Gregory XVI.

Gregory XVI (1831-1846).—Gregory XVI had to cope with the nationalist movement in Italy, which threatened the existence of the Papal States. This Pope vigorously opposed such leaders of the Italian unification movement as Mazzini and Garibaldi (page 247). There was considerable turmoil during these years, but when Gregory died, the Papal States was enjoying material security, and the societies of the Italian revolutionists were being suppressed. Gregory is also noted as a patron of learning and as a builder of many noble monuments in Rome.

Pius IX (1846-1878).—This Pontificate of thirty-two years is the longest in the history of the Church and ranks among the most memorable. During the reign of Pius IX, the Hierarchy was reëstablished in England and in Holland. Concordats were signed with all the Christian states of the Eastern and Western Hemispheres. On December 8, 1854, the dogma of the Immaculate Conception of the Blessed Virgin was proclaimed as an article of faith. This proclamation actually taught nothing new, for Christians had always believed in the Immaculate Conception. However, the proclamation was most opportune for it affirmed a truth in clear terms and made it an article of faith in an age when the Church was reviving from the infidelity of the eighteenth century.

In the *Syllabus* of 1864, Pius condemned many of the errors of the age and claimed the complete independence of the Church from state control.

The crowning event of Pius' reign was the Twentieth Ecumenical Council, which convened in Rome on December 8, 1869 and closed on October 20, 1870. The Council was attended by 719 representatives, including almost three-fourths of all the Bishops in the world. Doctrinal matters were defined, proving the harmony between reason and revelation and between faith and science. Atheism, pantheism, materialism and rationalism were condemned. The most important business of the Council, however, was the proclamation of the dogma of Papal Infallibility in a Bull entitled *Pastor aeternus*. We have already seen that this dogma aroused considerable opposition, especially in Germany. Some of the delegates opposed it during the discussions, believing it to be premature. However, all but two Bishops voted for it finally. It must be understood that the Pope claims infallibility as the head of the Universal Church; and that the infallibility extends only to matters of faith and morality which the Pope teaches *ex cathedra* (that is, in his official capacity).

We have already considered the relations of Pius IX with Germany during the *Kulturkampf* (page 245), and with the Kingdom of Italy (page 247).

Leo XIII (1878-1903).—Leo XIII stands out as one of the greatest Popes of modern times. "Throughout a quarter of a century," comments one writer, "Pope Leo proved himself on every occasion an accomplished diplomat, a polished scholar, a profound thinker, a friend of the laboring class, and a holy man." [2] He is most noted, perhaps, for his many constructive recommendations regarding economic reforms to benefit the working classes. For this reason, he is often referred to as the "Workingman's Pope." He dealt with these matters in a number of encyclicals, of which *Rerum novarum,* issued in 1891, was the most influential. Among the reforms advocated were old-age pensions, factory laws for children, a minimum wage in some industries, and other social innovations which have become realities in our generation.

During his Pontificate, Leo improved diplomatic relations with Germany, France, Poland, Russia, Japan and the United States, thus gaining important advantages for the Church. The *Kulturkampf* in Germany was finally settled by his skillful efforts (page 246). Largely through the influence of Pope Leo, Thomistic philosophy was restored to prominence and the writings of St. Thomas Aquinas became official texts in colleges and seminaries. Under his direction, also, fruitful missionary activities were carried out.

---

[2] Raemer, S. A., *Church History.*

CHAPTER 14

FAITH VERSUS UNBELIEF IN TWENTIETH-CENTURY EUROPE

"There is every reason to believe that there are more martyrs now for the Christian faith in a single year than during any twenty-five years of the Roman persecutions of the first three centuries."—BISHOP FULTON J. SHEEN "Communism and the Conscience of the West," 1948)

CHARACTER OF THE TWENTIETH CENTURY

A Period of Turmoil.—The twentieth century, thus far, has been a period of great turmoil. Although science has made extraordinary progress in mastering our physical environment, the destructive spiritual forces abroad in the world have prevented the nations from living in peace and happiness. Thus, we find that the twentieth century is characterized by class struggles, economic depressions, revolutions, social unrest, and above all, war. The world has been ravaged in this century by two global wars, and a third threatens as Communist aggression seeks new victims. All these upheavals are a symptom of an even more fundamental conflict—the conflict between faith and Godless unbelief. Fifty million Catholics are now suffering persecution.

Types of Government.—The Catholic Church does not regard any particular type of government as necessarily or unqualifiedly superior to all others. As one Catholic writer expresses it: "The salvation of the world does not depend on the form its government may take but on a return to those eternal principles of truth and justice without which there can be no lasting peace."[1] None the less, the Catholic Church encourages patriotism and teaches full respect for duly established temporal authorities.

---

[1] Forner, B. N., *The Story of the Church*.

In the world today, we find two basic forms of political authority which are directly opposed to each other—*democracy* and *dictatorship*. In the totalitarian states, a dictator is invested with supreme power in both temporal and spiritual matters. Stalin is the dictator of Communist Russia, together with its satellites—Hungary, Poland, Lithuania, Rumania, Czechoslovakia, and Soviet Germany. Communist Yugoslavia, under the dictatorship of Tito, has revolted against Stalin but is persecuting the Church. Mao Tse-tung's Red China offers exile or house arrest to foreign missionaries, and attempts to organize a National Church. Two other dictators, Mussolini of Fascist Italy and Hitler of Nazi Germany, met violent and inglorious deaths in 1945. These totalitarian tyrants had been guilty of the most brutal cruelty and disregard of human rights.

The only large nations which have democratic governments today are Great Britain (including the Dominions), France, and the United States. Smaller democratic nations include Sweden, Switzerland and Eire (Ireland). Democracy rests on self-government by the people and guarantees certain inalienable rights to all men, including freedom of worship.

There are a number of nations which cannot be adequately described as either totalitarian or democratic. The Franco regime in Spain, for example, inclines toward totalitarianism, but it is still an experiment and differs in many respects from Italian Fascism or German Nazism. (Some writers refer to Spain as an *authoritarian* state.) Similarly, the governments of Latin America are democratic in form, but some of them have totalitarian tendencies.

The Second World War.—The Second World War began on September 1, 1939, when German forces invaded Poland. Although Great Britain and France immediately declared war on Germany, they could offer no substantial assistance to the hard-pressed Poles. On September 17, Soviet Russia invaded Poland from the east. The Polish armies fought gallantly but they were overwhelmed by larger, better equipped forces. After the fall of Warsaw, Poland was partitioned between Germany and Russia. This was a hard blow for the Catholic Church.

In April, 1940, Germany attacked and soon overpowered Denmark and Norway. These small countries were the victims of aggression and internal treachery.

Up to this point, Italy had not taken part in the war. Pope Pius XII and the democratic governments, including the United States, pleaded with Mussolini, the Italian dictator, to keep out of the conflict. They warned him that entering the war on the side of Germany would mean only misery and ruin for Italy. Mussolini, however, disregarded all warnings and appeals; in June, 1940, he declared war on Great Britain and France.

German forces, violating the neutrality of Belgium, Holland, and Luxemburg, marched into France, and soon crushed all organized French resistance. France surrendered and became a vassal of the Nazi conquerors.

In September, 1940, Japan formed an alliance with Germany and Italy. The treacherous Japanese attack on Pearl Harbor (December 7, 1941) brought the United States into the war on the side of the Allies.

American forces played a major part in the defeat of the Germans in North Africa in the spring of 1943. Then, with British assistance, they invaded Sicily and later crossed over onto the Italian mainland (September, 1943). The unbroken string of military disasters led to the fall of Mussolini and his imprisonment by the Italians. The new Italian government, led by Marshal Badoglio, repudiated its alliance with the Germans and signed a truce with the Allies. In October, 1943, Italy declared war on Germany, joining the Allies as a "co-belligerent."

German forces invaded Italy from the north and occupied Rome. A major campaign was shaping up on the Italian peninsula. President Franklin D. Roosevelt issued a message to Rome, promising to respect the neutrality of Vatican City and to do everything possible to preserve the Catholic treasures of Rome. On July 19, 1943, however, a suburb of Rome near a railroad station was bombed, causing damage to the Basilica of San Lorenzo. A month later, the district of San Giovanni was bombed. On November 5, 1943, there was an explosion within Vatican City, attributed to Mussolini's Fascists. These ordeals, however, were soon to come to an end. On June 4, 1944, while all Rome prayed, the Allies entered the city victoriously, while the Nazi invaders fled. The Eternal City remain undamaged throughout this critical period.

Meanwhile, Hitler had turned on his fellow-dictator Stalin and staged a vast invasion of Russia (June, 1941). Many bitter battles were fought on Soviet soil. In February, 1943, the Germans suffered a major defeat at Stalingrad. Then the Soviet forces counter-attacked and drove the Germans westward.

In June, 1944, the Allies invaded France across the English Channel. Desperate German efforts could not prevent the Allies from landing or halt their surge eastward. Soon all of France was liberated. German resistance was weakening fast, and in the spring of 1945 it collapsed completely. On May 8, 1945 (V-E Day), the war in Europe was declared ended. Hitler was believed to be a suicide in the ruins of Berlin, and most of the other Nazi leaders were either killed or captured.

The war in the Pacific was not yet over. However, on August 6, 1945, an atomic bomb, the first used in warfare, was dropped on the city of Hiroshima, doing terrible damage there. Two days later, a second bomb obliterated a large part of Nagasaki. This led to the unconditional surrender of Japan, announced by President Truman on August 14, 1945. General Douglas MacArthur became the commander of the United States occupation forces in Japan and served in that capacity until 1951.

Catholics played a major part in every phase of the war effort of the United States during World War II. Approximately 24% of all the men and women in the Armed Forces were of the Catholic faith. There were 3036 Catholic chaplains serving in the Armed Forces, of whom 83 died in service.

FRANCE

Anti-Catholic Legislation.—During the twentieth century the insidious anti-clerical spirit which had been present in France since the Revolution continued and grew bolder. This was shown in 1905, when the Franch government set aside the Concordat of 1801, without even consulting Rome. Under this Separation Act, the state ceased to take part in the appointment of Priests and Bishops, and also discontinued financial payments to the Church. Pope Pius X rejected this high-handed and unfair law.

In 1907, the French government passed another law which stated that while the clergy might continue to use churches and other religious edifices, the ownership of these buildings resided in the state, not in the Church. The anti-Christian spirit of the legislators was shown in a provision that no religious sign or emblem might be added to any public building or monument.

We have already seen that the Ferry Laws of 1881-1886 restricted the right of the clergy to teach (page 241). In 1901, an *Associations Act* provided that no religious order would be allowed to exist in France without a government permit, and that only authorized orders might maintain schools. In 1904, another law decreed that after ten years, no member of any religious association would be permitted to teach. As a result of these infamous laws, thousands of Catholic schools were forced to close.

The Conquest of France.—In spite of this anti-Catholic legislation, Christian faith burns high in the hearts of the masses of the French people during the twentieth century. The French clergy is second to none in its ardor and ability. Before 1940, Catholic newspapers, youth organizations, charities, etc., were very active, and there was a Catholic political party (the *Action Libérale Populaire*) with a large following.

None the less, the insidious forces of Godless skepticism and anti-clericalism were undermining the moral foundations of France. This was made evident in many different ways: the existence of radicalism in the government; the appearance of Communist and Fascist groups openly calling for bloody revolution; the sneering contempt for religion evinced by many so-called "intellectuals"; the power of Freemasonry; the low moral tone of certain phases of French social life. This spiritual collapse, in large measure, explains the military collapse of France when attacked by Hitler's army in 1940.

After this defeat, France was under the Nazi heel and went through a period of terrible travail. In this time of suffering and humiliation, the people of France turned again to Mother Church for solace and for guidance.

The Liberation of France.—We have already noted how the Allied forces invaded France in June, 1944 and drove out the Nazi conquerors. A new French government, the Fourth Republic, was formed. Although the forces of Communism and anti-clericalism have remained active in France, there is abundant evidence that the Church is experiencing a spring-like revival of faith in Catholic Action. A good book dealing with this theme is *Mission to the Poorest* by M. R. Loew (Sheed-Ward, 1950).

GERMANY

The Position of the Church before 1933.—During the early part of the twentieth century, the Catholic Church in Germany was hampered by laws which invaded religious rights. Attempts were made by the state to curtail the Church's power over marriage, education and other similar matters. The Church, naturally, protested vigorously and with some success.

After Germany's defeat in the First World War, the rule of the Hohenzollerns over the Empire came to an end. A Republic was declared. Under this so-called Weimar Republic, some of the earlier grievances of the Church remained, but on the whole there was religious toleration. The Catholic Center Party was a potent force in politics.

The Hitler Dictatorship.—In 1933, Adolf Hitler, leader of the National Socialist (Nazi) Party came to power. Hitler immediately instituted one of the most ruthless dictatorships that mankind has ever known. His aim was to de-Christianize Germany, to make of it a nation devoted only to brute power and to the fulfillment of his unholy ambitions. These ambitions were nothing more or less than the conquest of the world, and the substitution of paganism for Christianity throughout Europe, the Western Hemisphere, and any other regions he might be able to dominate.

Hitler began by trying to crush all opposition within Germany, religious, political and social. Those who dared oppose him were subjected to dreadful tortures. In spite of this reign of terror, many faithful Catholics asserted openly that their duties to the state did not transcend their duties to God; and that they could not recognize Hitler's right to dominate all education, to persecute minorities, such as the Jews, and to interfere with such sacred institutions as the family. Because of this valiant stand, Catholic clerics and laymen were persecuted with a savagery that had not been seen in Europe since the days of the Protestant Reformation. Out of approximately 20,000 Priests in Germany during the Nazi era, Hitler's minions killed, imprisoned, exiled, or otherwise persecuted 14,364. There were 885 separate instances of attacks by Nazi agencies on Catholic churches; and a total of 140 churches were desecrated. The number of martyrs is yet to be ascertained. (Figures from *The Register*, Denver, Colo., June 22, 1951.)

Hitler and World War II.—As soon as Hitler had built up a powerful military machine, he began a program of ruthless military aggression. His first conquest, in 1938, was Austria, one of the states carved out of the old Austro-Hungarian Empire after World War I. Most of Austria's population was Catholic, and the people suffered severely under the Nazi heel. Even Cardinals were subjected to indescribable indignities. Later in 1938 and in 1939, Germany absorbed most of Czechoslovakia.

We have already described how Hitler's attack on Poland in September, 1939 was the immediate cause of World War II. For a time, the Nazi forces swept everything before them, and seemed to be well on the way toward realizing Hitler's evil dreams of world conquest. Then, gradually but inevitably, the tide turned. By May, 1945, the mighty Nazi armies were fleeing in wild disorder on every front, and the great cities of Germany lay in ruins as a result of Allied bombardment. Hitler's career came to an ignominious end by suicide, and Germany surrendered.

Occupied Germany.—Under the Allied occupation, the Church in Germany is reviving, except in the Soviet (eastern) zone, where persecution is the order of the day. One of the great problems with which the Church has had to cope in Germany is the influx of refugees. Under the Potsdam Agreement of 1945, Russia was authorized to send back into German territory certain German ethnic (racial) groups living in Poland, Czechoslovakia, Hungary, Rumania, East Prussia, and Pomerania. This was done in the most inhumane manner by mass expulsion. Also, many Germans voluntarily fled the Russian zone of Germany. In all, about 12 million refugees swarmed into West Germany (occupied by the United States, Great Britain, and France), although this region was still suffering severely from the aftermath of the war. Many of these newcomers were Catholics. Thus, today it is estimated that Germany's total population of 65 million includes about 20 million Catholics.

The exiled Catholics (known as *Diaspora Catholics*) did not receive a very warm reception in the predominantly Protestant regions of North Germany. There were no homes, schools, or churches available for them. However, the Church has labored mightily to attend to the spiritual and material needs of the newcomers. A total of 6400 Mass stations have been set up, often in a Lutheran Church or a school building. In many cases, a Priest will celebrate four Sunday Masses in four different stations located many miles apart. Catholics prepare each place with clean linens and fresh field flowers, as symbols of the people's love of God. Cardinal Frings has allotted 31,000 acres of land as sites for homes to be erected by Catholic building organizations. In 1950, there were still about 8,500,000 refugees in Western Germany.

The Church in Germany has not only been shouldering this vast responsibility of caring for refugees but also has been sending forth missionary workers, chiefly to South Africa. In 1950, Germany had about 7500 individuals engaged in missionary work, as compared to 8019 before the war.

JAPAN

Japan's Defeat in World War II.—Trusting in the might of Germany, Japan attacked the United States at Pearl Harbor, Hawaii, on December 7, 1941. For a time after this attack, Japan was able to spread destruction and terror throughout southeast Asia and the islands of the western Pacific, but the tide of battle soon turned against her, as the greater resources of the United States began to tell. The use of the atomic bomb in August, 1945 led to Japan's unconditional surrender.

Japan Under American Occupation.—United States occupation forces moved in under the leadership of General Douglas MacArthur, who remained as Supreme Commander until 1951. These have been fruitful years for Christianity in Japan. The Japanese Diet (parliament) has allotted funds to build a university at Hiroshima, as a symbol of peace. Prominent Buddhists have requested the Jesuits to erect a palace of prayer as a memorial of World War II. The Franciscan Adoration Monastery of Cleveland, Ohio will provide perpetual adoration. These are concrete instances of a nationwide revival of Catholicity in Japan.

In 1951, the Sisters of the Presentation, a community of native Japanese received final approval from the Holy See. The order was founded by Rev. Albert Breton of the French Foreign Missionary Society, a retired Bishop of Fukuoka (Japan). He was recuperating in California at the time, so that the place of foundation was in the United States. A house was established in Tokyo in 1921. The Motherhouse is now in Kamakura.

In 1956, there were a total of 185,284 Catholics in Japan, with 1144 Priests, of whom 292 were natives. There were 3349 Sisters, of whom 2464 were natives; and 334 Brothers, of whom 228 were natives.

> NOTES: On August 3, 1951, six Japanese novices made their first vows at the Dominican Novitiate in Sendai. This was the first such Dominican ceremony in Japan. The Order previously had several Japanese members, but they made their Novitiates abroad.
>
> Seven Japanese of the Franciscan Order made their solemn vows recently at the Franciscan monastery at Urawa. Three other Japanese have been preparing for the priesthood at a Carmelite monastery in France.

ITALY

The Settlement of the Roman Question.—Benito Mussolini became dictator of Italy in 1922. He instituted a form of totalitarian government called *Fascism*. A great deal of friction developed between this government and the Papacy, but since the Italian people were almost all devout Catholics, Mussolini was forced to respect the rights of the Church. In 1929, Pope Pius XI and the Italian government settled the vexing Roman Question (page 248), by negotiating the *Lateran Treaty*, as well as a Concordat and a financial agreement. The Italian government acknowledged the complete sovereignty of the Papacy and recognized Vatican City as an independent state. Catholicity was declared to be "the sole religion of the state," and the state was to continue to pay the salaries of the clergy. Important rights of the Church were guaranteed with regard to marriage and education. The government also agreed to compensate the Papacy for the loss of revenues from the city of Rome since 1870. On the other hand, the Papacy recognized the legal right of the Kingdom of Italy to the city of Rome.

Conflict with the Church.—During the years of Fascist rule of Italy, Mussolini violated both the spirit and the letter of the Concordat of 1929. For example, he imposed certain restrictions on marriage on the basis of race. He also interfered with religious education and showed in various other ways that he wished his totalitarian state to be supreme over the Church. The Church, although anxious for amicable relations with the Italian government, refused to sanction such violations of its rights.

Postwar Italy.—We have already referred to Italy's unfortunate entry into World War II, her military reverses, the overthrow of the Fascist regime, and her re-entry into the war on the side of the Allies. Mussolini was "rescued" by the Nazis from his Italian jailers and announced the formation of a "government in exile," headed of course by himself.

With the collapse of Nazi resistance in the spring of 1945, Mussolini attempted to flee to Switzerland, but he was captured and shot by a group of Italians. His corpse was thrown into the streets of Milan, and thousands of his former victims fought for a chance to subject the mortal remains of the *Duce* to indignities. As the magazine *America* stated in an editorial at the time (May 12, 1945): "It is scarcely possible that any of Fascism's victims was as degraded in death as the founder of Fascism himself."

With the coming of peace, Italy turned to the job of reconstruction. In a national referendum (June, 1946), the people voted to end the monarchy and to become a republic. In February, 1947, the Allies signed a peace treaty with the Republic of Italy. Under the new constitution, Catholicism is the state religion and is the only one receiving state support. Religious education is required in the elementary and secondary schools.

Communism, however, is very strong in poverty-stricken Italy, and a bitter struggle has been taking place between the Communist Party and anti-Communist forces under the leadership of the Church. In 1948, there was a critical election for the National Assembly (parliament) of Italy. The Communists were determined to win and waged an aggressive campaign, making all sorts of wild accusations and fantastic promises to the poorer classes. The Church stood firm against this unscrupulous propaganda, Pope Pius XII warning his beloved fellow-citizens of the dangers of Communism. The United States government made it clear that we would not be able to continue our aid to Italy if a Communist regime came into power. Also, many Americans of Italian descent wrote to their relatives and friends in Italy, appealing to them not to vote for Communism. As a result, the Communists were decisively defeated. The Christian Democrats won 307 seats in the parliament and Alcide de Gasperi became Premier. The Communists won 182 seats.

In spite of this reverse, the Communists in Italy are still strong and aggressive, and the Church continues its relentless fight against this great evil of the modern world. For a heart-warming picture of this contest in a small Italian village, read *The Little World of Don Camillo* by Giovanni Guareschi.

GREAT BRITAIN

Status of the Church in Great Britain.—Catholicity has flourished in Great Britain during the twentieth century. Many illustrious converts have been made, including such brilliant writers as Noyes, Chesterton and Baring. These men have wielded influential pens in support of Catholic philosophy. Other prominent converts include Sheila Kaye-Smith, Shane Leslie, Owen Francis Dudley and Dr. Robert Braun.

Within the Anglican Church, a more friendly spirit to Rome has been evident. Indeed, certain important elements of the Anglican Church have seriously considered union with Rome.

After Hitler's victories in the Second World War, leaders from such predominantly Catholic countries as Poland, Belgium and France took refuge in England and continued to work and fight for the liberation of their homelands from the pagan yoke.

In 1956, England had a total population of about 44,000,000, of whom 3,661,429 were Catholics. There were 7040 Priests in 3963 churches and chapels. Education was provided for 460,000 students in 575 secondary schools and 1380 elementary schools. Catholics in British East and West Africa and in Indian Ocean Islands numbered 3,775,000 plus about 737,000 catechumens, in a total population of 67,440,000.

Ireland.—The long and bitter struggle of Catholic Ireland to win national independence was crowned with success in 1937. In that year, Ireland became a sovereign state, under the name of *Eire*. In 1949, Ireland was declared a republic, completely free of any connection with England. The six northern counties of Ulster remained part of the Kingdom of Great Britain.

In the twentieth century, Ireland remained solidly and ardently Catholic. Moreover, English-speaking Irish immigrants to the United States and England did magnificent Apostolic work for the Faith.

Scotland.—Scotland's total population of 5,351,782 in 1956 included 753,022 Catholics. There were 1086 clergy in eight dioceses.

POLAND

Poland as an Independent Nation.—The tyranny of the Russian Tsars could not weaken Catholicity in Poland. When the nation regained its independence in 1918, it continued as a bulwark of the Faith. Three-fourths of the 30,000,000 people were Catholics. In 1925, a Concordat was negotiated with Rome which settled satisfactorily all questions between the Church and the Polish state.

Conquest by Germany and Russia.—But Poland was not to be allowed to live in Christian peace and happiness. In 1939, Nazi Germany invaded this peaceful land. In spite of the gallant resistance of the Poles, the more numerous and powerful German army was soon completely victorious. Then began one of the saddest chapters in the history of the church. Poland was divided between Germany and Communist Russia. In both sections, Christians were persecuted with indescribable barbarism. Executions, tortures, imprisonments and mass deportations became daily events. It is known that 3100 Priests died as a result of Nazi terrorism alone. Pope Pius XII protested vigorously against the mistreatment of the clergy in German-occupied Poland. In spite of this horrible ordeal, the Polish people remained unswerving in their faith. They are the descendants of martyrs and canonized saints, and they know that deliverance is certain.

Poland After the War.—After the close of the war, Poland was re-established as a supposedly independent country, but with a Communist government completely subservient to the Soviet Union. Since the total population of 24,000,000 includes 21,540,000 loyal Catholics, Russia has been attempting to divert the religious fervor of the people to her own nefarious purposes by setting up a "National Church" and by enlisting the support of so-called "patriotic Priests" who would "cooperate" with the Communist government. The overwhelming majority of the people and of the 10,300 Priests have resisted this pressure in spite of severe persecutions. The "patriotic Priests" have been described by Catholics as "in conflict with their consciences, with their moral and canonical duties, and . . . under Church penalties."

RUSSIA

The Communist Revolution.—In 1917, the Tsarist government of Russia was overthrown in a revolution led by the Communists. The so-called *Soviet* regime which came into power at that time has controlled the country ever since.

The basic principles of Communism or Marxism are: (1) **a** completely materialistic philosophy; (2) abolition of all **private** property; (3) concentration of absolute power in the hands of a small group of Communist leaders, headed by a dictator (at first Lenin, now Stalin); and (4) the destruction of religion—not any particular religion, but all religion.

Communist Russia covers one-sixth of the earth's surface and has a population of 193 millions. Although most of the people belonged to the Greek Orthodox Church, there were many Roman Catholics. One can well imagine the sad fate which overtook these Christians under the Godless Communist dictatorship.[2] All public divine services were forbidden, and no religious instruction was permitted to anyone under eighteen years of age. This was part of a diabolical program which emphasized primarily corrupting the minds of the younger generation. Hundreds of Priests and Bishops were murdered in cold blood, imprisoned, or exiled. In 1922 all Church property was confiscated. In 1929, 1500 churches were closed to divine services and converted into public buildings to be used as theatres, fire stations, gymnasiums, museums, etc. All this while, the government kept up an incessant stream of virulent anti-religious propaganda. An avowedly atheistic newspaper called *Bezboshnik* ("The Godless") was distributed.

Communist Russia and the War.—Communist Russia helped to bring on the Second World War by entering into a pact with Germany in August, 1939. As a reward for this, Russia was allowed to share in the partition of Poland after that unhappy nation had been conquered. The Catholic Poles who came under Russian domination were subject to brutal persecutions. In 1940, for example, 100,000 inhabitants of Lwow, one of the largest cities of Poland, were deported to Siberia. Their homes were taken over by persons coming from Soviet Russia.

In June, 1941, Hitler suddenly turned on his fellow-dictator and launched an invasion of Soviet Russia. One of the bloodiest and most ferocious struggles in all history resulted, ending in the utter defeat of Germany.

Russia's Satellites.—During and after World War II, Russia became dominant over a vast area, including three small Baltic

---

[2] Two novels which give vivid pictures of the sufferings of Catholics in Soviet Russia are *The Pageant of Life* by Owen Francis Dudley, and *Silver Trumpets Calling*, by Lucille Borden.

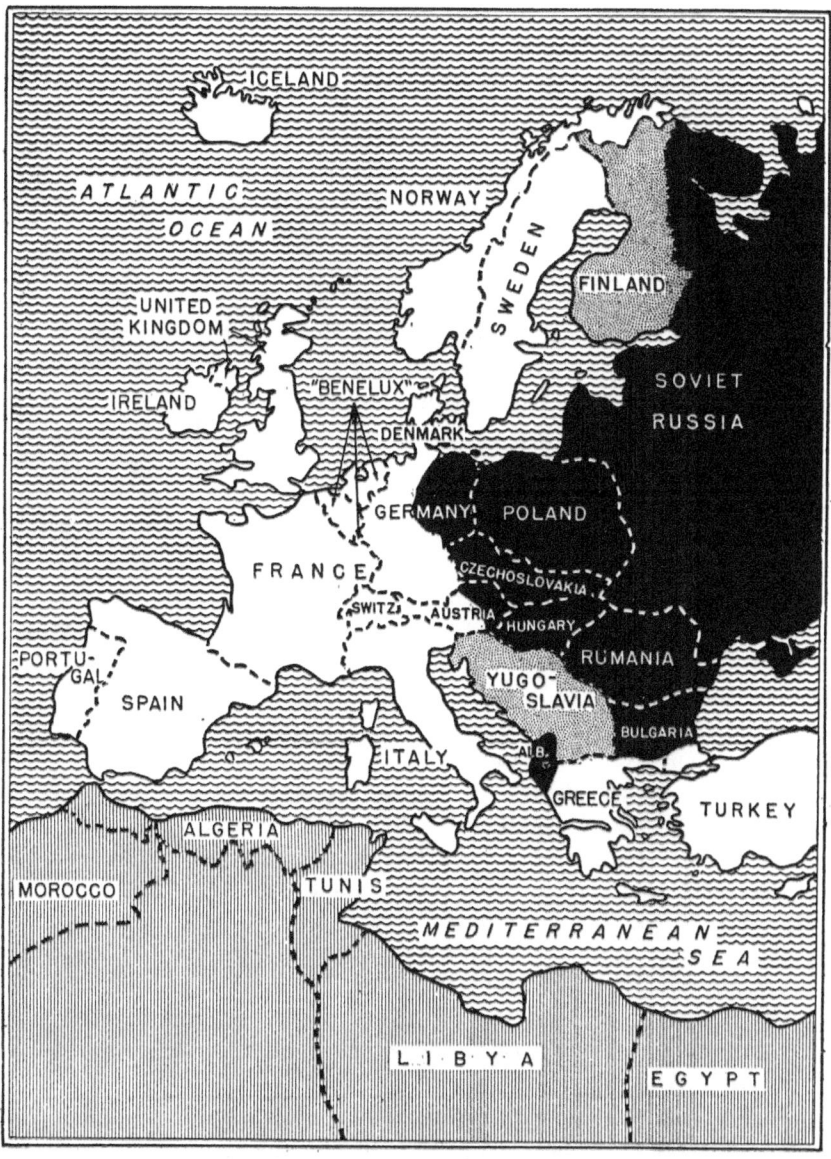

The regions of Europe which are Communist or Communist-controlled are shown in black on this map. The countries (or parts of countries) shown in white are actively opposed to Communism. Yugoslavia is Communist but not now dominated by the Soviet Union. Finland, although subjected to much Russian influence because of her geographic position, is not Communist.

countries (Estonia, Latvia, and Lithuania), the Balkans (Bulgaria, Rumania, Albania, and Yugoslavia[3]), and Poland, Czechoslovakia, and Hungary. The Communist governments of all these countries (and the Communist parties of other nations) are linked together in an organization known as the *Communist Information Bureau* (*Cominform*). Together with Soviet Germany, these satellite countries are inhabited by at least 50,000,000 Catholics, possibly by as many as 65,000,000. Moreover, there are 9,000,000 Eastern Rite Catholics in Russia proper.

Russia has erected an *Iron Curtain* to shut off herself and her satellites from the Western world. Every effort is made to prevent news from entering or leaving this area and to shut off all cultural contacts with the outside world. It is clear that the Russian leaders are afraid to allow the people under their control to be exposed to the influence of the West. The enemy which they fear and hate the most is the Church. Thus, Catholics in Russia and in the satellite lands are persecuted cruelly, and the vast power of the totalitarian state is being used in an attempt to eliminate the Church. What Stalin, Molotov, Malik and the others fail to realize is that their campaign is foredoomed to utter failure because Communism is merely human in its power, while the Church is divine.

In every country where the Communists have attained power, they have followed essentially the same tactics. First, they use force to seize control of the government. Opposition leaders of all types are tortured, exiled, imprisoned, or simply put to death. All political parties, except the Communist Party, are dissolved, and all non-Communist cultural organizations are either dissolved or paralyzed in their activities. The press, radio, and all other means of influencing public opinion are made the tools of Communist propaganda. Most important of all, religion is subjected to persecution, and an utterly unprincipled effort is made to discredit it in the eyes of the people.

Persecution of Churchmen.—Thousand of loyal Catholics have suffered persecution in the satellite countries of Russia,

---

[3] Yugoslavia, under the leadership of Tito, broke away from Russian domination in 1948. Tito is still a Communist and a dictator, but he is an enemy of Russia and her satellites, and for that reason has received some help from the United States.

but three men have become world symbols of the resistance of the Church to Communist despotism. These men are ARCHBISHOP ALOYSIUS STEPINAC of Yugoslavia, JOSEF CARDINAL MINDSZENTY of Hungary, and ARCHBISHOP JOSEF BERAN of Czechoslovakia. In the treatment which has been accorded these noble men, there is a well-defined pattern of persecution which shows a carefully designed plan. The first step is to organize a propaganda campaign against the victim, using the press, the radio, word-of-mouth rumors, and any other means available. The charges made include "sabotage," "treason," and "espionage." This is followed by house arrest and by the seizure of all private documents. Then, the victim "disappears," and is subjected for weeks to unremitting questioning, accompanied by Heaven only knows what diabolical forms of physical and psychological torture. When the victim has finally broken down, as a result of utter exhaustion of body, mind, and spirit, the arrest and the subsequent "confession" are triumphantly announced.

Then begins the "trial"—a perversion and mockery of all principles of law and justice. A standard feature, with which the Communists hope to impress the outside world, is a dramatic self-denunciation on the part of the accused. After a few days of this tragic farce, the accused is found guilty, and is sentenced to a long term of imprisonment (perhaps life) or to death. It is now well known how the Russian Communists have perverted the findings of modern psychology and chemical science to achieve such results as the courtroom "confessions." Religious and political prisoners are "conditioned" by means of drugs and various forms of psychological suggestion so that they will say or do anything that their torturers wish them to. The *London Tablet* of February 5, 1949 has provided a fine report on this subject.

Archbishop Stepinac of Zagreb (Yugoslavia).—Among the innumerable victims of Communist tyranny since the close of the war, this eminent Churchman (who was created a Cardinal in 1953) was the first to be given world-wide sympathy. His case is representative of the fate shared by hundreds of Bishops and thousands of Priests behind the Iron Curtain.

Yugoslavia evolved as a political unit after World War I. Its population of 16,000,000 is made up of various nationalities, and includes approximately 7,000,000 Catholics. In 1941, this country was overrun by Hitler's armies, and in the ensuing occupation 500 Priests were killed, wounded, or jailed by the Nazis.

In 1946, a Communist named Tito (Josip Broz) came to power with the aid of his Soviet Russian masters. Subsequently (1948), Tito rebelled against Stalin, but he is still a Communist and a bitter opponent of the Church. His regime has murdered 378 Priests and about 400 are now known to be in prison. The aim of Tito, as of Communist dictators everywhere, is to stamp out religion by eliminating its leaders.

The most eminent of Tito's victims is Archbishop Stepinac. He was born to a Croat peasant family of eleven children. After serving in the Austrian Army in World War I, he became a Priest and studied in Rome in 1924. Then in 1937, he became an Archbishop—universally loved and respected as a patriot, an angel of charity, and a defender of the oppressed.

In 1946, Archbishop Stepinac was accused by the Communists of wartime collaboration with the Nazis. After a farcical trial of the type referred to above, he was found "guilty" and sentenced to serve sixteen years in prison. World opinion knows him to be an intrepid defender of the rights of man, and many attempts were made, under both private and governmental auspices, to secure his release. Finally, in December, 1951, Archbishop Stepinac was freed from jail. The Communists announced that he would have to remain in his native village of Krasic, and also that he would not be allowed to wield any authority in the Yugoslav Church. The Archbishop said simply: "No government can deprive me of my rank."

Cardinal Josef Mindszenty of Budapest (Hungary).—This noble figure is loved throughout the Catholic world as a living Christian martyr. His case in 1948 was the first historical example of a Cardinal being brought to trial in a secular court since the trial of St. John Fisher of England in the sixteenth-century persecution of Catholics.

Hungary has a total population of 9,200,000, of whom about 6,000,000 are Catholics. The people practice their faith zealously and deeply love their Cardinal Mindszenty, a true son of the people, for his father was a peasant farmer. The courageous Cardinal incurred the wrath of the Communists as a sequel to his uncompromising opposition to the nationalization and secularization of the Church schools of Hungary.

Cardinal Mindszenty was arrested in December, 1948 and accused of "treason." At his trial, fantastically irrelevant charges were brought up, such as the claim that he had "relations" with the United States government and that he favored a monarchy for Hungary. The trial was along the usual Communist lines, and the indignities to which the Prelate was subjected are not for the young to read. The Cardinal was, of course, found "guilty" (February, 1949), and since then has been imprisoned by the Communists.

Later, Cardinal Mindszenty's successor, Archbishop Josef Groesz, the acting Primate of Hungary, was tried with eight co-defendants in a notorious Communist "group trial." The Archbishop was convicted and sentenced to jail (June, 1951).

Archbishop Josef Beran of Prague (Czechoslovakia).— Czechoslovakia has a total population of 12,300,000, which includes 8,500,000 Catholics. After the Communists took over this democratic country in 1948 by an infamous use of trickery and brute force, Archbishop Beran refused to accede to the demands of the new regime. Accordingly, he was dispossessed of his diocese and a "patriot priest" was installed in his place by the Communists.

The *Congressional Record* for July, 1951 contains a description of the Church in each of the slave states controlled by the Soviet Union. Of conditions in Czechoslovakia, this report speaks as follows:

> Communism ... is in the process of destroying religion in Czechoslovakia by fostering schism, by encroaching ruthlessly on the freedom of religious worship and religious expression, by subjugating to political control the discharge of clergymen, priests and bishops of their duties as preachers of the word of God and spiritual counsellors of men, by imprisoning, intimidating, and terrorizing the duly authorized leaders of the Christian religion which has been the priceless heritage of the Slovak and the Czech people, by seeking to establish schismatic religious associations and to disrupt them from within and control from without the freedom and the independence of the churches, destroying religious schools and eliminating the religious instructions of the children, by introducing Marxist-Leninist doctrine into the theological seminaries and by deifying Stalin.

Communist Persecution Will Not Conquer Christianity.— The persecution which the Church suffers under Communism

THE CHURCH IN COMMUNIST COUNTRIES

Country	Total Population	Catholic Population	Martyrs; Confessors
Poland	26,000,000	20,000,000	Millions in forced labor.
Germany	65,000,000	20,000,000	12 million Diaspora Catholics.
Czechoslovakia	12,300,000	8,500,000	Archbishop Josef Beran
Hungary	9,200,000	6,000,000	Josef Cardinal Mindszenty Archbishop Groesz.
Yugoslavia	16,000,000	7,000,000	Archbishop Aloysius Stepinac; Catholic churches, schools, homes dynamited.
Russia	193,000,000	8,250,000	One priest in Moscow to say Mass in small apartment.
Albania	1,000,000	113,000	Bishop exiled; 30 Priests killed, 40 in prison.
Bulgaria	7,000,000	45,000	Priests, Nuns, laity in labor camps in Siberia.
Rumania	20,000,000	3,100,000	600 Priests refused to join Russian Orthodox Church; have been imprisoned.
Estonia	1,137,000	3,000	Two Priests alive in 1940.
Latvia	1,950,000	506,500	34 of 110 Priests killed.
Lithuania	3,033,000	2,100,000	More than half of 800 Priests liquidated.
Ukraine	39,000,000	4,500,000	13 Prelates martyred.
Korea	30,000,000	500,000	135 Priests and Nuns have been martyrs.
China	445,000,000	3,275,000	Missionaries under house arrest, or exiled; natives killed; "National Church" being organized.

Statistics from *National Catholic Almanac* (1951). Other data mainly from information supplied by American embassies in these countries.

in the 1950's is not new; nor is the perseverance of the martyrs. Jesus Christ prophesied this action and reaction both by word and by work. He said on the eve of His crucifixion: "I will strike the shepherd, and the sheep of the flock shall be dispersed (Matt. 26:31). But the Divine Founder also said: "All power in heaven and on earth has been given to Me . . . and behold, I am with you all days, even unto the consummation of the world" (Matt 28:18-20).

While such movements as Nazism and Communism have given millions of martyrs to the Church, missionaries have given spiritual birth to millions of converts. The Encyclical of Pope Pius XII on the missions (June 2, 1951) reports that in 25 years missions have grown from 400 to 600 districts; missionary Priests have increased from 14,800 to 26,800, and the faithful in these missions from 14,500,000 to 28,000,000.

These facts, and many other facts as well, corroborate the unshakable truth that human Communism will never conquer divine Christianity.

OTHER EUROPEAN COUNTRIES

Spain.—Spain's population of 28,000,000 is almost entirely Catholic. Every family has memories of martyrs.

From 1936 to 1938, Spain went through a terrible Civil War, during which the Communists massacred 13 Prelates and 14,000 Priests and Religious, and destroyed 22,000 churches and chapels. The war ended with the defeat of the Communists by the forces under General Franco.

During World War II, Spain remained neutral. When the United Nations was formed in 1945 Spain was not invited to become a member. Furthermore, in 1946, the UN adopted a resolution, sponsored by Russia, which requested all member states to withdraw their ambassadors from Madrid. In 1951, in the face of Communism's threat to Europe and to the entire world, the UN General Assembly revoked this resolution. President Truman thereupon appointed Stanton Griffis to serve as our Ambassador to Madrid, while Spain sent José Felix Lequerica to Washington.

Catholic Spain has many problems to solve, including poverty for the masses of the people, but she stands firm as a stronghold of the Catholic Faith and a bulwark against Communism.

Belgium.—Belgium's population of about 8,330,000 includes more than 8,238,000 Catholics. All religions are granted full toleration.

Since the close of World War II, Belgium has been outstanding among the nations of Europe for its domestic stability and economic recovery. This excellent record has been the result, in large part, of organized Catholic activity. The specialized Catholic Action, so important in the world of today, including the United States (page 338), is modeled upon the Belgian Jocist movement led by Canon Joseph Cardijn. A recent example of its effectiveness was the first postwar election in February, 1946, when the Christian Social Party, under the leadership of A. E. de Schrijver, won control of the government, in spite of the opposition of the Communist and Socialist Parties. The Christian Social Party is the successor of the old Catholic Party in Belgium.

Holland.—Holland's population of 10,435,631 (1956) included 4,019,995 Catholics. The Catholic school system in Holland is a model of social justice for the entire Catholic world, especially for countries like the United States, whose population is chiefly Protestant. The Catholic people of Holland receive their just share of public funds for school purposes. No principle is sacrificed in this way, either by the church or the Netherlands government.

Switzerland.—The 1956 census revealed that of the Swiss population of 4,714,992, about 1,900,000 were Catholics.

Sweden. —Sweden lost its Catholic faith about 400 years ago, when Gustav Vasa liberated his people from the rule of the Danish Kings. He introduced the Lutheran religion. In 1946, Sweden's population of about 7,000,000 included only 6,000 Catholics served by forty Priests of whom only six were Swedish. The years since then, however, have seen a great change. Immigrants from Latvia, Poland, Hungary, Czechoslovakia, and Italy have increased the number of Catholics to 16,000 (1951). In 1951, a new law for religion was enacted which removed many restraints on Catholics. Vatican war relief work and the Catholic attitude toward Communism have resulted in this heartening change of attitude. The Lutheran Church, however, is still the national church of Sweden.

POPES OF THE TWENTIETH CENTURY

Introduction—The four Pontiffs of the twentieth century have all been men of great wisdom and goodness, and have been generally recognized as the moral rulers of the civilized world. "When one turns from the turmoil and strife of our modern world to the foot of the Papal throne, it is like passing from the streets of a busy city into the quiet of a great cathedral. However mad men may become, we find there the same quiet assurance, wisdom, understanding and helpfulness that men found in Christ Himself."[4]

Pius X (1903-1914).—Pius X, the "Pope of the Eucharist," promulgated the early reception of the Eucharist by children, and its daily reception by all Catholics. This was intended to help overcome the low moral tone of the age. Its success may be gauged by the fact that the great moral evils which characterize the modern world (*e.g.,* divorce and birth control) are usually less prevalent among Catholics than among non-Catholics.

Pope Pius X was canonized on May 29, 1954.

Benedict XV (1914-1922).—Benedict XV served as Vicar of Christ during the First World War, and did much to alleviate the sufferings of all peoples during that tragic period. He acted as an intermediary in effecting exchanges of prisoners; provided civilian refugees with the necessities of life; aided soldiers in prison camps; and performed many other services greatly appreciated by both sides in the war. Benedict also worked tirelessly to put an end to the bloody strife and to arrange a just peace. Unfortunately, the temporal rulers of the world were not willing to listen to him.

Pius XI (1922-1939).—The long Pontificate of Pius XI was marked by great accomplishments in various fields.

As we have seen, it was Pius XI who solved the Roman Question by negotiating the Lateran Treaty and Concordat of 1929 with the Italian government (page 264). The spiritual gains which the Church registered by this agreement were a source of rejoicing to the entire Catholic world. Mussolini's faithlessness in violating the spirit of this agreement has been described above.

Pius XI is also known as the "Pope of the Foreign Missions." With great ardor and practical wisdom, he encouraged missionary

---

[4] Forner, B. N., *The Story of the Church.*

activities in the far corners of the world. He made possible a native clergy and native hierarchies for the missions in the Far East.

Pius XI was much concerned over the economic problems of the day, such as unemployment, low wages, industrial disputes, etc. One of his best known encyclicals on these problems is *The Reconstruction of the Social Order* (Latin title, *Quadragesimo anno*), issued in May 1931. In this encyclical, Pius pointed the way to practical, Christian reforms which would eliminate social and economic evils.

Toward the end of his reign, Pius was much saddened by the growth of international dissension and the threat of war. Although in failing health, he labored ceaselessly to avert the catastrophe. On several occasions, he condemned the excesses of the Nazi dictatorship in Germany.

Pius XI was a man of the purest character, filled with love for his Faith and for mankind. When he died, he was sincerely mourned throughout the civilized world, not only by Catholics but also by Protestants and Jews.

Pope Pius XII (1939-   ).—The elevation of Cardinal Pacelli to the throne of St. Peter on March 2, 1939, marked the second time in a generation that a new Pontiff was elected in a year darkened by the outbreak of a great world conflict.

Eugenio Pacelli was born in Rome on March 2, 1876. He studied for the Priesthood in the Eternal City, and was ordained in 1899. After years of fruitful labor, he was consecrated an Archbishop in 1917. As a Papal Nuncio, he served in the capacity of diplomatic representative of Pope Benedict XV, who made unsuccessful efforts to mediate between the Allies and the Central Powers during the First World War. In 1929, Archbishop Pacelli was raised to the Cardinalate by Pope Pius XI and, in the following year, was appointed Papal Secretary of State. While holding this important office, he paid visits to the principal countries of the world. In 1934, he attended the International Eucharistic Congress at Buenos Aires, Argentina, as a Papal Legate. In 1936, he visited the United States and made an extensive tour of the nation, covering 8000 miles. He was the official Papal representative at the coronation of King George VI at London in 1938. In 1939, Cardinal Pacelli was elected by sixty-two Cardinals as the 262nd Vicar of Christ.

An incident which occurred in December, 1918, at Munich, Germany, illustrates the reigning Pontiff's great courage and commanding personality. He had been preaching against Bolshevism, thus incurring the enmity of the "Spartacists," as the most radical German Communists were known. A number of these Communists, pistols in hand, broke into Archbishop Pacelli's home. Calmly, clad in the robes of his holy office, he faced the revolvers levelled at his breast. Then he said, smilingly, to the intruders, "You're on extra-territorial ground. It is never wise to kill a diplomat."[5] The confused radicals lowered their revolvers, then offered their apologies and departed. This is typical of the valor and selflessness which Pius XII has manifested throughout his entire career.

Eucharistic Congresses.—The International Eucharistic Congresses, which are attended by delegates from all over the world, are public demonstrations of faith to honor the Blessed Sacrament. They have been called the "most splendid manifestation of the loftier heights to which Catholic life has reached."[6]

The first of these Congresses was held in Lille, France in 1881. The twenty-eighth Congress was held in Chicago in 1926. The thirty-fourth Congress took place in Budapest, Hungary in 1939. No meetings were held during the troubled war years that followed, but the thirty-fifth Congress was held in 1952 in Barcelona, Spain, and the thirty-sixth in 1955 in Rio de Janeiro, Brazil.

The Holy Year in Rome, 1950.—This event was a source of joy during days of great sorrow. A total of 3,700,000 pilgrims from the whole globe, except the persecuted Catholics from behind the Iron Curtain, visited Rome and the Pope, giving a magnificent manifestation of Church unity. This truly incomparable year, which has left a profound mark on the life of the Church, was characterized by the grandeur of great liturgical functions. Even more impressive was the invisible splendor of souls renewed and sanctified in tears of repentance and love. Solemn canonizations and beatification ceremonies paid witness to the great achievements of human nature strengthened by Divine grace and resulting in numerous beneficent works to

---

[5] Dinneen, J. S., *Pius XII, Pope of Peace*.

[6] Lortz, J. and Kaiser, F. C., *History of the Church*.

which the Church has given birth in every age. Extensive excavations concluded at this time have proved scientifically the location of the tomb of St. Peter, the Apostle, and have established beyond any doubt that Rome was the center of Christianity from the beginning. The proclamation of the dogma of the Assumption of Mary was the crowning event.

The original idea of the Holy Year was that of Moses, who designated every 50th year as a time of pardon for sinners, liberation for slaves, and remittance for debtors. The year 1950 marked the 25th official Christian Jubilee year.

The Proclamation of the Dogma of the Assumption.— Pope Pius XII proclaimed this dogma on November 1, 1950, in a Bull entitled *Munificentissimus Deus,* a 6000-word document which was witnessed by 37 Cardinals, 500 Prelates, and thousands of the laity. One sentence contains the essence of the proclamation:

> By the authority of Our Lord Jesus Christ, of the Blessed Apostles Peter and Paul, and by our own authority, We pronounce, declare and define it to be divinely revealed dogma: That the Immaculate Mother of God, the ever Virgin Mary, having completed the course of her earthly life was assumed body and soul into heavenly glory.

Sacred writings (Isaias 60:13), ecclesiastical worship, and the wisdom of theologians (St. Albert the Great) explain and expound what is now proclaimed of this privilege of the Blessed Virgin. In the definition of the Immaculate Conception, the Church had to remind the world that perfection is not biologically inevitable, as people who optimistically deny original sin seem to believe. So now, in the definiton of the Assumption, the Church gives hope to individuals who might otherwise succumb to despair. This is the interpretation of Bishop Fulton J. Sheen in *The Thomist,* January, 1951.

Canonizations by Pope Pius XII.—Pope Pius XII during his pontificate, has canonized thirty-three saints and beatified almost 100 (as of 1955). Those canonized (see *Chronology*—page 285) include an eleven-year old virgin martyr of twentieth-century Italy. She is St. Maria Goretti, a model of incomparable virtue in an age of sex crimes. St. Vincenzo Strambi, a Bishop who defied Napoleon, is an inspiration to suffering

Bishops of the present century. Several of those canonized were founders and foundresses of religious communities, such as St. Francis Xavier Cabrini who died in Chicago in 1917. Among those canonized was Pope Pius X (page 285). If you are interested in the life of Pope Pius X, read *The Great Mantle* by Katherine Burton (Longmans, Green, 1951).

Conclusion.—Thus we see that in the troubled years of the twentieth century the Church has passed through many trials and endured innumerable persecutions, but has met each new challenge with undiminished strength and faith. These glorious experiences amply prove the wisdom of the words which Pope Pius XII delivered on June 3, 1946: "The Church, taken as a whole, reveals itself as united and solid internally and externally. In every place, where, because of well-planned persecutions or because of the terrific destruction of the war, she was deprived of all support and of her legitimate properties the faithful rallied ever more closely around their leaders and showed an ever more fervent zeal. . . . We do not hesitate to assert that the Church of the present can favorably compare with the Church of the past."

CHRONOLOGICAL TABLE OF PRINCIPAL EVENTS IN CHURCH HISTORY

YEAR	EVENT
1789	French Revolution broke out, beginning an era of social upheaval, bloodshed, and anti-clericalism
1800	Pius VII became Pope, reigning until 1823
1801	Concordat between France and Rome negotiated by Napoleon and Pope Pius VII; Church reëstablished in France; remained in effect until 1905
1809	Pius VII made prisoner in France, where he was held until 1813; Napoleon at height of power
1814	Pius VII returned to Rome; Jesuit Order restored by Pope
1815	Congress of Vienna ended Napoleonic Era; Papal States restored to Church
1817	Concordat negotiated between Rome and Bavaria
1821	Concordats negotiated between Rome and various German states (Wurtemberg, Baden, Hessias, and Prussia)
1824	Concordat negotiated with German state of Hanover
1825	Leo XII condemned Freemasons (previously condemned in 1738 by Clement XII, and in 1751 by Benedict XIV)
1829	Catholic Emancipation Act passed in England, under leadership of Daniel O'Connell
1830	Pope Pius VIII issued regulations concerning mixed marriages; much opposition in Germany
1831	Pope Gregory XVI confirmed legislation on mixed marriages; Mazzini organized Young Italy Society, beginning his conflict with Church
1835	Beginning of Oxford Movement, led by John Henry Newman
1836	Archbishop von Dunin and Bishop Droste imprisoned for enforcing Papal decree regarding mixed marriages
1845	John Henry Newman entered Catholic Church
1846	Pius IX became Pope; reigned until 1878, longest of all Pontificates
1848	Revolutionary uprisings throughout Europe; Pius IX forced to flee Rome
1850	Restoration of Hierarchy in England; Cardinal Wiseman appointed Archbishop of Westminster

SUPPLEMENTARY MATERIAL FOR UNIT VI

Year	Event
1853	Restoration of Hierarchy in Holland
1854	Dogma of Immaculate Conception promulgated
1858	Blessed Virgin appeared to Bernadette Soubirous eighteen times in Grotto at Lourdes
1861	Italy became a united kingdom; death of Lacordaire, great Dominican orator
1864	Pope Pius IX issued *Syllabus,* condemning errors of age
1869	Anglican Church disestablished in Ireland; Twentieth Ecumenical Council met at Rome (lasting until 1870)
1870	Dogma of Papal Infallibility proclaimed at Twentieth Ecumenical Council; Pope Pius IX became "Prisoner of the Vatican" as protest against seizure of Rome by Italian government
1871	Prussia conquered France and established German Empire
1872	Beginning of *Kulturkampf* in Germany; Catholics persecuted; Jesuits expelled from Germany
1873	May Laws enacted in Prussia, giving state control over Catholic education and appointment and discipline of clergy
1878	Bismarck acknowledged virtual defeat in conflict with Church; most anti-Catholic legislation withdrawn
1891	Leo XIII issued Encyclical *Rerum novarum*
1901	Anti-clerical Association Laws passed in France
1905	Concordat of 1801 revoked in France
1907	Pius X issued Encyclical *Pacendi,* condemning Modernism
1914	Benedict XV elected Pope, serving until 1922; outbreak of First World War
1916-1921	Irish Revolution, culminating in establishment of Irish Free State in 1921
1917	New Code of Canon Law adopted, compiled chiefly by Cardinal Gasparri; Jesuits returned to Germany; Communist revolutionists seized power in Russia and began persecution of Church
1918	End of First World War
1922	Pius XI elected Pope, serving until 1939
1925	Concordat negotiated with Poland
1929	Roman Question settled by Lateran Treaty and Concordat; signed by Mussolini and representative of Pope Pius XI; Pius issued Encyclicals on Marriage and on Christian Education

Year	Event
1931	Pius XI issued Encyclical *Quadragesimo anno,* on relations of capital and labor
1933	Hitler siezed power in Germany and began persecution of Church and of various minorities
1936	Beginning of Civil War in Spain; Cardinal Pacelli, future Pope, visited United States
1937	Pius XI issued Encyclical on Communism
1938	Catholic Austria annexed by Nazi Germany
1939	Pius XII elected to St. Peter's throne; outbreak of Second World War; Nazis and Russians partitioned Poland and began horrible persecution of Polish Catholics
1940	Norway, Denmark, Belgium, Holland and France conquered by Nazis
1941	Soviet Russia invaded by Nazis; United States entered Second World War after attack by Japan
1943	Mass deportations of Catholics in Eastern European countries to concentration camps of Germany and to Soviet slave labor camps in Siberia
1944	Canonization of St. Margaret of Hungary; Rome liberated by Allies from Nazis and Fascists
1945	End of World War II; death of dictator-persecutors Mussolini and Hitler; beginning of American occupation of Japan, beneficial to Christian missions; Diaspora Germans suffer for Faith
1946	Canonization of Saint Francis Xavier Cabrini, who died in Chicago in 1917; St. Anthony of Padua proclaimed 29th Doctor of Church; creation of 32 Cardinals; Archbishop Aloysius Stepinac of Yugoslavia sentenced to 16 years of imprisonment by Tito; China raised from mission status
1947	Canonization of seven: Nicholas von Flue, John Di Britto, Bernardino Realino, Joseph Cafasso, Elizabeth Bicher des Ages, Louis de Montfort, Catherine Laboure.
1948	Cardinal Mindszenty of Hungary imprisoned for life by Communists; fierce persecution of Catholics in Albania, Hungary, and Yugoslavia.
1949	Canonization of Saint Jeanne de Lestonnac and Saint Maria Giuseppa Rosello. Decree of excommunication for all Communists. 600 Byzantine Rite Priests refuse to join schismatic Orthodox Church in Rumania; imprisoned

SUPPLEMENTARY MATERIAL FOR UNIT VI

1950   Holy Year. 3,700,000 pilgrims visit Rome. War in Korea, with 135 Priests and Nuns martyrs. Proclamation of the Dogma of Assumption. Canonization of eight saints: Jeanne of Valois, Vincenzo Strambi, Maria Goretti, Ana Maria Paredes, Anthony M. Claret, Emilie de Rodat, Bartolomeo Capitanio, Vincenzia Gerosa

1951   Canonization of St. Domenico Mazzarello and of Emilie de Vialar; beatification of Pope Pius X; particularly severe persecutions in Czechoslovakia and Hungary.

1954   Canonization of Pope Pius X.

1955   Thirty-sixth International Eucharistic Congress at Rio de Janeiro.

REFERENCES

BROWNE-OLF, L., *Pius XI*

CURRAN, E. L., *Great Moments in Church History*, pp. 80-83, 86-101

DINNEEN, J. S., *Pius XII, Pope of Peace*

DREHER, T., *Outlines of Church History*, pp. 103-110, 112-117

FORNER, B. N., *Story of the Church*, pp. 264-267

GUGGENBERGER, A., *A General History of the Christian Era*, Vol. III, pp. 98-122, 146-354

GULOVICH, S. C., *Windows Westward*

JOHNSON, G. W., HANNAN, J. D., DOMINICA, SR., *Story of the Church*, pp. 380-418, 432-484

KAUFMANN, A., *Modern Europe*, pp. 177-600

LAUX, J., *Church History*, pp. 517-544, 612

LOEW, M. R., *Mission to the Poorest*

LORTZ, J., KAISER, E. G., *History of the Church*, pp. 441-561

MINDSZENTY, J., *Four Years Struggle of the Church*

ORSKA, I., *Silent is the Vistula*

RAEMER, S. A., *Church History*, pp. 448-496, 520-545

SHEEN, F. J., *Communism and the Conscience of the West*

SISTERS OF NOTRE DAME, *Compendium of Church History*, pp. 129-143

SPALDING, B. J., *Church History*, pp. 618-684

SWANSTROM, E. E., *Pilgrims in the Night*

WEBER, N. A., *Christian Era*, A.D. 1517 to Present, pp. 304-697

WHITE, H. C., *To the End of the world* (a novel)

Catholic Encyclopedia, "Eucharistic Congresses," "France," "Germany"

QUESTIONS

1. (*a*) What was the basic underlying cause of the French Revolution? (*b*) Discuss fully at least five specific factors which helped to bring about the Revolution.

2. (*a*) Why was the French Estates-General convoked in 1789 after a lapse of almost two centuries? (*b*) Explain how the Estates-General was converted into the National Assembly. (*c*) State the provisions of the *Civil Constitution of the Clergy* (1790). (*d*) What was the attitude of the Pope and the great majority of the Clergy toward this Constitution? (*e*) State one other important action taken by the National Assembly.

3. (*a*) What was the *Reign of Terror?* (*b*) Who was the most notorious figure connected with this sad chapter of history? (*c*) What desecrations were committed against the Church during this period? (*d*) Describe one episode in which the loyal Catholics of France resisted these outrages. (*e*) What was the attitude of Pope Pius VI toward the French Revolution?

4. (*a*) It has been said that the epoch-making career of Napoleon Bonaparte was a "strange mixture of good and evil." Discuss this statement fully, pointing out both the good and the bad features of Napoleon's career. (*b*) What factors helped to make it possible for Napoleon to become the dominant figure in all Europe?

5. (*a*) State the main provisions of the Concordat of 1801. (*b*) Why did Napoleon enter into this Concordat? (*c*) How long did it last?

6. (*a*) What were the *Ferry Laws?* When were they enacted? (*b*) What tendencies or characteristics of French life did these laws reflect? (*c*) What laws, passed early in the twentieth century, extended these restrictions on the rights of the Church?

7. Summarize the life of each of the following great personalities in the history of nineteenth-century France: (*a*) Louis Pasteur, (*b*) Lacordaire, (*c*) the Curé of Ars, (*d*) **Bernadette of Lourdes**, (*e*) St. Therese of Lisieux.

8. (*a*) State three basic provisions which were common to all the Concordats negotiated between the Church and the German states in the early nineteenth century. (*b*) What was the nature of the dispute between the Church and Prussia over the question of mixed marriages? What was the outcome of this dispute?

9. (*a*) What was the *Kulturkampf?* (*b*) Describe the origin and history of the *Kulturkampf,* including the manner in which it was finally settled. (c) What was the role of Bishop von Ketteler in the *Kulturkampf?*

10. (a) Describe the outstanding events in the national unification of Italy. (b) What was the *Roman Question?* (c) When and how was the Roman Question settled?

11. (a) What was the *Catholic Emancipation Bill,* passed by the English Parliament? (b) Describe the part played by Daniel O'Connell in the enactment of this bill. (c) During most of the nineteenth century, the Anglican Church was the established church in Ireland. Why was this flagrantly unfair to the Irish people? When was the Anglican Church in Ireland disestablished?

12. (a) What was the *Oxford Movement?* (b) Name a great leader of this movement and describe his life work. (c) When was the Catholic Hierarchy restored in England, and by whom? (d) Describe the part played by Cardinal Wiseman in the restoration of the Catholic Hierarchy in England.

13. Describe the fate of Catholicity in each of the following European countries during the nineteenth century: (a) Holland, (b) Belgium, (c) Poland, (d) Spain, (e) Austria-Hungary, (f) Scandinavia.

14. Describe the life work of each of the following distinguished Popes of the nineteenth century: (a) Pius VII, (b) Gregory XVI, (c) Pius IX, (d) Leo XIII.

15. (a) Does the Catholic Church regard any particular form of government as unqualifiedly superior to all others? Explain. (b) Distinguish between *totalitarianism* and *democracy.* Name two countries living under each of these forms of government today.

16. (a) Describe the anti-Catholic legislation enacted in France in the twentieth century. (b) What Godless forces existed in contemporary France which undermined the moral foundations of the nation and helped to bring about its military defeat in 1940?

17. (a) What was the position of the Catholic Church in Germany before the rise of Hitler? (b) What were the aims of the Hitler dictatorship? (c) Describe the measures adopted by Hitler to put his domestic program into effect. (d) Summarize the series of military aggressions committed by Nazi Germany since 1938. (e) What are the principles of Communism, or Marxism, as adopted in Soviet Russia? (f) Describe the fate of religion under the Soviet regime.

18. (a) What was the *Lateran Treaty?* When was it negotiated? (b) Summarize the provisions of the Lateran Treaty. (c) Have the provisions of this treaty been fully observed in recent years? Explain.

19. (a) What has been the status of the Catholic Church in England in the twentieth century? (b) Name several prominent English converts to Catholicity during this period. (c) When did Ireland become a fully sovereign state? What is its official name?

20. Summarize the life and achievements of each of the following Popes of the twentieth century: (a) Pius X, (b) Benedict XV, (c) Pius XI, (d) Pius XII.

21. (a) Describe the type of martyrdom in the Russian satellite states of Eastern Europe in the decade 1940-1950. (b) Summarize the lives of Cardinal Mindszenty and Bishops Stepinac and Beran. Compare the martyrdom which they suffer at the hands of the Communists with the martyrdom of the early Roman Christians.

22. (a) Describe the Holy Year Pilgrimages to Rome in 1950. (b) Define the Dogma promulgated in 1950. (c) Name three of the many Saints canonized by Pope Pius XII.

MATCHING TEST

In the parenthesis next to each name in column **A**. *write the number of the item in column* **B** *which is most closely associated with it.*

A

( ) Pope Pius XII
( ) Pope Pius VII
( ) Archbishop Stepinac
( ) Cardinal Newman
( ) Pope Pius IX
( ) Pope Leo XIII
( ) Daniel O'Connell
( ) Pope Pius XI
( ) Don Bosco
( ) Cardinal Mindszenty

B

1. Leader of Oxford Movement
2. Negotiated Concordat of 1801 with Napoleon
3. "Workingman's Pope"
4. Member of "Old Catholics"
5. Secured passage of Catholic Emancipation Bill
6. Italian Priest who furthered education for poor boys
7. "Pope of the Foreign Missions"
8. French Dominican orator
9. Victim of Yugoslav Communists
10. Reigning Pontiff
11. Proclaimed dogma of the Immaculate Conception an article of faith
12. Living martyr in Hungary

SUPPLEMENTARY MATERIAL FOR UNIT VI 289

CHRONOLOGY TEST

Number the items in each of the following groups in their proper chronological order.

A

( ) Twentieth Ecumenical Council
( ) Encyclical *Rerum novarum* issued.
( ) Encyclical *Quadragesimo anno* issued
( ) Pius XII elected Pope
( ) Settlement of Roman Question

B

( ) Apparitions at Lourdes
( ) Franco-Prussian War
( ) Associations Act
( ) Louis Napoleon becomes Emperor
( ) Revocation of Concordat of 1801

C

( ) Conversion of John Henry Newman to Catholicity
( ) Restoration of Hierarchy in England
( ) Ireland becomes independent nation
( ) Anglican Church disestablished in Ireland
( ) Daniel O'Connell secures passage of Catholic Emancipation Act

D

( ) Invasion of Poland by Nazi Germany and Soviet Russia
( ) Outbreak of World War II
( ) Entry of United States into War
( ) Tito Rebellion against Stalin
( ) Trial of Archbishop Stepinac

COMPLETION TEST

Complete each of the following statements by supplying the correct word or phrase.

1. Danton and Robespierre were leading figures in the phase of the French Revolution known as the . . . .

2. The . . . . . . are an international secret society opposed particularly to the Catholic religion.

3. One of the writers of eighteenth-century France whose virulent opposition to the Catholic Church helped bring about the Revolution was ....

4. The Society of Jesus was restored in the year 1814 by Pope ....

5. The members of the clergy who refused to take an oath supporting the Civil Constitution of 1790 in France were called the ...... clergy.

6. The extreme radicals of the French Revolution were the .....

7. The reigning monarch in France at the outbreak of the French Revolution was ....

8. The "Iron Chancellor" of Germany was ....

9. A great French Catholic layman who has often been called the "Apostle of Health" is ....

10. St. ...... is sometimes known as the "Little Flower."

11. Italian patriots who struggled to free Italy from Austrian domination formed a secret society known as the ....

12. Cardinal Newman is remembered for his inspiring autobiography entitled ....

13. The most important business of the Twentieth Ecumenical Council was the proclamation of the dogma of ....

14. Don Bosco founded an Order of Priests known as the ....

15. The dominant religion in the Austro-Hungarian Empire was ....

16. Jean Marie Vianney is better known as the ....

17. Eucharistic Congresses are demonstrations of faith to honor .....

18. Two Catholic countries conquered by Hitler were ...... and ....

19. The hymn *Lead Kindly Light* was written by ....

20. Three countries in which Catholics are suffering persecution today are: (a) ......, (b) ......, and (c) ....

21. Diaspora Catholics are exiles in ....

22. A Community of native Japanese Sisters received approval of the Holy See in the year ....

23. The Iron Curtain is an effort to cut off communication between the outside world and the regions under the control of ....

24. Three men have become world symbols of Communist persecution. They are (a) ......, (b) ......, and (c) ....

25. The Bull, *Munificentissimus Deus*, proclaimed the Dogma of ....

UNIT VII
CATHOLICITY IN AMERICA

PREVIEW

THE Catholic Church has played an important and a glorious role in the history of the United States, from the very beginning to the present day. As we have seen, Catholic missionaries accompanied the discoverers and early explorers of the New World. The Spanish and French brought the Faith to these shores long before the English colonists arrived. The first permanent settlement in the United States was a Catholic parish at St. Augustine, Florida, founded in 1565. In 1601, Mass was celebrated in California; in 1608, there were 8000 Catholic Indians in New Mexico. More than 100 Catholic missionaries died as martyrs, and not all at the hands of the Indians. Father Rale, S. J., was killed by English Protestants in 1724.

There were about 25,000 Catholics living in the thirteen English colonies along the Atlantic seaboard. These valiant souls, a small minority among a population of 3,500,000, were often the victims of persecutions motivated by bigotry and ignorance. The colonial governments did not encourage these persecutions; for the most part, also, considerable elements of the non-Catholic population did not approve of them. But comparatively small groups of evil-minded men took advantage of popular prejudices and ignorance to stir up savage mob action against the Catholics.

American Catholics played a prominent part in the Revolutionary War, which freed our land from the tyranny of the

English crown. When our national government was formed, the Constitution, the supreme law of the land, guaranteed complete religious freedom to all persons living in the United States. Gradually, all the states adopted similar legislation. Thus, the Church was free to carry on its great work, and became well established in every state in the Union. A prominent Catholic layman has written: "Religious liberty—the complete separation of Church and State and the non-application of any form of religious test of citizenship or of fitness for public office—is in principle and practice the unique contribution of the United States to the political and social theories and customs of the world" (Michael Williams, Editor of the *Commonweal*).

In the glorious period of national growth and development that followed the winning of independence, Catholics made innumerable important contributions. We shall mention some of the outstanding individuals in the following chapters. Today, American Catholics are living up to their proud heritage. There is not a field of worthwhile endeavor (medicine, law, business, labor organization, literature, art, etc.) in which we do not find Catholics among the foremost leaders and workers.

The United States is no longer a missionary country. Most of our Priests and Bishops are now trained in our own schools and seminaries. Young American Priests are going forth to carry the Faith to India, China, Japan and other far-off lands. Here, at home, there are fruitful fields for missionary work among the Indians and Negroes. In many rural districts there are great opportunities for high school and college graduates to help plant the seeds of Faith and carry the torch of truth for the greater glory of God.

CHAPTER 15

MISSIONARIES AND MARTYRS IN COLONIAL AMERICA

"The Catholic Church in this country does not begin her history after the colonies were formed, and men had looked to their temporal well-being. Her priests were among the explorers of the coast, were the pioneers of the vast interior; with Catholic settlers came the minister of God, and Mass was said to hallow the land and draw down the blessing of heaven before the first step was taken to rear a human habitation. The altar was older than the hearth."
—J. G. SHEA ("The Catholic Church in the United States")

SPAIN IN AMERICA

Introduction.—The region which now forms the southwestern and far-western part of the United States, as well as the State of Florida, was discovered, explored, settled, and for many years governed, by Spanish Catholics. Among the treasures of the Cathedral of Seville in Spain is a chalice made from the first gold which Columbus brought from America to Europe. As early as 1511, the Church in the New World was governed and guarded by Spanish Bishops. Spanish missionaries labored fruitfully among the people inhabiting the region which comprises Florida, New Mexico, Arizona, Texas and California. Spanish geographical names are very common today in this section of the United States. It is to be noted that many of the names have a religious background—for example, *Santa Fe* ("Holy Faith"), *San Francisco* ("Saint Francis"), *Los Angeles* ("The Angels"), *San Antonio* ("Saint Anthony"), and *San Diego* ("Saint James").

Florida.—Florida early became the center of intensive missionary activities. In 1549, a Dominican, Father Louis Cancer, landed here but was immediately martyred by the club of a savage Indian. Soon thereafter the Jesuits came, and the Indians were won to the Faith by their heroic efforts. The first parish within the United States was St. Augustine, founded in 1565. (This is also the oldest existing settlement in our country.) The first Bishop of Florida was a Franciscan, Juan Juarez, appointed in 1568. For two centuries, the Catholic missionaries labored zealously in Florida, bringing Christ to the Indians, and also giving them medical care and teaching them improved methods of farming and craftsmanship. In 1763, however, England took possession of Florida. The English Protestant colonists and administrators soon undid all the good work of the Spaniards. Catholic activity, however, did not cease entirely. In 1783 at St. Augustine, Father Thomas Hassett, an Irish priest from the Irish college at Salamanca, organized the first free school in America. This school was attended by both whites and Negroes. The Indians, for the most part, deserted the settlement and became wanderers in the Everglades. They took the name of *Seminoles*. In 1956, Florida had over 173,000 Catholics.

New Mexico.—Santa Fe, founded in 1609, is the second oldest city in the United States. Even before the city was founded, however, four Franciscan Fathers shed martyrs' blood in this region. The first martyr in the United States was Father Padilla, a Franciscan, who died a glorious death in 1542 near the present site of Kansas City. (This was then considered within the New Mexico Territory.) The missionaries continued their work undaunted and met with splendid success. Whole tribes became Christianized. In 1956, there were over 290,000 Catholics in this sparsely settled state, including 7500 Indians.

Arizona.—Jesuit missionaries in Arizona labored among the fierce Apache Indians. Near the end of the seventeenth century, Father Kino, aided by Father Campos, baptized no fewer than 48,000 Indians. Many other Jesuits followed these two until 1767, when Spain suppressed the Jesuits and destroyed their work in Arizona. In 1956, Arizona had a Catholic population of over 190,000, with a full organization, except a seminary. The life of a Catholic Priest or Sister here is that of a missionary.

Texas.—A Franciscan, Father de Olmos, visited Texas in 1544 and converted several Indians but organized missionary activity did not begin until 1688. The missions did untold good, but in 1798 the Spanish government secularized them. Now, Texas has an Archdiocese, San Antonio, and six Dioceses, Amarillo, Corpus Christi, Dallas, El Paso, Galveston, and Austin. The Catholic population in 1956 was almost 1,600,000.

California.—Franciscan missionaries from Mexico visited California in 1535; many attempts at colonization failed. The Jesuits came in 1697 and persuaded wealthy Spaniards to establish the Pius Fund to support the missions. After the Jesuits had been suppressed in 1767, the Mexican government seized this money, robbing the Church of it. In 1869, the Church tried to regain the fund. The United States and Great Britain supported the Church

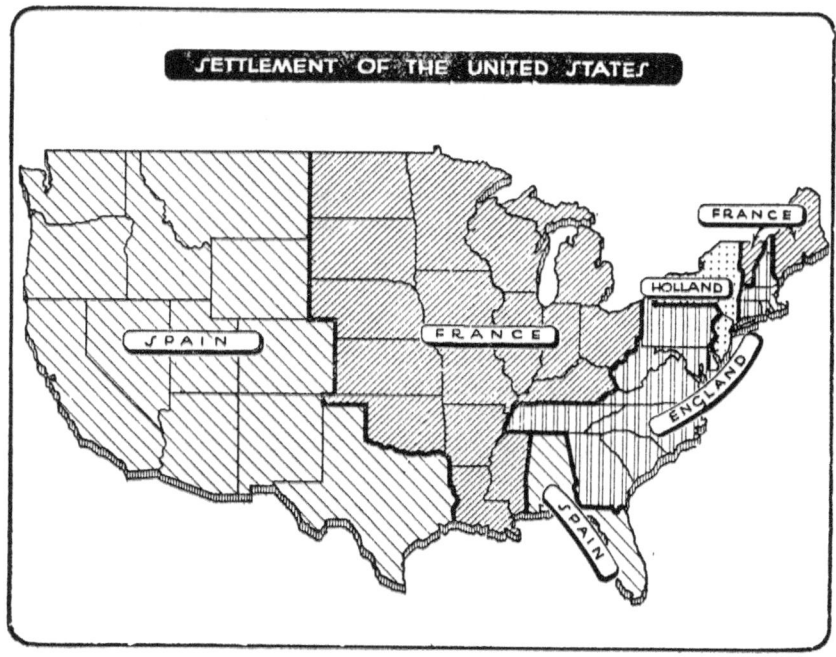

Settlement of the United States by European Nations.

in this matter and the issue was submitted to the Hague Tribunal. In 1902, this Tribunal decided that Mexico would have to pay $43,000 annually until the entire sum due the Church (about $1,420,000) was accumulated.

Between 1769 and 1845, a series of more than twenty missions was erected in California along the Pacific Coast. These extended from San Diego in the south to San Francisco in the north. The missions were the first settlements in California, and many of them became the sites of large cities. The guiding genius in the construction and administration of these California missions was a Franciscan Father named Junipero Serra. This servant of Christ, assisted by a small band of Franciscan Friars, founded the first mission at San Diego in 1769. He made his headquarters at Monterey and frequently visited all the missions, always making the long journeys between them on foot. He died in 1784, worn out by his arduous labors.

Each mission consisted of a church, school and hospital. These buildings were constructed in a distinctive style of architecture which is still very popular in California and elsewhere; it is called "Mission architecture." The Franciscan Fathers not only brought the word of Christ to the Indians, but also instructed them in agriculture and in various handicrafts, such as carpentry and metal work, and in the fine arts. The affection and esteem of the Indians for their Priests can scarcely be exaggerated.

Early in the nineteenth century, Mexico (which then included California) became independent of Spain. The missions were neglected and most of them were allowed to fall into ruins.[1] Nevertheless, the good which they accomplished is still evident in California. In 1950 there were more than 2,134,000 Catholics in this state. Moreover, the Catholic population is increasing at a more rapid rate than the non-Catholic population. San Francisco and Los Angeles are Archdioceses, while San Diego, Monterey-Fresno, and Sacramento are Dioceses. In 1951, under the provisions of a new law, California ceased taxing Catholic school property.

Latin America—The region which we now call Latin America (Mexico, Central America, the West Indies and South America) was colonized for the most part by Spain and Portugal. The Catholic missionaries who came to this region introduced many plants and animals to the New World, including oranges, lemons, cotton, sugar cane, horses and cattle. They also established many schools and colleges. The oldest institutions of higher education in the Western Hemisphere are the University of Mexico and the University of San Marcos at Lima (Peru). Both institutions were founded in 1551, and thus are about 90 years older than Harvard. The University of Santo Tomas de Aquino was founded in 1538 by Dominicans in Santo Domingo. The seeds of faith were sown so well that today Latin America, inhabited

---

[1] Several missions, such as San Luis Rey and Santa Barbara, are still in a good state of preservation and are being preserved as historical treasures.

by about 150 million souls and comprising twenty independent countries, is largely Catholic. Since Latin America is still sparsely populated and is bound to grow rapidly in the future, it should become one of the most important strongholds of Catholicity. Catholics are very much interested in the "Good Neighbor" movement, which aims to bring about improved relations between the United States and her sister republics to the south.

Puerto Rico.—Puerto Rico was colonized in 1508 by Ponce de Leon leading an expedition of 50 men. In the years since then it has grown to a community of about 2,200,000 of Spanish-American culture. The island has been favored by a brilliant constellation of natives who have distinguished themselves in religion, in civil life, and in the armed forces. Prominent among them is Rt. Rev. Juan Alejo Arizmendi y de la Torre (1760-1814), who guided the diocese of San Juan for eleven years.

For more than 400 years the island was under Spanish rule until it became a possession of the United States in 1898. San Juan is the oldest diocese in the Americas, being granted that status by Pope Julius II in 1511. The first Bishop was Alonso Manso, who took possession of the See in 1513. The four centuries of Spanish rule were rich in cultural traditions but included much which was unfavorable to the development of a robust Catholic faith.

The missionary area of Puerto Rico is now cared for by twelve Orders of men, of which eight are from the United States—Redemptorists, Capuchins, Marianists, Holy Ghost Fathers, Benedictines, Salesians, Augustinians, and Carmelites. There are twenty-seven Orders of Sisters, of which sixteen are from the United States, including Charity Sisters, Dominicans, Notre Dames, St. Joseph, and Madames of the Sacred Heart. There are about 300 Priests and Brothers; the Sisters number about 700. There are very few native Sisters or Priests. The first Sisters, however, were natives, belonging to a Carmelite community established in 1651; this community still exists with twenty-four members. Many missionaries are from Spain. The Dominican Fathers are from Holland. A new seminary is conducted by the Jesuits.

In 1948, at Ponce, the first Catholic University on the Island was founded by Bishop James E. McManus, C.SS.R. and Monsignor Vincente Murga. In 1956, the school year closed with

2513 students (3933 including the summer school and 143 professors. Bishop James Peter Davis of San Juan is establishing schools and churches, a crying need for the economically handicapped people. There are only 57 Catholic schools with about 35,000 students conducted by Religious on the island.

After class hours, the teaching Sisters, aided by native lay catechists, go up into the mountains to teach religion to children who attend public schools or no schools at all. After taking care of their regular parish duties, the Priests also go up into the mountains to little chapels to celebrate Mass and to administer the sacraments. The need for mission work is very great.

FRANCE IN AMERICA

Introduction.—French Catholic missionaries toiled valiantly in the region which is now the northeastern part of the United States and in Canada. They also traveled west to the Mississippi and sailed down this mighty stream to its mouth, the Gulf of Mexico. The founders of the French empire in America were almost always accompanied by missionaries. As early as 1609, there was a Catholic chapel in Maine for the Abnaki Indians. These missionaries were supported not by the French government but by the generosity of private individuals. Among those engaged in this missionary work were Franciscans, Jesuits, Dominicans, Sulpicians, Carmelites, and Secular Priests.

"Saint Among Savages."—One of the best known of the French missionaries was a Jesuit named Isaac Jogues—the "Apostle of New York." In 1935, Francis Talbot, S. J., wrote a fascinating biography of this soldier of Christ entitled *Saint Among Savages*. You will be well rewarded if you read this book. It tells how Isaac Jogues, a young Priest, spent ten years of his life in the primeval forests of Canada, among the savage Mohawks. He and his companions were taken prisoners. After fifteen months of captivity, during which Father Jogues was tortured and his companions put to death, the Dutch ransomed the valiant Jesuit. He then visited New York State, the first Catholic Priest to do so. In 1643, he returned to France, but in 1645 gladly came back to his missionary work in America. He traveled to the present site of Schenectady, where the Mohawk Indians again seized him. These superstitious savages believed that a little box which St. Isaac had left there on his last visit had been the cause of various misfortunes, such as sickness and crop failures. After a day of terrible torture, a tomahawk blow sent the Priest to his heavenly rewards. This happened in 1646 when St. Isaac was only thirty-nine years of age.

In 1930, Pope Pius XI canonized this Jesuit, as well as seven other Jesuit martyrs of North America. The sufferings of these Saints have not been in vain. In 1643, St. Isaac Jogues found just two Catholic laymen in New York City; today the great metropolis has more than 1,458,000 Catholic laymen and 2312 Catholic Priests. In the state of New York, there are over 4,825,000 Catholics. New York City is an Archdiocese, while Brooklyn, Buffalo, Albany, Ogdensburg, Rochester, and Syracuse are Dioceses.

In Canada, where St. Isaac also labored, the Faith flourishes. In 1951, when the population stood at about 14,000,000, there were about 6,260,000 Catholics, many of them French-speaking. Since then, the Catholic population has grown considerably.

Russian persecutions have added many Catholic Ukrainians to the population.

Thus the Apostle of New York again fulfills the prophecy of Tertullian that the "blood of martyrs is the seed of the Church."

Marquette and Joliet.—The martyrdom of St. Isaac Jogues inspired other French Priests to come to the New World and carry on his holy work. The missionary journeys which these valiant men undertook were of great importance in the exploration and mapping of America. One of the best known of these pioneer Priests was a French Jesuit named Jacques Marquette. He arrived in Canada in 1666. For ten years, he labored among the Indians of Michigan and Illinois. In 1673, Father Marquette accompanied a layman named Louis Joliet on a voyage of exploration down the Mississippi River. They sailed downstream in canoes for a distance of over 2700 miles, coming within 700 miles of the Gulf of Mexico. Although the Mississippi had been discovered more than a century earlier by de Soto, this was the first time that white men had traveled over any considerable portion of the mighty stream.

During the journey, both Father Marquette and Joliet made maps and wrote minute descriptions of all that they observed. Father Marquette's papers were a veritable treasure for early American historians. They described vividly the Indians and the plant and animal life, and also contained an explanation of lake tides which science has not been able to improve upon to this day.

Father Marquette returned to Illinois and resumed his missionary labors among the Indians. But the hardships of frontier life were too much for him, and he died in 1675, in his thirty-eighth year. His last winter was spent on the present site of the city of Chicago.

Today, the city of Chicago has about 1,900,000 Catholics and 2455 Priests. This is the mighty harvest of the seed planted by the lonely Jesuit almost 300 years ago.

Catherine Tekakwitha.—This saintly Indian maiden was born in 1656, in the same Mohawk village in which St. Isaac Jogues had met his martyrdom. When she was four years of age, her Mohawk father and Christian Algonquin mother died of small-pox. When Catherine was eleven years old, her village was visited by two Jesuit missionaries. The Indians at the time were engaged in intemperate carousing, and only Catherine extended courtesy to the Priests. Eight year later, another missionary came to labor in this Mohawk settlement. For many years, Catherine had longed for baptism. Now she timidly and modestly approached the Priest and informed him of her desire. On Easter Sunday, 1676, after several months' instruction, this pure Mohawk maiden was baptized.

The pagan Mohawks made life unbearable for Catherine and she was forced to flee to an Indian village in Canada. For the few remaining years of her life, she practiced the most heroic virtue. When she died in 1680, at the age of twenty-four, she was loved and reverenced by all who knew her.

In 1843, after many miracles had occurred at the intercession of Catherine Tekakwitha, a majestic cross twenty-five feet high was erected over her tomb. The chant of the Church, the thunder of cannon and the joyous cries of the people attested to her reputation of sanctity.

THE ENGLISH IN AMERICA

The Maryland Colony.—The first Catholics to visit Maryland were eight Spanish Jesuits who arrived there in 1570 and were martyred by the savages. These martyrs did not die in vain. Maryland was destined to become a stronghold of the Faith and a refuge for English Catholics.

Such a refuge was needed because Catholics in England had been the victims of severe persecution. In spite of this, a Catholic named George Calvert had become prominent at court and had gained the title of Lord Baltimore. This influential and high-minded man, distressed by the sufferings of his co-religionists, decided to found a settlement in America in which Catholics would be able to live in peace and safety. An unsuccessful attempt was made to establish such a colony in Newfoundland. Nothing daunted, Lord Baltimore decided to make another attempt in Virginia, where the climate was much milder than in Newfoundland, but he died before he could carry out his plans.

The project was carried on, however, by Baltimore's oldest son Cecil, who succeeded to his father's title. King Charles I authorized him to establish the colony, to be called Maryland, in honor of the King's wife. Cecil Calvert became the "proprietor" of the colony, with the right to appoint the governor, establish courts, propose laws to the Assembly, etc. In 1633, a group of 200 souls, about half of whom were Catholics, set sail for Maryland in two ships. They were accompanied by two Jesuit missionaries, Father Andrew White and Father John Altham, and by a younger son of the first Lord Baltimore, Leonard Calvert.

SOME EARLY INFLUENCES ON CATHOLICITY IN AMERICA

The first colony was established at St. Mary's on Chesapeake Bay. Leonard Calvert served as Governor. This colony was the true birthplace of religious liberty in America. The Protestant Pilgrims and Puritans who settled in Massachusetts were extremely intolerant; they persecuted everyone who did not unquestioningly accept their religious doctrines. In contrast to this, the Maryland Assembly in 1649 passed the famous *Toleration Act,* insuring complete religious liberty for all those who believed in the Holy Trinity.[2] Many Puritans and members of other Protestant sects took advantage of this provision and settled in Maryland. In fact, after a time the non-Catholic element constituted a majority and passed laws which prohibited the practice of the Roman Catholic religion. The Catholics of Maryland, however, remained loyal to their Faith. Led by such valiant

---

[2] The Maryland Assembly which passed the Toleration Act contained a good many Protestants, probably a majority. However, the influence of the Catholic Baltimores was decisive in bringing about the passage of the Act.

Jesuits as Father White, they withstood the persecutions, until the adoption of the Federal Constitution ended religious persecution in our land for all time.

In their relations with the Indians, the Catholics of Maryland stand in sharp contrast to the Protestants of Massachusetts. In Massachusetts, for the most part, there was only bitter enmity between the white man and the Indians. Blood flowed freely, and very few conversions were made. In Maryland, on the other hand, the Catholics and the Pascatoway Indians lived in peace and brotherhood. Father White and his fellow Jesuits converted many Indians, as well as a good number of Protestants, who gladly returned to the Faith of their forefathers. Today in the state of Maryland, there are over 600,000 Catholic laymen and more than 1560 Priests.

Catholics in the Other English Colonies.—In most of the other English colonies, Catholics were severely persecuted. Only in Rhode Island and Pennsylvania was there some measure of toleration. At the time of the American Revolution, there were only 25,000 Catholic laymen in all the English colonies, ministered to by twenty-five missionary Priests. There was no resident Bishop, and no communication with the Bishop in England to whom the English colonial possesions were assigned. Only in Maryland and Pennsylvania were there chapels for Mass.

In spite of these unfavorable conditions, the Catholics clung loyally to their religion and valiant missionaries strove to sow the seeds of the Faith far and wide. One of the most illustrious of these missionaries was Father Rale, S.J., who was riddled by the bullets of English Protestants while ministering to the Indians of Maine in 1724. Other well-known missionaries include Father Druillettes and Father Masse.

The American Revolution was a great turning point in the history of the Catholic Church in America. The great majority of the Catholics in the colonies supported the cause of independence and many fought for it in the armed forces. George Washington appreciated the loyal support of the Catholics and set a good example of respect and toleration for the Catholic religion. Among the signers of the Declaration of Independence was a Catholic, Charles Carroll of Carrolton, Maryland. Catholic Indians of Maine joined the American army. The active help of a Catholic country, France, was an essential factor in the success of the Revolution. Other Catholic countries (Spain, Poland and Ireland) provided money and volunteers for the forces of Washington and also gave moral support to the hard-pressed American colonists.

The victory of the Revolutionary army was followed by the formation of a new nation—the United States of America. The fundamental law of this nation, the Federal Constitution, framed in 1787, guaranteed complete religious freedom to all creeds. Among the fifty-five framers of the Constitution were two Catholics, Daniel Carroll and Thomas FitzSimons. Article VI of this document reads: ". . . no religious test shall be required as a qualification to any office or public trust under the United States." The First Amendment, adopted in 1791, provides that "Congress shall make no law respecting an establishment of religion, or prohibiting the free exercise thereof." Similar guarantees of religious freedom are found in the constitutions of the various states.

CHAPTER 16

THE CATHOLIC CLERGY OF THE UNITED STATES

"Nay, we make progress by means of reverses; our griefs are our consolations; we lose Stephen to gain Paul, and Matthias replaces the traitor Judas."—CARDINAL NEWMAN

THE HIERARCHY

Members of the Hierarchy.—"The Catholic Hierarchy, or the governing body of the Catholic Church, consists of His Holiness the Supreme Pontiff, assisted by the Sacred College of Cardinals and by several Sacred Congregations, or permanent ecclesiastical committees, of which the Cardinals are the chief members; by the Patriarchs, Archbishops and Bishops; by the Apostolic Nuncios and Delegates, Vicars and Prefects; and by certain Abbots and other Prelates."[1]

In ecclesiastical gatherings in the United States, the *Hierarchy* usually refers to Cardinals, Archbishops, Bishops, and Abbots. But in the technical terms of the Council of Trent, the *Hierarchy* also includes the Priesthood.

Why is it important to be familiar with the structure and organization of the Hierarchy? In the life of an individual Catholic layman today, there may be need to refer to the authorities of the Church as a means of regulating one's daily actions in our complex society. The first step in consulting Church authorities in such matters is to refer to one's pastor, who enjoys authority by virtue of his office. But there are dispensations for an individual layman that must come from higher authority (a Bishop or the Pope). Also, to appreciate the news in the Catholic press, one must know the various titles of persons in authority and appreciate their differences of rank within the Hierarchy. Lastly, God willing, a Catholic boy now in school may eventually bear one of these titles of authority and responsibility; thus, they should be of immediate interest and significance to all young Catholics today.

---

[1] From Official *Catholic Directory,* 1951.

Thus, the term *Hierarchy*, as it touches our daily lives, refers to the organization of the Catholic clergy into three grades of spiritual power—*Ministers, Priests,* and *Bishops*. Ministers of the Hierarchy of the United States are found in the seminaries where young Americans are preparing for the Priesthood. Ministers include those who have minor orders (page 59), as well as those who have major orders below the Priesthood. A necessary preliminary to taking minor orders is tonsure. The chief duties of Priests and Bishops are preaching, teaching, the offering of the sacrifice of the Mass, and the administration of the Sacraments; a Priest does not ordinarily have the power to administer Confirmation and Holy Orders. In addition, a Bishop consecrates places of worship and has the right to delegate the duties of preaching and teaching to others.

Seminaries and Priests.—A Catholic young man who wishes to become a Priest must enter a seminary. No profession today offers a training or education which is superior to that received by a Catholic ordained Priest. The requirements which a candidate for the Priesthood must have are the willingness to serve God and souls, and the intellectual capacity to render this service properly. There is also a third requirement which may be lacking even when the other two are present: namely, "the providential circumstances that render it indicated in a particular case." This is the opinion of the late Bishop James Anthony Walsh, co-founder of the Maryknoll Fathers (page 308). The canonical age for ordination to the Priesthood is twenty-four years.

The oldest seminary in the United States is St. Mary's Seminary at Baltimore, founded in 1791 by the Sulpician Fathers. This cradle of the American Hierarchy was opened with four Priests and five Seminarians, all exiles from the Reign of Terror in Revolutionary France. The manner in which the founding of the American Hierarchy resulted from a terrible tragedy in France calls to mind the words of Cardinal Newman that "we lose Stephen to gain Paul." The first Priest ordained within the organized thirteen colonies was Theodore Badin, at Baltimore in 1793. In 1795, Prince Demetrius A. Gallitzin, a Russian, was ordained by Bishop Carroll. For forty years, this Prince-Priest labored in the missions of Maryland and Pennsylvania.

In 1956, there were some 505 seminaries in the United States, preparing more than 34,000 students for the Priesthood. Our country in 1956 was served by 48,349 Priests and 8868 Brothers. In previous generations, Priests came to the United States from almost every country in Europe, but today American Catholics are being pastored almost entirely by Priests born and trained in America. If you will consider these facts and compare them with those given in previous chapters, you will see that the words of the Holy Scripture are literally true: "The harvest indeed is abundant, but the laborers are few. Pray therefore the Lord of the harvest to send laborers into his harvest" (Luke 10, 2).

Missionaries.—In true Apostolic fashion, the American clergy today not only are preserving our Catholic heritage of truth and sanctity and handing the torch to future generations, but are also going forth to foreign missions and to home missions (there are 70 dioceses within the United States which have mission needs) as zealous missionaries. In 1950, 4123 American Priests and 9331 Brothers traveled to the far corners of the globe. They labored in 596 foreign mission territories inhabited by more than 31,000,000 Catholics (including such lands as China, Japan, and India, Africa, and South America) to carry the word and work of God to less favored portions of humanity. They were assisted by 61,577 Sisters and 82,863 Catechists (lay assistants).

These young Priests go to fill vacancies left by the martyrs who walked before them. Some martyrs shed their blood because of the violence of the ignorant or malicious. Other Priests are victims of circumstances, such as climate, disease or physical hardships. But all are motivated by the zeal of the Apostles and the grace of God.

In 1950-1951 the Korean War added 135 martyrs to the record. Communists in Russia, China, and the enslaved countries of Eastern Europe are also creating many new martyrs by their brutal persecutions.

> NOTE: Some Religious Orders are devoted entirely to missionary labors. All Orders undertake a certain amount of missionary work.

The Maryknoll Society.—The Maryknoll Fathers, the first foreign missionary society in the United States, now have seven Bishops, 636 Priests, 160 Brothers, and 631 Seminarians. Many of the personnel are natives of the foreign missions, since the purpose of missionary labor is not merely to preach and baptize, but also to organize and establish the Church with a native hierarchy. The Maryknoll Society was founded in 1911. The cofounders were the late Bishop James Anthony Walsh of Boston and Father Thomas F. Price of North Carolina, with the approval of the American Hierarchy and of Pope Pius X. The first student to enter Maryknoll was Francis X. Ford of Brooklyn. He went to China in 1918 and today is Bishop of Kaying, a prisoner of the Chinese Communists.

MISSIONARY AMERICA

Another of the original students was Daniel McShane of Indiana. In 1919 Father McShane went to China where he engaged in arduous and highly successful missionary activity for eight years. Through his holy zeal, thousands of souls were brought to Christ, and many schools, churches, and convents were erected. He baptized 2483 babies. In 1927, however, Father McShane, afflicted with smallpox, gave his soul back to God. In the book entitled *The Man of Joss Stick Alley,* by Rev. James Edward Walsh (Longmans, Green, 1947), you may read a most delightful and instructive story telling of a typical Catholic American boy, destined to become a Priest and a missionary in China.

The Maryknoll Fathers are assisted by the Maryknoll Sisters, founded in 1912 by Mother Mary Joseph of Jamaica Plain, Massachusetts. In 1951, there were 1032 Sisters in missions in

Hawaii, Korea, China, Japan, the Philippines, the Caroline and Marshall Islands, Bolivia, Chile, Guatemala, Panama, Nicaragua, Ceylon, and Africa. Some Sisters work in the United States with foreign groups.

Missionary Activity Within the United States.—In 1588, a Bull of Pope Sixtus V classified America as a missionary country under the jurisdiction of the *Propaganda Fide*. This status continued until 1908, when Pope Pius X decreed that the United States was no longer to be considered a missionary country but rather was to be ranked with the Catholic nations of the world under the Consistorial Congregation.

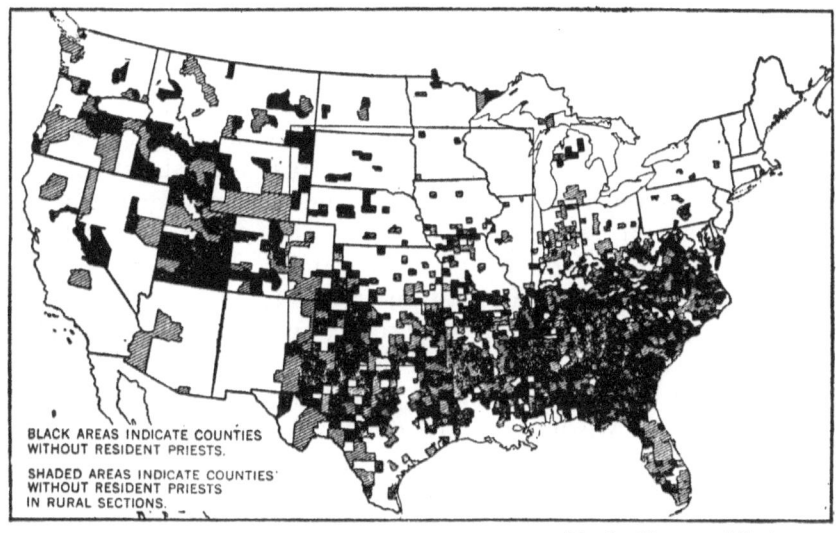

Map by Glenmary Missioners

Counties in the United States without Resident Priests

None the less, there is still much missionary work to do in the United States. Of approximately 3000 counties in this nation, 897 have no resident Priest, and another 572 have no resident Priest in the rural sections, but only in the cities. There are 70 dioceses which still receive "mission assistance." Since 1924, 40 cents of each dollar collected on Mission Sunday in October has been distributed to our home missions. The Catholic missionaries of today travel abroad, preaching from a trailer, chapel car, or sound truck. They celebrate Mass in the small towns through which they pass, and they distribute Catholic literature to inquirers.

The Glenmary Missioners.—This organization, centered at Cincinnati, Ohio, propagates the Faith in rural sections of the United States, much as the Maryknoll Society spreads it in foreign lands. The Glenmary Missioners were founded in 1937 by Rev. W. Howard Bishop of Washington, D. C. In 1956, 34 Priests, 83 Seminarians, 34 Brothers, and 50 Sisters served in 21 counties. The home mission field of the United States comprises not only the continental United States, but also Alaska, Hawaii, Puerto Rico and that portion of Panama (the Canal Zone) under United States control. In 1951, Catholic schools were authorized by law in the Panama Canal Zone. The people had been struggling for this privilege for 30 years.

Missionary Activity and the Laity.—Catholic missionary activity begins with the school child who is told about the foreign missions and the home missions and is encouraged to make small sacrifices for the support of these institutions. The children in the class rooms are urged to contribute at least a penny a month to the Pontifical Association of the Holy Childhood.

Catholic adults are motivated to contribute to the mission activity by means of periodical literature printed by various societies which train missionaries. One Sunday a year in October is designated as Mission Sunday; on this day, a special collection is taken up and the funds received are devoted to the needs of the missions. Since 1918, the United States have been the principal contributors to the general fund of the Society for the Propagation of the Faith.

Bishops in the United States.—The first resident Bishop in the United States was the Most Reverend John Carroll, D.D., consecrated in 1790. Baltimore was his See. In 1808, he was made an Archbishop. He died at Baltimore in 1815. In 1956, there were 173 Bishops and thirty-seven Archbishops in the United States. Each of the forty-eight states had at least one Bishop.

The twenty-four Archbishops preside over twenty-two Provinces, the Archdiocese of Washington, D. C., and the Apostolic Delegation in Washington, D. C. Dioceses and Archdioceses, in turn, are divided into parishes and missions. Parishes are served by resident Priests, who often also minister to nearby missions. Archbishops and Bishops have equal spiritual powers, but Archbishops have precedence in honor in ceremonial functions and usually bear heavier responsibilities and have larger flocks to shepherd. Some Archdioceses in densely populated districts are quite small in territory (*e.g.*, New York and Chicago). Note that an Archbishop is the shepherd of his own Archdiocese, but not of the suffraganites.

Can You Identify these Representative American Churchmen?

The first and most important duty of a Bishop is the governing of his diocese. His particular duties are to administer the Sacraments of Holy Orders and Confirmation, and to dedicate and consecrate Church buildings and other Church properties. Every five years, a Bishop must pay an official visit to Rome to inform the Holy Father of the conditions and needs of his flock. Since the Church in the United States is supported by the spontaneous offering of its faithful followers, the Bishops must take active charge of temporal affairs involving the raising and expenditure of funds. They must supervise the construction and maintenance of churches, schools and various types of charitable institutions. This important administrative work, combined with the responsibility for the spiritual welfare of 33,574,017 souls (1956), is indeed a heavy burden for the Bishops of the United States. It is, however, a burden which they bear joyously and well.

AMERICAN CARDINALS

Introduction.—A Cardinal is a prince of the Church and a counsellor and assistant of the Pope. Cardinals are the highest dignitaries of the Church next to the Pope. The position of Cardinal dates from the very early days of our Faith, for by the end of the fifth century the title was being applied to prominent Priests of important parishes. (The word *Cardinal*, incidentally, comes from the Latin word *cardo*, meaning "hinge.")

The full membership of the Sacred College of Cardinals is 70. In 1946, there were 70 Cardinals, but by 1951, as a result of deaths, this had dropped to 49. By 1956, it had risen to 60.

A meeting of the Pope with the Sacred College of Cardinals is called a *Consistory*. At a secret Consistory, the Pope nominates new Cardinals. When the assembled Cardinals have indicated their approval, the new dignitary waits upon the Pope, who invests him with a scarlet *zucchetta* (skullcap) and a scarlet *biretta*. A few days later, the new Cardinal's red hat is conferred upon him in a public Consistory. This is immediately followed by another secret Consistory, in which the last ceremonies are completed. Public Consistories are also held to complete canonization ceremonies and to give audiences to sovereigns or ambassadors.

During a vacancy of the Holy See, the College of Cardinals administers the Church. They also meet in a *Conclave* and elect the new Pope. (The election of the Pope by the Cardinals dates from the eleventh century.) Cardinals fill certain permanent offices, such as Chancellor and Penitentiary in the Papal Curia. They may be sent as Legates to foreign countries on extraordinary occasions. They have seats in the councils and tribunals which deal with the affairs of the Church.

There are three grades of Cardinals—Cardinal-Deacons, Cardinal-Priests and Cardinal-Bishops. Cardinal-Priests are the most numerous grade. All of our American Cardinals have been Cardinal-Priests. We shall now describe briefly the careers of the American Churchmen who have risen to this eminent position.

John Cardinal McCloskey (1810-1895).—John Cardinal McCloskey, the first American Cardinal, was born in Brooklyn, N. Y., the son of Irish immigrants. He was educated at St. Mary's College, Emmitsburg, Md., and was the first native of New York

State to become a Secular Priest. As a young Priest, he studied in Rome and traveled in Europe for three years. During this period, he made the acquaintance of the truly great Churchmen of the day—Wiseman, Newman, Lacordaire, Gorres and the late Archbishop Hayes of New York. He served as the first President of Fordham University, established in 1841, and was made Archbishop of New York, succeeding Archbishop Hughes. In 1875, he was created a Cardinal by Pope Pius IX. Cardinal McCloskey was a gentle, scholarly character whose years as Prelate covered a relatively peaceful period in American history. As Cardinal, he devoted himself successfully to conserving and increasing the Catholicity of New York.

James Cardinal Gibbons (1834-1921).—James Cardinal Gibbons, considered by many to be the greatest of all American Churchmen, was born in Baltimore. His early education was received in Ireland, but he studied for the Priesthood at St. Charles' College and St. Mary's College in Baltimore, where he was ordained in 1861. He served as volunteer Chaplain to Northern troops during the Civil War. After this, he held various important offices, in all of which he manifested an exemplary Priestly zeal. In 1877, he became Archbishop of Baltimore. The Third Plenary Council of Baltimore in 1884 owed its momentous success largely to Cardinal Gibbons, who presided over it. It was this Council that decreed a Catholic school for every parish in the United States, determined the six holy days of obligation to be observed in the United States, and provided for the establishment of the Catholic University of America at Washington, D. C. Such a university had long been a dream of Cardinal Gibbons, and he became the first Chancellor and President of the Board of Trustees. In 1886, Pope Leo XIII made him a Cardinal.

Cardinal Gibbons was a great American patriot and a true friend of the workingman. He opposed and defeated various attempts which were made to organize immigrants into national groups under European control. He championed sane and orderly reforms realistically designed to improve the conditions of the poorer classes. He took up the cause of a labor organization known as the Knights of Labor and defended it successfully when there was some fear of Papal condemnation. All his activities were marked by true Christian piety and extraordinary prudence and practical ability. In 1911, this great man held his

Silver Jubilee as a Cardinal and his Golden Jubilee as a Priest. On this occasion, noted men of all faiths gathered in Washington to do him honor.

Cardinal Gibbons was also a noted author. One of his books called *The Faith of Our Fathers* provided an explanation of the Catholic Faith, intended particularly for Protestants. It passed through more than 100 editions and was responsible for many conversions.

John Cardinal Farley (1842-1918).—John Cardinal Farley was born in Ireland but lived most of his life in New York. His only ambition was to attain the honor of the Priesthood, but in 1895 he became a Bishop and in 1902, Archbishop of New York. In this latter office he succeeded such great Churchmen as Archbishop Hughes, "the Hero," Archbishop McCloskey, "the Sage," and Archbishop Corrigan, "the Saint." In 1911, Pope Pius X made him the third American Cardinal, to multiply the fruits of the Apostolate "over the hospitable land which receives all the people of the world, and with well-ordered liberty provides for their universal well-being." As Priest, Bishop and Cardinal, this pure, unworldly man labored with extraordinary zeal to advance the cause of Christ.

William Cardinal O'Connell (1859-1944).—In 1934 Cardinal O'Connell published his autobiography, *Recollections of Seventy Years,* in which he tells of a saintly, active, thoroughly American life that should be an inspiration to present-day American youth. He was born in Lowell, Mass., the youngest of eleven children—"strong, hearty, and healthy children . . . lively and boisterous and full of gaiety, and sometimes of mischief, too." He tells how in his boyhood he was instructed by "strict Puritanical teachers, in an atmosphere of fear, where everything Catholic was distrusted and suspected." In the public high schools, there was less bigotry but still "concealed antipathy" for Catholics. He was ordained in Rome at the American College in 1884. In 1907, he became Archbishop of Boston. In 1911, after long and distinguished service to the Church, he was made a Cardinal by Pope Pius X, at the same time as Cardinal Farley.

Dennis Cardinal Dougherty (1865-1951).—Cardinal Dougherty was born in Girardville, Pennsylvania in 1865. He was ordained in 1890 and spent many years as a professor at Overbrook College in Pennsylvania before he was consecrated Bishop in 1903. From 1903 to 1915, he labored valiantly in the Phillippine Islands. In 1915, he was appointed to the diocese of Buffalo; in 1918, he became Archbishop of Philadelphia, one of the oldest dioceses in the United States, with 1,000,000 Catholics and 1761 Priests at the time of the Cardinal's death. Pope Benedict XV created him Cardinal in 1921. His 61 years in the priesthood are an honor shared by few and an inspiration to all.

Patrick Cardinal Hayes (1867-1938).—Patrick Cardinal Hayes, one of the most lovable characters in the history of the American Hierarchy, was born in New York City. He was educated in the Catholic schools of that metropolis, including Manhattan College. He was ordained in 1892, and like Cardinal Dougherty spent some time as an educator, serving as President of Cathedral College of New York for eleven years. He also served as Chancellor of the New York Archdiocese for many years before being consecrated its Bishop in 1914. In 1917, he was appointed Chaplain Bishop over 1000 Priests, who served during the First World War. In 1919, he became Archbishop of New York, and in 1924, together with his boyhood friend George Cardinal Mundelein, he was elevated to the Cardinalate. He did splendid work in raising and administering funds for various charities, and became known as the "Cardinal of Charities." Deeply loved and venerated by all, including non-Catholics, he died in 1938.

George Cardinal Mundelein (1872-1939).—This truly great Churchman was born in New York City. After studying in the schools of that city, in St. Vincent's Seminary at Beatty, Pa., and in Rome, he was ordained in 1895. In 1909, he was consecrated a Bishop, and in 1915 became Archbishop of Chicago. In 1924, as we have seen, he was raised to the Cardinalate, together with Cardinal Hayes. Throughout his career, Cardinal Mundelein showed a concern for the rights and interests of workingmen that brings to mind the work of Cardinal Gibbons. He was greatly interested in intelligent social reform and had an extremely keen understanding of current issues and problems. His opinions were greatly respected by workingmen, employers and government officials.

When George Cardinal Mundelein died in 1939, he left Chicago with the greatest Catholic population of any single Archdiocese in the United States, 1,400,000 communicants. Among the institutions which perpetuate his memory are St. Mary's Seminary at Mundelein, Ill., and Mundelein College for Women in Chicago. An even greater monument is the memory of his saintly personality and indefatigable zeal. Chicago will never forget its great Archbishop.

John Cardinal Glennon (1862-1946).—This Archbishop of St. Louis, Missouri, died 14 days after being created Cardinal.

James Francis Cardinal McIntyre (1886-   ).—The Archbishop of Los Angeles was born in New York City. Until he was 29, he worked and supported his invalid father. He was ordained in 1921, and consecrated Bishop in 1941. As Auxiliary and then Coadjutor Bishop, he served in New York for 25 years. He was appointed Archbishop of Los Angeles in 1948, and was created Cardinal in 1953. Within five years, he organized 26 new parishes and built 83 new schools.

Edward Cardinal Mooney (1882-   ).—This Archbishop of Detroit is a scholarly diplomat of keen judgment. He was born in Mount Savage, Maryland, and spent his youth in Youngstown, Ohio. His ordination took place in Rome in 1909. He was a seminary professor in Cleveland and Spiritual Director at the American College in Rome. In 1926, he was consecrated Bishop. As Apostolic Delegate, he spent five years in India, where he increased the number of native Priests. In 1931, duty took him to Japan; later, he was active in Korea. As Bishop, he went to Rochester, New York in 1933. His regime in Detroit began in 1937. At that time, the Diocese of Detroit was financially embarrassed by a debt of $20,000,000. Moreover, the city itself faced critical problems in such fields as labor-management dealings and social relations. Bishop Mooney made a major contribution toward solving these problems. He established a branch of the Association of Catholic Trade Unions (ACTU) in Detroit, and took a vital, truly constructive interest in various foreign population groups. Moreover, his excellent administrative ability greatly improved the organization and financial position of the Diocese.

Bishop Mooney was made a Cardinal in 1946. In 1951, as Detroit celebrated its 250th birthday in glory, all classes of the population acknowledged the contributions of this great "Apostle of the Workingman."

Samuel Cardinal Stritch (1887-   ).—Chicago's Archbishop was born in Nashville Tennessee, August 17, 1887. His studies for the Priesthood were carried on at St. Gregory Seminary, Cincinnati, and in Rome, where he was ordained in 1910. This genial brilliant scholar served as a Priest in Memphis, where he was greatly loved. In 1921, he was consecrated Bishop for Toledo, Ohio. In 1930, the Bishop was transferred to Milwaukee. Here and in Chicago, to which he was appointed in 1939, he is known as the "Cardinal of Charity, Catholic Action, and Youth." On his arrival in Chicago, his baggage consisted of an oil painting of his mother and a few cherished books. He has an ardent interest in missions, and established the first mission for the Chinese people in Chicago. He was created Cardinal in 1946.

Francis Cardinal Spellman (1889-   ).—The Archbishop of New York was born in Whitman, Massachusetts, in 1889. He attended the public schools and Fordham University. Then he went to Rome, where he studied for the Priesthood and was ordained in 1916. He spent some years in Boston, where his talents and his gentle nature won him widespread respect. Then he was appointed to the secretariat in Rome. Here, his work was of a diplomatic nature. In July, 1931, Pope Pius XI entrusted him with a precious encyclical to be conveyed from Rome to Paris. This document denounced the interference of the Fascist government of Italy in purely spiritual matters. (See page 264 for a discussion of this conflict between the Church and the Mussolini dictatorship.)

In 1932, Father Spellman was consecrated Bishop by Cardinal Pacelli. In 1936, when the future Pope Pius XII made a tour of the United States, Bishop Spellman accompanied him. In 1939, he was appointed Archbishop of New York. Since 1939, he has been Military Vicar of the Armed Forces of the United States. He was created Cardinal in 1946.

Cardinal Spellman has traveled all over the earth, using virtually every imaginable means of transportation. Wherever he goes, he uses his remarkable talents as a writer, orator, publicist, and organizer to win a greater audience for the message of Christ.

CHAPTER 17

THE CATHOLIC LAITY IN AMERICA; CATHOLIC EDUCATION

"The part taken by those of the Catholic Faith has been an honorable, deserving and, we may fairly say, an indispensable one in bringing the country that we love to her present state of development."
—ADMIRAL W. S. BENSON

THE CATHOLIC LAITY

What Is the Laity?—The term *laity* refers to all members of the Roman Catholic Church outside of the Hierarchy. The Hierarchy, as we have seen, includes Ministers, Priests and Bishops, all of whom have power to govern. The laity are those who are governed. The distinction between those who govern and those who are governed is essential to every organized society. Some members of the laity bind themselves to observe the evangelical counsels under the guidance of the Church by withdrawing from the world and entering one of the many religious houses. Such people, however, were not originally in the ranks of the clergy and, strictly speaking, are not so considered now.

Achievements of the Catholic Laity.—From the very beginning of our nation until the present day, Catholics have always been a minority religious group. At the time of the American Revolution, there were about 25,000 Catholics in the thirteen colonies, out of a total population of 3,500,000. In 1956, with the population of the United States approximately 165,000,000, there were 33,396,647 Catholics.

In spite of the fact that they are a minority numerically, Catholics have made a mighty contribution to the development of this country. There is no important phase of American life in which Catholics have not served with honor and distinction. In the following pages, we shall prove this claim by describing briefly the careers of a few outstanding Catholic laymen in various fields, from the days of the Revolution until the present. Space limitations, of course, permit us to mention only a handful of representative figures. An exhaustive listing would have to include tens of thousands of names.

> NOTE: The student should become familiar with *Catholic Builders of the Nation,* published in 1935. This authoritative five-volume reference work contains accounts of the lives and achievements of thousands of Catholics who have distinguished themselves in various phases of American life.

Catholics in Public Life.—Catholics have played an honored role in the political life of the United States since colonial times. Under the American system of free, representative government, they have filled many offices, both high and low, and for the most part have served the people with devotion and ability. Some representative figures follow.

CHARLES CARROLL of Carrolton, Md. (1737-1832) was one of the outstanding statesmen of the Revolutionary and post-Revolutionary period. He was a signer of the Declaration of Independence and a close personal friend of George Washington. The last act of his public life was the laying of the corner stone of the Baltimore and Ohio Railroad on July 4, 1828. Charles Carroll was also a most capable businessman and was, perhaps, the richest American of his times. He was a devout Catholic and lived an ideal family life, being the father of seven children.

DANIEL CARROLL (1733-1829) was one of the fifty-five men who drew up and signed the Constitution. He owned one of the four farms offered and accepted for the site of our national capital in Washington, D. C. In 1791, Carroll with one other official commissioner of Congress, laid the corner stone of the first government building to be erected on that site.

ROGER B. TANEY (1777-1864) was the fifth Chief Justice of the United States Supreme Court. Born in Baltimore, Taney began the practice of law in that city and was highly successful. He held various public offices in Maryland, and then was appointed Attorney-General and Secretary of the Treasury by President Andrew Jackson. The Senate refused to confirm his appointment to the latter post, but President Jackson in 1836 named him Chief Justice of the Supreme Court, in which position he served for almost thirty years. Taney is generally considered to have had one of the most brilliant legal minds in all our history, and exercised a profound influence on the development of American Constitutional law. It was he who rendered the famous Dred Scott decision in 1857.

FRANCIS KERNAN (1816-1892) was one of the outstanding citizens of New York State during a most stormy period of American history. He occupied many trusted posts: manager of the New York State Hospital, official reporter of the Court of Appeals, Regent of the State University, member of the State Constitutional Convention of 1867, and member of the State Assembly. With this rich background of experience, he was elected to the national House of Representatives and to the Senate, where he served with distinction. Francis Kernan was a charitable, devout Catholic and reared ten children in a truly Christian home.

In our own day a great many Catholics have held important positions in Federal, state and local governments. One of the best known was ALFRED E. SMITH (1873-1944), four times Governor of New York State. Mr. Smith is universally considered one of the most able chief executives that the Empire State has ever had. During his administrations, he secured the passage of much legislation to protect workingmen, such as laws providing for compensation in case of injuries. In 1928, Mr. Smith was the nominee of the Democratic Party for President of the United States. He made a strong campaign but was defeated, largely because of bigoted, anti-Catholic propaganda. Throughout his life, Mr. Smith was active in Catholic charities and other Catholic affairs. He was a Papal Knight, a Knight of Malta, and a Catholic Action Medalist.

The 82nd Congress (1950-1952) included 67 Representatives and 8 Senators who were Catholics. In 1951, President Truman's Cabinet included two Catholics—Secretary of Labor MAURICE TOBIN, formerly Mayor of Boston and Governor of Massachusetts; and Attorney-General J. HOWARD MCGRATH, who served three terms as Governor of Rhode Island. A third Catholic member of the Cabinet, Secretary of the Navy FRANCIS P. MATTHEWS, resigned in 1951 to assume the important post of Ambassador to Ireland.

LOUIS CHARLES RABAUT is an admirable example of a Catholic statesmen of the present day. Mr. Rabaut was born in Detroit in 1886. He attended the parochial schools and the University of Detroit, conducted by the Jesuits. He entered the law and practiced with great success. He married a Catholic and has reared a family of three sons and six daughters. One son is now Francis Dermott Rabaut, S.J. Three daughters are nuns: Marie Celeste is now Sister M. Palmyre, IHM; Stella Marie is Sister Stella Maris, IHM; and Martha is Sister Martha Marie, IHM. The other children, Louis III, Mary Jane, Vincent, Carolyn, Joan Marie and Martha, are all cultured Catholics.

Mr. Rabaut has been elected to Congress seven times and has served there with rare distinction. His entire career reflects the ideals of the highest type of Catholic, deeply spiritual, and unquestionably loyal to God, country, and family. He is certainly worthy of imitation by Catholic boys and young men, especially those who hope to enter public life.

Governor PAUL A. DEVER of Massachusetts recently declared in public: "All my life I have been a Catholic. All my life I have been an American. Most of my adult life has been given to the department of public service called politics." This statement was to refute the charges made by such anti-Catholic writers as Paul Blanshard that the religious duties of Catholics interfere with their civic duties.

Catholic Writers.—Talented Catholic writers have contributed a wealth of high-minded literature to the cultural treasures of the United States.

JOEL CHANDLER HARRIS (1848-1908) wrote a series of delightful sketches dealing with a quaint old Negro named "Uncle Remus." This lovable character and his stories about animals (such as "Brer Rabbit") have endeared themselves to untold thousands of children and grown-ups.

ORESTES BROWNSON (1803-1876) is probably the most profound thinker and writer among all the Catholic authors of the United States. He was not born to the Catholic Faith, but for many years he studied intensively, seeking a religion that would satisfy his craving for truth. Finally, in his forty-first year, he was converted to Catholicity. Brownson left a voluminous body of writings, most of them philosophical essays dealing with religious, political and literary topics. He was utterly fearless, and his pen was a mighty weapon in defense of religion, the rights of the laboring man, and lofty literary standards. It is quite possible that if Brownson had not become a Catholic, he would today be receiving the honors accorded to Ralph Waldo Emerson as the greatest American essayist. Notre Dame University has honored the remains of Orestes Brownson by burying his remains on the University campus.

CARLTON J. H. HAYES (1882-   ) is a distinguished historian, born in New York City and educated at Columbia University. In 1904, inspired by his profound studies of European history, he became a Catholic. For many years, he served as Professor of History at Columbia and, through his teachings and prolific writings, exercised a profound and highly beneficial influence on the thinking of historians and on the teaching of this subject at all levels from the primary school to the university. From 1942 to 1945, he served as the United States Ambassador to Spain.

FULTON JOHN SHEEN (1895-   ) was born in southern Illinois, attended St. Mary School in Peoria and the Seminary at Bourbonnais, Illinois. Later he studied at Louvain and at Rome. After twenty-three years as Professor of Philosophy at the Catholic University in Washington, D. C., he was consecrated Bishop in Rome (June, 1951). Bishop Sheen has written more than 30 books, presenting various phases of Catholic thought and doctrine in a style of matchless charm and clarity. He is also the most persuasive orator for Catholicity on the radio in the United States. He has instructed many people who have received the gift of Faith as converts.

WALTER FARRELL, O.P. (1902-1951) is a Dominican philosopher who was born in Chicago and educated at a parochial school conducted by Dominicans and at the Quigley Seminary in that city. He was ordained in Washington, D. C. in 1927. He studied at Fribourg and Rome, and from 1943 to 1946 served as a Navy Chaplain. Father Farrell is noted as the author of *Companion to the Summa,* a four-volume work which is a twentieth-century version of the philosophy of St. Thomas Aquinas.

THOMAS MERTON (1915-   ) is a Cistercian of Kentucky (a Trappist) who was born in France of an American mother and a British father. He lived in Paris, Bermuda, and England, and as a young man came to America, where he was educated at Columbia University. He became a Catholic in 1939 and a Priest in 1949. His book entitled *Seven Storey Mountain* is a most vital and remarkable autobiography of a young man groping desperately in the chaotic world of today and finally finding spiritual peace and assurance in the Faith. He is also a talented poet.

Catholics in Industry.—There is not an industry in the United States which does not owe a great deal to skilled and diligent Catholic workingmen. Catholic labor was particularly important in the construction of the canals and railroads that made possible our national growth in the nineteenth century. Catholics, moreover, have been among the leading spirits in the organization and guidance of labor unions. Among the many Catholics engaged in this important work at the present time, perhaps the most prominent is PHILIP MURRAY, President of the Congress of Industrial Organizations (CIO).

Thousands of Catholic business men, large and small, have also contributed to the growth of the United States.

EDWARD CREIGHTON (1810-1874) and JOHN CREIGHTON (1831-1907) were two brothers who acquired great wealth by helping to build up the transcontinental telegraph system and by engaging in the meat-packing business. Much of their wealth was donated to philanthropic works, such as Creighton University, St. Joseph's Hospital, and the Poor Clare Monastery, all in Omaha, Nebraska.

HENRY FORD II (1917-   ) heads the great Ford Motor Company, founded by his distinguished grandfather. Mr. Ford was not born a Catholic, but in 1940 he was instructed in the Faith and married Anne McDonnell, a Catholic. After a term of service in the Navy during World War II, he assumed control of the family business. He has promoted the idea of joint management-labor responsibility, in accordance with Catholic social principles, as taught by the encyclicals of the recent Popes for an industrialized world. This is as significant an innovation in American industry as Henry Ford's introduction of a base wage of 5 dollars a day in 1914.

JOHN HENRY PHELAN (1877-   ) is a prominent executive in the petroleum industry and a generous philanthropist who has given more than $1,000,000 to the Church. Notre Dame University recognized him as the outstanding Catholic layman of 1951 by awarding him the Laetare Medal. Mr. Phelan is an example of an American who has attained great success in the business world and has retained his humble devotion to his Faith.

Can You Identify these Representative Members of the American Catholic Laity?

Catholics in Medicine.—In the noble profession of medicine, Catholics have been prominent since colonial times.

THOMAS ADDIS EMMET (1789-1840) was a distinguished surgeon and gynecologist. He invented several surgical instruments and wrote a widely used textbook.

WASHINGTON L. ATLEE (1808-1878) of Lancaster, Pa., was another prominent gynecologist. His brother JOHN L. ATLEE was also a distinguished physician.

WILLIAM V. KEATING (1821-1881) was a professor at Jefferson Medical College in Philadelphia, and one of the outstanding teachers of his time. His son, JOHN M. KEATING (1852-1893), was a highly successful specialist in children's diseases.

HORATIO R. STORER (1829-1922) was a leader in the medical world for many years. He practiced in Boston.

JOHN B. MURPHY (1857-1916) was one of the greatest surgeons of his generation. He developed the so-called "Murphy button," a device which greatly facilitates intestinal surgery. He reintroduced into America the pneumo-thorax method of treating tuberculosis. This is still widely used. His brilliant clinical research helped to improve bone surgery.

HENRY J. BLANKEMEYER is one of the outstanding authorities on the detection and treatment of tuberculosis of the larynx. He has given courses of instruction at the world-famous Trudeau School of Tuberculosis in the Adirondack Mountains of New York State.

One of the best-known clinics in the United States today is that of the Mayo Brothers in Rochester, Minn. The Mayos were not Catholics, but they attributed much of their success to the Catholic Sisters' Hospital in Rochester, where the surgical work is done.

In 1951, there were 871 Catholic hospitals in the United States.

Catholics in Time of War.—Catholics in the United States have never hesitated to fight gallantly and to shed their blood in the defense of our nation. The names of Catholics are found on the roll-call of heroes in every war in which the United States has participated. Today, many thousands of Catholics are carrying on this traditon, serving in the armed forces of their country.

1. *Revolutionary War.*—The services of Catholics during the American Revolution were attested to by no less an authority than George Washington. Many of the 25,000 Catholics then living in the Colonies fought in the army, and those who could not render military service helped in other ways. One of the best known Catholic soldiers in this struggle for independence was STEPHEN MOYLAN (1737-1811), who held the high rank of Quartermaster-General and commanded all the cavalry regiments in the Continental Army. FATHER PETER GIBAULT helped to save the Western territories for the Colonists. Catholic Indians of Maine fought valiantly for the American cause. Among the European Catholics who contributed greatly to the final success of the Revolution were the Frenchmen LAFAYETTE, ROCHAMBEAU, and DE GRASSE, and the Poles PULASKI and KOSCIUSKO.

During the Revolution, Congress officially attended Mass at St. Mary's Church in Philadelphia four times. Two of these visits were for funerals, and two for formal thanksgivings.

2. *The War of 1812.*—The greatest American land victory during the War of 1812 was General Andrew Jackson's brilliant

defense of New Orleans in 1815. On the eve of this battle, BISHOP DUBOIS of New Orleans publicly prayed for an American victory. After the battle, General Jackson acknowledged the efficacy of Catholic prayer by expressing his thanks to the Bishop, and by visiting the Convent of the Ursuline Sisters to deliver his thanks personally.

3. *The Civil War.*—The Catholic Church officially supported neither side in the American Civil War. Catholics fought valiantly both for the North and for the South. Among the Northern officers of the Catholic Faith, perhaps the best known was GENERAL PHILIP SHERIDAN (1831-1888), a brilliant cavalry leader who was one of General Grant's most trusted lieutenants. Others included ROSECRANS, CORCORAN, SHIELDS, and COPPINGER. One of the most successful Southern generals was P. G. T. BEAUREGARD (1818-1893), a daring Louisianan of French ancestry, who commanded and won a notable victory at the first battle of Bull Run. Another prominent Southern general, JAMES LONGSTREET (1821-1904), was converted to Catholicity after the war. STEPHEN MALLORY, a former United States Senator from Florida, was a Catholic who served as Secretary of the Navy in the Cabinet of President Jefferson Davis of the Confederate States of America.

Among the Catholic Priests who served as army chaplains during the war were FATHER CORBY, FATHER JOHN IRELAND (later Bishop Ireland), and Father ABRAM RYAN, the noted poet. ARCHBISHOP HUGHES of New York served the North in a diplomatic capacity. He was appointed by President Lincoln to travel to Europe and obtain proclamations of neutrality from Spain and France. He succeeded in this important mission.

Many Sisters served as nurses on the battlefields during the bloody struggle. Among them were about 100 Sisters of Charity, sixty Sisters of the Holy Cross, as well as Sisters of Mercy and Sisters of St. Joseph. None of these devout, self-sacrificing women sought individual fame, but one of them, SISTER ANTHONY, became known as the "ministering angel of the army of the Tennessee."

4. *The First World War.*—American Catholics today are justly proud of the splendid records which Catholic men and officers made during the First World War. One of the first Americans

to be killed in action was a Catholic volunteer from Pittsburgh, CORPORAL THOMAS F. ENRIGHT. The last American officer to be killed was a Catholic chaplain, REV. WILLIAM F. DEVITT, of Holyoke, Mass. General Pershing's Chief-of-Staff was MAJOR GENERAL JAMES W. MCANDREWS. Ten other Catholics served as Major Generals, and fifteen as Brigadier Generals. The Chief of Naval Operations was a distinguished Catholic, ADMIRAL WILLIAM S. BENSON (1855-1932). In all, there were more than a million Catholics in the American armed forces, of whom hundreds of thousands went overseas. While in France, they observed their religious duties in a manner that inspired admiration throughout that Catholic land.

5. *The Second World War.*—In this great struggle, approximately 24 per cent of the millions of men and women who served in the Armed Forces of the United States were Catholic. A total of 130,679 Catholics were killed in the war.

There were 3036 Catholic chaplains in our Armed Forces, of whom 83 sacrificed their lives. The Chief of Army Chaplains during the war was BRIGADIER GENERAL WILLIAM R. ARNOLD, who was consecrated Bishop and appointed Military Delegate in 1945. The first Priest to die in the military service was FATHER ALOYSIUS SCHMITT, who went down with the U.S.S. *Oklahoma,* sunk at Pearl Harbor on December 7, 1941. The first Congressional Medal of Honor ever given to a Chaplain of the Armed Forces was awarded to FATHER JOSEPH T. O'CALLAHAN, S.J., for services abroad the U.S.S. *Franklin.*

By October, 1946, a total of 67 Catholics had received the Congressional Medal of Honor. Among those receiving high honors were BRIGADIER GENERAL PAUL G. WURTSMITH of the Air Force, the first man of his rank to win the Distinguished Service Cross in combat; CAPTAIN RICHARD E. FLEMING, first Marine officer to win the Congressional Medal of Honor; SERGEANT JOHN BASELONE, first Marine enlisted man to win the Congressional Medal of Honor; and LIEUTENANT ELIZABETH P. HOISINGTON, first WAC officer to win the Bronze Star in the European Theater.

Among the many Catholics who served their country nobly in this greatest of wars, we should mention MRS. LEO M. VAN COUTREN of St. Louis, who gave nine sons and three daughters to serve in the Armed Forces.

PROPAGATION OF THE FAITH IN AMERICA

1850

1950

Position of the Catholics in the United States.—As we have seen, the persecution of Catholics during colonial times came to an end with the adoption of the Federal Constitution in 1789. Since then, Catholics have been guaranteed exactly the same rights and privileges as the members of any other religious group.

Of course, equality under the law does not mean that bigotry and intolerance no longer exist. In the main, however, the trend of the public attitude in the United States has been toward full tolerance for the Catholics in all fields—political, social and economic. It is true that there have been strong organizations with viciously anti-Catholic aims, such as the "Know-Nothing" Party in the 1850's, and more recently, the Ku Klux Klan. (The activities of the Klan in attempting to suppress Catholic education are discussed on page 336.) All such organizations, however, have been abhorred by the great majority of non-Catholics, who realize that intolerance of *any* religious or racial minority is un-American.

It may be said that, in general, anti-Catholic feeling survives principally in rural districts. This is to be expected, because attitudes and prejudices of any kind change more slowly in the country than in urban areas. The flare-up of bigotry that marred the 1928 Presidential campaign (in which Alfred E. Smith was a candidate) centered largely in the small towns. The Church, however, is keenly aware of this situation and is taking active steps to counteract it. Missionaries are going forth in ever-increasing numbers to disseminate truth in rural sections. Many college youths have volunteered for this holy work. The radio is also being employed for this purpose. The splendid program known as *The Catholic Hour* has been heard in forty-one states, carrying the voice of such magnetic personalities as Bishop Fulton J. Sheen into millions of homes of all kinds.

And these efforts are not in vain! The *Official Catholic Directory* reveals that there were 121,950 converts to the Faith in 1950.

CATHOLIC EDUCATION IN THE UNITED STATES

Introduction.—The Catholic Church is the divinely appointed guardian of truth, and one of the most important avenues to truth is formal education. For this reason, one of the basic functions of the Church is to educate children and young people.

To a Catholic, education means the complete development of the individual (morally, intellectually and physically) to enable him to play his part well in the drama of life on earth, and then to return to God, his Maker, for a happy eternity.

The Catholic educational system in the United States is a great monument to Catholicity and is the chief wealth of the Catholic Church. Catholic schools are established and maintained by the free-will offerings of Catholics. The manner in which these offerings are made differs at various times and places, but they are always spontaneous and always imply some kind of sacrifice. It is to be noted that Catholics, as loyal citizens, also pay taxes to support the regular public schools. However, Catholic parents prefer to send their children to schools in which they will learn all that is good and useful in a Catholic atmosphere where religion is revered and faith is nourished by those who love it.

Why Catholics Have Established Their Own Schools.— The first institutions of learning in the United States were Catholic schools. During the early years of our national history, there was comparatively little free public education. In the decade of the 1830's, however, widespread organization of public school systems began under the leadership of such educators as Horace Mann. These schools, unfortunately, were of such character as to be dangerous to the faith of Catholic children. The first protest of Catholics was against the requirement that all children in school read the Protestant version of the Bible. Catholics requested that Catholic children be permitted to read the Douay Version. This request and others were not granted.

During the 1840's, Bishop (later Archbishop) John Hughes of New York, to whom our parochial school system is deeply indebted, strove to bring about a compromise. His plan was to allow Catholics the use of special schools within the public school system; these schools were to be supported by public taxes, to which Catholics of course contributed. None of the states saw fit to adopt this plan, and Catholics had no alternative save to build and maintain their own schools.

Extent of Catholic Education.—A tabulation made in 1956 listed the following Catholic institutions of learning: 9051 parochial (elementary) schools; 2383 high schools; and 254 universities and colleges. The total enrollment in these institutions was about 6,805,000 students, including those attending vacation schools and released-time classes. If we exclude these last two categories, the total enrollment was about 4,500,000. In spite of this, many Catholic children, including more than half of those of primary school age, are attending public schools. There are various reasons for this. One of the most important, no doubt, is that 20% of the Catholic population lives in rural districts, and very often the Church cannot maintain schools in such districts because the Catholic population is too sparse and scattered, or because funds may not be available. It is evident, therefore, that a great many more Catholic schools are needed. The same is true of religious teachers. There is not a community of teaching men or women which is able to meet all the requests which are made of it for teachers. In short, while Catholic education in the United States has great achievements to its credit, there is much which remains to be accomplished.

1. *Parochial Schools.*—As early as 1640, the Catholic colony of Maryland had elementary schools conducted by the Jesuits. The First Synod of Baltimore in 1791 considered the problem of schools; and in 1829, at the first Provincial Council, the responsibility for establishing schools for children was placed on the shoulders of the Bishops. In 1866, the aim of a "school in every parish" was enunciated but an insufficiency of qualified teachers made it impossible to carry out this purpose immediately. In 1884, the Third Plenary Council of Baltimore, under the leadership of Archbishop Gibbons, adopted legislation providing for a Catholic elementary school near every church. Parents were to be required to send their children to these schools, unless the Bishop specifically permitted otherwise in particular cases. In 1951, there were over 4,000,000 students enrolled in 8710 parochial schools in the United States.

2. *High Schools.*—There are now over 2400 Catholic high schools, with a total enrollment of more than a half million students. Many more institutions of this type are now urgently needed, and expansion is being carried on steadily. The scope of this program may be indicated by reference to a single city, Cleveland, Ohio. In September, 1951, three new high schools opened their doors in this city: the Dominican Sisters of Adrian, Michigan opened the Hoban-Dominican High School for girls

(capacity, 1000 students) ; the Marianists of Dayton, Ohio opened Saint Joseph High School for boys (capacity, 2300 students) ; and the Holy Cross Brothers of Notre Dame, Indiana opened St. Edward High School (capacity, 1200 students). Each of these schools is a modern, fully equipped institution of American-Catholic secondary education. Similar development is now taking place from coast to coast.

3. *Colleges.*—The first Catholic college in the United States was *Georgetown College,* founded by the Jesuits in 1789. Now known as *Georgetown University,* it is located in Washington, D. C., and is an outstanding institution of higher education. Another renowned institution is *Notre Dame University* of South Bend, Ind. This school, which has been called the "American Oxford," was founded in 1841 by the Rev. Father Edward Sorin, O.S.C., aided by six Holy Cross Brothers from France. It was first housed in log cabins. Now, thousands of young men from every section of the country study in two score handsome buildings, which, as the Holy Cross Brothers tell us, were built by "Hail Mary's." *Fordham University* of New York City was also founded in 1841 as St. John's College, and has been conducted since 1846 by the Society of Jesus. The first president was Father McCloskey, later to become America's first Cardinal. Thousands of young Catholics now receive instruction at Fordham. Its graduate school and professional schools are particularly noted. The *Catholic University of America,* located in Washington, D. C., was founded by Pope Leo XIII in 1889. It is a pontifical university, conducted by the Catholic Hierarchy of the United States. It has been called the "Queen" of the twenty-two Catholic universities that flourish in our country today.

The few colleges mentioned above are representative of hundreds of Catholic institutions of higher education, all of which are doing a splendid work. The facilities for Catholic higher education are constantly being expanded. The year 1940, for example, witnessed the opening of Barry College in Miami, Fla. This was the first Catholic college for women in Florida.

The Faculties of Catholic Schools.—The members of Religious Orders of men and women are the teachers in our Catholic schools. Recently, laymen have been teaching, especially in the larger universities and colleges, but their number is limited.

SOME OF THE CATHOLIC TEACHING SISTERHOODS IN THE UNITED STATES[1]

ORDER OR CONGREGATION	WHERE AND WHEN FOUNDED	FIRST FOUNDATION IN THE U.S.A.	APPROXIMATE NUMBER OF MEMBERS (1956) [2]
Ursuline Nuns	Italy, 1535	Louisiana, 1727	3,847
Visitation Nuns	France, 1610	Maryland, 1799	777
Sisters of Charity	France, 1633	Maryland, 1809	22,000
Sisters of Loretto	Kentucky, 1812		1,186
Religious of the Sacred Heart	France, 1800	Missouri, 1818	1,003
Dominican Sisters	France, 1206	Kentucky, 1822	15,100
Sisters of St. Joseph	France, 1650	Missouri, 1836	17,650
Sisters of Notre Dame de Namur	France, 1803	Ohio, 1840	2,817
Sisters of Providence	France, 1762	Maryland, 1829	4,387
Sisters of Mercy	Ireland, 1831	Pennsylvania, 1843	12,563
Holy Cross Sisters	France, 1841	Michigan, 1843	2,876
Good Shepherd Sisters	France, 1641	Kentucky, 1843	1,387
Precious Blood Sisters	Switzerland, 1834	Ohio, 1844	2,707
Sister Servants of I.H.M.	Michigan, 1845		4,742
Sisters of Notre Dame	Germany, 1833	Milwaukee, 1850	7,252
Franciscan Sisters	Italy, 1212	Wisconsin, 1849	33,500
Benedictine Sisters	Italy, 529 (?)	Pennsylvania, 1852	6,471
Presentation Nuns	Ireland, 1777	California, 1854	2,092
Sisters of the Holy Name	Canada, 1843	Oregon, 1859	1,560
Blessed Sacrament Sisters	Pennsylvania, 1891		550

[1] In 1956, there were 159,545 Sisters in the United States, of whom 93,518 were engaged in teaching.
[2] Data based on *Official Catholic Directory* (1951 edition).

There are now more than 84,000 Religious women teaching in the United States, and about 11,700 Religious men. They come from fifteen Congregations of Brothers (see the chart on page 335), 234 Orders and Congregations of women, and seventy-three Orders and Congregations of men. Many Secular Priests are also professional teachers.

Some of the Orders and Congregations of women which play a leading role in Catholic education today are as follows:

1. *The Ursuline Sisters.*—The Ursuline foundation was made in New Orleans in 1727, under the leadership of Mother Mary Augustine Tranchepain. New Orleans was then a French possession. President Thomas Jefferson, whose own daughters attended a convent in France, insured the security of the Ursulines when he purchased the entire Louisiana territory from France in 1803. We have already noted how Andrew Jackson expressed his thanks for the prayers of the Ursuline Sisters after the battle of New Orleans in the War of 1812. In 1956, there were 3847 Ursulines teaching in the United States.

2. *The Visitation Nuns.*—The first convent of the Visitation Nuns was established in Georgetown, Md., in 1799. Miss Alice Theresa Lalor of Philadelphia was the foundress. In 1814, the invading British troops spared this convent when they burned the government buildings in Washington. The convent was also in the battle-zone during the Civil War but it remained untouched, due largely to the influence of General Winfield Scott, whose daughter Virginia was a deceased Visitation Nun. The convent has been the Alma Mater of many distinguished women. In 1956, 777 Visitation Nuns were teaching in this country.

3. *Sisters of Charity.*—This community was founded in 1809 in Emmitsburg, Md. The foundress was a New York woman, Mother Elizabeth Ann Seton. Today, more than 2400 women, known as the *Cornet Sisters of Charity,* belong to this community. They are active not only in education, but also in hospitals and in charitable and social-service work. They have distinguished themselves particularly by their services on the battlefields in times of war. Other foundations have sprung from the original one, and there were about 22,000 Sisters of Charity in 1956.

The cause of canonization of the foundress of the Sisters of Charity, Mother Elizabeth Ann Seton, is now being considered in

CATHOLIC TEACHING BROTHERHOODS IN THE UNITED STATES

Congregation	Where Founded	When Founded in United States	Approximate Number in U. S. (1956)	Location of Mother House in America
Holy Cross Brothers	France	1841	820	Washington, D. C.
Brothers of Christian Schools	France	1845	2659	Baltimore, Md.
Brothers of Mary Marianists	France	1849	999	Dayton, O.
Xaverian Brothers	Belgium	1854	583	Baltimore, Md.
Franciscan Brothers	Ireland	1858	219	Brooklyn, N. Y.
Brothers of Charity	Belgium	1865	261	Boston, Mass.
Poor Brothers of St. Francis Seraphicus	Holland	1866	64	Cincinnati, O.
Marist Brothers	France	1885	651	Poughkeepsie, N. Y.
Brothers of Christian Instruction	France	1886	164	Alfred, Me.
Christian Brothers of Ireland	Ireland	1916	712	West Park, N. Y.
Brothers of the Sacred Heart	France	1847	891	Metuchen, N. J.

Note: There were approximately 8868 Brothers in the United States in 1956. Some were engaged in nursing.

Rome. Her beautiful life has been the inspiration of much current literature. One such book which you will want to read is a novel, *White Noon*, by Sigrid Van Sweringen.

4. *The Dominican Sisters.*—The Dominican Sisters were founded in this country by the Dominican Fathers in Kentucky, in 1822. Other related and unrelated foundations were established from time to time in various parts of the United States. Moreover, Dominican Sisters came from Europe as missionaries and began new and flourishing foundations, with the result that in 1956 there were about 30 distinct foundations, with over 15,000 teaching Sisters. And this does not include cloistered Dominican Sisters, nor the various affiliated branches of the Order which have been established in recent years.

5. *Sisters of St. Joseph.*—The first Sisters of St. Joseph came to this country from France. In 1836, eight of them established a foundation at St. Louis, Mo., then a rude frontier town. Today, more than 17,600 successors of these valiant pioneer women continue to train young Americans for Faith and for country.

6. *The Franciscan Sisters.*—The first community of Franciscan Sisters in the United States was established in Milwaukee, Wisc. in 1849. The founders were six noble women from Germany. In 1956, there were more than 200 such communities in the United States, and fully 33,500 Franciscan Sisters labor fruitfully, teaching and nursing. They manifest all the traditional love of the Franciscans for God's poor and humble creatures.

7. *The Sisters of Mercy.*—The Sisters of Mercy began their work in the United States in the year 1843, when seven pioneers from Carlon, Ireland, arrived in this country. They were graciously received by the Most Reverend John Hughes, then Bishop of New York. Led by their superior, Mother Francis Xavier Warde, they established their foundation in Pittsburgh. As of 1956, more than 15,500 Sisters of Mercy were carrying on this work.

The Oregon Compulsory Education Law.—There have been, at various times in the past, organized political attempts to suppress the Catholic schools in the United States. In 1920, Ku Klux Klan agitation led to an attempt to insert into the constitution of Michigan an amendment suppressing all parochial schools. This attempt, fortunately, was defeated at the polls. In 1923, however, the Klan forces in Oregon, taking advantage of the machinery for popular initiative, managed to secure the enactment of a state law compelling universal attendance at public schools. The law was to go into effect in September, 1926. In 1925, two private schools brought suit against the law, contending that it was unconstitutional. A Federal District Court upheld this contention, and declared the law void. The case was finally taken to the Supreme Court of the United States. The Supreme Court, by a unanimous decision, pronounced the Oregon Compulsory Education Law unconstitutional.

The voiding of this anti-Catholic legislation furnished convincing proof that the Catholic schools of the United States are well protected by the Constitution.

Bus Transportation for Parochial School Students.—Some years ago, a New Jersey town, acting under a state law, reimbursed parents of school children for the bus fares they had spent to send their children to and from school. This included parents whose children were attending parochial schools. A resident of the town sued to prevent such payments to parents of parochial school children, claiming that they violated the Constitution.

This suit reached the Supreme Court. In 1947, in the *Everson Case*, the Court decided by a 5-to-4 vote that use of tax funds to provide transportation for parochial school children is legal. This established a long-needed precedent for equal treatment of *all* American boys and girls, no matter what school they may attend.

At present, all the states provide free bus transportation from public funds for public school children, but only nineteen states offer this same help to Catholic school children. In 1949, Wisconsin rejected a proposal to extend its system of free bus transportation to students in parochial schools.

The Question of Federal Aid to Education.—At present, public education in the United States is supported almost entirely by the states and by subdivisions of the states (cities, counties, etc.). In recent years, there has been much agitation in favor of alloting Federal funds directly to the states and their subdivisions for support of the schools.

In 1950, Congress defeated the Thomas Bill, providing a grant of 300 million dollars to the states for aid to education. The states were to have full authority to administer the funds. Alert Catholics helped to defeat this bill. Catholic opinion did not consider the projected program of aid acceptable unless it guaranteed equal treatment to parochial school children. Discrimination, such as Wisconsin had practiced in the matter of school bus transportation, was considered undemocratic and unfair.

The "Released Time" Program.—The public schools of Champaign, Illinois, set up a program by which children of all faiths were "released" from regular classes at specified times to receive religious instruction. Mrs. Vashti McCullom, a resident of Champaign, sued to stop this program, claiming that it violated the Constitution. In March, 1948, the Supreme Court handed down a verdict by an 8-to-1 vote ruling in favor of Mrs. McCullom. The Court held that it is unconstitutional to hold classes of religious instruction on public school property during school hours.

Although this was a blow to the "released time" program of religious instruction, the program is still flourishing. It was estimated in 1951 that almost 2,000,000 students in about 2500 communities were receiving instruction in this way. Children are still "released" from their classes for this purpose, but the classrooms and other facilities of the public schools are not used.

CATHOLIC ACTION IN THE TWENTIETH CENTURY

The Nature of Catholic Action.—Catholic Action was defined by Pope Pius XI in 1922 as the participation of the laity in the apostolate of the Hierarchy. It has been approved and advocated by the last six Pontiffs.

Canon Cardijn of Belgium designed a program and a pattern for Catholic Action. Under this program, the Church is no longer on the defensive, merely trying to prevent losses and encroachments. Instead, the Church takes the offensive, in a great, positive drive to win souls for God.

Under this program, the laity are organized by parishes, by dioceses, and also on a national scale. Units are formed on the basis of age, sex, and occupation. Within a given unit (let us say, men working in a factory), a Priest serving as Chaplain will usually select five or six leaders. These individuals form a "cell." Each leader selects five or six workers who form a "team." The members of the "cell" meet every week to exchange observations, discuss problems, and decide on modes of action. Each leader or worker tries to exert influence on the people around him by word and by example.

The Hierarchy of the United States in 1935 issued a joint statement entitled *Catholic Action and Catholic Activities* in which they indicated their will that the National Catholic Welfare Council (NCWC) serve as the instrument through which the official actions of the laity are to be developed. The NCWC issues *Catholic Action*, a monthly report that serves as a clearing house for information about Catholics and Catholic activities in the United States. Each Bishop officially approves the form that Catholic Action is to take in his diocese. A very good exposition of the procedure is to be found in *Fire in the Rain*, by Rev. William L. Doty (Bruce, 1951).

Newman Clubs.—The first Newman Club was formed in 1894 by a group of medical students at the University of Pennsylvania, led by Joseph Walsh. Father John Keough, their Chaplain, spread the idea. In June, 1950, a national conference of the Newman Clubs at Cleveland was attended by 1000 delegates, representing 450 colleges and universities.

Newman Clubs strive to promote an adult knowledge of the Faith and a frank recognition of Catholic social principles among the student communities of secular institutions of higher education, including state universities. In such secular institutions, "truth is taught as tentative, religion as an emotional observation, dogmatic authority as archaic and undemocratic, and moral principles as the product of group expedience" (*America*, 83:263, June 3, 1950). Newman Clubs do much to counteract these harmful tendencies among Catholic students attending secular colleges and universities.

Religion Vacation Schools.—Religion vacation schools are conducted during the summer vacations for elementary and high school students in need of further religious training. Sisters, Seminarians, and other suitably trained personnel serve as the faculty. In 1950, there were 9000 such schools with about 600,000 pupils. Modern pedagogical methods are used, and a happy companionship prevails between teachers and students. For example, Mass may be dramatized by the class; then a game of baseball may follow. A session is four weeks, five days a week; or the same plan can be completed in two weeks, with a full day's schedule. Most Rev. Edwin V. O'Hara, Bishop of Kansas City, introduced the idea of religious vacation schools in 1921, in Oregon. The Confraternity of Christian Doctrine is a division of NCWC that now supplies information about this activity.

Cana Conferences.—A Cana Conference is a day of discussion for married couples in a parish. Couples intending to marry may also attend. This is a form of Catholic Action designed to cope with the secularization of the family and other destructive tendencies in modern life. A typical Conference includes the reading of reports, workshop discussions, and informal corridor discussions, all intended to encourage and inspire people to make their marriages a means of attaining great holiness and happiness. The men and women attending learn the goals of marriage and the means of achieving them.

The idea of Cana Conferences originated with John P. Delaney, S.J., of New York City, who first met with eleven couples in March, 1943. Chicago invited Father Delaney to propagate the idea. St. Louis heard of this, and Father Dowling, S.J., took over the program in that city. By 1947, Cana Conferences constituted a full-fledged "movement." By 1949, 4393 couples had made Cana Days in the Chicago area alone.

The program is organized on a Diocesan basis. Today, nineteen Dioceses have special directors for this activity. The work, in origin and in purpose, is local rather than national—a parochial responsibility. Within the NCWC, the Family Life Bureau under the direction of Rev. Edgar Schmiedeler, O.S.B., sponsors this phase of Catholic Action.

Catholics on Radio and Television.—In 1951, there were about 93 million radio receiving sets in the United States; there were also about 10 million television receiving sets, with the number constantly growing. These modern means of communication are a potent instrument for reaching and influencing vast numbers of people. The Church has been utilizing them with great effectiveness.

National Catholic religious radio programs were inaugurated on March 2, 1930. The National Council of Catholic Men, a division of the NCWC, sponsors the programs. Bishop Fulton J. Sheen for twenty years has been the outstanding figure on these programs, with his matchless eloquence. In 1950, a new feature was added; well-known laymen participated in the program, including Henry Ford II, Dr. George Sperti, Judge Michael Walsh, and Howard Mitchell, leaders respectively in industry, science, law, and music. Regional programs have been in operation since 1943. In these, a question-and-answer type of discussion, conducted between a Priest and a layman, has proved very popular. The *Family Theater*, conducted by Rev. Patrick Peyton, C.S.C., has been carried by 500 stations throughout the world since February, 1947. Another program, *The Greatest Story Ever Told*, has been conducted by Fulton Oursler, a Catholic layman, since March, 1947. This program dramatizing incidents in the life of Christ, is commercially sponsored. Vatican City Station was inaugurated on February 12, 1931, broadcasting the voice of Pope Pius XI. More recently, Catholic ceremonies have been televised in New York and Chicago.

In 1951, Rev. Patrick Peyton, a modern Apostle of the Family Rosary, had approximately 5,000,000 people pledged to recite the family rosary daily. This is the fruit of two years of intensive activity utilizing radio and television, as well as moving pictures and other modern media. The success has been world-wide. Father Peyton has promoted the rosary crusade in Alaska, bringing the prayer program within three miles of the territory of Communist Russia. Even 1000 Protestants are pledged to recite the rosary daily.

It is a common experience, today, to find groups in private homes, in office buildings at lunch hour, in hospital rooms, in schools, and elsewhere, reciting the rosary in unison with voices coming over the radio.

CHRONOLOGICAL TABLE OF PRINCIPAL EVENTS IN CHURCH HISTORY

Year	Event
1511	First diocese in the Americas, in San Juan, Puerto Rico
1526	Dominican Friar said first Mass in Virginia
1535	Franciscans arrived in California
1542	Father Padilla, a Franciscan, became first martyr in what is now United States (near present site of Kansas City)
1549	Father Louis Cancer became proto-martyr of Florida
1565	St. Augustine, Fla., oldest city and parish in the United States, founded by Spanish Catholics

VISUALIZED CHURCH HISTORY

1569   Jesuits arrived in South Carolina
1597   Church in New Mexico erected by Reverend Martinez
1601   Mass offered in California
1604   Catholic chapel built in Maine; Mass offered by Father Aubry
1609   Santa Fe, N. M. founded; second oldest city in United States
1634   Maryland settled by group of 200, including many Catholics, with Father Andrew White, S.J., as their spiritual leader
1646   Mohawk Indians killed Father Isaac Jogues, S.J., "Apostle of New York"
1649   Toleration Act in Maryland granted religious freedom to all Christians
1671   Father Jacques Marquette (1637-1675) arrived in Michigan, carrying the Faith to the Indians
1673   Father Marquette and Joliet sailed down Mississippi, coming within 700 miles of Gulf of Mexico
1674   Father Marquette spent winter on present site of Chicago
1680   Catherine Tekakwitha, pious Mohawk maiden, died.
1685   Jesuit Catholic school established in New York City
1690   Reverend Eusebius Kino, S.J., arrived in Arizona
1701   Detroit founded by French Catholics; St. Anne's Church erected
1724   Reverend Sebastian Rale martyred in Maine by English colonists
1727   Ursulines, first Nuns in United States, arrived at New Orleans
1733   First Catholic Church built in Pennsylvania, under leadership of Father Joseph Greaton, S.J.
1755   French Catholic Acadians expelled from Canada by British
1769   First of twenty-one Spanish missions in California established by the Franciscan Father Junipero Serra
1770   Reverend Pierre Gibault founded first Catholic church in St. Louis, Mo.
1783   First free school in America founded by Father Thomas Hassett in Florida.
1789   Father John Carroll of Baltimore chosen first American Bishop; Federal Constitution adopted, containing guarantee of religious freedom to all
1791   First seminary in United States opened by Sulpician Fathers at Baltimore
1793   First Priest ordained in the United States (Theodore Badin at Baltimore)
1795   Prince Gallitzin, a Russian, ordained Priest; labored for forty-one years as "Apostle of the Alleghenies"

SUPPLEMENTARY MATERIAL FOR UNIT VII

- 1799 Visitation Nuns established at Georgetown, Md.
- 1806 Dominican Fathers established in Kentucky
- 1809 Mother Elizabeth Ann Seton founded Sisters of Charity at Emmitsburg, Md.
- 1817 Vincentian Seminary founded at Perrysville, Mo.
- 1820 Trusteeism in New York, Baltimore, and Philadelphia
- 1822 Dominican Sisters founded in Kentucky
- 1822 First Catholic newspaper established in the United States, *The United States Miscellany*, edited by Bishop England
- 1829 First Provincial Council met at Baltimore
- 1840 Pierre DeSmet, S.J. (1801-1873) became missionary to Indians in the Rocky Mountains.
- 1841 Fordham University founded in New York City, Reverend John McCloskey serving as first president
- 1841 Notre Dame University founded in Indiana by Reverend E. Sorin, C.S.C.
- 1842 Most Reverend John Hughes became Bishop of New York, where he organized a parochial school system; destroyed trusteeism
- 1843 Sisters of Mercy from Ireland settled in Pittsburgh
- 1844 Orestes Brownson (1803-1876) became a convert to the Faith
- 1859 North American College founded at Rome
- 1875 Archbishop McCloskey of New York (1810-1885) made first American Cardinal
- 1882 Knights of Columbus organized at New Haven, Conn.
- 1884 Third Plenary Council met at Baltimore
- 1886 Archbishop Gibbons of Baltimore (1834-1921) became the second United States Cardinal
- 1889 Catholic University founded at Washington, D. C.; Mother Katherine Drexel founded the Blessed Sacrament Sisters to teach Indians and Negroes
- 1892 Josephite Fathers founded at Baltimore to conduct Negro missions
- 1893 Apostolic Delegation appointed for United States
- 1908 United States raised above status of missionary country
- 1909 *America*, Catholic weekly, founded by Jesuits at Fordham University
- 1911 Archbishops John Farley of New York (1842-1918) and William O'Connell of Boston (1858-1944) raised to Cardinalate; Maryknoll Foreign Mission Society founded by Fathers Walsh and Price

344 VISUALIZED CHURCH HISTORY

1914 *Catholic Encyclopedia* published under American editorship

1916 System of nominating Bishops of the United States established

1921 Archbishop Dennis Dougherty of Philadelphia (1865-1951) created Cardinal

1924 Archbishops Patrick Hayes of New York (1867-1938) and George William Mundelein of Chicago (1872-1939) created Cardinals; *Commonweal*, a weekly publication, established by Catholic laymen of New York City

1925 United States Supreme Court declared unconstitutional the Oregon School Law of 1923, whose purpose was to force Catholic children under fourteen years of age to attend public schools

1926 Twenty-eighth International Eucharistic Congress held at Chicago (the first in the United States)

1930 Jesuit Martyrs of North America canonized by Pope Pius XI

1935 American Hierarchy protested religious persecution in Mexico

1936 Cardinal Pacelli, Papal Secretary of State (now Pope Pius XII) toured United States

1937 Dennis Cardinal Dougherty served as Papal Legate at thirty-third International Eucharistic Congress, held at Manila in the Philippine Islands; United States Hierarchy founded Montezuma Seminary at Las Vegas, N. M., for Mexican clergy

1940 Barry College, first Catholic college for women in Florida, founded by Bishop Barry, conducted by Dominican Sisters; Philip Murray became President of C.I.O.; New Bishops installed in United States included: Joseph Hurley, St. Augustine, Fla.; Samuel A. Stritch, Archbishop of Chicago, Ill.; Joseph C. Plagens, Grand Rapids, Mich.; Moses E. Kiley, Archbishop of Milwaukee, Wis.; William A. Griffin, Trenton, N. J.; A. J. Schwertner, Wheeling, W. Va.

1941 New Bishops installed in United States included: Robert E. Lucey, Archbishop of San Antonio, Tex.; James J. Sweeney, first Bishop of Honolulu, Hawaii; Francis J. Magner, Marquette, Mich.; Joseph C. Willging, first Bishop of Pueblo, Colo.; Peter W. Bartholomew, St. Cloud, Minn.; Edward G. Hettinger, Columbus, O.; National Eucharistic Congress of Eastern Rite Catholics held in Chicago, attended by 50,000 in 5-day session; St. Theresa School for Chinese Catholics established in Chicago

1943 Archbishop Francis Spellman (Military Vicar) toured the fighting fronts throughout the world, visiting Chaplains and men in service

SUPPLEMENTARY MATERIAL FOR UNIT VII

1944 American troops liberated Rome from Nazis; 6,000,000 pounds of clothing collected in the United States for people of Italy

1946 Elevation to rank of Cardinal for Francis Spellman of New York, Samuel Stritch of Chicago, Edward Mooney of Detroit and John Glennon of St. Louis; Senator Robert F. Wagner of New York, long a national political leader, became a Catholic convert

1947 In Everson Case, United States Supreme Court supported use of tax funds to provide free bus transportation for parochial school children as a constitutional right; Archbishop Ritter of St. Louis opened parochial schools to Negroes

1948 Santa Maria University at Ponce, Puerto Rico founded by Bishop James E. McManus, C.SS.R., the first Catholic University in Puerto Rico; first group of DP's (refugees) from Europe, including many Catholics, arrived in United States

1949 First Trappistines in the United States at Wrentham, Massachusetts; ten American women canonically trained in Waterford, Ireland

1950 Death of Archbishop John T. McNicholas of Cincinnati; General J. Lawton Collins, Army Chief of Staff, received the Laetare Medal at Notre Dame; 90,000 Pilgrims from United States visited Rome for Holy Year; parochial schools opened in Panama Canal Zone; 5,000,000 pounds of clothing collected during Thanksgiving week for relief work in Korea

1951 Fulton John Sheen consecrated Bishop in Rome; Francis P. Matthews, Secretary of Navy, appointed Ambassador to Dublin, Ireland; first native Eskimo Nun, Sister Naya Pelagie in Community of Grey Nuns of Nicolet

1952 The 35th International Eucharistic Congress was held at Barcelona, Spain.

1953 Several new Cardinals created, among them James Francis Cardinal McIntyre of Los Angeles, California.

1954 Canonization of Pope Pius X (May 29); his feast day is September 3.

1955 The 36th International Eucharistic Congress was held at Rio de Janeiro, Brazil; Peron government in Argentina was responsible for burning and destruction of several churches, imprisonment of over 100 Priests, and exile of members of the Hierarchy; later in the year, after the Peron tyranny had been overthrown, the Argentine government officially restored the rights of the Church.

1956 New Canon Law for the observance of the Easter Week liturgy.

REFERENCES

BOARDMAN, A. C., *Such Love Is Seldom* (Mother M. Walsh, Cincinnati)
CURRAN, E. L., *Great Moments in Catholic History*, pp. 73-100
DINNEEN, J. S., *Pius XII, Pope of Peace*
DOTY, W. L., *Fire in the Rain* (Catholic Action in the United States)
FINN, B., *Twenty-four Cardinals of the United States*
LAUX, J., *Church History*, pp. 545-577, Appendix pp. 1-11
LORTZ, J., KAISER, E. G., *Church History*, pp. 515-519
MEEHAN, T. A., *Christ's Career Women*
MERTON, T., *The Seven Storey Mountain*
MURRAY, J. O., *The Catholic Church in the United States*
O'CONNELL, WILLIAM CARDINAL, *Recollections of Seventy Years* (an autobiography)
RAEMER, S. A., *Church History*, pp. 497-515
ROSALITA, SR. M., *No Greater Service*
SARGENT, D., *Our Land and Our Lady* (essays)
SHEA, J. G., *The Catholic Church in the United States*
SISTERS OF NOTRE DAME, *Compendium of Church History*, pp. 1-97
VAN SWERINGEN, S., *White Noon* (a novel about Mother Elizabeth Ann Seton)
WALSH, J. E., *The Man of Joss Stick Alley*
WILLIAMS, M., *Shadow of the Pope* (an analysis of the Presidential election of 1928)
Catholic Encyclopedia, "Baltimore," "Cardinals," "Laity," "Taney," "Texas."

QUESTIONS

1. Describe the missionary activities of Spanish Catholics in the following territories during the sixteenth and seventeenth centuries. In each case, state when organized missionary activities began and name the outstanding missionaries engaged in this holy work: (a) Florida, (b) New Mexico, (c) Arizona, (d) Texas, (e) California.

2. Explain fully how each of the following helped to plant the seeds of Faith in the New World: (a) St. Isaac Jogues, (b) Father Jacques Marquette, (c) Catherine Tekakwitha.

3. (a) Which English colony in America was established by Catholics? (b) What circumstances impelled the Catholics to establish this colony? (c) Tell the story of the founding of this colony, naming the

outstanding personalities who played a part in it. (*d*) How did the English Catholics in America differ from the Puritans of New England in their treatment of religious minorities and in their attitude toward the Indians?

4. (*a*) What was the general status of Catholics in the thirteen English colonies? (*b*) Describe the role of American Catholics in the Revolutionary War. (*c*) Name a Catholic who was a signer of the Declaration of Independence. (*d*) Describe the provisions of the Federal Constitution which relate to religion.

5. (*a*) What is the meaning of the term *hierarchy*? (*b*) What are *subordinate ministers*? (*c*) Describe the chief duties of Priests and Bishops. What powers are exercised by Bishops which are not granted to Priests? (*d*) What requirements must a candidate for the Priesthood have?

6. (*a*) What is the oldest seminary in the United States? When and by whom was it founded? (*b*) Approximately how many seminaries are in existence in the United States today? How many students are preparing for the Priesthood in these seminaries? (*c*) When and by whom was the Society of the Maryknoll Fathers founded? (*d*) Describe the career of Father McShane of Maryknoll.

7. (*a*) What is a *consistory*? (*b*) By whom is a candidate for the Cardinalate nominated? Describe the procedure followed in the selection of a Cardinal. (*c*) What is a *conclave*? (*d*) Name the three grades of Cardinals.

8. (*a*) Name the eminent American Churchmen who have become Cardinals. (*b*) Summarize the careers of three of these Princes of the Church.

9. Name and describe the achievements of three American Catholic laymen who have distinguished themselves in each of the following fields: (*a*) public life, (*b*) literature, (*c*) industry, (*d*) medicine, (*e*) the armed forces of the United States.

10. Name four outstanding Catholic institutions of higher learning in the United States. When and by whom were they founded?

11. (*a*) Discuss fully the situation of Catholics in the United States today, with regard to political, social, and economic discrimination. (*b*) What efforts are being made to combat anti-Catholic bigotry?

12. (*a*) Name six Religious Orders and Congregations of women which are playing a leading role in Catholic education in the United States today. (*b*) When was each of these organizations established in the United States and by whom?

13. (a) Name four American Cardinals created in 1946. (b) Outline the life of one of these.

14. (a) Define *Catholic Action.* (b) Give three examples of Catholic Action in the United States. (c) Name three outstanding Catholics on radio and television programs.

15. State the ruling of the United States Supreme Court in regard to the following issues: (a) the Oregon Compulsory Education Law; (b) use of tax funds to provide bus transportation for parochial school children; (c) the "released time" program for religious instruction.

SELECTION TEST

In each of the following groups, select the name that does not apply.

1. *Catholic Missionaries:* Louis Cancer, Isaac Jogues, Junipero Serra, Louis Joliet, Jacques Marquette.

2. *American Cardinals:* John McCloskey, James Gibbons, Charles Carroll, William O'Connell, Patrick Hayes.

3. *Catholic American Statesmen:* Charles Carroll, Roger B. Taney, Andrew Jackson, Francis Kernan, Alfred E. Smith.

4. *Catholic Universities:* Notre Dame, Harvard, Fordham, Georgetown, Creighton.

5. *Catholic Periodicals:* "American," "Commonweal," "Sunday Visitor," "Atlantic Monthly."

6. *Catholic American Military Heroes:* Thomas F. Enright, W. S. Rosecrans, Philip Sheridan, Robert E. Lee.

7. *Catholic Hierarchy:* Archbishop Hughes, Cardinal Mundelein, Father Badin, Mother Elizabeth Ann Seton, Father Gallitzin.

8. *Catholic American Leaders in Industry and Labor:* Henry Ford II, John Henry Phelan, Charles W. Stoddard, Creighton Brothers, Philip Murray.

9. *Catholic American Writers:* Joel Chandler Harris, Fulton J. Sheen, Thomas Merton, Ralph Waldo Emerson, Orestes Brownson.

10. *Catholic American Medical Authorities:* Mayo Brothers, Henry J. Blankemeyer, Horatio R. Storer, John B. Murphy, Thomas A. Emmet.

SUPPLEMENTARY MATERIAL FOR UNIT VII

CHRONOLOGY TEST

Number the items in each of the following groups in their proper chronological order.

A

( ) Father Isaac Jogues, S.J., martyred, by Mohawks
( ) Father Louis Cancer, O.P., martyred in Florida
( ) Father Rale, S.J., martyred by English Protestants
( ) Father Padilla, O.F.M., martyred in New Mexico Territory
( ) Death of Father Marquette, S.J.

B

( ) Archbishop McCloskey selected Cardinal
( ) Archbishops O'Connell and Farley selected Cardinals
( ) Archbishop Gibbons selected Cardinal
( ) Archbishops Hayes and Mundelein selected Cardinals
( ) Archbishop Dougherty selected Cardinal

C

( ) First California mission founded at San Diego
( ) Maryland settled by Catholics
( ) St. Augustine, Fla., founded
( ) Mississippi explored by Father Marquette
( ) Santa Fe, N. M., founded

D

( ) Georgetown University founded
( ) Catholic University of America founded
( ) Notre Dame University founded.
( ) Ursuline Sisters founded in United States
( ) Sisters of Charity founded in United States

COMPLETION TEST

Complete each of the following statements by supplying the correct word or phrase in the blank space.

1. The Catholic population in the American colonies at the time of the Revolutionary War numbered ....

2. The unique contribution of the United States to the political and social theories and practices of the world is the separation of ...... and ....

3. The first martyr in the United States was a Franciscan Priest named ....

4. The religion of Latin America today is predominantly ....

5. The first resident Bishop in the United States was ....

6. The first Priest ordained in the American colonies was ....

7. There are, at present, ... Archbishops in the United States.

8. ...... was known as the "Cardinal of Charities."

9. The first American Cardinal was ....

10. There are at present (*how many?*) ...... living Cardinals in the United States. Their names are ....

11. The city of ...... has, at present, the largest Catholic population in the United States.

12. The Catholic population in the United States today numbers more than ....

MATCHING TEST

In the parenthesis next to each name in Column A, write the number of the item in Column B which is most closely associated with it.

A

( ) Bishop Carroll
( ) Cardinal McCloskey
( ) Bishop Hughes
( ) Cardinal O'Connell
( ) John B. Murphy
( ) Roger B. Taney
( ) Louis Cancer
( ) Junipero Serra
( ) St. Isaac Jogues
( ) **Charles Carroll of Carrolton**

B

1. Signer of Declaration of Independence
2. Jesuit missionary
3. Catholic American statesman
4. First Cardinal of United States
5. Cardinal of Boston
6. Dominican missionary
7. Catholic American physician
8. Established parochial school system in United States
9. Franciscan missionary
10. Great Catholic American general
11. First American Bishop of United States
12. First Priest ordained in United States

RECENT DEVELOPMENTS

Pope John XXIII (1958-   ).—On October 28, 1958, following the death of Pope Pius XII, a conclave of 51 Cardinals chose Angelo Giuseppe Cardinal Roncalli, Patriarch of Venice, to ascend the throne of St. Peter. This came on the third day of the proceedings after 11 ballots. The new Pontiff selected the name of John XXIII.

Angelo Roncalli was born November 25, 1881, the third of 10 children in a farmer's family in the Alpine foothills of Northern Italy. After ordination on August 10, 1904, in Rome, he served as secretary to his own Bishop for 10 years, during which time he acquired a polish and poise which, with his open, affable, warmhearted character, would later make him an effective diplomat.

The years from 1915 to 1919 were spent in military service, chiefly as chaplain. Until his 44th year, Italy was the setting for his priestly labors. Then for 30 years he was a papal diplomat in Bulgaria, Greece, and France. In 1953 he became Patriarch of Venice, Italy. Five years later he was elected Pope and now wears the triple diadem that symbolizes the powers to teach, to rule, and to sanctify in the Church.

His Holiness has been likened in character to Pope Pius X and to Abraham Lincoln. The Pontiff's words and deeds are those of an energetic shepherd of souls. On October 29, in his first radio message to the world, he quoted four definitions of peace: "ordered harmony of men" (St. Augustine); "tranquillity of order" (Aquinas); peace is a blessing; and "peace is tranquil liberty" (Cicero).

In December, 1958, the Pontiff elevated 23 prelates to the College of Cardinals, making the total 74 for the first time in history. By January, 1961, the membership of the College of Cardinals stood at 86. In January, 1959, Pope John announced three major projects: a diocesan synod of Rome, the 21st Ecumenical Council, and the modernization of the Code of Canon Law.

The Pope emphasizes his duties as Bishop of Rome, a city of 2 million souls. He says: "It needs a pastoral refresher of everything for which We as Bishop of Rome bear responsibility before God." He makes it a practice to leave the Vatican, and on one occasion visited a jail in Rome, to whose 1500 inmates he said: "You could not come to me, so it is right that I come to you."

Observing some tourists in Rome, he suggested wisely but humorously: "Italy ... is not on the equator, and even there, by the way, lions wear their coats, and crocodiles are lined with their most precious hides." He has canonized five saints: St. Charles, an Italian Franciscan; St. Joaquina, a Spanish Carmelite Nun; St. Gregory Barbarigo (1625-1697) ; St. John de Ribera (1532-1611); and St. Bertilla Boscardin (1888-1922), an Italian Nun. Two beatifications are those of Sister Elena Guerra, an Italian who died in 1914; and Mother Marie Marguerite d'Youville, born near Montreal, Canada, in 1701.

Many serious problems face the Holy Father, including the "silent church," the persecuted church in Eastern Europe, and the threat of schism in Communist China. Since 1946, in China, 4 million Catholics have suffered brutal persecutions. In March, 1959, reports indicate, the Red Chinese forced 300 native Catholic nuns to work the furnaces in the steel mills of Shanghai with an undisclosed number of priests. There is evidence that the Chinese Catholics are loyal to their faith under such severe persecution. Latin America lacks sufficient priests to shepherd the more than 170 million Catholics now living in that part of the world. Pope John's motto is to see everything, to turn a blind eye to much of it, to correct a little.

His devotion to the United States has been shown by the selection of Archbishop Egidio Vagnozzi to be Apostolic Delegate to our country, as a successor to Archbishop Cicognani, recently elevated to the rank of Cardinal after 25 years of service. The new delegate spent nine years in Washington in the Vatican delegation and also acted as counselor to Angelo Roncalli, the papal diplomat, in France. He loves the American ideals and spirit, as well as the ideals of the Holy Father.

American Cardinals.—In January, 1961, the United States had six living Cardinals. The careers of Francis Cardinal Spellman and James Cardinal McIntyre are described on pages 316 and 317. The careers of the other four Cardinals, as well as that of John Cardinal O'Hara, who died August 28, 1960, are summarized below.

Richard Cardinal Cushing (1895-   ).—The Archbishop of Boston was born a Bostonian on August 24, 1895. After education in his native city, he was ordained in 1921 and served as a parish Priest for nine years. His consecration as Auxiliary Bishop of

Boston occurred in 1939; he became Archbishop of Boston in 1944 and Cardinal in 1958. He has been characterized as the "Candid Cardinal" and has been outstandingly active in civic, relief, and welfare work in the Boston area.

Cardinal Cushing says of himself that he is still following his father's advice given when he was of high school age and not doing particularly well in school. "Carry on," the older Cushing admonished him. "Just work." At 63 this magnetic prelate said of himself: "That's all I've done since—work."

His work now centers about his interest in missions for Latin America. Bishop Fulton Sheen said of him: "He is the priests' bishop. And the 50,000 priests in the United States feel this. There are three reasons: his poverty is the twin-sister of his suffering; he is totally indifferent to praise; he is rich in the affections of the priests of the United States."

John Cardinal O'Hara (1888-1960).—From Ann Arbor, Mich., to international eminence sums up briefly the life and the priestly career of John Cardinal O'Hara, C.S.C., Archbishop of Philadelphia, who received the red hat at the December, 1958, Consistory. Born in Ann Arbor on May 1, 1888, he lived for a short time in Peru, Ind. In 1905, while his father was in the United States consular service, he attended the Jesuit Colegio de la Sagrada Corazón in Montevideo, Uruguay. Argentina and Brazil were his next homes. In 1909-1911, he attended Notre Dame University, where he received a Ph.B. He then entered the Congregation of the Holy Cross, and ordination followed in 1916. Until 1934 he was prefect of religion at Notre Dame. In this capacity, he served as presiding judge of unforgettable sessions in his famous "gripe room" in the Sorin Tower. The student body affectionately nicknamed him "The Pope." In 1934 he was elected Notre Dame's president. He was consecrated Bishop in 1939 and served as Bishop of the Army and Navy diocese. Buffalo was his diocese in 1945, Philadelphia in 1951.

When visiting the Notre Dame International School in Rome, Cardinal O'Hara spoke to 270 lads from 35 nations on a favorite theme of his—what you find on the first page of the catechism.

Albert Cardinal Meyer (1903-   ).—Albert Gregory Meyer, Archbishop and third Cardinal of Chicago, was born in Milwaukee. He attended Catholic schools in Milwaukee and completed his studies in philosophy and theology at the North American College in Rome. He was ordained in Rome, July 11, 1926, and remained a Scripture student for three years more. A Sacred Scripture expert, he functioned as parish priest, seminary professor, and rector from 1931 to 1946. In 1946 he was consecrated Bishop of Superior, Wisc., and in 1953 became Archbishop of Milwaukee. In 1958 he became Archbishop of Chicago with the spiritual care of 2 million Catholics and in 1959 was created a Cardinal. In an official letter to the people of his Archdiocese, he said: "Rightly we rejoice in the extraordinary vitality of Catholic life here in our great Archdiocese."

Aloysius Cardinal Muench (1889-   ).—Milwaukee is also the birthplace of this kindly prelate. He prepared for the priesthood at St. Francis Seminary in Milwaukee. His ordination on June 8, 1913, was followed by a professorship and a term as rector at his Alma Mater. In 1935 he became Bishop of Fargo, N. Dak., and in 1951, was appointed Papal Nuncio to Bonn, Germany. In 1959 he was created a Cardinal and made a member of the Curia, the Church's "Cabinet," in Rome. He was the first native-born citizen of the United States to serve as Papal Nuncio. When Chancellor Adenauer admired a purple cape he was wearing, the Cardinal said, "I'll see that you get something purple," and promptly delighted the Chancellor with a necktie made of the same material.

Joseph Cardinal Ritter (1892-   ).—This Archbishop of St. Louis, Mo., was born in New Albany, Ind., and was ordained in May, 1917. He was consecrated Auxiliary Bishop of Indianapolis in 1933 and was transferred to St. Louis in 1946.

In 1947 Archbishop Ritter integrated the St. Louis Catholic schools, seven years before the Supreme Court ordered desegregation in the public schools. When a group of Catholics organized for opposition, the Archbishop effectively checked it by a persuasive warning and the laymen disbanded.

In 1955 this determined prelate took action to relieve the shortage of priests in Latin America. His Archdiocese established and supported a mission in Bolivia staffed with three volunteer Priests of the St. Louis Archdiocese. He has been forceful in promoting the dialogue Mass in his churches. The Archbishop points out that the Church's social teachings are designed to let laymen know how "Christ would act if He were a banker, a baker, a broker, or a bricklayer." He was created a Cardinal in January, 1961.

New Diocese of Miami, Florida.—Pope Pius XII on August 13, 1958, canonically erected the Diocese of Miami, with Bishop Coleman F. Carroll as its Ordinary. The 16 southern counties of Florida's 67 counties constitute the area of the new Diocese.

Catholicity has had an inspiring history of growth in southern Florida. Henry M. Flagler, railroad and real estate magnate, donated the land for the first church in the area. The first railroad reached Miami in 1912. In 1926, Monsignor William Barry established St. Patrick's Church in Miami Beach. Temporary accommodations were found in a converted polo stable. Today, dynamic Bishop Carroll and 86 priests function in 60 parishes in the fastest growing diocese in the United States. There are 331,000 Catholics in the diocese, of whom 85,000 are Spanish-speaking. The Bishop and Priests are assisted by 563 Sisters of 16 communities who conduct schools and hospitals. In the summer of 1959, six new communities assumed duties, including two communities of Brothers, who, for the first time in the Diocese, undertook the education of boys. A minor seminary opened in Miami in September, 1959.

Hawaii.—Catholicity in Hawaii, which became the 50th state in 1959, has had a long history, marked by persecution, war, and heroic sanctity. Today the Church in Hawaii is thriving. There are 155,000 Catholics in a total population of more than 550,000. Bishop James W. Sweeney of Honolulu directs the labors of 145 Priests, 58 Brothers, and 424 Sisters. There are a minor seminary with 70 seminarians, a coeducational college, 10 Catholic high schools, and 25 elementary schools.

The Catholic faith was introduced to the islands in July, 1827, by three Priests of the Congregation of the Sacred Hearts of Jesus and Mary, two Frenchmen and an Irishman. United States Protestant missionaries had entered the area in 1820. Persecution followed. The French government intervened, and on July 9, 1839, an ultimatum was accepted that secured religious freedom for

Catholics. When the Hawaiian Islands were taken over by the United States in 1898, the freedom of the Church in this part of the world was assured. Under statehood, the Church will continue to carry on its mission with renewed vigor.

Alaska.—Alaska was admitted to the Union as the 49th state in 1959. At the time of statehood, there were about 29,500 Catholics living among a total population of 187,000. There are two Bishops, 49 Priests, 90 Sisters, and eight Brothers spreading the Faith in this vast northern area, which at one point is only a few miles from territory of Soviet Russia.

Jesuits from Oregon have been the missionaries in 27 parishes and 68 missions and mission stations. In four secondary and 10 elementary schools there are over 1700 pupils, while an equal number of public school students are in religious instruction classes. Rome in 1951 divided the mission vicariate into two dioceses. The Most Rev. Francis D. Gleeson, S.J., is one bishop; the other is the Most Rev. Dermot O'Flanagan in the new Diocese of Juneau.

The Church in Norway.—The first monastery to be built in Norway since the Reformation has been planned by Dominicans. The first Dominican monastery in Norway, St. Olaf's of Gamblebyen, built in the 1220's, is being restored and preserved as a national monument. In 1958, there were eight Dominican fathers in Oslo, capital of Norway; of these, four were Norwegian-born.

The Church in Denmark.—Prior to the Reformation, Denmark had nearly a thousand churches. Today, only 2% of Denmark's population attends church on Sunday. There are 26,000 Catholics in the country, with about 100 Priests. Priests are generally respected for their personal qualities, but not for their positions.

INDEX

Abelard, 126
Absolutism, royal, 211-217
Acolytes, 59
Action, Catholic, 338-341
Acts of the Apostles, 10
Adrian I, Pope, 54
Adrian II, Pope, 54
Adrianople, battle of, 65
Agnes, St., 23
Alans, 65
Alaric, 65
Albert the Great, St., 126
Albigenses, 54, 108-109
Alcuin, 83, 92
Alexander III, Pope, 54
Alexander VI, Pope, 155
Alexander, Bishop of Alexandria, 44, 45
Alexander I, of Russia, 240
All Saints' Day, 6
Altar, liturgical development of, 29
Alva, Duke of, 187-188
Ambrose, St., 54, 56, 58, 68
America, colonization by Spain, 293-298; colonization by France, 298-301; colonization by English, 301-304; establishment of independent nation, 304; *see also* "United States"
American Revolution, effects on French Revolution, 230; role of Catholics in, 303-304, 325
Amiens, Peace of, 139
Anabaptists, 182
Anagni, tragedy of, 141
Andrew, St., 14
Angela Merici, St., 207, 210
Angelico, Fra, 157-158
Anglican Church, 191 ff., 249-250, 266
Ansgar, St., 94
Anthony, St., 68
Apocalypse, 6, 10
Apostasy, definition of, 40
Apostles, 6-9, 14-15
Apostles' Creed, 28, 44, 47
Apse, 28, 61
Aquinas, St. Thomas, 40, 121, 125, 254
Archbishops, 59, 310-311
Archdioceses, 59, 310-311
Arianism, 43-45, 46, 47, 52
Arizona, missionary activities in, 294
Ars, Curé of, 242
Art, in Middle Ages, 126-128; of Renaissance, 153, 157-159
Associations Act, in France, 259
Assumption, Dogma of the, 280
Athanasius, St., 44, 45, 53, 68
Atlee, Washington L., 324
Attila, 65
Augsburg, Confession of, 182-183; Peace of, 183
Augustine, St., 49-50, 52, 53, 68, 92
Augustinians, 118, 122
Aurelian, Emperor, persecution of Christians, 23, 25
Ausculta, fili, 140

Austria, Josephism in, 214-215; in nineteenth century, 251-252; conquered by Hitler, 261
Avignon, 142, 145, 146

"Babylonian Captivity," 142-145
Bacon, Roger, 120, 126
Baltimore, Lord, 301-302
Baltimore, Third Plenary Council of, 313, 331; First Synod of, 331
Barbarian invasions, 63-67
Baring, Maurice, 250, 265
Bartholomew, St., 14; St. Bartholomew's Massacre, 185-186
Basil, St., 46, 53, 68
Basilicas, 27, 29, 61-62
Basle-Florence, Council of, 55, 149-150
Bavaria, conquered by Charlemagne, 83; in Protestant Revolt, 182; Concordat with (*1817*), 243-244
Beatitudes, 6, 30
Beguards, 55
Beguines, 55
Belgium, in Protestant Revolt, 187-188; in nineteenth century, 251; in twentieth century, 276
Bellarmine, St. Robert, 210
Benedict, St., 68, 69; Rule of, 69
Benedict XI, Pope, 142
Benedict XII, Pope, 143-144, 147
Benedict XV, Pope, 277
Benedictine Order, 69
Beran, Archbishop Josef, of Prague, 273, 274
Bernadette of Lourdes, 242-243
Bishop of Rome, 8-9, 59-60; *see also* "Papacy"
Bishops, 59, 60, 305, 310-311
Bismarck, Otto von, 245, 246
"Black Cardinals," 237
Black death, 144
Blankemeyer, Henry J., 325
"Bloodless Revolution," 196
Boccaccio, 159, 160-161
Bogoris, Prince, of Bulgaria, 86, 96
Bohemia, 83, 96, 149, 197
Bologna, University of, 122
Bonaparte, Napoleon, 234, 236-240
Bonaventure, St., 120, 126
Boniface, St., 92-94
Boniface VIII, Pope, 138-141
Borromeo, St. Charles, 202, 207, 210
Bosco, Don, 248-249
Boston, 314
Bourbon dynasty, 185, 186
Bramante, 155, 156
Breda, Compromise of, 187
Bridget, St., 145, 146
Brotherhoods, Catholic teaching, 334-335
Brownson, Orestes, 321-322
Bruno, St., 99-100
Bulgaria, 86, 96, 270, 274
Bus transportation for parochial school students (Everson Case), 337
Burgundians, 67
Byzantine architecture, 62

xi

California, missionary activities in, 295-296
Calixtus II, Pope, 54, 105
Calvert, George (Lord Baltimore), 301
Calvin, John, 184-185
Cana Conferences, 340
Canada, Catholicity in, 298-300
Candace, Queen, 11
Canisius, St. Peter, 206-207, 208
Cappadocian Doctors of Church, 46, 47, 53
Capuchins, 120
Carbonari, 247
Cardinals, nature of office, 59, 312; American, 312-317
Carmelites, 118, 121-122, 207
Carroll, Charles, 303, 319
Carroll, Daniel, 304, 319
Carroll, Most Rev. John, 310
Carthage, Council of, 48, 49, 52
Catacombs, 18, 26-28
Catechumens, 60
Cathari, *see* "Albigenses"
Cathedrals, construction of, 126-127
Catherine of Alexandria, St., 23, 25
Catherine of Siena, St., 121, 146
Catherine of Aragon, 191
Catherine di Medici, 187-188
Catherine Tekakwitha, 300-301
Catholic Center Party (Germany), 260
Catholic Emancipation Act, 249
Catholic University of America, 292, 332,
Cavaliers, 195
Cavour, 247
Cecilia, St., 25
Celestine I, Pope, 54, 71
Center Party (Germany), 245, 246, 260
Chalcedon, Council of, 51, 52, 53, 54
Châlons, battle of, 65
Charity, Sisters of, founding of, 208; in United States, 333, 334
Charlemagne, 82, 83-84; and Greek Schism, 86
Charles Borromeo, St., 202, 210
Charles V, Emperor, 116, 181, 182, 183, 187
Charles I, of England, 194
Charles II, of England, 196
Charles VII, of France, 167
Charles X, of France, 240
Charles Martel, 82, 90
Chesterton, Gilbert K., 250, 265
Children's Crusade, 113
Chicago, 300, 311, 315-316
China, 145, 206, 308
Christ, Jesus, 4, 5; and Gospels, 8; and heresy, 42, 43
Christmas, beginning of celebration of, 61
Church, definition of, 2; charter of, 3; constitution of, 3-4; as a corner stone of, 4; as a perfect society, 4-5; Founder of, 5 (*For further references, see specific items in Index*)
Cistercians, 100, 109
Citeaux, monastery of, 100, 109
Civil Constitution of the Clergy, 232
Civil War (American), Catholics in, 326
Clement, St., Pope, 59
Clement V, Pope, 55, 142
Clement VI, Pope, **144**
Clement VII, Pope, 191
Clement VII, anti-Pope, 146
Clericis laicos, 139
Clermont, Council of, 111
Clonard, monastery of, 71
Clovis, 67
Cluny, monastery of, 98
Colonna, Sciarra, 141, 142, 143

Columba, St., 92
Communion, 55
Communism, 267-275
Conciliar theory, 144, 149, 150
Conclave, 312
Concordat, of Worms (*1122*), 105; of *1801* with France, 237-238, 239, 258; with German States, 243-244; with Austria-Hungary, 252; negotiated by Pius VII, 252; negotiated by Leo XII, 252; negotiated by Pius IX, 253; with Italy (*1929*), 264; with Poland (*1925*), 266-267
Confessors, 60-61
Confirmation, 60, 306, 311
Confirmation of the Charters, 139
Consistory, 312
Constance, Council of, 55, 147-148, 149
Constantine, 28, 30, 62
Constantinople, founding of, 30; summary of Councils at, 54; basilicas in, 62; Sixth Council at, 53; center of Greek Schism, 84 *ff.*; attacked in Fourth Crusade, 112; fall of to Turks, 154
Constantinople, First Council of, 47; Second Council of, 53; Third Council of, 53; Fourth Council of, 88 (*See also pages 54-55 for summary of Ecumenical Councils*)
Constitution, of United States, and religious freedom, 304
Converts, in Great Britain, 250, 265-266; in United States, 329
Copernicus, 163, 164
Cornelius, 12
Councils, General or Ecumenical, First (Nicaea), 30, 44, 52; Second (Constantinople), 47; Third (Ephesus), 51, 52; Fourth (Chalcedon), 51, 52, 53; Fifth (Constantinople), 53; Sixth (Constantinople), 53; Seventh (Nicaea and Constantinople), 85; Eighth (Constantinople), 88; Ninth (Lateran), 105; Tenth (Lateran), 52, 109; Twelfth (Lateran), 107, 128; Fifteenth (Vienne), 142; Sixteenth (Constance), 147-148, 149; Seventeenth (Basle-Florence), 149-150; Eighteenth (Lateran), 156; Nineteenth (Trent), 176, 200 *ff.*; Twentieth (Vatican), 245, 246, 253-254 (*See also pages 54-55 for summary of all the Ecumenical Councils*)
Counter-Reformation, definition of, 200; and Council of Trent, 200-202; Popes of, 202-204; other leaders of, 204-208, 209, 210.
Coventuals, 120
Cranmer, Thomas, 192
Creighton Brothers, 323
Cromwell, Oliver, 195
Cromwell, Thomas, 191, 192
Crusades, background of, 111; summary of leading events, 112-113; reason for failure, 114; results of, 114-115
Cusa, Cardinal, 159, 161
Cyril, St., of Alexandria, 56
Cyril, St., of Jerusalem, 56

Damasus I, Pope, 47, 54
Dante, 127-128, 141
Da Vinci, Leonardo, 158
Deacons, 11, 59
Decameron, 160-161
Decius, Emperor, persecution of Christians, 22, 25
Defense of the Seven Sacraments, 191
Deism, 224

Democracy, 256
Denmark, propagation of the Faith in, 94; Protestantism in, 183; in Thirty Years' War, 197; invaded by Nazis, 256
Dever, Gov. Paul A., 321
Diaspora Catholics, 262
Diderot, 227-228
Di Medici, Catherine, 185
Diocletian, Emperor, persecution of Christians, 23, 25
Directory, in French Revolution, 234, 236
Disputa, 157, 158
Divine Comedy, 127-128, 141
Divine right of kings, 194
Doctors of Church, 53, 56-59
Dominic, St., 109, 120-121
Dominicans, 109, 118, 120-121
Dominican Sisters, 336
Domitian, Emperor, persecution of Christians, 20, 24
Donatism, 48, 52
Dougherty, Dennis Cardinal, 314-315
Dualism, 108
Dual Monarchy of Austria-Hungary, 252
Duns Scotus, 120

Easter, 61
Ecumenical Councils of Church, see "Councils, General or Ecumenical"
Education, Catholic, by monasteries, 92, 97-98; by Jesuits, 205-206; in United States, 329 ff.
Edward I, of England, 139
Edward VI, of England, 192
Eire, 266
Elizabeth, St., Queen of Hungary, 120
Elizabeth, Queen of England, 193-194
Encyclopedists, 228
England, propagation of the Faith in, 90-92; and Hundred Years' War, 166; and Protestantism, 190-196; Catholic emancipation in, 249; restoration of Hierarchy in, 250; in twentieth century, 265-266; colonization by in America, 301-303
Ephesus, Council of, 54
Ephrem, St., 56
Epiphany, feast of, 61
Episcopal Church, see "Anglican Church"
Epistles, in New Testament, 6, 10
Erasmus, 159, 161
Estates General, in France, 140, 231
Eucharistic Congresses, 279
Eugenius IV, Pope, 55, 149, 158
Eusebius, supporter of Arius, 44
Eusebius of Caesarea, 47
Eutychianism, 51, 52
Evangelists, 6
Exorcists, 59
Exsurge Domine, 181

Fabian, St., 22
Faithful, 60
Farley, John Cardinal, 314
Farrell, Walter, O.P., 322
Ferdinand II, Emperor, 197
Ferdinand, of Spain, 168-169
Ferry Laws, 241, 259
Feudalism, 79, 100-102
Fisher, St. John, 191, 208
FitzSimons, Thomas, 304
Florence, Council of, 55, 149-150
Florida, missionary activities in, 293-294

Flotte, Peter, 140, 141
Ford, Henry II, 323
Fordham University, 332
France, foundation of nation, 67; settlement of Norsemen in, 95; monasteries in Early Middle Ages, 98-100; heresies in, 106-109; conflict of Philip the Fair and Boniface VIII, 138-141; and "Babylonian Captivity," 142-145; and Hundred Years' War, 166-167; and Protestant Revolt, 185-187; and Thirty Years' War, 197-198; under Louis XIV, 212-213; and the Revolution of *1789,* 226-235; under Napoleon, 236-240; after Napoleon, 240-241; in the twentieth century, 258-259; colonization by, in America, 298-301
Francis of Assisi, St., 119-120
Francis de Sales, St., 209
Francis Xavier, St., 206
Franciscans, establishment and work of, 118-120; in America, 294-296
Franciscan Sisters, 336
Franks, 67, 81-84
Frederick Barbarossa, Emperor, 105-106, 112
Frederick II, Emperor, 106, 113
Frederick II (the Great), of Prussia, 214, 216, 228
Freemasons, 228
French Clergy, Declaration of, 213
French Revolution, 226-235
Friars, 118 ff.
Friars Minors, 120
Fulda, monastery of, 93-94

Galileo, 163-164
Gallicanism, 213
Garibaldi, 248, 253
General Councils, see "Councils, General or Ecumenical"
Geneva, Calvin's dictatorship in, 185
Genseric, 65
Gentiles, propagation of the Faith among, 11
Georgetown University, 332
Germanic barbarians, 63-64
Germany, propagation of the Faith in, 92-93; Protestant Revolt in, 179-183; Catholic revival in nineteenth century, 244; unification of, 244-245; *Kulturkampf* in, 245-246; in twentieth century, 260-262
Gibbons, James Cardinal, 313-314
Gift of tongues, 9
Giotto, 127, 141
Glenmary Missioners, 310
Glennon, John Cardinal, 316
Gorkum, martyrs of, 188-189
Gorres, Josef von, 244
Gospels, 6, 8
Gothic architecture, 98, 126-127
Grand Chartreuse, monastery of, 99
Great Britain, see "England"
Great Schism, 146-148
Greek Doctors of Church, 53
Greek Schism, causes of, 85-88
Gregorian calendar, 204
Gregory I, Pope (St. Gregory the Great), 53, 66, 80-81
Gregory VII, Pope, 103-105, 111
Gregory IX, Pope, 109, 110
Gregory X, Pope, 55
Gregory XI, Pope, 121, 145
Gregory XII, Pope, 147, 148
Gregory XIII, Pope, 186, 203-204
Gregory XVI, Pope, 253

Gregory, St., of Nazianzus, 47, 53
Gunpowder Plot, 194
Gustavus Adolphus, 197
Gutenberg, John, 162

Harris, Joel Chandler, 321
Hayes, Carlton J. H., 322
Hayes, Patrick Cardinal, 315
Hegira, 89
Henry IV, Emperor, and lay investiture, 104-105
Henry V, Emperor, 105
Henry VII, of England, 168
Henry VIII, of England, 190-192
Henry IV, of France, 186
Heresy, definition of, 40; causes of, 41-42; action of Church against, 42-43; early struggles of Church against, 43 ff.; in twelfth and thirteenth centuries, 107-110; in fourteenth century, 148-150
Hermits, 68, 120
Hierarchy, defined, 4, 59; restoration of in England, 250; restoration of in Holland, 251; in the United States, 305-311
Hilary, St., of Poitiers, 56
Hildebrand, see "Gregory VII"
Hitler, 260-262
Hohenstaufen family, 106
Holland, Protestantism in, 187-188; restoration of Hierarchy in, 251; in twentieth century, 276
Holy Orders, 60, 306, 311
Holy Ghost, 9, 86
Holy Roman Empire, 82, 104, 105, 106, 143, 144, 181, 182, 187, 197, 198, 245
Holy Rosary, Feast of, 203
Holy Year *(1950)*, 279
Huguenots, 185, 186, 187
Humanism, 154 ff.; radical and Christian schools contrasted, 159-162
Hundred Years' War, 166-167
Hungary, 96, 251-252; persecution of Church, 272-273
Huns, 64, 65-66
Hus, John, 149
Hymns, Latin, 128

Iceland, 95
Iconoclasts, 54, 84-85
Ignatius Loyola, St., 200, 205-206, 209
Ignatius, Patriarch of Constantinople, 86-88
Illuminated manuscripts, 97
Index, 42
India, missionary activities in, 14, 206
Indulgences, 180, 181
Industry, American Catholics in, 323-324
Ineffabilis, 139
Infallibility of Pope, Dogma of, 55, 84, 164, 253-254
Innocent II, Pope, 54
Innocent III, Pope, 55, 106-107, 109, 128
Innocent IV, Pope, 55
Innocent VI, Pope, 144
Inquisition, Episcopal, 109-110; Spanish, 110
Institutes of the Christian Religion, 184
Ireland, propagation of the Faith in, 71; during Protestant Revolt, 196; disestablishment of Anglican Church in, 249; in twentieth century, 256, 266
Isaac Jogues, St., 298-300
Isabella, Queen, of Spain, 168-169
Islam, see "Mohammedanism"
Italy, relations with Papacy in nineteenth century, 247-248; in twentieth century, 264-265

Jacobins, 232, 233
James, the Greater, Apostle, 6, 8, 14
James, the Lesser, Apostle, 14
James I, of England, 194
James II, of England, 196
Japan, 206, 254, 263
Jerome, St., 53, 58-59, 68
Jerusalem, Council of, 8, 16
Jesuits, see "Society of Jesus"
Jews, and Jesus Christ, 5; propagation of Christianity among, 10-11; and Council of Jerusalem, 16; and Mohammedan doctrines, 88; and Spanish Inquisition, 110; protected by Pope Clement VI, 144; persecution of in Nazi Germany, 257, 260
Joan of Arc, 166-167
John, St. (the Evangelist), 6, 8, 10, 14
John Baptist de la Salle, St., 209
John Chrysostom, St., 53, 56
John of Cologne, St., 188-189, 208
John Dominic, Cardinal, 147, 148
John XXII, Pope, 143
John XXIII, anti-Pope, 146, 147
John, of England, 106
Joliet, Louis, 300
Joseph II, Emperor of Austria, 214-215
Josephism, 214-215
Juarez, Juan, 294
Jubilee, of *1300*, 141
Judas Iscariot, 8, 15
Jude, St., 6, 15
Julius II, Pope, 55, 155-156, 159
Julius III, Pope, 55
Justinian, Emperor, 53
Justinian Code, 43

Kernan, Francis, 320
Ketteler, Bishop Wilhelm Emmanuel von, 246-247
Knighthood, 115-116
Knights of St. John, 116
Knights Templars, 55, 116, 142
Knox, John, 189
Koran, 88, 89
Korea, War in, 307
Ku Klux Klan, 329, 336-337
Kulturkampf, 245, 246, 254

Lacordaire, 242
Lafayette, 325
Laity, defined, 4; and missionary activities, 310; in United States, 318-329
Langton, Stephen, 106
Lateran, Council of, First, 105; Second, 52, 109; Fourth, 107, 128; Fifth, 156 (See also pages 54-55 for summary of Ecumenical Councils)
Lateran Treaty *(1929)*, 264
Latin America, 296-297
Latin Doctors of Church, 49-50, 53, 56-59, 80-81
Latin translation of Bible, 58, 202
Laud, Archbishop, 194
La Vendée, Catholic revolt in, 234
Lawrence, St., 22
Leo I, Pope (St. Leo the Great), 51, 54, 56, 65, 66
Leo II, Pope, 54
Leo X, Pope, 55, 156, 181
Leo XII, Pope, 252
Leo XIII, Pope, 254
Lepanto, battle of, 203
Liberius, Pope, 45-46; basilica of, 62

INDEX

Literature, preservation of ancient, by monks, 97; of Renaissance, 159-162; contributions of American Catholics to, 321-323
Liturgy, 61, 86
Lollards, 149
Lombard League, 105-106
Lombards, 66, 81
Lord's Prayer, 6
Louis Cancer, Father, 293
Louis IX (St. Louis), of France, 113, 120
Louis XIV, of France, 186-187, 212-213, 229
Louis XV, of France, 229
Louis XVI, of France, 229, 231, 232, 233
Louis XVIII, of France, 240
Louis Napoleon, Emperor of France, 240-241
Louis the Bavarian, Emperor, 143, 144
Loyola, St. Ignatius, see "Ignatius Loyola"
Luke, St., 6, 8, 10
Luther, Martin, 179-181
Lützen, battle of, 197
Lyons, Ecumenical Councils at, 55

Macedonius, 47, 54
Magna Carta, 140
Major orders, 59, 306
Manichaeism, 49, 52, 108
Manor, in feudal system, 101
Marat, 232
Marcus Aurelius, Emperor, persecution of Christians, 21, 24
Marie Antoinette, of France, 233
Mark, St., 6, 8
Marquette, Father, 300
Martel, Charles, 82
Martin V, Pope, 55, 148
Martyrs, in early days of Church, 10, 14, 16; of Roman persecution, 18 *ff.*; in iconoclastic dispute, 85; among missionaries in early Middle Ages, 94; of the Protestant Revolt and Counter-Reformation, 208-210; in countries controlled by Communists, 270-275; among missionaries in America, 293 *ff.*
Maryknoll Fathers, 307-309, 310
Maryland colony, 301-303
Mary Queen of Scots, 189
Mary Tudor, Queen of England, 187, 192-193
Mass, 6, 10, 18, 22, 23, 61, 306
Matthew, St., 6, 8, 15
Matthias, 15
Maximinus, Emperor, persecution of Christians by, 22, 25
May Laws, 245-246
Mazzini, 247, 253
McCloskey, John Cardinal, 312-313
McManus, Bishop James E., 297
McShane, Father Daniel, 308
Medicine, American Catholics in, 324-325
Medieval civilization, 117-118
Melanchthon, Philip, 183
Mendicant Orders, 96, 97, 118-122
Mercy, Sisters of, 333, 336
Merton, Thomas, 322-323
Methodius, St., 95-96
Metternich, Prince, 240, 251-252
Mexico, dispute with church over Pius Fund, 295
Michelangelo, 155, 156, 159
Middle Ages, meaning of, 77-78; character and leading events of Early Middle Ages, 79-90; propagation of Faith in Early Middle Ages, 90-96; monasticism in Early Middle Ages, 96-100; influence of feudalism on, 100-102;

Pontificates of Gregory VII and Innocent III, 103-107; heresies of twelfth and thirteenth centuries, 107-110; Crusades, 111-117; height of Medieval civilization, 117-128; Later Middle Ages, 137 *ff.*
Milan, Edict of, 18, 28, 30
Military Orders, 115-118
Military service, by American Catholics, 325-327
Mindszenty, Cardinal Josef of Budapest, 271, 272-273
Minor orders, 59, 306
Mission architecture, 296
Missionary activity, early propagation among Jews, 10; early propagation among Gentiles, 11-13; and growth of Church, 32; in Ireland, 71; in Early Middle Ages, 90-96; by Mendicant Orders, 118-122; in Far East, 145, 206; during Counter-Reformation, 204-210; under Pius XI, 277-278; in colonial America, 291-304; by American clergy today, 307-310; within United States today, 309-310, 328-329
Mohammedanism, 88-90
Monasteries, see "Monasticism"
Monasticism, early history of, 68-69; structure of typical monastic enclosure, 70; in Ireland, 71; services of in Early Middle Ages, 96-98; famous monasteries, 98-100; Protestant attack on, 181
Monophysitism, 51, 54
Monothelite heresy, 84
Monte Cassino, 69, 98
Montfort, Simon de, 109
Mooney, Edward Cardinal, 316-317
More, St. Thomas, 159, 161-162, 191, 209
Mundelein, George Cardinal, 315-316
Murray, Philip, 323
Mussolini, Benito, 256, 264-265

Nantes, Edict of, 186-187
Napoleon Bonaparte, 234, 235, 236 *ff.*
Napoleon III, Emperor, 240-241
National Catholic Welfare Council, 339
Nazism, 256, 260-261
Nero, persecution of Christians, 20, 24
Nestorianism, 50-51, 52
Newman, Cardinal, 250
Newman Clubs, 339
New Mexico, missionary activities in, 294
New Testament, 6-8
Newton, Sir Isaac, 164
New York, 188, 298, 299, 311, 315
Nicaea, First Council of, 44, 54; Second Council of, 54, 85
Nicene Creed, 44, 45, 47, 54; and Greek schism, 86
Nicholas V, Pope, 150, 154
Nicholas of Cusa, Cardinal, 161
Ninety-five Theses, of Luther, 180-181
Non-juring clergy, 232
Norway, propagation of the Faith in, 95; Protestantism in, 183; in World War II, 256
Notre Dame University, 332

O'Callahan, Father Joseph T., S.J., 327
O'Connell, William Cardinal, 314
Odoacer, 63, 66
Oregon Compulsory Education Law, 336-337
Ostrogoths, 66
Oxford Movement, 249-250

INDEX

Pacelli, Cardinal, *see* "Pius XII"
Pachomius, St., 68
Padilla, Father, 294
Painting, 127, 157-159
Papacy, origins of, 8-10; in primitive Church, 59-60; election of Popes by Cardinals, 103, 312 *(The various Popes are listed in this Index under their individual names, and also under other specific headings.)*
Papal Infallibility, *see* "Infallibility of Pope"
Papal Legates, 60
Papal States, 82, 106, 235, 238, 240, 247-248, 252, 253, 264
Paris, University of, 122-123
Parishes, 60-61
Pasteur, Louis, 241-242
Pastor aeternus, 253
Patrick, St., 71
Paul III, Pope, 55, 191, 200, 202-203
Paul, St., 6, 12, 15
Peasants' War, in Germany, 181-182
Pelagianism, 48-49, 52
Pentecost, 9, 61
Pepin, 82, 86
Persecution of Christians, Roman, 17-25
Peter, St., 6, 8, 10, 12, 14
Peter Canisius, St., 206-207, 208
Peter Chrysologus, St., 56
Peter the Hermit, 111, 112
Petrarch, 159, 160
Phelan, John Henry, 323-324
Philip, the Deacon, 11, 14
Philip Augustus of France, 106
Philip IV (the Fair), of France, 138-139, 140-141, 142
Philip II, of Spain, 193-194
Philip Neri, St., 210
Photius, 54, 88
Pisa, Council of, 55, 147
Pius II, Pope, 154-155
Pius IV, Pope, 55
Pius V, Pope (St. Pius), 200, 203
Pius VI, Pope, 234-235
Pius VII, Pope, 238, 252
Pius VIII, Pope, 253
Pius IX, Pope, 55, 247, 253
Pius X, Pope, 277, 281, 309
Pius XI, Pope, 277-278
Pius XII, Pope, 265, 278-279
Pius Fund, 295
Plunket, Oliver, 195
Poland, propagation of the Faith in, 95; partitions of, 215-216; in nineteenth century, 251; in twentieth century, 266-267, 270, 274
Polycarp, St., 21
Popes, *see* "Papacy"
Pragmatic Sanction, 55
Presbyterianism, 189
Priests, 59, 60, 306-307
Printing, invention of, 162-163
Propaganda Fide, 309
Protestant Revolt, causes of, 177; in Germany, 179-183; in Scandinavia, 183; in Switzerland, 184-185; in France, 185-187; in the Netherlands, 187-189; in Scotland, 189; in England, 190-196; results of, 198-199; Counter-Reformation, 200-210; and absolutism, 212
Protomartyr, 11
Provisors, Statute of, 190
Prussia, 117, 198, 213-214, 243-245

Ptolemaic system, 163
Puerto Rico, 297-298
Puritans, 194, 195

Rabaut, Louis Charles, 320-321
Radio and television, 329, 340-341
Raphael, 156, 157, 158
Reign of Terror, 233-234
"Released time" program (McCullom Case), 338
Renaissance, characteristics of, 151-152; Popes of, 153-156; art and literature of, 157-162; political events of, 164-169
Rense, Decision of, 143-144
Rerum novarum, 254
Rights of Man, Declaration of, 231
"Robber Synod," 51
Robert of Molesme, St., 100
Robespierre, 233, 234
Rollo, 95
Roman Empire, and the foundation of Christianity, 5 *ff.*; and persecution of Christians, 17-28; toleration of Christianity in, 29-30; and establishment of a universal Church, 32; invasion and downfall of, 63-67
Roman Question, 247; settlement of, 264
Rome, city of, introduction of Christianity into, 17; basilicas in, 62; in World War II, 257; *see also* "Bishop of Rome," "Papacy," "Papal States," "Roman Question," and "Roman Empire"
Rosary, Devotion to, 122, 341
Roses, War of, 167-168
Rousseau, Jean Jacques, 227
Rule, of St. Basil, 46, 68; of St. Benedict, 68, 69
Russia, propagation of Faith in, 96; under Peter the Great, 215; in twentieth century, 267-268; satellites of, 268-270

Sacraments, 10, 60, 306, 311
Salerno, University of, 122
Salesian Fathers, 249
Saul of Tarsus, *see* "St. Paul"
Savonarola, 164-165
Scapular, Devotion to, 122
Schism, definition of, 40; *see also* "Great Schism" and "Greek Schism"
Schmalkald, Protestant League of, 183
Scholastica, St., 69
Scholasticism, 125-126
Scotland, propagation of Faith in, 92; revolt against England, 166; Protestantism in, 189; in twentieth century, 266
Semi-Arianism, 45-46
Seminaries, in United States, 306-307
Seminoles, 294
Separation Act, in France, 258
Septimius Severus, persecution of Christians, 22, 24
Serfdom, 100-101
Sermon on the Mount, 6
Serra, Father Junípero, 296
Servites, 118
Seton, Mother Elizabeth Ann, 334-335
Seven Years' War, 214
Sheen, Bishop Fulton J., 322, 329, 340
Simony, 104
Simon Zelotes, Apostle, 15
Sisterhoods, teaching, 334-336
Sistine Chapel, 155, 159
Sixtus II, Pope, 22, 25

INDEX

Sixtus IV, Pope, 155
Sixtus V, Pope, 204, 309
Smith, Alfred E., 320, 329
Sobieski, John, King of Poland, 215
Society of Jesus, establishment and work of, 205-206; suppression of, 228-229; restoration of, 238-239; missionary activities in America, 293 ff.
Soviet regime, 267 ff.
Spain, national inquisition in, 110; unification of, 168-169; revolt of Netherlands against, 187-188; wars with England in sixteenth century, 193-194; in Thirty Years' War, 197; role in Counter-Reformation, 200 ff.; in nineteenth century, 251; in twentieth century, 275; missionary activities in America, 293-298
Spellman, Francis Cardinal, 317
Spires, Diet of, 182
Stephen, St., 11
Stepinac, Archbishop of Zagreb, 271-272
Stritch, Samuel Cardinal, 317
Suetonius, 14
Sueves, 65
Summa Theologica, 125
Supremacy, Act of, 191
Sweden, propagation of the Faith in, 94; Protestant Revolt in, 183; in Thirty Years' War, 197; in nineteenth century, 252; in twentieth century, 276
Switzerland, Protestant Revolt in, 184-185; Catholic population in, 276
Syllabus of *1864*, 253
Sylvester I, Pope, 54
Symbols, of Apostles, 14-15; use of in Catacombs, 27

Talleyrand, 240
Taney, Roger B., 319-320
Tekakwitha, Catherine, 300-301
Television and radio, 340-341
Ten Commandments, 6, 30
Tertullian, 17, 19, 31
Tetzel, John, 180
Teutonic Knights, 116
Texas, missionary activities in, 294
Thaddeus Jude, Apostle, 15
Theodore, 92
Theodoric, 66
Theodosius I, Emperor, 47, 54
Theodosius II, Emperor, 51, 54
Theresa of Avila, St., 207, 209
Theresa of Lisieux, 243
Thirty-Nine Articles, 193
Thirty Years' War, 197-199
Thomas, St., Apostle, 14
Thomas Aquinas, St., 40, 121, 125, 254
Three Chapters, 53, 54
Toleration Act, in Maryland, 302
Totalitarianism, 256
Tours, battle of, 82, 90
Tracts for the Times, 249-250
Trajan, persecution of Christians, 20-21, 24

Trent, Council of, 55, 200-202, 203
Truce of God, 102
Tudor dynasty, 168

Unam Sanctam, 140
United States, colonial period, 293 ff.; establishment of independent government, 304; Hierarchy of, 305-311; Cardinals of, 312-316; Catholic laity in, 318-329; Catholic education in, 329-338
Universities, of Middle Ages, 122-125; Catholic, in United States, 332
Urban II, Pope, 99, 111
Urban V, Pope, 144-145
Urban VI, Pope, 146, 147
Ursuline Nuns, 207, 333, 334
Utopia, 161-162
Utrecht, Union of, 188

Vacation schools, 339-340
Valerian, persecution of Christians, 22, 25
Vandals, 65
Vassals, 100
Vatican, Council of, 55, 253-254
Vatican City, 264
Venerable Bede, 92
Vernacular languages, 137
Verona, Council of, 109
Vienna, Congress of, 240
Vienne, Council of, 55, 142
Vigilius, Pope, 54
Vincent de Paul, St., 207-208, 209
Vincentians, 208
Visigoths, 64-65
Visitation Nuns, 333, 334
Voltaire, 227, 228
Vulgate, 58, 202

Waldenses, 54, 107-108
Walsh, Rev. James Edward, 306, 308
War of *1812*, Catholics in, 325-326
Washington, George, 325
Weimar Republic, 260
Westphalia, Treaty of, 188, 197-198
White, Father Andrew, 302, 303
William I, of Germany, 245
William of Orange, 188
William and Mary, of England, 196
Williams, Michael (quoted), 292
Wiseman, Cardinal, 250
Wolsey, Cardinal, 192
World War, First, 255, 277, 278; Second, 256 ff.
Worms, Concordat of, 105; Diet of, 181
Wycliffe, John, 148-149

Xavier, St. Francis, 206, 209
Ximenes, Cardinal, 168-169

Yugoslavia, 269, 270, 271-272

Zwingli, 184